LANDMARK CASES IN LABOUR LAW

This book features essays by leading legal scholars on 'landmark' labour law cases from the mid-19th century to the present day. The essays are acutely sensitive to the historical and theoretical context of each case, and the volume provides original and sometimes startling new perspectives on some familiar friends.

There are few activities as distinctively human as work and labour. The book traces the development of labour law through the social struggles and economic conflicts between workers, trade unions and employers. The narrative arc of its landmark cases reveals the richness and complexity of the human story played out in the working lives of real people. It also charts the remarkable transformation of the constitutional role of courts in labour law, from instruments of class oppression to the vindication of workers' fundamental rights at work.

The collection will be of interest to students, scholars, and legal practitioners in labour and equality law, as well as students in management studies, industrial relations, and labour history.

Landmark Cases in Labour Law

Edited by
Jeremias Adams-Prassl
Alan Bogg
and
ACL Davies

•HART•
OXFORD • LONDON • NEW YORK • NEW DELHI • SYDNEY

HART PUBLISHING

Bloomsbury Publishing Plc

Kemp House, Chawley Park, Cumnor Hill, Oxford, OX2 9PH, UK

1385 Broadway, New York, NY 10018, USA

29 Earlsfort Terrace, Dublin 2, Ireland

HART PUBLISHING, the Hart/Stag logo, BLOOMSBURY and the Diana logo are trademarks of Bloomsbury Publishing Plc

First published in Great Britain 2022

A catalogue record for this book is available from the British Library.

A catalogue record for this book is available from the Library of Congress.

Library of Congress Control Number: 2022944258

ISBN: HB: 978-1-50994-426-2
ePDF: 978-1-50994-428-6
ePub: 978-1-50994-427-9

Typeset by Compuscript Ltd, Shannon

Foreword

WHAT MAKES A landmark case? The authors of this fascinating set of essays could not come up with a clear definition and gave persuasive reasons why the task is more difficult in labour law than in other common law subjects. Perhaps a workable solution is to adopt a variation of Desert Island discs: what (in this case) 14 decisions would you wish to have with you on your desert island? The academics should choose; barristers would select the cases they won. And the luxury would of course be this volume of essays!

Inevitably, each reader will have their pet cases which he or she believes ought to have been included but has not. I suspect that, in part at least, the choice will depend significantly on when the reader studied labour law. Those who studied the subject in what Professor Kahn Freund famously characterised as the period of 'collective laissez faire', when worker protection was afforded more by trades unions rather than by legislation, landmark cases will include the great union cases which led to the development and stabilisation of that system, such as *Taff Vale* and the *Crofter* case. But with an increasing focus on individual rights and discrimination in labour law courses, other important cases fight for attention. Further, when the closed shop was in force, the relationship between trade unions and their members was an important aspect of every labour law course. Cases such as *Bonsor v Musicians Union* and *Edwards v SOGAT*, concerning the rights of members to sue their union, would trip off the labour law student's tongue rather as *Johnson* and *Malik* do for today's students. They now seem from another world.

There are some fascinating choices here. I confess to not even having been aware of the case discussed by Zoe Adams, *Riley v Warden*, an early case on the Truck Act 1833. She gives a wonderful historical account of the development of what we now define as the employee, starting with *Riley* and up to and including *Uber*. The significance of *Riley* is that the court focused on socio-economic status when determining who should be covered by protective legislation. Zoe's thesis (at the risk of oversimplification) is that shifting the focus to the contract has weakened the protection in a number of important respects, principally because the employer typically determines what is in the contract. Whether *Riley* is truly a landmark case, as opposed to what ought to have been a landmark case had its potential significance been fully recognised, is questionable. But why worry when it results in such a stimulating discussion. A similar stretching of the concept of landmark case is found in Catherine Barnard's contribution. She has selected three inter-related cases. (Can a landmark case be constituted from three cases, none of which would justify that status? Discuss). Again, it matters not; this is a typically enlightening discussion of recent cases from the CJEU dealing with the highly contentious area of whether and when employers can discipline women workers who insist on wearing Islamic scarves for religious reasons.

Two other landmark cases deal with employment status – perhaps reflecting the potential complexities of this topic. Anne Davies applies her rigorous intellect to the Court of Appeal decision in *O'Kelly v Trusthouse Forte*, important not only because of its (arguably) baleful influence on the issue of employment status but also, as she points out, because of its emphasis on the obligation on appellate courts' loyally to accept tribunal findings not only on primary facts but also inferences from those facts, unless they are obviously unsustainable. That was critical to the result in *O'Kelly* and to many cases since. The discussion inevitably raises the relevance of mutuality of obligation (although I confess that I believe that many academics have misunderstood and exaggerated its significance). *Autoclenz*, which requires courts to focus on economic realities and bargaining power as well as contractual language, is the third status case. As Jeremias Adams-Prassl argues, its significance may with hindsight be seen to be its importance as a stepping-stone to *Uber*, surely a landmark case in its own right even if, in my view at least, its impact on the issue of status remains far from clear.

There are a number of other cases which focus on the nature of the contract and individual rights. Astrid Sanders considers a case over a century old, *Devonald v Rosser*. This is not perhaps an obvious choice for a landmark case but she makes a strong argument for including it. Should an employer pay a piece worker even if no work was available? Perhaps surprisingly, particularly at that time, the court implied a term requiring payment in favour of the worker. As the author says, perhaps the potentially most far-reaching significance of the case – but rarely noted – is the judicial observation that 'apart from authority, it would be strange if such a right is not implied; for otherwise the bargain is of a very one-sided character'. She argues that the courts should, and could, have made more of this principle in the context of implying terms.

Some modern cases more obviously justify the epithet 'landmark'. Joe Atkinson discusses *Johnson*, a case that has divided the academic community on the very fundamental issue of whether the existence of the statutory right to unfair dismissal has fettered the development of the common law. Subsequent cases have sought to identify the contours of the so-called 'exclusion zone' but it is so difficult to pin down that it might be the legal reflection of Heisenberg's uncertainty principle. *Malik v BCCI* was not so much breaking new ground but was confirming and to some extent expanding the scope of the trust and confidence term, which Douglas Brodie surely correctly claims has transformed our understanding of the contract of employment. Douglas argues that the concept leaves lots of loose ends and still has much potential for growth. In *Iceland Frozen Foods* Phillipa Collins discusses the development of, and the arguments justifying or otherwise, the adoption of the 'range of reasonable responses' test in unfair dismissal law, again a highly controversial area. She makes a good case for its replacement by what seems to me at least to be a similar, but intellectually more principled, proportionality test. Finally, Sandra Fredman has provided a penetrating analysis of the *Enderby* case. She has also highlighted the problems which women have had, and still have, in enforcing the right to equal pay, particularly when they are doing what has traditionally been seen as 'women's work'. She argues, with some justification some may think, that post-*Enderby* too many employers have been running specious legal arguments to undermine the force of *Enderby*, all of which have led to quite unacceptable delays in bringing closure to these important cases.

There are five cases which focus primarily on collective labour issues, using that term broadly. Whereas the cases on individual labour law primarily tend to provide a critique of the legal reasoning of the court, and the subsequent development (or missed opportunities for development) of the principle enunciated in the case, in these collective cases the decision itself is only part of the story. Equally important are the circumstances leading to the decision and the reaction to it, which typically involves unions (successfully) pressing Parliament for change. In each of the cases (except *Grunwick*) the adverse effect has been reversed by subsequent legislation. The essays on these decisions are as much vignettes of social and labour history as critiques of legal reasoning (although they are that too).

Hornby v Close established that trades unions were unlawful bodies at common law, being in restraint of trade. This did not make them criminal organisations but on the facts it meant that they could not take advantage of a procedure which would have enabled them to recover moneys from a defaulting official. In one sense the significance of this decision is its consequence; it led to the passage of the Trade Union Act 1871, which was vital in putting the unions on a proper legal footing. But the doctrine of restraint of trade, which lay at the heart of the decision, still underpins collective labour law. Joanna McCunn shows how, in developing the concept, the courts broadly reflected the economic and political thinking of the time which was notoriously hostile to collective interests. The idea that unions might be able to compel their members to strike was an anathema. Joanna makes the interesting observation that a number of judges – including Campbell LCJ – expressed concern about having to make decisions on such a highly charged political concept which they did not feel they were particularly equipped to make.

David Cabrelli considers *Osborne*, without doubt a historical landmark case. The House of Lords, on the highly dubious ground of defining the scope of union powers from the statutory definition, restricted the right of trades unions to raise funds for political purposes. This was very damaging not just to the unions but also to the fledgling Labour Party which relied heavily on union financial support to fight elections and for other purposes. There was a successful drive for legislation to reverse the effect of the decision. However, in some respects it remains something of a political hot potato, particularly on the question of whether individuals should have to opt out of the fund or whether they should opt in – a factor of real practical significance given the power of the force of inertia.

Alan Bogg's essay on the decision in *Wilson and Palmer* is a tour de force. He has interviewed participants and lawyers involved in the legal proceedings and shows that in law, as in life, so much depends on serendipity, as well as the courage and commitment of those prepared to fight for their rights. The case raised an important issue about whether employers could lawfully agree to pay workers more if they were willing to have their terms and conditions determined independently of the collective bargaining process. Whatever the aim, the effect was certainly to weaken trades unions. There is a detailed analysis of all four stages of the domestic proceedings, from tribunals to the House of Lords (where the unions lost); and then of the challenge before the Strasbourg Court (where it won). It is perhaps that Court's decision, involving what at the time was perceived to be a surprisingly generous construction of Article 11 on freedom of association, which is really the landmark here. Article 11 has been further developed by later Convention jurisprudence. Indeed, not least because of the commitment of Lord Hendy and Keith Ewing, international standards gradually being given more consideration by the domestic courts than was the case then. Legislation was passed to give effect to this Strasbourg ruling and reverse the effect of their Lordship's ruling. As Alan points out, in hindsight it can be seen that the defeat in the Lords may have been in the long-term interests of the union movement.

Grunwick was a cause celebre of the 1970s. It was centre stage in the media and sparked widespread and conflicting political debates. It involved an ultimately unsuccessful strike which went on for over a year involving heavy mass picketing which followed the dismissal of the strikers. The legal aspect involved the question of whether ACAS, in the course of making a recommendation for union recognition, had acted procedurally lawfully. The House of Lords held that it had not and this resulted in the repeal of the statutory recognition provisions then in force; ACAS itself thought that in the light of the Lords' ruling, they were a hindrance rather than a help. But in addition to this, there was an inquiry under Lord Scarman who made various proposals, many sympathetic to the union and the dismissed striking workers, but an obstructive employer frustrated them. All these aspects are discussed in a superb contribution from Keith Ewing who focuses in particular on some of the wider constitutional issues in the case, and discusses the different concepts of the rule of law which emerge from the political and social debates then current.

Perhaps the essay which most surprised me was the analysis of *Rookes v Barnard* by Roderick Bagshaw, who is primarily a tort rather than labour lawyer. Those of us brought up in the classic collective labour law culture then dominated by Lord Wedderburn almost universally (me included) shared – and no doubt still share – the assumption that *Rookes* was an example of a wholly unjustified judicial creation of a new tort by the House of Lords, the tort of intimidation, and a perverse failure to find that the so called 'golden formula' provided an immunity to it. Lord Wedderburn was vitriolic not only about the alleged anti-union Law Lords but also about fellow academics, and in particular

Tony Weir, who supported the court's analysis. As Roderick shows, however, there is a powerful case for saying that in principle the use of an unlawful threat to achieve one's objective ought to be a tort, even where the unlawful act is a threat of breach of contract. Should the court have said that even if that is so, since trade unions will be the primary victims of its development, the law should not be developed in that way? It is far from self evident that it would have been right for any court to adopt such a policy driven approach to the arguments. And given the way in which the immunities had been granted in the Trade Disputes Act 1906, it would have been difficult to construe them in a manner that covered this particular wrong. In the light of the historical development of union immunities, it is understandable why unions thought that they had been given effective immunity from tort liabilities arising in the course of a strike. But the question is whether that expectation was justified as a matter of law; the expectation cannot itself be the source of a legal submission.

Whatever the proper solution to this problem, Roderick has demonstrated convincingly, to me at least, that it is at the very least far from obvious that the Law Lords were in their reasoning wrong, let alone deliberately or perversely hostile to union interests (whatever their personal views may have been). It may sometimes be difficult for labour lawyers, who are typically attracted to the subject because of emotional sympathies for workers and unions, to view critical cases like this dispassionately. Lord Wedderburn was highly persuasive and a fine doctrinal lawyer – I would in fact put both him and Tony Weir among the very best I have met– but this essay shows that there is another less jaundiced critique of the decision. Perhaps the judges were seeking to act in a principled way, leaving any adverse consequences to Parliament, who did indeed soon provide the requisite immunity in this case. It is important that assumptions are challenged, and this is precisely what this contribution does. Congratulations to the editors for including this important essay in the volume.

All in all, this is an outstanding collection of essays. They are without exception engaging and intellectually challenging. Above all, they are a treat to read. I recommend this book with great enthusiasm.

Sir Patrick Elias

Acknowledgements

THE EDITORS WOULD like to thank the Faculty of Law, University of Oxford, for funding a workshop at which the contributors were able to present their draft chapters, and Brasenose College, Oxford, for hosting the event, one of the first in-person events many of us had been able to attend after pandemic restrictions were lifted. We were lucky to have such wonderful surroundings to discuss the chosen cases and understand the broader story of labour law told through them. It was also a pleasure that the three editors could meet and work together again in familiar surroundings. Rather like a band reforming, the old hits sounded just as good and the banter was undimmed. We were all slightly older, of course, but that never stopped The Rolling Stones. We would also like to express our appreciation for Hart Publishing's management of this project with their usual speed and efficiency and their support for the workshop dinner. We record our particular thanks for the excellent editorial work of Dr Eleni Katsampouka. She was a research assistant in the preparation of the final manuscript for submission, and her deft and reliable touch ensured that it arrived at the publisher in excellent shape and on time. Sir Patrick Elias very kindly agreed to prepare a foreword to the collection. As one of the leading appellate judges specialising in labour law in the modern era, it is entirely fitting that he should deliver judgment on the book.

Contents

Contributors

Zoe Adams is an Affiliated Lecturer in Law at the University of Cambridge and Admissions Tutor and Fellow at King's College, Cambridge.

Jeremias Adams-Prassl is a Professor of Law at the University of Oxford and a Fellow of Magdalen College, Oxford.

Joe Atkinson is a Lecturer in Law at the University of Sheffield.

Roderick Bagshaw is an Associate Professor of Law at the University of Oxford and a Tutorial Fellow at Magdalen College, Oxford.

Catherine Barnard is a Professor of European Union Law and Employment Law at the University of Cambridge and a Fellow of Trinity College, Cambridge.

Alan Bogg is a Professor of Labour Law at the University of Bristol and an Emeritus Fellow of Hertford College, Oxford.

Douglas Brodie is a Professor of Law at the University of Strathclyde.

David Cabrelli is a Professor of Labour Law at the University of Edinburgh.

Philippa Collins is a Senior Lecturer in Law at the University of Bristol.

ACL Davies is a Professor of Law and Public Policy at the University of Oxford and a Fellow of Brasenose College, Oxford.

Keith Ewing is a Professor of Public Law at King's College London.

Sandra Fredman FBA, QC (hon) is a Professor of the Law of the British Commonwealth and the United States at the University of Oxford and a Fellow of Pembroke College, Oxford.

Joanna McCunn is a Senior Lecturer in Law at the University of Bristol.

Astrid Sanders is an Associate Professor of Law at the London School of Economics.

Introduction: A Brief Cartography of Landmarks in Labour Law

JEREMIAS ADAMS-PRASSL, ALAN BOGG AND ACL DAVIES

IT IS A great pleasure to present this volume, *Landmark Cases in Labour Law*, to our readers. In the course of preparing it, we have reflected on the multiple meanings of the term 'landmark'. When the project began, we proceeded on the basis that the idea of a 'landmark' case was a settled and obvious proposition. As we drew up the list, and encountered our own disagreements about which cases should be included, we soon realised that the notion of 'landmark' was rather more elusive and contested. In these short reflections, we will set out our own thinking on 'landmark' status. As editors, we reached the conclusion that those early disagreements were in fact integral to the concept of 'landmark'. 'Landmark' encompasses a range of dimensions. It is not reducible to a single idea. As such, our task is to clarify that range of meanings, rather than to stipulate a simple and reductive definition that conjures the real conceptual difficulties away.

I. LABOUR LEGISLATION, THE COMMON LAW, AND THE POLITICS OF LABOUR LAW

Before doing so, it is unusually important to justify the treatment of 'landmark cases' in a field such as labour law. *Landmark Cases in Labour Law* is a relatively late arrival to a highly successful and well-established series. It is worthwhile reflecting on why that might be so, aside from the dilatoriness of the editorial team and the disruption of the pandemic. Landmark cases in common law-based disciplines such as the law of contract or the law of torts scarcely needs to be explained: they are the lifeblood of the common law. In many ways, however, labour law emerged as a reaction to the restrictions and limitations of the common law in the sphere of work and employment. During the formative and mature periods of labour law's flourishing, captured in Kahn-Freund's theory of collective laissez-faire, the legal complexion of the discipline was rooted in statute. Its history was one of legislative, rather than common law, development. This statutory base provided the foundations for collective bargaining between trade unions and employers, which remained the main regulatory instrument for much of the twentieth century. From time to time, the common law encroached upon the disciplinary field, as in cases like *Rookes v Barnard*[1] or *Hornby v Close*.[2] However, the juridical repair of labour law then depended upon a neat statutory intervention to restore the equilibrium of social forces. The common law (and the judges) were the barbarians at the gate of labour law. This had significant methodological consequences. Scholars cautioned of the importance of going *through* the cases but not getting stuck in them. Purely doctrinal analysis was the poor relative of sociological, economic, and 'law in context' approaches. And the authoritative histories of labour law were histories of legislative development and governmental activity.[3] When judges appeared in the story, it was often as disruptive eruptions from labour law's looming 'unconscious' material, the latent common law.

This account is, of course, somewhat stylised. The great intellectual figures of labour law were also great doctrinal lawyers. For example, any account of the *oeuvre* of Lord Wedderburn would be incomplete without acknowledging his prodigious body of sophisticated 'case notes' on the leading cases of the day. These were bravura pieces of precise doctrinal analysis. The leading UK journal, the *Industrial Law Journal*, has a long-established and successful 'Recent Cases' section that attracts outstanding contributions. Moreover, leading generalist journals such as the *Modern Law Review* and the *Law Quarterly Review* have always published case notes on the labour cases of wider interest to the legal community. And from the late 1970s, driven both by the ascendancy of deregulatory politics and an increasing legislative emphasis on individual, rather than collective, rights, courts have become an increasingly important site of worker-protective strategic engagement by workers and trade unions. This was supported by the increasing importance of EC and eventually EU law as well as the European Convention of Human Rights in the domain of labour law, key elements in the reconfiguration of labour law around a discourse of fundamental rights.

While juridification does not necessarily entail judicialisation, courts are obviously important constitutional actors in defining and vindicating fundamental rights. All of this means that modern labour law has become much more recognisable as a case-based legal discipline. However, the historical range of the cases examined in this volume, from the nineteenth through to the twenty-first century, also reveals a narrative arc for the discipline that can be traced through shifting ideologies of judicial decision-making. Our contemporary familiarity with the modern 'landmark case' has perhaps allowed us to see a hidden jurisprudential history told through the cases more clearly than before.

[1] *Rookes v Barnard* [1964] AC 1129 (HL). See Bagshaw, ch 5 in this volume.

[2] *Hornby v Close* (1866–67) LR 2 QB 153 (QB). See McCunn, ch 2 in this volume.

[3] PL Davies and MR Freedland, *Labour Legislation and Public Policy* (Oxford, Oxford University Press, 1993).

II. IDENTIFYING THE LANDMARKS

Having established that 'landmark cases' are an appropriate focus of enquiry, how does one identify a 'landmark' case in labour law? We suggest that the idea of a 'landmark' is more complex and contested here compared with other common law-based legal disciplines. Ask any contract or torts lawyer the 'landmarks' of their discipline and they perhaps reach for those cases in which the deep common law principles of the subject are to be found: privity, consideration, duty of care, the measure of damages, and so forth. Matters are less clear-cut in labour law. There are a number of factors that complicate the identification of 'landmarks'. First, there is the relative dominance of legislation in legal development. Coupled with this dominance of statute as regulatory technique is the greater (overt) politicisation of labour law. This means that the shape of the discipline is much more liable to profound realignment by the government of the day. This politicisation also means that there are fewer stable and uncontested fundamental principles. As such, the fundamental building blocks of the discipline – for example, whether we are concerned with contracts of employment, or work relations, or the law of the labour market – is also much more keenly contested. While this is not to deny the presence of vigorous normative contestation in other disciplines, those disagreements are orientated around the best account of a roughly accepted set of rules and principles. In labour law, on the other hand, the principles themselves may be much more contingent because they have been exposed to regular, extensive legislative modification. This accounts for the contested idea of 'landmark' in labour law.

For all that contestation, each of the chapters in this volume makes a strong case for the landmark status of the case(s) under discussion. After many a joyful discussion, we still cannot provide a simple definition of a 'landmark' in labour law – but we did learn a great deal about the different dimensions of 'landmarks' in the field.

The first aspect is the importance of *statutory interpretation* to landmark cases. Even if the legal history of labour law is predominantly a legislative history, statutes must be interpreted by courts. This is reflected in many of our landmark cases which are concerned directly with statutory interpretation. In this vein, *Iceland Frozen Foods Ltd v Jones*[4] and *Wilson v Associated Newspapers Ltd*;[5] *Palmer v Associated British Ports*[6] are landmark judgments on statutory interpretation. Even where a decision is not concerned directly with statutory interpretation, the presence of a statute can exert a gravitational pull on the

[4] *Iceland Frozen Foods Ltd v Jones* [1983] ICR 17 (EAT). See Collins, ch 7 in this volume.

[5] *Wilson v Associated Newspapers Ltd* [1995] 2 AC 454 (HL). See Bogg, ch 10, section II in this volume.

[6] ibid.

development of common law doctrines. Examples of these 'indirect' statutory landmarks include *Johnson v Unisys*[7] and *Autoclenz v Belcher*.[8]

A second aspect is the '*bad*' or '*disruptive*' *landmark case*. In common law fields, landmarks are often associated with the fundamental principles they stand for. In labour law, however, the battle lines are more sharply drawn because even key principles often do not attract any kind of consensus. In cases like *O' Kelly v Trusthouse Forte*,[9] for example, a formalistic and contractualised approach to employment status led to the exclusion of casual workers from the scope of the fundamental labour right to freedom of association. From a worker-protective perspective, *O' Kelly* set a terrible precedent, with the potential to undermine the entire statutory scheme of protections for vulnerable workers. Not everyone shares that normative vision of labour law: from the deregulatory vantage point of the government circa 1983, *O' Kelly* would have been welcomed as a liberalisation of labour market rigidities. The landmark status of *O' Kelly* is less in its enduring value as a source of legal guidance, and more in its exposure of a neuralgic point in the contested politics of labour market regulation. It is also important to recognise that the disciplinary specialisation of a scholar can colour her evaluation of a landmark case. For example, *Rookes v Barnard*[10] has always been an object of severe criticism by labour lawyers who viewed it as an unwarranted judicial incursion into the politically sensitive area of strike law. In this volume, a leading torts scholar provides a very different perspective on that case and paints it in a light that will be unfamiliar to many of our labour lawyer readers.[11]

A third aspect is the critical interactions between different legal orders through the medium of landmark cases. The landmark quality of *Wilson and Palmer*[12] evolved over time. The House of Lords judgment is another instance of a 'bad' landmark, a regressive judgment that revealed a disconnect between the individualism of the common law and the collectivism of trade union legislation. In due course, it led to another landmark in *Wilson v UK*,[13] when the European Court of Human Rights found that UK law was in breach of trade union rights under Article 11 of the European Convention on Human Rights. The role of the Court of Justice of the European Union has also been pivotal in modern labour law, both in the Union's legal order and domestically, tackling fundamental questions of labour market regulation, from the interpretation of equal pay legislation in *Enderby v Frenchay*[14] to the role of discrimination law in

[7] *Johnson v Unisys* [2001] UKHL 13, [2003] 1 AC 518. See Atkinson, ch 12 in this volume.

[8] *Autoclenz v Belcher* [2011] UKSC 41, [2011] 4 All ER 745. See Adams-Prassl, ch 13 in this volume.

[9] *O' Kelly v Trusthouse Forte* [1984] QB 90 (CA). See Davies, ch 8 in this volume.

[10] (n 1).

[11] Bagshaw, ch 5 in this volume.

[12] (n 5).

[13] [2002] 35 EHRR 20. See Bogg, ch 10, section III in this volume.

[14] Case C-127/92 *Enderby v Frenchay HA* [1994] ICR 112 (ECJ). See Fredman, ch 9 in this volume.

regulating manifestations of faith in *Achbita*,[15] *Bougnaoui*[16] and *WABE*.[17] Even at the domestic level, the development of litigation through specialist labour courts to general appeal courts provides interesting insights into wider debates about whether the effective adjudication of labour law depends upon specialist expertise or, alternatively, whether law is always just law. Sometimes, the most significant and enduring judgments have issued from the Employment Appeal Tribunal, as with the ubiquitous *Iceland Frozen Foods* decision.[18] It would be relatively unusual in other fields to find a 'landmark' in an appeal court that sits beneath the Court of Appeal in the court hierarchy.

A fourth aspect is how landmarks can be politically salient in the story of labour law even when the legal points in the case have been long forgotten. The phenomenon of the 'political' landmark is especially pronounced in the judicial development of collective labour law. In *Hornby v Close*,[19] *Osborne*,[20] *Rookes v Barnard*,[21] and *Grunwick*,[22] the specific legal points have long been superseded by legal changes. However, the cases remain of the first importance in understanding the politics of judging, and the difficulties of translating common law values into the domain of trade union regulation.

A final aspect is the transformative evolution of the common law as it relates to the personal employment contract. The chapters on *Riley v Warden*,[23] *Devonald v Rosser*,[24] and *Malik v BCCI*[25] chart different common law responses to problems in the employment contract. *Riley* represents a wonderfully hidden landmark, rather like stumbling into St Sepulchre's graveyard in Oxford and pulling back the ivy and finding AV Dicey's gravestone. It identifies an alternative way of thinking about personal work that has now been all but forgotten, yet could usefully be retrieved in dealing with modern problems of substitution clauses. Both *Devonald* and *Malik* provide important insights into a worker-protective conceptualisation of the common law, and one that is at odds with the traditional picture of a regressive common law that threatens the dignity and autonomy of workers.

[15] Case C-157/15 *Achbita v G4S Secure Solutions NV* [2017] 3 CMLR 21 (CJEU). See Barnard, ch 14 in this volume.

[16] Case C–188/15 *Bougnaoui v Micropole SA* [2017] 3 CMLR 22. See Barnard, ch 14 in this volume.

[17] Joined Cases C–804/18 and C–341/19 *IX v WABE eV* [2022] 1 CMLR 11. See Barnard, ch 14 in this volume.

[18] (n 4).

[19] (n 2).

[20] *Amalgamated Society of Railway Servants v Osborne (No 2)* [1911] 1 Ch 540 (CA). See Cabrelli, ch 4 in this volume.

[21] (n 1).

[22] *Grunwick Processing Laboratories Ltd v Advisory, Conciliation and Arbitration Service* (ACAS) [1978] AC 655 (HL). See Ewing, ch 6 in this volume.

[23] *Riley v Warden* (1848) 2 Ex 59, 154 ER 405. See Adams, ch 1 in this volume.

[24] *Devonald v Rosser* [1906] 2 KB 728 (CA). See Sanders, ch 3 in this volume.

[25] *Malik v BCCI* [1998] AC 20 (HL). See Brodie, ch 11 in this volume.

Above all, each chapter is a poignant reminder that work is surely the most human of activities, and landmark cases are nothing without the remarkable people that make those cases. First and foremost, of course, there are the workers themselves who bravely fought for freedom and justice, sometimes at great personal cost. Their stories include a myriad supporting cast of managers, employers, trade union officials, politicians, lawyers, and judges. These moving and inspiring portraits of real people are vital. The chapters bring these figures back to life. They remind us that labour is not a commodity. When workers sell their labour, their very personhood is at stake. Sometimes, the idea of labour as a distinctively human activity has been obscured by the relentless contractualisation of labour law.[26] The most fitting legacy of *Landmark Cases in Labour Law* would be to remind us of the humanity of labour law, and the many ways in which courts can support (or undermine) the dignity of labour.

[26] J Gardner, 'The Contractualisation of Labour Law' in H Collins and V Mantouvalou (eds), *Philosophical Foundations of Labour Law* (Oxford, Oxford University Press, 2019) ch 2.

1

Riley v Warden – *A Landmark Case?*

ZOE ADAMS

I. INTRODUCTION

RILEY V WARDEN,[1] it will be argued, expresses a turning point in the evolution of modern labour law, for it is one of the earliest cases in which we see the emergence of a coherent, legal conceptualisation of wage-dependent labour, and, in turn, the establishment of a link between that conceptualisation and emerging beliefs about labour law's function, and/or rationale. The context of the case is also important: the case arose in the context of the Truck Act 1831, one of the first pieces of 'modern' labour legislation in the sense that this term is understood today: a piece of legislation designed, expressly, for the regulation of the distinct power-relation that lies at the heart of the wage-relation. So too it is one of the first pieces of labour legislation in which we see a clear, coherent, *legal* concept of the wage-dependent person differentiating itself from every-day concepts linked with particular occupations and/or socio-economic groups.[2] The Truck Act, and the particular interpretation that the Act received in *Riley*, not only reflected a major staging post in the evolution of labour law, therefore, and in judicial approaches to questions of employment status, but also in the evolution of the juridical form.[3]

The conceptualisation of the scope of the Truck Act that emerged from *Riley v Warden* did not only influence how subsequent cases were decided under

[1] *Riley v Warden* (1848) 2 Ex 59, 154 ER 405.

[2] The Factory Acts can also be included in this category, although the use of legal definitions emerged only with the later Acts; the scope of the Act was linked more with the sphere in which work was performed, than the status of the person performing it, and the Acts only applied, initially, to children, and later, to women and young people. Thus, the Truck Act 1831 stands out as innovative at both a policy and legal level.

[3] E Pashukanis, *Law and Marxism: A General Theory* (London, Pluto Press, 1989). For a critical discussion of the role of the legal form in shaping labour law's development, see: Z Adams, *Labour and the Wage: A Critical Perspective* (Oxford, Oxford University Press, 2020).

the Truck Acts;[4] it had a profound impact on how beliefs about the scope of the emerging regimes of statutory labour and social welfare legislation were to develop. The premise, taken for granted today, that a worker, and indeed an employee, is someone who provides their work or services personally, and that, as such, the application of statutory labour law presupposes the provision of personal work or services, has its origins in *Riley v Warden*, and the unique legal, and socio-economic environment, in which it was decided. This idea, and the legal tests that developed in relation to it, continue to play a role in the way in which the scope of labour law is conceptualised.[5]

In order to grasp the significance of *Riley v Warden*, it is necessary to engage, at a more abstract, conceptual, level with the 'test' of personal 'labour' or 'service', to better appreciate how, and why, that test might have developed, given the nature and function of labour law, and the contexts to which it has been applied. Having explored this 'test' at a conceptual level, the next task is to explore the background and context of *Riley* in more detail. This will enable us to explore in more detail the case, and judgment, itself. From here, the legacy of *Riley*, and the subsequent evolution of the ideas that emerged through the case, will then be explored, with a view to shedding new light on some of the confusions, and conceptual contradictions, in modern labour law.

II. PERSONAL SERVICE IN MODERN LABOUR LAW

In UK labour law, the concept of the 'worker', a concept that denotes the scope of a number of significant pieces of statutory labour regulation, requires the personal performance of work. Broadly speaking, there are two dimensions to this requirement: first, a person who undertakes to get work done and then employs other persons to do the work is not a worker even if he or she does some of the work personally; and second, the individual cannot be a worker if they are contractually entitled to appoint a substitute, and so, need not perform the work themselves. While these two aspects of the 'test' of personal service are distinct, in practice, particularly since the 1970s, they have tended to be conflated. As a result, the test is today seen, predominantly, through the lens of so-called

[4] Truck Act 1831; Truck Act 1896; and the Hosiery Act 1874. See, also, *Sharman v Sanders* (1853) 13 CB 166, 138 ER 1161; *Sleeman v Barrett, Executors of Bennett* (1864) 2 Hurl& C 934, 159 ER 386; *Squire v Midland Lace Co* [1905] 2 KB 448 (KBD).

[5] In *The Independent Workers Union of Great Britain v The Central Arbitration Committee* [2021] EWCA Civ 952, [2022] ICR 84 the Court of Appeal re-enforced the centrality of the requirement for personal service, at least when it comes to trade union rights, suggesting that the impact of *Uber*, at least outside the context of minimum wage and working time claims, is likely to be limited. However, *Uber* was handed down after the hearing and oral submissions in *Deliveroo*, and the proceedings were only given permission to proceed on a narrow point concerning Article 11 ECHR. This itself might have limited the significance of *Uber* to the case.

substitution clauses.[6] The focus thus tends to be on the extent to which a 'substitution' clause (that expressly empowers the individual to appoint a substitute) reflects the reality of what was agreed between the parties; and the extent to which the power of substitution is unfettered, or subject to various limits. While the courts will take the relative bargaining power of the parties into consideration when determining this question, what remains relevant to the legal assessment is what the 'true agreement' between the parties on this point was, regardless of the *reasons* for which a right of substitution may or may not have been agreed.[7]

The requirement that the individual contract to perform work 'personally' receives legislative backing in section 230(3) ERA, which defines a limb(b) worker as someone who has entered into, or works under, a contract … 'Whereby the individual undertakes to do or perform personally any work or services for another party to the contract whose status is not by virtue of the contract that of a client or customer of any profession or business undertaking carried on by the individual.'[8] This requirement had, however, been incorporated in various ways into the definition of the *workman*, from the beginning of the twentieth century.[9]

We will return to a discussion of the modern interpretation and application of this test towards the end of this chapter. For now, we take a step back, so as to explore, at a more abstract level, why such a test might have developed, and why it might make sense, given labour law's broader structure, and underlying rationale.

In asking why this test might have developed, we are asking two different, but inter-related questions. First, what were the historical circumstances that led to its articulation; Second, how do we make sense of this test in light of labour law's broader function? The first, historical, question will be answered when we explore the pre-history, and legacy, of *Riley*. For now, we focus on the second.

At this level of analysis, we are not concerned with why specific labour law rules, or statutes, came to apply to specific groups; nor are we concerned with the purposes, or policies, behind them. Instead, we are thinking at a much more abstract level about the function that labour law performs more generally, and

[6] Key cases include *Express & Echo Publications Ltd v Tanton* [1999] ICR 693 (CA); *Autoclenz v Belcher* [2009] EWCA Civ 1046, [2010] IRLR 70; *Pimlico Plumbers Ltd v Smith* [2018] UKSC 29, [2018] 4 All ER 641; Case C-692/19 *B v Yodel Delivery Network Ltd* (Court of Justice, 22 April 2020).

[7] *Autoclenz v Belcher* [2011] UKSC 41, [2011] 4 All ER 745, particularly [35].

[8] The status of the statutory wording remains somewhat unclear after the Supreme Court's decision in *Uber v Aslam* [2021] UKSC 5, [2021] 4 All ER 209 because the Court, while endorsing the premise that the statutory wording must be the starting point for legal analysis, went on to determine the question of worker status without drawing on any elements of the statutory definition at all. Until we have a new case concerning substitution clauses and raising issues about personal service, however, we are left to conclude that the statutory definition remains important, although how it will now relate to the factors (of vulnerability, subordination, and dependence) relied upon in *Uber*, remains unclear.

[9] See the discussion below.

about what that function implies about its general scope of application; not the particular persons to which specific labour law rules, or labour law in general, should apply, but the sorts of persons, or rather relations, to which its function is *relevant*.

The starting point for this analysis is the observation that labour law is, ultimately, the law of dependent labour; it applies to wage-relations, relations between those who must work for others for a living, and thus, those who are able to hire others with a view to making a profit (or accumulating a surplus, as in public sector employment). Labour law's development corresponded with the generalisation of exchange, and the emergence of a class of persons with no choice but to sell their labour power in the labour market in order to have access to the means of subsistence.[10] These persons thus became dependent on those with the means to hire those workers, and deploy them productively, to live; persons in a position to profit from their work.[11] The dependence that is characteristic of these working relations, combined with the competitive pressures to which both parties are subject, creates an incentive, and opportunity for the 'employing' party to use the labour of the worker in such a way as to interfere with the process of social reproduction – to subject the worker to various socio-economic and physical risks, against which the worker is largely powerless to protect him/herself. This is not because employers are greedy and malicious, but because of the imperative towards accumulation that is inherent in the structure of capitalism, and which is 'enforced' through the competitive market. The 'intervention' of labour law, placing limits on how labour power can be used in the production process, can thus be seen as a collective attempt to regulate the way in which the power-relation between capital and labour manifests in the context of the wage-relation in the interests of capital in general, and, by implication, of society. It thus recognises the need by workers (and, by implication, capital) for decent working conditions and adequate wages, and the need by firms for productive labour and profit – minimising, or controlling for, these risks, and doing so in such a way as to secure a sustainable supply of labour power over time, while, at the same time, minimising the social and economic conflict intrinsic to capitalist relations of production.[12]

Given these observations, there are two ways in which we might understand why labour law, which attempts to align itself with the power relation unique to capitalist work relations, requires, as a condition for its own application,

[10] S Deakin, 'The Contribution of Labour Law to Economic and Human Development' in BA Langille and G Davidov (eds), *The Idea of Labour Law* (Oxford, Oxford University Press, 2011); S Deakin, 'The Contract of Employment: A Study in Legal Evolution' [2001] *Historical Studies in Industrial Relations* 1.

[11] The generalisation of wage-dependence also placed others, not employed by capital, such as domestic servants, in a similar position of dependence, and such persons have often also been included within the scope of aspects of labour law by way of analogy.

[12] This conception of labour law is elaborated in detail in Adams (n 3).

the provision of *personal* labour or service. On the one hand, we might see the requirement for personal work or service as emphasising the distinction between someone who provides their labour power – their 'personal labour' – and someone who, not dependent on working for others to access to the means of subsistence, is in a position to sell the product of their labour with a view to making a profit. From this perspective, then, 'personal service' functions as a proxy for wage-dependence, or rather, a juridical technique for identifying an exchange of labour *power*, and so, helps to identify members of a particular socio-economic class: wage-dependent labour. This, as we shall see, is the meaning implicitly attributed to 'personal labour' in *Riley*, where the requirement for personal labour functions to distinguish those who sell their labour power for wages, from those who agree to secure some outcome, or result, from which they are in a position to profit.

From a different perspective, the notion of personal service or labour expresses something about how the wage-relation is, or has come, over time, to be legitimised in law: as a highly personal relationship in which the nature and quality of the labour, and the identity and needs of the worker, are legitimised, and attributed importance, by each party.[13] From this perspective, the idea that a worker is someone who provides his personal labour or services does not necessarily imply that the individual should not be classed in law *as* a worker unless this 'personal' element is present; rather, it expresses the normative ideal, the hoped for result, of labour law's application – a more personal relation in which the dignity of the worker is, and can be seen to be, upheld and respected, a prerequisite, moreover, for society's sustainable reproduction.

In what follows, we will see that it is this latter interpretation of the requirement for personal labour that has prevailed in the case law, but that it has become inverted, or distorted, as labour law has developed. Rather than seeing the personal nature of the labour relationship as a normative ideal projected onto working relationships with a view to shaping them, the courts have begun to make this personal element a factual precondition for labour law's application; for *finding* worker status in the first place.[14] This position is what is reflected in the emphasis placed today on substitution clauses, on whether the contract allows for an unfettered right of substitution. By recovering the analysis employed in *Riley*, however, and the role that the test of personal labour performed in that context, we can, it will be argued, go some way towards better aligning labour law's function, with its scope of application, making socio-economic criteria central to questions of employment status.

[13] This perspective underpins the recognition of the implied duty of mutual trust and confidence, see *Malik v Bank of Credit and Commerce International SA (in liq)* [1998] AC 20 (HL).

[14] N Contouris, 'Uses and Misuses of "Mutuality of Obligations" and the Autonomy of Labour Law' in A Bogg and others (eds), *The Autonomy of Labour Law* (Oxford, Hart, 2015). See also ch 8 in this volume.

III. EMPLOYMENT STATUS: A PRE-HISTORY

Labour law does not directly refer to the individual's socio-economic status when determining whether someone meets the legal criteria for worker or employee status. Not only is a direct engagement with the structural origins of that status, and thus, the inequalities inherent in the capitalist system, largely precluded by the assumptions of freedom and equality that are so integral to the law's legitimacy, but so too are questions of socioeconomic status extremely difficult to answer in practice. That is, while, conceptually, the distinction between labour and capital is clear, in practice, not only does wage-dependence manifest itself in a myriad of ways, in the context of a variety of forms of working arrangements, but so too will the court not always be presented with sufficient information to make such an elaborate and complex assessment. As such, and out of a need to facilitate efficiency and consistency in legal reasoning, the courts inevitably develop certain *proxies* for wage-dependence, factors which are often associated with wage-dependence, and which can be relied on to facilitate decision-making in practice. These so-called proxies might then crystallise into a set of tests, or factors to be considered, when assessments about employment status are made.

Not only are these tests inherently imperfect, then, abstracted as they are from the diverse circumstances in which questions of status arise, but each 'proxy' or 'test' for establishing employment status is influenced by the particular socio-historical context in which different labour law rights developed, and, relatedly, in which particular kinds of cases came before the courts.[15] Thus, the nature and policy behind particular pieces of legislation, as well as the nature and structure of industry and the wider economic framework, necessarily influences which 'proxies' are identified, and persist, at different times. At the same time, however, these proxies necessarily express certain common, or recurrent, features of capitalist work relations, and so allow, however imperfectly, the legal system to identify wage-relations without, necessarily, engaging with questions of socio-economic status directly.

In early modern labour law, at a time when the legal form was relatively under-developed (there was an absence of political, or legal, equality, and many groups remained excluded from participation in social and economic life) labour legislation made an individual's socio-economic status the reference point for determining the scope of the Act's application, and this enabled the courts to engage with socio-economic criteria more or less directly when it came to determining the scope of the legislative duty to work.[16] It was thus

[15] S Deakin, 'Juridical Ontology: The Evolution of Legal Form' [2015] *Historical Social Research/Historische Sozialforschung* 170.

[16] The Statute of Labourers 1351 (25 Ed 3 c 1) applied to 'every man and woman of our kingdom of England, of whatever condition, whether bond or free, who is able bodied and below the age of sixty years, not living from trade nor carrying on a fixed craft, nor having of his own the means of living, or land of his own with regard to the cultivation of which he might occupy himself, and not

the socio-economic status of the parties, and the lack of economic independence of the 'servant' that explained the different rights and obligations to which each were subject in the context of the 'master and servant' relation. Not only did this lack of economic independence justify a legal duty to work, so too did it justify the individual's subordination to the control of his master, and the latter's obligations of maintenance and protection. In such a context, it was evidence of factual subordination to a master's control, that gradually came to be associated with the subordinate socio-economic status required by the legislation.[17]

Socio-economic criteria remained central to determining the scope of protective labour and social security legislation throughout the fourteenth to the eighteenth centuries.[18] Things began to change, however, with the introduction of the master and servant legislation of the eighteenth and nineteenth centuries. By the early-mid eighteenth century, successive waves of land enclosure had brought into being a large class of propertyless persons with no choice but to work for others to live.[19] The result was a rapid growth in the numbers of persons moving to the towns in search of work, and thus, the numbers of those hired in predominantly manual, or industrial, employment. In this context, labour law's function began to change.[20] While this legislation included a number of provisions similar to those contained in the Statute of Artificers 1563, the entire rationale, and structure, of the legislation was quite different. Far from forming part of a comprehensive system of social and labour legislation whereby a legal obligation to work was coupled with a right to subsistence (statutory wages and access to poor relief), the master and servant acts were concerned, principally, with matters of work discipline.[21]

The master and servant legislation was enacted at a time when wage-labour was increasingly being associated with ideas about *free labour*, rather than social, and economic, subordination.[22] In such a context, and in the absence of any legal compulsion to work, it was by reference to occupation, rather than socio-economic position, that the scope of master and servant legislation came to be delimited. The legislation was, however, founded on a contradiction.

serving another'. The Statute of Artificers 1563 (5 Eliz 1 c 4), s 3 similarly, applied to all those 'not having Tenements Rentes or Hereditamentes Copieholder or Freeholder of an Estate of Inheritance or for the terms of ante Life or Lives of *the clear value of fourty shillings, nor being worthy of his own Gods the clear value of ten pounds*' (emphasis added).

[17] Similar approaches were applied under the Statute of Labourers 1351 (25 Ed 3 c 1), the Statute of Artificers 1563 (5 Eliz 1 c 4) and the 1834 Poor Law.

[18] Adams (n 3).

[19] For a detailed history of this process, see MA Žmolek, *Rethinking the Industrial Revolution: Five Centuries of Transition from Agrarian to Industrial Capitalism in England* (Leiden, Brill, 2013).

[20] For a detailed analysis, see S Deakin and F Wilkinson, *The Law of the Labour Market: Industrialization, Employment and Legal Evolution* (Oxford, Oxford University Press, 2005)

[21] RJ Steinfeld, *Coercion, Contract, and Free Labor in the Nineteenth Century* (Cambridge, Cambridge University Press, 2001).

[22] RJ Steinfeld, *The Invention of Free Labor: The Employment Relation in English and American Law and Culture, 1350–1870* (London, University of North Carolina Press, 1991).

While the legal status, and thus autonomy, of the worker was now taken as given, the substantive provisions of the legislation still presupposed a difference of status – and it was this difference of status that justified subjecting workers, but not employers, to criminal sanctions for contract breach. It was workers' lack of financial independence that meant workers could not be trusted to hold to the terms of their agreement, by not being in a position to pay damages in the event of a breach.[23]

Having abandoned socio-economic criteria as a basis on which to determine the scope of the Acts, Parliament resorted instead to factual or vernacular descriptors – listed occupations – making it extremely difficult to abstract generalisable criteria for the Acts' application. And yet, the ability to do this was essential to the legislation's legitimacy; there had to be some basis on which to distinguish those *within* and those *without* the Act's scope, and thus, to justify why certain persons were subject to criminal penalties, and others were not.

It was in the course of establishing such generalisable criteria that the courts determined that 'high status' workers in a position of relative economic independence could not be within the scope of the legislation: persons such as the clerk in *Bramwell v Penneck*, clearly not being within the class contemplated by the Act.[24] To better distinguish between these groups, the courts began to focus less on the list of occupations and trades enumerated in the Acts, and more on the description of the way in which they were contracted to work:[25] on the *manner in which the work was procured*. Given common law associations between the notion of service, and the private, patriarchal relationship of service, however, this meant that the courts began delimiting the scope of the Act by reference to the degree of exclusive control to which the servant was subject. The Acts were thus interpreted not as applying to all persons who freely agreed to work for another, nor to persons who were wage-dependent per se, but, as a proxy for this latter category, all those whose wage dependence was such as to compel them to *enter into the service* of another, this entry being both an explanation, and justification, for their subjection to the penal provisions of the Act.[26] In effect, despite Parliament's clear intention to extend the Act to all wage-dependent persons working for emerging capitalist firms, the courts applied the Act only to those wage dependent persons hired under a contract of service, and so, who were subordinate or dependent to a particular employer, now, not so much because of their legal and social inferiority, but by reason of the subordination implied by the specific form of contract by which they were hired.

[23] That this was the rationale is particularly clear from the Select Committee Report on the master and servant legislation: Great Britain Parliament and others, 'Report from the Selected Committee on Master and Servants; Together with the Proceedings of the Committee, Minutes of Evidence, Appendix, and Index'. For discussion, see Steinfeld (n 21).

[24] (1827) 7 B & C 536, 108 ER 823.

[25] This was also reflected in the statutory wording: Master and Servant Act 1823, s 3 (4 Geo 4 c 34).

[26] *Johnson v Reid* (1840) 6 M & W 124, 125; 151 ER 348, 350.

In order to extend the scope of the Acts beyond those entering service, to include all the dependent 'employed', and thus, to overcome what was effectively a judicial gloss on the statute, Parliament gradually modified the wording of the Acts to remove all references to *serving* and *service*. In the Hosiery Act 1843, for example, the term *serve* was replaced with the term *to work* and the term *service* with 'work or employment'. In effect, Parliament was trying to establish a formulation that would have the effect of bringing within the scope of the Act a particular *social class*, without, however, making express reference to the parties' respective socio-economic status. In the absence of a clear legal conceptualisation of the wage-dependent person, or of the relationship through which such persons worked, however, the only way they could do this was by exhaustively listing the occupations in which wage-labour was dominant, and the various forms of arrangement by which workers might be hired. The result was considerable inconsistency, and complexity, in the way in which the Acts came to be applied.[27]

By the mid-1800s, it was becoming clear that the concept of service could no longer do the conceptual work required to encompass the full scope of dependent working relations to which the Acts were intended to apply: workers were increasingly being hired under forms of contract that deviated from the way such contracts had been conceived, given the prevalence of piecework, putting out and other sub-contracting arrangements. It is no surprise, then, that a conceptual break was to occur, and labour legislation to move away from the notion of *master and servant*, towards ideas about work, labour, and employment.[28]

It is against this background that the novelty, and significance, of the Truck Act 1831 must be appreciated. The modern Truck legislation was introduced in the 1830s[29] with a view to combatting what was seen as a highly abusive practice, namely, the substitution, by employers, of monetary wages, for payment in kind; a strategy that enabled them to gain a competitive advantage by artificially depressing the wages of their workers, while, simultaneously, keeping

[27] For detailed analysis of this law, see Steinfeld (n 21).

[28] The Factory Acts are outside the scope of this article. However, it is important to note that the Factory Acts also moved away from the language of master and servant, referring to persons 'employed' in a factory and a particular trade/industry (originally, textiles). Only later was 'employed' defined to refer to persons who were *hired* to perform work of a particular kind, whether or not for wages (and, implicitly, irrespective of the type of contract). The Factory Acts did not, however, develop a clear legal concept to conceptualise the sorts of persons working in factories, and later, workshops, and so, was less innovative in this respect than the Truck Act. Despite this, in establishing limits to the working day, policymakers were giving expression to the boundaries of the commodity labour power, and the time in the factory was conceptualised as time under the control of an alien power – machinery. By implication, then, like the Truck Act, the Act was novel in that they did implicitly recognise a class of persons to whom protective labour legislation of various sorts ought to apply, by reason of the fact that they alienated their 'personal labour' or labour power, subjecting themselves to the 'tyranny' of capital (or rather, the machine).

[29] Examples of truck legislation go back to the fifteenth century, but the 1831 legislation was the first generalised truck legislation to be applied outside specific industries.

them in a position of dependence by preventing them from accessing necessary consumption goods other than via the employer.

Importantly, the Truck Act 1831 was the first labour legislation to define its scope of application through a *legal concept* subsequently defined in the Act, rather than by reference to the socio-economic status of the parties (as in the Statute of Labourers 1351 and the Statute of Artificers 1563) and rather than by listing exhaustively the sorts of work arrangements included (as in the master and servant Legislation). But so too was the Act the first to self-consciously conceptualise itself as legislation designed to 'protect' wage-dependent persons against abuse by the economically more powerful party: the employer. As a result, a distinction between the beneficiaries of the Act – the workman, or artificer – and the employer, was integral to the Act's entire structure.

The Act applied to all artificers, defined as including 'all Workmen, Labourers, and *other Persons* in any Manner *engaged* in the Performance of any Work, Employment, or Operation, of what Nature soever, in or about the several Trades and Occupations aforesaid' and provided such artificers with an absolute right to be paid by their employers, all wages due and payable in monetary form. These persons were distinguished from their employers, who were defined as all those 'Masters, Bailiffs, Foremen, Managers Clerks, and other Persons engaged in the Hiring, Employment, or Superintendence of the Labour of such Artificers.'[30]

Despite the clear statutory definitions, itself a novelty in the labour law field, the reality of the division between workers and employers in the trades to which the Act applied was highly complex. The sub-contracting system was still so common that many persons who might be thought to meet the definition of 'Artificer' would often also be 'super-intending' others in the performance of the work. As a result, the courts were forced to interpret the definition of the 'Artificer' in light of the Act's purpose, which, they assumed was linked with the socio-economic status of the Artificer, as a member of the 'unprovided class' and the vulnerability this status created vis-a-vis attempts, by employers, to avoid their contractual obligations.[31]

The courts derived this understanding of the legislation's purpose from the use of other terms invoked in the Act, namely, the terms *wage* and *labour*. Artificers, the courts said, must be persons for whom a payment for work constitutes a *wage*, and thus, whose work could be conceptualised as a form of personal *labour*. What they meant by this was that, given their wage-dependence, that they 'earned their bread by the sweat of their brow', the persons within the scope of the Acts were persons with nothing *but* their personal labour from which to live, persons with no capital to deploy, and thus, no capacity with which to hire others, in order to make a profit.

[30] Truck Act 1831, s 24 (1 & 2 Will 4 c 37) (emphasis added).
[31] See the discussion below.

By these means, the courts distinguished between persons who provided their personal labour for wages, and who were wage-dependent and within the scope of the Act (Artificers), and those who were not wage-dependent, and so, were paid a price for some contracted for result. It was this premise that underpinned the decision in *Riley*, a case followed in all subsequent decisions about scope decided under the Acts.

IV. RILEY V WARDEN

Riley arose from an action for work and labour. The defendants had contracted to make part of the Oxford, Worcester, and Wolverhampton railway, at a certain sum per cubic yard. The defendants had divided the contract into several smaller portions, and sub-contracted them to various persons, one of whom was the plaintiff. Tickets for goods were supplied by the defendants to the plaintiff, who gave them to his men as payment. The plaintiff then engaged eight or nine men to work with him in the construction of the railway, including in removing clay from the soil for the making of bricks (an activity expressly included within the Truck Act). It was accepted by both sides that, in practice, the plaintiff worked alongside his men doing the work of a 'common labourer' – removing clay from the soil.

The case arose when the defendants pleaded a set-off in goods to the amount of 16l. 8s in respect of clay provided to the plaintiff for the purposes of making bricks. The plaintiff objected that the set-off was in respect of goods delivered to the plaintiff in lieu of payment of wages due to him as a workman, and that such a demand was illegal under the Truck Act (which provided an absolute right to be paid all wages due and payable in monetary coin). The key question in the case was whether, as the plaintiff contended, the plaintiff was a workman within the meaning of the Truck Act, or whether, as the defendants contended, he was not, him being a sub-contractor who further sub-contracted work to his men.

The Court's starting premise was that the Act applies to those who 'strictly contract as labourers'.[32] By this was meant 'to such as enter into a contract to employ their personal services and to receive payment for that service in wages'.[33] Parke B suggested that this question referred to the *condition* of the plaintiff, and to answer this question, he turned to analyse the purpose of the Act, arguing that:

> [T]his act was intended to be applied to those who engage to do a work by their own personal labour, and that the object of it is to protect such men as earn their bread by the sweat of their brow, and who are, for the most part, an unprovided class, and

[32] *Riley* (n 1) (1848) 2 Ex 59, 68;154 ER 405, 409 (Parke B).
[33] ibid.

> that it was not intended to have any application whatever to persons who take work upon a great scale.[34]

This question was different, he suggested, from the question under the master and servant legislation as to whether the *relation* of master and servant was present – a question that continued to imply the existence of (social) subordination and control, by the master, over the performance of work. This view was echoed by Rolf B who emphasised that the Act

> applies only to those persons who are to receive wages as the price of their labour, and that the term "wages" is to be understood in its popular sense and does not include wages which are the price of a contract. … The 19th section seems to me to have reference to workmen and labourers who earn wages by their own personal labour, and not to those who, although they join in the work, derive a profit from the exertions of others.[35]

Two core principles can be derived from this judgment. First, the Truck Act was deemed to apply to an 'unprovided class' unable to protect themselves by contract.[36] This inability to protect themselves was linked with the fact that these persons 'earned their bread by the sweat of their brow',[37] and so, had no choice but to work in exchange for wages to live. Second, those who were in such a position, or 'condition', were persons who had nothing *but* their personal labour to sell, and as such, could be said to have contracted to provide their work personally. Persons in this position would not be able to take on contracts of a large scale, which would require considerable capital investments, and, potentially, the hiring of a number of additional labourers, and so, could not be said to be artificers within the meaning of the Act.

Through the cases decided under these Acts, and their interpretation of the Act's scope, the courts elaborated a rationale for the existence of the Truck Act 1831, as a limited exception to the principle of freedom of contract, by reference to the worker's socio-economic status: his wage-dependence.[38] This wage-dependence thus became the reference point when it came to determining the scope of the Act, because its presence was the factor legitimising the Act's, or rather, the legislature's, 'intervention' with free labour. The statutory terms 'artificer' and 'workman' were to be construed as referring to wage-dependent persons, a useful proxy for which, they assumed, was the criterion of personal service: persons who are dependent on wages for subsistence are persons who, by definition, have no choice but to sell their 'personal' labour to others to live. While the Court conceptualised the requirement for personal service, or 'labour',

[34] ibid.

[35] ibid (1848) 2 Ex 59, 69–70;154 ER 405, 409–10 (Parke B).

[36] See also *Archer v James* (1859) 2 Best and Smith 67, 72–73; 121 ER 998, 100 (Keating J).

[37] *Riley* (n 1) (1848) 2 Ex 59, 68;154 ER 405, 409 (Parke B).

[38] *Archer* (n 36); 121 ER 998, 100 (Keating J). This is consistent with the debates in Parliament surrounding the passage of the legislation, see, eg, HC Deb 17 March 1830, vol 23, cols 461–74.

as a requirement that the individual have contracted to provide work personally, the existence of an obligation to provide work personally was derived from an analysis of the status of the parties; a wage dependent person who worked for another simply was, in other words, someone who contracted to provide their personal labour. This was not merely a distinction between someone who contracts to provide a specific result, and someone who agrees to provide a given quantum of work. It was a distinction between persons in a position to profit from their work, and those able, merely, to access the means of subsistence, reproducing their wage-dependence, and thus, their necessity to work for wages on an ongoing basis.

The problem, however, was that after these ideas were first articulated, they crystallised into a highly contractualised test of *personal service*, which, while initially invoked as a proxy for wage-dependence, soon came to be viewed through the lens of the contract. By the time that *Ingram v Barnes*[39] was decided, therefore, the courts were arguing that, to fall within the scope of the Act, an individual must be expressly required by their *contract* to provide their work personally, and thus, be prevented by that contract from hiring others to assist them in their work. Personal service no longer functioned to identify the provision of labour *power*, that labour was being provided by someone dependent on wages for subsistence; instead, it expressed a particular contractual obligation to which the parties may or may not have agreed. Particularly where there was a written contract, therefore, this meant that, in the absence of an express undertaking to provide work personally, the Truck Act 1831 would not apply. While the existence of a contractual right to provide a substitute was still not considered, the absence of an express contractual obligation to provide work oneself was deemed to negate employment status for the purposes of the Truck Act 1831.

The problem with this 'juridified' notion of personal service, viewed through the lens of the parties' agreement, was that, in a context where most individuals were paid by the piece, it was often not necessary for the employer to specify in the contract that the worker had to do the work him/herself to guarantee that the work would be performed to specification. While the test may have worked well in the case of *Riley*, a contractor hiring a large number of workers to perform the work for which he was paid, it worked less well when the test was applied to a homeworker who shared the burden of the work with her family because if she did not do so, she simply would not be able to meet the employer's production quota, and so, would not be paid at all.[40] In this latter context, rather than an expression of economic independence, hiring others could actually be an expression of desperation, of an extreme state of dependence that was becoming increasingly invisible to the law because it did not need

[39] *Ingram v Barnes* (1857) 7 El & Bl 115, 119 ER 1190.

[40] For a particularly extreme example of this, see *Squire v Midland Lace Co* [1905] 2 KB 448 (KBD).

to be given an explicit contractual basis in order to be of potential benefit to the capitalist employer. While the Truck Act 1831 thus expressed an increasing formalisation and systematisation of legal discourse, this went hand in hand with a diminishment in the legal system's capacity to perceive, and conceptualise, differences of *socio-economic* status in practice. However integral questions of socio-economic status may have been to the decision in *Riley*, therefore, the premise that was to be taken forward, and thus, to guide future cases, was that an individual must have contracted to provide their personal service for the Truck Act 1831 to apply, and this was now something that could only be ascertained through an analysis of the parties' agreement.

V. THE SUBSEQUENT FATE OF THE 'TEST' FOR PERSONAL SERVICE

In *Riley*, the courts had recognised that labour law's rationale was rooted to the unique socio-economic position of labour in the social structure of capitalism. In order to articulate this observation in law, however, some explanation for socio-economic inequality – for wage dependence – had to be found that was consistent with the legal system's emerging assumptions about formal freedom and equality. This 'explanation' was found by giving expression to the notion of wage-dependence through the idea of a contractual obligation to provide work personally: the provision of labour power to capital thus became a function of the parties' free agreement, rather than a function of their respective socio-economic positions. As the case law developed, then, emphasis shifted away from the socioeconomic realties of the relationship, and the structural pressures characterising its dynamics, to the particular form in which that relationship was given juridical expression.

It was in light of the difficulties of this reframing of the personal service test that a new way of giving expression to this ideal developed as it became embedded in the concept of the 'workman', a concept which became the focal point for determining the scope of protective labour legislation as it developed throughout the late nineteenth and early twentieth centuries. This approach circumvented the highly contractualised interpretation of personal service by reading it through the lens of a requirement for 'manual labour'. Because manual labour was, by definition, work that had to be done personally (by one's own hands'), and because it was in the context of manufacturing that wage-labour was predominant, manual labour appeared to allow for a more nuanced analysis of the circumstances of each case. Increasingly, then, manual labour became central to statutory definitions of the workman, and to the courts' attempts to interpret such definitions in practice.

As wage dependence extended to new sectors, however, the limitations of the 'manual labour' proxy became apparent. As a result, in the mid- twentieth century, the requirement for personal service began, once again, to assume central stage, accompanied, however, by the notion of *control*. In practice, the two concepts were closely related: the requirement that the individual be under the control of their employer expressed the premise that workmen, as persons who provided their personal labour to their employers were necessarily persons who had no choice but to cede control over their working processes to their employers,[41] and so, were in a fundamentally different position from 'the manager of a bank, a foreman with high wages, persons … in the position almost of gentlemen'.[42]

This conception of control continued to inform the courts' interpretation of the 'workman' concept after 1906, when the definition of the workman was narrowed so as to apply only if the individual was employed under a contract of service or apprenticeship, rendering the status of 'workman' not a socioeconomic status, associated with manual forms of work, but a legal status derivative of the form of contract by which they were hired (a contract of service of apprenticeship).[43] The effect of this was, ultimately, to introduce a second set of criteria by which to determine the Act's scope; the Act still applied to 'workmen' in the 'ordinary sense of the word', that is, wage dependent persons and/or persons earning little by way of wages or salary,[44] but only if those persons were also hired under a contract of service (or apprenticeship), rather than a contract *for services.*

The result of this shift was that the contract of service came to be associated with the criteria which, previously, had developed to denote the *socioeconomic* status of a workman – notions such as personal service, predominantly manual work, and subordination to an employer's control.[45] Thus, what had once been criteria relied on to identify membership of a particular class, became instead a description of a particular *form* of contract, the existence of which was a precondition for the application of rights under protective labour legislation. As such, in time, the courts began implying that what makes someone a workman *is* the form of contract by which they are hired. Thus, in the same way that a servant became, in the seventeenth and eighteenth centuries, a wage dependent person *hired under a particular form of contract*, so too did the workman become someone hired under a particular form of contract, someone who, *by virtue of his contract* was in a relationship of subordination with an employer, the latter being someone who, *by virtue of that contract*, had control over the work.

[41] This link is clear from the discussion by Dillon J in *Humberstone v Northern Timber Mills* (1949) 79 CLR 389 (HCA) 404; *Ready Mixed Concrete (South East) Ltd v Minister of Pensions and National Insurance* [1968] 2 QB 497 (QB) 523.

[42] *Yewens v Noakes* (1880) 6 QBD 530 (CA) 538. The idea of 'control' was also implicit in the discussion surrounding the Factory Acts, where 'work' was conceptualised in terms of a particular 'compulsion' to an 'alien power', imposing on the worker unnatural, and inhuman, conditions of work.

[43] Workmen's Compensation Act 1906, s 13.

[44] The Act further reinforced this point by excluding anyone earning over £250 per year, see Workmen's Compensation Act 1906, s 13.

[45] As summarised in *Ready Mixed Concrete (South East) Ltd* (n 41).

In practice, these changes meant that the courts no longer had to refer directly to questions of social status to determine the scope of the emerging body of labour law's application. Rather than focusing on the question of the individual's wage dependence, therefore, and thus, their class position, the courts increasingly *deduced* that class position (their status as 'workmen') *from* an analysis of the contract by which they were hired, the presumption being that wage dependent persons *were* persons whose contracts reserved their employers a general power to direct the work, *and* whose contracts obliged them to provide their work personally.

With the introduction of the National Insurance Act 1911, the entire structure of social insurance legislation was to change. As part of this, the rights were extended beyond the contract of service to encompass an entire socio-economic class, persons who 'are engaged in some regular occupation and are wholly or mainly dependent for their livelihood on the earnings derived by them from that occupation' *regardless* of the form of the contract by which they were hired.[46] For these persons then, the Act recognised a distinct class of persons whose status was not derivative of the contract through which they provided their work, persons in need of the Act's protection.

Following the war, the scope of social insurance was extended. Given that different forms of work arrangement necessitated a different system for administrating contributions and payments, a new distinction was created between persons gainfully occupied *in employment*, hired under a contract of service, and all others in gainful occupation *other than by way of a contract of service*. The result was that all express references to wage-dependence, or socio-economic status, disappeared, and the key distinction came to be the form of contract by which labour was hired.

It was a result of this new distinction between the employed and the self-employed that the courts were forced to broaden their conception of the contract of service, so as to bring within the scope of the 'employed' not only those 'workmen' who were hired under a contract of service, whose employers exercised control over the manner in which they did their work, but also the growing number of skilled, and professional, persons, unable to earn an income *other than* by providing their work or services through a large public, or private, firm or organisation. To do this, they reconceptualised the sort of control which the structure of the contract of service was deemed to imply, so as to include *organisational* control, and thus, the integration of the individual into another's business, rather than direct supervision over working processes, and it is this idea that is today expressed in the modern concept of the employee. This notion of integration helped support an idea of employment as inherently personal, for it saw the employee – his individual qualities and personality – as an *integral* part of the employer's organisation.

[46] National Insurance Act 1911, s 1.

This distinction, between persons providing work under this reconceptualised contract of service, and those providing 'work' under some other arrangement, allowed for the development of a new body of labour protections that attached to the contract of service or employment, rather than being contingent on the socio-economic status of the person providing work. Thus, as labour law developed, new rights came to be conferred on *employees*, and could be justified not by reference to the socio-economic status of the person providing work, but by reference to the nature of the legal form under which they did so: a particular form of contract in which personal subordination and direct, *contractually mediated* mechanisms of control, were implied. In this context, that employment implied the provision of *personal* service, and thus, a highly personal, and co-operative relationship, was coming to be taken for granted in juridical discourse, as one of the 'hallmarks' of the *regulated* relationship that was employment. In effect, through legal regulation, the law had realised the idea of a more personal employment relationship for a sub-class of the dependent employers, and they had done so through the lens of the concept of the contract of employment.

It was in *Ready Mixed Concrete*[47] that the Court attempted to elaborate clear criteria for distinguishing between contracts of service, and contracts for services, and it is in this context that a clear link is made between the idea that employment implies that the individual provide his/her own work or skill, and the notion of a contractual power of delegation/substitution. While the Court suggested that a freedom to do the job by the hands of another is inconsistent with a contract of service, although a limited *power* of delegation may not be, the authority cited in support of this proposition is Atiyah's book on Vicarious Liability.[48] Here, Atiyah states that a contract of service requires that the individual provide *at least some* of the work him/herself, and that an *obligation* (ie rather than a power) to provide a substitute is just one of the factors that will point away from the existence of a contract of service.[49] Atiyah in no way suggested, therefore, that the existence of a power to substitute was necessarily decisive when it came to questions of employment status. While the idea that contracts of service are highly personal was thus persistent at this time, 'substitution' clauses were not seen to be particularly significant in the overall assessment of the nature of the parties' relationship, and thus, the question of employment status. While an obligation to provide a substitute might point away from employment status, a mere power to do so need not.

Throughout the mid-twentieth century, the contract of service had thus become central to questions of employment status, and thus, to the scope of the emerging set of protective labour legislation. This was, to a large extent, due to the *nature* of many of the rights developed – rights that presupposed

[47] *Ready Mixed Concrete* (n 41).
[48] PS Atiyah, *Vicarious Liability in the Law of Torts* (London, Butterworths, 1967).
[49] Citing *Braddell v Baker* (1911) 104 LT 673 (DC) in support. See Atiyah (n 48) 59.

a long-term, stable relationship, between a single employee and a single firm. When the Industrial Relations Act was introduced in 1971 ('IRA 1971'), however, Parliament recognised that the right to join a trade union could not be justified by reference to the particular form of contract by which someone was hired. Rather, the right was required in respect of all persons dependent on wages (or salaries) to live, and for this, the concept of the employee was deemed inappropriate.[50] In the end, having dismissed the concept of the employee as too narrow, and the concept of person as too broad, the concept of the 'worker' was chosen as the appropriate concept through which to include an *entire* socio-economic class, something they intended to capture through a statutory definition that drew, in many respects, on the earlier definition of the *workman*.

While drawing on the earlier concept of the workman (renamed 'worker' in the wages Councils Act in the mid-1940s) the IRA 1971 introduced two important innovations: first, a new exception excluding professionals providing services to a client; and second, an express inclusion of not only those who *actually* work under a contract for personal work (etc) but also those who *normally work*, or are *seeking* to work under such a contract – an approach that very much mirrors the socio-economic criteria used in the National Insurance Act 1911. The definition thus made explicit the intention to extend unionisation rights to persons enjoying a status that was *not* dependent on the contract by which they were hired but attached to an individual by reason of his position in the broader social structure.

The IRA 1971 definition is still used today in the context of legislation concerning rights relating to trade unions (Trade Union and Labour Relations (Consolidation) Act 1992 ('TULRCA 1992'). The definition used in the context of individual employment rights, by contrast, is that originally formulated in the context of the Wages Act 1986. Not only did the Wages Act 1986 add the requirement that the other party to the contract not be a client or customer of any business or profession carried on by the individual, but because the rights provided under the Act were relevant only as between individual workers and firms, it only applied to individuals *actually* hired by a particular firm, and not people who would *ordinarily* work under a contract to provide personal services. For this reason, the formulation that was adopted, while intended to capture all wage-dependent persons, no longer expressed the status of worker as if it predated the contract. Instead, the status appeared as if it were derivative of that contract; it is this definition that can be found in section 230(3) of the Employment Rights Act 1996 ('ERA 1996') today, and which is usually the reference point when determining the scope of modern labour legislation as it applies to workers.[51]

[50] See particularly HL Deb 04 May 1971, vol 318, cols 160–349; HL Deb 05 April 1971, vol 317, cols 4–192; HC Deb 14 December 1970, vol 808, cols 961–1076.

[51] Wages Act 1986, s 8. See now ERA 1996, s 230(3) and similar provisions in the National Minimum Wage Act 1998 and the Working Time Regulations 1998.

The process by which the legal system has given juridical expression to a particular socio-economic status, has thus, over time, transformed the socio-economic status of the worker into something deemed, in law, to derive not from a power relation that has its origins in the wider class structures in which contracts for work are concluded, but in a power relation that arises because of the contract under which work is actually procured. As such, the existence of this status is to be determined not from an analysis of the circumstances of the parties, or the socio-economic function of the work performed, but from the terms of the agreement. While the trade union definition still refers to persons *normally working* under a particular contract, even this has been interpreted by the courts in a way that makes the status derivative of the contract, and not antecedent to it. As a result, what we see in practice is an assimilation of the tests used in relation to both definitions (that is, the definition in the IRA 1971 and in the Wages Act 1986/ERA 1996): the courts refusing to recognise the existence, or significance, of any distinction between them.[52] The inclusion in trade union legislation of those who 'normally work' under the contract therein described has thus been interpreted, somewhat artificially, to refer not to the idea that a worker is someone who, were they to be in work, would likely be working under a contract of that form (given their socio-economic status) but to those who are already in a contractual relationship with a firm, who, when working, are doing so under that form of contract. One of the core questions in all cases concerning collective or individual labour rights, then, is thus whether there exists a *contractual* obligation to provide work personally; whether the parties *agreed* that the individual must provide their work personally, or whether, instead, the worker is free by his contract to decide if, and if so, when and how much, to work, and whether or not to do so personally, or by providing a substitute.[53]

The difficulties that arise from focusing on the terms of a written contract in the context of employment, particularly when determining matters related to substitution, were explicitly acknowledged by the Supreme Court in *Autoclenz*,[54] where the Court expressly stated that the inequality of bargaining power between the parties must be considered when determining the true agreement between the parties. This case was important for distinguishing between the written contract, and the *actual* contract, that is, the parties' agreement, where circumstances effectively limit the capacity of one party to influence the written terms. Importantly, however, what *Autoclenz* did not do is explore the *structural origins* of this inequality of bargaining power, and explore how, and why, this might influence the options available to the parties, and thus, what they *actually* agree – what legal relationship is actually brought into being in practice.

[52] *IWGB v RooFoods Ltd (t/a Deliveroo)* [2018] IRLR 84 (CAC) [90]–[91]. For critiques of this conflation, see J Atkinson and H Dhorajiwala, 'IWGB v RooFoods: Status, Rights and Substitution' (2019) 48 *Industrial Law Journal* 278; M Freedland and N Kountouris, 'Some Reflections on the "Personal Scope" of Collective Labour Law' (2017) 46 *Industrial Law Journal* 52.

[53] ibid.

[54] *Autoclenz* (n 7), [2011] 4 All ER 745.

This progressive 'juridification' of the socio-economic status of the worker, and the resulting distortion of the test of personal service, has had a profound influence on how the 'tests' commonly associated with that status have been conceived. Rather than the courts interpreting the contract by reference to the socio-economic status of the parties, and/or the socio-economic function of the work, that status is determined 'backwards', so to speak, from an analysis of the parties' agreement. Thus, rather than classifying a contract as a contract to do work personally when the person providing the work 'earns their bread by the sweat of their brow', as implied by *Riley*, the courts instead *require* as a condition for worker status a contract that requires the worker to provide work personally, and so, will exclude from the scope of labour law anyone whose contract provides for an (unfettered) right of substitution.[55]

Perhaps the clearest articulation of this premise is the case of *IWGB v CAC* ('*Deliveroo*').[56] As part of the application to the CAC for statutory recognition for the purposes of collective bargaining, the CAC had to decide whether Deliveroo Riders were 'workers' for the purposes of section 296 of the TULRCA 1992. The CAC concluded the Riders were not workers, arguing that

> [t]he central and insuperable difficulty for the Union is that we find that the [unconditional] substitution right to be genuine, in the sense that *Deliveroo have decided* in the New Contract that Riders have a right to substitute themselves both before and after they have accepted a particular job; and we have also heard evidence, that we accepted, of it being operated in practice. Deliveroo was comfortable with it.[57]

The Court's reasoning in this case is consistent with earlier cases concerning substitution clauses and the statutory requirement that the contract be one that requires the person to personally perform work. It expresses particularly well, however, the distortive effects of the juridical form. On the one hand, a right to substitution could reflect the fact that Deliveroo is merely purchasing services from the Rider, with the Rider being an independent business in a position to invest their own capital in their venture, and thus profit from their arrangement with Deliveroo. On the other hand, however, a right to substitution could reflect the fact, in a casualised labour market, not only is a right to substitution the only way that riders can practically earn enough to cover their living costs, given the inherently irregular, and precarious, nature of the engagement, but so too does it reflect the inherent substitutability of labour power – the tendency for firms to treat all labour as homogenous, and thus, to be indifferent to *who* works, caring only that the work is done, and that it is done with the requisite intensity and efficiency to secure a profit.

[55] *IWGB v CAC* [2018] EWHC 1939 (Admin), [2018] IRLR 911.

[56] The Court of Appeal has recently handed down its appeal of this decision, focusing on a narrow question relating to the relevance of Article 11 ECHR to the way in which the personal scope of TULRCA 1992 is interpreted: *The Independent Workers Union of Great Britain v The Central Arbitration Committee* (n 5). See below.

[57] *IWGB v RooFoods Ltd* (n 52) [100].

In the course of its judgment, the CAC acknowledged that 'Few if that, Riders use substitutes'.[58] It gave an example of one driver, however, who did use a substitute, and who did so because it allowed him to take 15–20 per cent of the fee, passing on the balance to his friend. This, the CAC concluded, suggested that the driver used the substitute for his own personal profit. The problem with this conclusion, however, is that, if one is only paid for the time one works, and it is practically impossible for someone to work enough shifts to earn a living, the use of a substitute will often be an expression not of financial independence, but of an extreme state of dependence, produced, and reinforced by the company's refusal to provide sickness and holiday pay, and its inability to *guarantee* drivers a minimum amount of work. What initially emerged as an indicator of wage dependence, and thus, one's inability to hire others to do work, is thus being used in a fundamentally distorted, or abstracted way, and this is because it is being applied in abstraction from any engagement with the wider class structures in which contracts for work are concluded.

The contrast between the way the 'test' of personal service was conceived in *Riley* and the way it was conceived in *Deliveroo* is notable. In *Riley*, the courts' assumption that the Truck Act 1831 was intended to apply to wage-dependent persons structured their interpretation of the legal concepts invoked in the Act to determine its scope. As such, the 'test' of personal service, the requirement that the individual contract to provide their personal labour, was formulated and interpreted in light of this purpose as a way of distinguishing between those with nothing but their labour power from which to live; and those who had sufficient means with which to take on a large contracting project, and to advance capital, and employ labourers, with a view to earning a *profit* from its performance. In *Deliveroo* by contrast, there is no indication that the court even sees the concept of the worker as a proxy for a particular socio-economic status, that it sees labour law as applying to a particular socio-economic class. Instead, in part due to the codification of the worker concept in statute, the worker is seen to be someone who contracts to work under a particular type of contract, one of the characteristics of which is a *contractual* obligation to provide work personally, and thus, a contractually imposed limit on the freedom of that worker to ask others to perform work in his/her place.

It may be asked whether the Supreme Court decision in *Uber v Aslam*[59] signals a departure in this respect. In this case, the Court expressly suggested that questions of employment status are not questions of contractual interpretation, but questions of statutory interpretation.[60] This meant that the status of the parties could not turn on the terms of the parties' agreement. Rather, it depended on whether the individual in question was within the category of persons with whom the legislation was designed to protect. This, it was said,

[58] ibid [78].
[59] *Uber v Aslam* (n 8).
[60] ibid [69].

in relation to minimum wage and working time regulations in particular, and individual labour law more generally, was to be persons vulnerable to being paid excessively low wages, being made to work excessively long working hours, and/or to accept unfair terms, and who are unable to adequately protect themselves by way of contract.[61] This, the Court suggested, would be persons who are *vulnerable*, are in a state of subordination and dependence to their putative employer, something to which the existence of *contractually* mediated control would be strong evidence.

In discussing the notion of vulnerability, however, the Court suggested that employees, persons hired under a contract of employment, can be deemed to be vulnerable in the sense implied above, because subordination and control are juridically implied into the structure of the contract, and so, employees are a category of persons who can be assumed, generally, to be in need of labour law's protection. When it came to workers, therefore, the question of status did not depend on the form of the contract per se, but on whether workers were rendered subordinate and dependent as a result of the existence of contractual rights of control, something which could be inferred from an analysis of how the parties conducted themselves in practice.[62]

The problem with this approach, however, is that, yet again, it addresses the question of status backwards, by reference to the nature of the legal relationship actually brought into being between the parties, rather than by reference to the structural context that explains how and why that particular legal relationship came to be. This approach leads the court to completely mis-understand the normative relevance, and nature, of control in the context of the wage-relation. Labour law is not required simply because certain forms of working arrangement involve contractual rights of control, and contractually mediated forms of subordination and dependence. Labour law is required because of the *structural* power relation in which such working arrangements are embedded, power relations that enable firms/organisations to take advantage of workers in ways that are potentially harmful, and to do so regardless of the form of the contract by which they capture the benefit of their work.

The Supreme Court in *Uber* may well have rejected the idea that employment status depends on the way in which a relationship is represented in the contract, therefore, on the basis that, were this so, inequality of bargaining power would enable employers to mis-represent the nature of the legal relationship between the parties, excluding individuals from the scope of labour law's application; but it failed to take seriously the way in which inequality of bargaining power, because it is structural in nature, also empowers employers to decide how labour power will be contracted in the first place – the form which that legal relationship will actually take. For this reason, it was unable to appreciate that subordination and dependence might pre-exist the contract, and so, pre-exist the exercise

[61] ibid [71].
[62] Eg, ibid [97].

of any contractual right of control, and importantly, and by implication, any contractual rights and obligations concerning whether or not the individual is required to provide work personally.

Following *Uber*, then, employment status still seems to be something determined by the parties – by the decisions made about how to legally structure a working relationship – rather than something imputed to socio-economic relationships based on a recognition of the structural positions they occupy. Insofar as this is the case, labour law will continue to face a perennial problem: the *structural* inequality of bargaining power which explains the existence, and need, for labour law, will continue to exclude from labour law's application a large number of the relationships to which it is relevant. And this is exactly the conclusion which comes through clearly from the Court of Appeal's decision in *Deliveroo*, decided shortly after *Uber* was handed down.[63] Although the Court refused to consider the potential relevance of *Uber* to the case at hand, on the basis that issues of substitution were not in issue in *Uber*, and the *Deliveroo* case concerned questions of employment status solely in the context of Article 11 ECHR, its emphasis on the fact that the 'riders are genuinely not under obligations to provide their services personally and have a virtually unlimited right of substitution'[64] as sufficient to deny access to deny employment status in the context of Article 11, is perfectly consistent with the way in which employment status was approached in *Uber*. Rather than asking *why* a company, such as Deliveroo, would not need to impose a legal obligation to work personally in order to ensure its labour power needs are met; why it might be irrelevant to the firm *who* performs the work; and rather than exploring the reasons why a rider might, in practice, be reluctant to provide a substitute, particularly if such would entail surrendering or sharing their pay, the court simply focuses on the existence, or not, of a 'right' to substitution, and draws its conclusion accordingly. As in *Uber*, then, it simply ignores the reasons why the tests relied upon to determine employment status, here, the personal service test, ever became a part of juridical doctrine about employment status in the first place. It fails, in other words, to see these tests as proxies for the existence of a power-relation which is *structural* in origin, and which is unique to the way in which work relations manifest in the context of capitalism.

While we may welcome the more flexible approach to questions of employment status indicated in *Uber*, therefore, we are still a long way away from ensuring an alignment between labour law's scope, and the sorts of relationships to which it is relevant – still a long way, in other words, from the approach implicit in *Riley*, where employment status is conceptualised as a socio-economic status that depends on a structurally produced subordination and dependence, rather than a status that arises as a result of the free actions, and decisions, of

[63] *The Independent Workers Union of Great Britain v The Central Arbitration Committee* (n 5) [84].

[64] ibid [77] (Underhill LJ).

legal subjects. For these reasons, the Supreme Court would clearly benefit from revisiting the Court's discussion in *Riley*, to encourage them to rethink exactly what they are asking, and why, when they explore whether someone is within the class of persons to whom they believe labour law should apply, and the relevance, to this question, of the requirement for personal service. *Riley* may not be a well-known case, therefore, may be rarely cited, and indeed, rarely included in modern textbooks on labour law; but its 'landmark' status, and its potential significance for labour law analysis today, should not be under-estimated.

2

Hornby v Close *(1867): Freedom of Contract and Freedom of Trade*

JOANNA McCUNN*

I. INTRODUCTION

HORNBY V CLOSE (1867) was politically incendiary. In 1867, trade unions existed in a kind of legal limbo: decriminalised, but with few positive rights. Well-organised 'new model' unions strove for respectability,[1] but their illusions of security were 'completely shattered' when *Hornby*, 'to the general surprise of all concerned', established that all trade unions were illegal as restraints on trade.[2] More than that, it demonstrated that 'the working classes are not fairly incorporated into the nation as part of society'.[3] Yet while *Hornby* at first seemed disastrous for unions, it soon turned out to be a 'godsend'.[4] It galvanised the campaign for legal reform and led directly to the passing of the Trade Union Act 1871, 'one of the very few occasions on which the British trade unions demanded the positive intervention of the law in their own affairs'.[5] Thanks partly to *Hornby*, unions achieved 'collective freedoms unparalleled' anywhere in Europe:[6] a triumph for freedom of contract.[7]

This, at least, is the picture often painted by labour lawyers. To some others, the case has looked very different. *Hornby* was not new law, but the natural extension of a line of authority that stretched back to the fifteenth century.[8]

* University of Bristol. I am grateful to the participants in the Landmark Cases in Labour Law workshop for their comments, and especially to Alan Bogg and Jeremias Adams-Prassl.

[1] J McIlroy, 'Financial Malpractice in British Trade Unions, 1800–1930: The Background to, and Consequences of, *Hornby v Close*' [1998] *Historical Studies in Industrial Relations* 1, 18–19.

[2] S Webb and B Webb, *The History of Trade Unionism* (London, Chiswick Press, 1898) 245.

[3] F Harrison, 'The Illegality of Unionism: The Case of *Hornby v Close*' *Bee-Hive* (26 January 1867) 4.

[4] McIlroy (n 1) 43.

[5] O Kahn-Freund, 'The Illegality of a Trade Union' (1944) 7 *Modern Law Review* 192, 193.

[6] M Curthoys, *Governments, Labour, and the Law in Mid-Victorian Britain: The Trade Union Legislation of the 1870s* (Oxford, Oxford University Press, 2004) 7.

[7] Webb and Webb (n 2) 276–78.

[8] See generally WS Holdsworth, 'Industrial Combinations and the Law in the Eighteenth Century' (1934) 18 *Minnesota Law Review* 369.

It did not evince any particular hostility towards trade unions, but applied equally to workers and employers.[9] And the idea that it removed unions from the law's protection was all a misunderstanding.[10] As for the 1871 Act, it sounded the death knell for freedom of contract, and created a legal relationship between unions and their members that was foreign to established common law principle.[11]

This chapter bridges the gap between these two views of *Hornby*, situating the case in the context of previous law on contracts in restraint of trade. It argues that the restraint of trade doctrine required courts to make political decisions about the kind of freedom that was valuable in the labour market. The nineteenth-century courts developed a distinctively individualist conception of freedom that loaded the dice against trade unions, guaranteeing that they would be seen as a threat to the right kind of trade in labour. Moreover, while the 1871 Act may have immediately improved the position of unions, it also accepted the analysis of *Hornby*, ensuring that the prejudices of mid-Victorian judges remain the bedrock of trade union law today.

II. BACKGROUND

Charles Close was born on the outskirts of Bradford in the 1820s. The area was dominated by woollen and worsted mills and Close began his working life in the textile industry. In 1846, he married Nancy Holdsworth and joined her late father's profession: boilermaking.[12] This was a lucrative move. The Industrial Revolution ran on steam, and there was constant demand for boilers to power mills, factories, ships and locomotives.[13] Boilermakers were highly skilled metalworkers, part of the 'aristocracy of labour'.[14] In his new profession, Close could expect to earn at least twice the wages of a weaver.[15]

Close also joined the United Society of Boilermakers and Iron Shipbuilders. This trade union had been founded in 1834, and opened its Bradford branch in 1842. The Society's rules emphasised that its purpose was to provide for

[9] PS Atiyah, *The Rise and Fall of Freedom of Contract* (Oxford, Oxford University Press, 1985) 412.

[10] ibid 533.

[11] ibid.

[12] 1841 census record, Stockhill, Eccleshill, Bradford, West Riding of Yorkshire (PRO HO 107/1295/5), f 6, p 4; marriage certificate, Charles Close to Nancy Holdsworth, 19 October 1846, St Peter's Church, Bradford; 1851 census record, 26 Portland Street, Horton, Bradford, West Riding of Yorkshire (PRO HO 107/2309), f 295, p 18.

[13] JE Mortimer, *History of the Boilermakers' Society*, vol 1 (London, George Allen & Unwin, 1973) 27–30.

[14] ibid 36.

[15] See AL Bowley, *Wages in the United Kingdom in the Nineteenth Century* (Cambridge, Cambridge University Press, 1900) 117, 123.

mutual relief and other benevolent purposes;[16] in keeping with the boilermakers' elevated position, its entrance fees were 'very high' and its benefits 'extremely generous'.[17] It also supported its members during strikes,[18] which became increasingly frequent as trade boomed in the early 1860s.[19] By 1866, the Society had over 9,000 members and held almost £20,000 in funds.[20]

In 1865, Close was the treasurer of the Boilermakers' Bradford branch, entrusted with the key to its all-important cashbox.[21] Then disaster struck: the branch's accounts were audited by William Swan, a Society official, who found that Close owed the union almost £25. This was a sizeable sum, representing several months of a boilermaker's wages. The union initially sought to deal with the matter internally, but Close was unable to come up with the money. After six months, the Boilermakers lost patience; in January 1866, an information was laid against Close in the name of John Hornby, the branch president.[22] The Society, no stranger to thieving officers,[23] was determined to make an example of Close: its trade report stormed that he would not 'rob us with impunity'.[24]

Earlier in the century, the Society would have been less bullish. At common law, an unincorporated association could only take legal action if all of its members acted in concert, a difficult task for a union to orchestrate. Furthermore, it was not a criminal offence for a member to embezzle the association's joint property, since he was one of its owners.[25] Improved statutory protection, however, was gradually extended to favoured organisations. In 1793, Parliament had granted friendly societies the power to take legal action in defence of their funds.[26] Sixty years later, unions thought that they too had scored a decisive victory. Section 44 of the Friendly Societies Act 1855 extended friendly societies' special remedies to societies 'established … for any Purpose which is not illegal', as long as their rules had been deposited with the Registrar of Friendly Societies.[27] The origins of section 44 were murky, but union leaders believed that it had finally placed them on a par with friendly societies.[28]

The Boilermakers' Society was confident that it was covered by section 44. It deposited its rules with the Registrar in 1865,[29] a move seemingly prompted

[16] Mortimer (n 13) 51–53.
[17] ibid 22.
[18] ibid 52.
[19] ibid 61–64.
[20] ibid 71.
[21] ibid 21.
[22] 'The Bradford Boiler Makers' Society and Their Treasurer' *Leeds Mercury* (17 January 1866) 3.
[23] McIlroy (n 1) 28–29.
[24] Boilermakers' Society Trade Report (30 December 1865), cited in ibid 30.
[25] W Erle, *The Law Relating to Trade Unions* (London, Macmillan, 1869) 3–4; RY Hedges and A Winterbottom, *The Legal History of Trade Unionism* (London, Longmans, Green & Co, 1930) 55–56.
[26] Friendly Societies Act 1793 (3 Geo 3 c 53), s 11.
[27] 18 & 19 Vic c 63.
[28] McIlroy (n 1) 24; Curthoys (n 6) 61.
[29] McIlroy (n 1) 24–25.

by a case of embezzlement involving William Warner, the secretary of its Leeds branch.[30] The Society's faith in the Act was soon rewarded. It launched proceedings under section 44 and secured Warner's conviction in December.[31] Understandably, the Boilermakers were confident of another success in Close's case in January. Before the Bradford magistrates, however, Close's lawyer argued that the Society could not proceed under section 44 because it had illegal purposes. Hornby and Swan were cross-examined and admitted that the Society's funds were used to support striking workers; its rules were also produced and shown to be 'in restraint of trade'. After 'very long argument', the Society's case was dismissed.[32]

The Boilermakers were furious. The charge against Close was fully proved, they fumed, but 'with £25 of our money in his pocket' he now 'huzza'd and scoffed at our society'.[33] They blamed the result on the anti-union bias of the Bradford magistrates, both of whom were ironmasters.[34] Counsel for Hornby immediately applied for a case stated, sending the matter to the Queen's Bench,[35] and the Society imposed a 1*s* levy on its members to fund the appeal.[36] The case was heard in January 1867 by Cockburn LCJ and Blackburn, Mellor and Lush JJ. The Society was now represented by George Mellish QC, who argued that 'very many' of its rules were 'strictly for benevolent objects', and that any rules in restraint of trade did not take it outside the Act.[37]

Again, however, the Society was disappointed. Cockburn LCJ declared: 'We ought not to hesitate a moment in saying that we think the magistrates were perfectly right'.[38] The judges made two points. First, although section 44 specified that the society could have 'any Purpose which is not illegal', the *ejusdem generis* principle meant that this purpose must be analogous to that of a friendly society.[39] That was not the case for a trade union.[40] Second, and more importantly, the purposes of the Society were illegal. The Court held itself bound by the precedent of *Hilton v Eckersley* (1855)[41] to find that, although the Society's rules were not necessarily illegal in the sense that they were criminal, they were illegal in the sense that they were contrary to public policy and thus lacked

[30] ibid 29.
[31] ibid.
[32] 'The Bradford Boiler Makers' Society and Their Treasurer' (n 22).
[33] Boilermakers' Society Trade Report (31 January 1866), cited in McIlroy (n 1) 30.
[34] Curthoys (n 6) 68; Mortimer (n 13) 72.
[35] JV Orth, *Combination and Conspiracy: A Legal History of Trade Unionism, 1721–1906* (Oxford, Clarendon Press, 1991) 102.
[36] Mortimer (n 13) 72.
[37] *Hornby v Close* (1866–67) LR 2 QB 153 (QB) 157–58.
[38] ibid 158.
[39] Under the *ejusdem generis* principle, general words that follow particular words are taken to apply only to things of the same kind as the particular words: see *R v Edmundson* (1859) 28 LJMC 213, 215.
[40] ibid 159.
[41] *Hilton v Eckersley* (1855) 6 E&B 47.

legal status.[42] The Society was constituted by rules in restraint of trade and could not claim the protection of the 1855 Act.

This news came as a shock to trade unions. Frederic Harrison argued that the repercussions of *Hornby* reached far beyond the application of the 1855 Act. The judges had found that unions were 'in their nature contrary to public policy', to be 'condemned and suppressed by the law' just like 'public nuisances and immoral considerations'.[43] The judges, however, thought that their decision was unexceptionable. Two years later, Cockburn LCJ insisted that 'in the case of *Hornby v Close*, we had no alternative, – even had we been disposed to do otherwise, – than to follow the decision in the case of *Hilton v Eckersley*'.[44] It was well-established that the law disapproved of restraints on trade; as unions operated in restraint of trade, they could not hope for the courts' favour. So was this cataclysmic decision an open-and-shut case? To find out, we must delve into the law on contracts in restraint of trade, and the key authority of *Hilton v Eckersley*.

III. CONTRACTS IN RESTRAINT OF TRADE

It has long been the case that the law will refuse to enforce certain kinds of agreement.[45] Contracts to commit criminal offences are a clear example; 'immoral' contracts a somewhat hazier one; and more shadowy still is the category of contracts that are against public policy. Contracts in restraint of trade are the best-established example of the latter category.[46] The common law's hostility to restraints on trade stretches back to the Middle Ages.[47] It grew up at a time when trade was heavily regulated by law; the objection was to extra-legal interferences with this system, whether by individuals meddling with food supplies, guilds regulating professions, or the Crown granting monopolies.[48] By the early eighteenth century, it was established that many by-laws, charters and contracts in restraint of trade were legally unenforceable.[49] When older regulation was swept aside by nineteenth-century reforms, the restraint of trade principle was understood to guarantee each person's access to the free market.[50]

The working of the principle was simple, even simplistic. Trade was favoured by the law, so anything that encouraged trade was good and anything that restrained it was suspect. Thus, a promise by A not to work for anyone but

[42] *Hornby* (n 37) 158–59.
[43] Harrison (n 3).
[44] *Farrer v Close* (1868–69) LR 4 QB 602 (QB) 609.
[45] W Holdsworth, *A History of English Law*, vol 8 (London, Sweet & Maxwell, 1966) 53.
[46] ibid 56.
[47] *The Dyer's Case* (1414) YB Pas 2 Hen V pl 26, f5b.
[48] Holdsworth (n 8) 369; Orth (n 35) 100.
[49] *Mitchell v Reynolds* (1712) 10 Mod 130, 131–33.
[50] Holdsworth (n 8) 380; Orth (n 35) 100.

B was void, because if B did not give A any work, A could not work at all. In contrast, an agreement that A would work for B in perpetuity was good, because it guaranteed work for A.[51] Even if the latter arrangement impinged just as much on A's liberty, it was not a restraint on trade.[52]

Why was trade to be promoted? Two consistent themes emerge from centuries of case law: restraints on trade were both 'prejudicial to the individual restrained, and to the rights of the public'.[53] Early modern lawyers were especially keen to emphasise the public interest angle. Restraints on trade, they argued, led to unfair prices and shoddy workmanship.[54] They encouraged workers to be idle, and to beg and steal.[55] In contrast, trade was associated with order and good government, as workers performed their duties to their families, the monarch, and even God.[56] Preventing a worker from exercising his God-given trade was 'unnatural and unmeet';[57] one judge compared a contract in restraint of trade to a contract not to attend church.[58]

Later lawyers were less forthcoming about why there was a public interest in trade; they seem to have seen the point as self-evident.[59] However, there was clear continuity with these older ideas. During the eighteenth century, the discipline of economics evolved as a branch of theology.[60] Its proponents explained that God had instituted trade to fulfil his purposes for the world,[61] making restrictions on trade unnatural and even sinful.[62] As Adam Smith argued in *The Wealth of Nations* (1776), enabling individuals to engage in free trade was the best means of furthering the public interest.[63] In the following decades, 'money making became not only respectable, but a positive duty'.[64] Ideas of public duty continued to be invoked in the case law: one judge declared that a worker 'shall not be at liberty to deprive … the state of his labour, skill or talent'.[65]

[51] *Young v Timmins* (1831) 1 Cr & J 331.

[52] Erle (n 25) 46; F Pollock, *Principles of Contract at Law and in Equity* (London, Stevens and Sons, 1876) 291; JW Smith and others, *A Selection of Leading Cases on Various Branches of the Law*, vol 1, 7th edn (London, William Maxwell & Son, 1876) 432. Equivalent reasoning applied to contracts in restraint of marriage: see *Lowe v Peers* (1768) 4 Burr 2225.

[53] *Young* (n 51) 340; compare *Claygate v Batchelor* (1601) Owen 142, 142.

[54] *Davenant v Hurdis* (1599) Moore 576, 587; *The Case of Monopolies* (1602) 11 Co Rep 84b, 86b.

[55] *The Case of Monopolies* (n 54) 86b; *Darcy v Allin* (1602) Noy 173, 180; *The Case of the Tailors of Ipswich* (1614) 11 Co Rep 53a, 53b.

[56] *The Case of Monopolies* (n 54) 86a.

[57] *Darcy* (n 55) 180–81.

[58] *Claygate* (n 53) 142.

[59] *Mitchell* (n 49) 136; *Homer v Ashford & Ainsworth* (1825) 3 Bing 322, 326; *Young* (n 51) 1831; *Hitchcock v Coker* (1837) 6 Ad & El 438, 444.

[60] GR Searle, *Morality and the Market in Victorian Britain* (Oxford, Oxford University Press, 1998) 9.

[61] ibid 13–14.

[62] ibid 21–22.

[63] A Smith, *An Inquiry Into the Nature and Causes of the Wealth of Nations*, vol II (London, W Strahan and T Cadell, 1776) 35.

[64] Atiyah (n 9) 84.

[65] *Leather Cloth Co v Lorsont* (1869–70) LR 9 Eq 345 (Ch) 354; see also *Young* (n 51) 340.

It was also argued that the individual restrained was specifically harmed. The early modern courts often noted that restrictive by-laws and charters infringed 'the liberty of a free-man … against the statute of Magna Carta'.[66] This argument was difficult to apply to contracts: after all, if a worker had agreed to the restraint, he could hardly complain that it infringed his liberty.[67] The objection could be revived, though, if the restraint had not been freely agreed. Many cases appear to have involved oppressive restraints imposed by masters on their apprentices.[68] In the leading case of *Mitchell v Reynolds*,[69] Parker CJ noted two key problems with contracts in restraint of trade. First, they could deprive the obligor of his livelihood without securing any corresponding advantage to the obligee or the public;[70] second, they could be imposed abusively on an obligor 'forced by the necessity of his circumstances' to surrender his trade 'for a trifle'.[71]

While the obligor's interest was often invoked by the courts,[72] the fit was a tricky one. Not all contracts in restraint of trade were exploitative, and, as we have seen, other contracts could be just as detrimental to a party's freedom. Frederick Pollock wrestled with this point in his *Principles of Contract*.[73] Arguments that restraints on trade could be abused, he observed, 'might be applied to almost any bad bargain'.[74] Although such contracts did limit the obligor's freedom, every contract 'set bounds to the party's freedom of action'.[75] The real objection must therefore be that restraints on trade were 'against the public good',[76] because they raised prices, encouraged idleness, and so on.[77] Thus, 'individual citizens could not without general inconvenience be allowed to set bounds to their freedom' of trade.[78]

However, the law's hostility to contracts in restraint of trade was never absolute.[79] The courts recognised that some limited restraints on trade could, counter-intuitively, encourage trade. For example, it would facilitate the sale of

[66] *Claygate* (n 53) 142; see generally JH Baker, *The Reinvention of Magna Carta 1216–1616* (Cambridge, Cambridge University Press, 2017) 311–23.
[67] *Broad v Jollyfe* (1620) Cro Jac 596, 596; *Mitchell* (n 49) 134. This point has a slight air of unreality, given that the poor law effectively imposed a duty to work: see S Deakin and F Wilkinson, *The Law of the Labour Market: Industrialization, Employment and Legal Evolution* (Oxford, Oxford University Press, 2005) ch 3. I am grateful to Alan Bogg for this point.
[68] HM Blake, 'Employee Agreements Not to Compete' (1960) 73 *Harvard Law Review* 625, 631–7; see *Nordenfelt v Maxim Nordenfelt Guns and Ammunition Co* [1894] AC 535 (HL) 566.
[69] *Mitchell* (n 49).
[70] ibid 135.
[71] ibid 135, 137.
[72] *Homer* (n 59) 326; *Young* (n 51) 340; *Leather Cloth Co* (n 65) 354.
[73] Pollock (n 52).
[74] ibid 285.
[75] ibid 219–20.
[76] ibid 251.
[77] ibid 285.
[78] ibid 219.
[79] *Mitchell* (n 49) 133.

businesses if sellers could promise not to compete with the new owners,[80] while non-compete agreements between businesses could benefit the public by reducing wasted costs.[81] As a result, limited restraints on trade were 'allowed by the very same policy that forbids restrictions generally, and for the like reasons',[82] if they would 'encourage rather than cramp the employment of capital in trade'.[83]

It was for the courts to determine whether any particular contract restrained trade or encouraged it. This required judges to exercise a quasi-legislative function, deciding which kinds of contract would best foster trade and serve the public interest.[84] These were not necessarily questions that the judiciary was well-placed to answer.[85] Judges were aware of their own limitations: Campbell LCJ expressed his 'great apprehension' of considering 'questions of political economy',[86] while Hannen J admitted that he had 'no means of judicially determining … the interest of the whole community', since the decision would not rest on 'recognized legal principles' but on the controverted opinions of political economists.[87]

Indeed, such decisions placed judges in a fundamental dilemma. Free trade was a tenet of nineteenth-century economic thought, but so too was freedom of contract.[88] What should be done when parties exercised their freedom of contract to restrict their freedom of trade?[89] Faced with this quandary, the courts preferred to err on the side of freedom of contract, which they saw as the 'natural' state of affairs. Any interference with contracts was viewed as a restriction of the parties' freedom,[90] so the safest course of action was to enforce the bargain and uphold the restraint on trade.[91] As Jessel MR explained,

> you are not to extend arbitrarily those rules which say that a given contract is void as being against public policy, because if there is one thing which more than another public policy requires it is that men of full age and competent understanding shall have the utmost liberty of contracting.[92]

It was generally easy for the courts to sideline countervailing concerns about free trade. They usually encountered restraints on trade as appendages to contracts

[80] *Hitchcock* (n 59) 454–55; see Holdsworth (n 45) 58. Compare *Homer* (n 59) 326.
[81] *Wickens v Evans* (1829) 3 Y & J 318, 328, 330.
[82] Pollock (n 52) 285.
[83] *Homer* (n 59) 326.
[84] WA Jolly, *Contracts in Restraint of Trade*, 2nd edn (London, Butterworth, 1900) 2.
[85] ibid.
[86] *Hilton* (n 41) 64.
[87] *Farrer* (n 44) 613.
[88] Blake (n 68) 637–38; Orth (n 35) 99; Holdsworth (n 8) 377.
[89] Atiyah (n 9) 408–09; see *Leather Cloth Co* (n 65) 354.
[90] *Sixth Report of the Select Committee on Artizans and Machinery*, vol 5 (Parliamentary Papers 1824) 590; Searle (n 60) 21–22; Atiyah (n 9) 386.
[91] Jolly (n 84) 2; Blake (n 68) 640.
[92] *Printing & Numerical Registering Company v Sampson* (1874–75) LR 19 Eq 462 (Ch) 465.

of employment or sale,[93] where they were unlikely to impinge significantly on the public interest.[94] However, when the restraint of trade doctrine came into contact with trade unions, very different public policy concerns were at stake.

IV. *HILTON v ECKERSLEY*

It might seem odd that trade unions were dealt with by the same doctrine that governed employees' non-compete agreements. However, in the eyes of the law, a trade union was an unincorporated association, and its members were contractually bound to each other by its rules. The key legal feature of a union was therefore the agreement on which it was based, and the legal status of the union depended on questions of contract law. When Parliament criminalised combinations, it did so via their contracts: a series of eighteenth-century statutes, culminating in the Combination Acts 1799 and 1800,[95] had voided existing union agreements and made it an offence to enter such agreements in the future.[96]

It was not only unions that were seen through a contractual lens; contract was also coming to the fore in conceptions of the employment relationship. In the eighteenth century, employment was understood primarily as a status. For William Blackstone, the relationship between master and servant was part of the law of persons, and its essence was the servant's duty to work for the master. Contract was simply one way in which such a relationship could be formed.[97] By the mid-nineteenth century, however, contract was gaining pride of place; it no longer merely established a status regulated by law, but was itself coming to regulate the employment relationship.[98] Labour was not a status or a duty, but a commodity that the worker sold.[99] Following the lead of Smith and his disciples, Parliament decreed that there should be free competition in the labour market. Workers and employers must each make the best bargains that they could, and their contracts, not the law, would set the terms of their relationship.[100]

However, the rules of engagement for this bargaining process remained unsettled. As Sir James Fitzjames Stephen observed, while the principle of free trade in labour was widely accepted, it

> meant different things to different people. In the mouths of employers, and those who sympathise with them, it has commonly meant 'a course of trade free from pressure

[93] Pollock (n 52) 287.

[94] Jolly (n 84) 35, 38.

[95] 39 Geo 3 c 81; 39 & 40 Geo 3 c 106.

[96] Orth (n 35) 5–24.

[97] O Kahn-Freund, 'Blackstone's Neglected Child: The Contract of Employment' (1977) 93 *Law Quarterly Review* 508, 510–12.

[98] Orth (n 35) 124.

[99] ibid 2.

[100] W Cornish and others, *The Oxford History of the Laws of England, Vol XIII: 1820–1914, Fields of Development* (Oxford, Oxford University Press, 2010) 632.

> exerted by trade unions for the increase of wages.' In the mouth of workmen, and those who sympathise with them, it has commonly meant 'a course of trade free from all legal restrictions upon the operations of trade unions.'[101]

Collective action by unions could be understood either as an interference with individuals' freedom or as an expression of it.[102] When the Combination Acts were repealed in 1824 and 1825,[103] Parliament warned that unions must not 'interfere with that perfect freedom which ought to be allowed to each party, of employing his labour or capital in the manner he may deem most advantageous'.[104] It would no longer be an offence simply to join a trade union, but many union activities were still viewed as illegitimate, and were strictly curtailed by the criminal law.[105] Members were permitted to consult together on the wages and hours they would accept, and little else.[106]

Following repeal, union agreements were no longer illegal in the sense that it was criminal to enter them.[107] But another question now arose: how did the law on contracts in restraint of trade apply to union rules? Were they illegal in the sense that they lacked legal status? This point did not arise for decision immediately. Unions were keen to stay out of the courts as much as possible: we have seen that the Boilermakers' Society did not deposit its rules until circumstances forced it to do so. Informal social sanctions against members were usually a more effective threat than legal proceedings,[108] and workers were unlikely to have sufficient funds to be worth suing by their unions, let alone to sue them.[109] It is therefore no surprise that the first encounter between combinations and the restraint of trade doctrine came in a case involving employers.

Nathaniel Eckersley was from a very different social milieu to Charles Close. In 1853, he was mayor of Wigan and, as managing director of James Eckersley and Sons, one of the town's largest mill-owners. That autumn, the factory workers of Wigan began to strike for higher wages.[110] Their employers responded by establishing their own association to enforce a lockout. Thirteen cotton spinners of Wigan and five of neighbouring Hindley bound themselves to Caleb Hilton, a local lawyer, promising that for the next twelve months they would each conduct their business in accordance with the majority decisions of the

[101] JF Stephen, *A History of the Criminal Law of England*, vol 3 (London, Macmillan, 1883) 202; the same point is made by Hedges and Winterbottom (n 25) 34; Atiyah (n 9) 531.

[102] JR McCulloch, 'Combination Laws – Restraints on Emigration' 39 *Edinburgh Review* 315, 317–18; Orth (n 35) 100; Curthoys (n 6) 43; Cornish and others (n 100) 633.

[103] 5 Geo 4 c 95, s 1; 6 Geo 4 c 129, s 2.

[104] *Sixth Report of the Select Committee on Artizans and Machinery* (n 90) 590.

[105] Atiyah (n 9) 531.

[106] 6 Geo 4 c 129, ss 4 and 5.

[107] The common law of conspiracy, however, remained a threat: see Curthoys (n 6) ch 1.

[108] Kahn-Freund (n 5) 193.

[109] P Davies and M Freedland (eds), *Kahn-Freund's Labour and the Law*, 3rd edn (London, Stevens and Sons, 1983) 35.

[110] 'Riots at Wigan' *Hull Packet* (4 November 1853) 7.

association. If any member failed to do so, he would pay a £500 penalty.[111] Such arrangements between employers were well-known: Smith had noted that 'when masters combine together in order to reduce the wages of their workmen, they commonly enter into a private bond or agreement'.[112]

The Wigan employers met fortnightly to confer on their strategy, and consistently determined to refuse the strikers' demands. Tensions ran high: in November, Eckersley called in the army to quell a riot in which the houses of mill-owners were attacked.[113] By the end of the year, the workers were starving and desperate. A delegation met with Eckersley and offered to return to work in exchange for half the increase they originally sought.[114] Eckersley agreed. However, the other mill-owners refused to approve the arrangement. After failing to persuade his fellow employers, Eckersley resigned from the association and re-opened his mills.[115] Hilton duly brought an action on the bond, seeking the £500 penalty. This was the first time that a party had sought to enforce such an agreement,[116] and, unsurprisingly, Eckersley responded that the bond was 'in restraint of trade, illegal and void'.[117]

The case was heard by the Queen's Bench in April 1855, and judgment was handed down in June. By a majority of two-to-one, the bond was held to be void. Crompton J took a strong line against the association; he began his judgment by noting that such agreements, whether made by workers or employers, were 'illegal and indictable at common law', and had only recently been decriminalised.[118] Although criminal sanctions had now been lifted, the bond was still unenforceable.[119] It removed Eckersley's 'freedom of action' by requiring him to abide by majority decisions, even if he was 'perfectly satisfied that in doing so he is acting contrary to his own interests, as well as to the interests of the workmen, the trade and the public'.[120] This was bad enough among employers, but it also raised the spectre of enforceable contracts between workers, who would be bound to strike even if they feared that they were 'ruining' themselves and 'doing incalculable injury to the public'.[121] Crompton J emphasised that nobody could surrender to a collective 'their individual right of judging and acting for themselves in matters so greatly affecting the public'; 'the happiness

[111] *Hilton* (n 41) 48–50.
[112] A Smith, *An Inquiry Into the Nature and Causes of the Wealth of Nations*, vol I (London, W Strahan and T Cadell, 1776) 177; See also McCulloch (n 102) 324; M Lobban, 'Strikers and the Law, 1825-51' in P Birks (ed), *The Life of the Law: Proceedings of the Tenth British Legal History Conference, Oxford 1991* (London, Hambledon Press, 1993) 216–17.
[113] 'Riots at Wigan' (n 110).
[114] 'Termination of the Wigan Strike' *Morning Post* (2 January 1854) 3.
[115] 'The Wages Movement' *Morning Post* (12 January 1854) 6.
[116] Atiyah (n 9) 411.
[117] *Hilton* (n 41) 50.
[118] ibid 53–54.
[119] ibid 54.
[120] ibid 55–56.
[121] ibid 56.

of the working classes and the prosperity of the trade and commerce of the whole nation' depended on it.[122]

Campbell LCJ echoed many of these points, though much more diffidently. He thought that the bond was not criminal, even at common law.[123] This meant that it existed in a strange limbo: not punishable, but not enforceable if it would 'produce public mischief'. He was uncomfortable with the existence of this grey area,[124] but certain that, although its aim was 'very laudable', the bond was indeed mischievous. Like Crompton J, he invoked the spectre of workers making similar arrangements. If such agreements were good, all the workers in England could surrender themselves to 'the will of a single individual', or even to an imperial 'Labour Parliament'.[125] This, he warned, would have 'the most disastrous consequences' for 'the whole community'.[126]

Erle J, dissenting, took a very different approach to the bond. First, he argued, it was not made in restraint of trade but 'for the advancement of trade'. The only threat to trade had been made by the striking workers.[127] Second, if it were a restraint on trade, it ought to be valid, since it went no further than was necessary to protect the 'important interest' of the mill-owners.[128] When Parliament decriminalised such agreements, it must have intended them to become subject to the same rules as other contracts in restraint of trade: thus, they would be valid insofar as they were reasonable, and void if they pursued a 'purposeless evil'.[129]

Faced with three such disparate judgments, Hilton brought a writ of error. The case was heard in the Exchequer Chamber in November 1855. Counsel for Hilton could see the way the wind was blowing: he sought valiantly to dissociate the masters' association from trade unions, arguing that it was not illegal for parties to combine if they acted in the public interest.[130] Mellish, appearing for Eckersley, hammered home the opposite point: it was not the admirable aim of the bond but its substance that was key. If such agreements were good for employers, they must be good for workers too.[131]

Alderson B handed down judgment in February 1856. Eckersley had won the day: although the error court emphasised that the employers' aims were 'laudable',[132] their bond was unenforceable. Each individual, explained Alderson B, had the 'privilege' of regulating his own manner of trade, and 'no

[122] ibid 57.
[123] ibid 62.
[124] ibid 64.
[125] A 'Labour Parliament' had met in Manchester in 1854.
[126] *Hilton* (n 41) 65–66.
[127] ibid 58.
[128] ibid 59.
[129] ibid 60–61.
[130] ibid 68.
[131] ibid 71.
[132] ibid 76.

power short of the general law ought to restrain his free discretion'.[133] Like the Queen's Bench judges, Alderson B made his real fears plain: if such a bond was enforceable between employers, the courts would soon 'be giving a legal effect to combinations of workmen for the purpose of raising wages, and make their strikes capable of being enforced at law'.[134]

As Stephen noted, *Hilton* 'sets in a strong light the extreme difficulty of giving a consistent rational account of the law' on restraints of trade.[135] Yet while all four judgments took different views of the bond, they also had two strikingly consistent features. First, although the case involved a combination of employers, the judges were primarily concerned with the question of workers' unions. They frequently expressed their sympathy for the mill-owners, while lamenting that unions 'seduced' honest workers,[136] 'arbitrarily levied' funds 'by extortion', and infringed 'the just rights of the masters'.[137] The clinching argument against the bond was not that it was against the public interest per se, but that a similar contract made by workers would have 'disastrous consequences' for the nation. The only question was whether the employers' arrangement could be successfully distinguished from such an agreement.

Second, three of the four judges maintained that collective action per se was a threat to the public interest. Only if each individual acted by his own lights could the prosperity of the nation be secured.[138] Counsel for Hilton seems to have been baffled by this point, pointing to instances of majority rule among partners, ship owners and the Stock Exchange Committee.[139] However, by finding that it was necessarily objectionable to submit to the decisions of a collective, the judges neatly ducked their usual freedom of contract problem. A combination was not like other contracts, so the public interest arguments tugged only in one direction. Only Erle J, more conventionally, treated the decision as a balancing act, assessing the public interest in free trade against that in freedom of contract. The others, ostensibly concerned with the 'free discretion' of traders, skimmed lightly over the fact that the mill-owners had used that discretion to enter the bond. The contrast with the courts' usual tendency, to privilege a freedom of contract analysis, was striking.

V. *HORNBY v CLOSE*

As we have seen, *Hilton v Eckersley* was the key authority adopted in *Hornby v Close*. If the mill-owners' bond was illegal, so too was the boilermakers'

[133] ibid 74–75.
[134] ibid 76.
[135] Stephen (n 101) 219–20.
[136] *Hilton* (n 41) 77.
[137] ibid 65.
[138] ibid 57.
[139] ibid 68–69.

agreement. It included objectionable terms that prohibited members from strikebreaking, entitled them to benefits during strikes, and made them liable to fines for assisting non-members.[140] Mellish QC, who had acted for Eckersley and now represented the Boilermakers, conceded that, following *Hilton*, such rules were not enforceable in contract law. The point was taken as read by every judge in *Hornby*.[141]

Mellish attempted to dodge *Hilton* by arguing that *Hornby* concerned a very different issue. The Society was not seeking to enforce its rules, but to gain the protection of the 1855 Act. The fact that some of its rules were in restraint of trade did 'not render the purpose of the society itself illegal'.[142] However, the Court was unimpressed. Cockburn LCJ agreed that, if the 'main purpose' of the Society were benevolent, 'one or two' rules in restraint of trade would not be a problem. Here, though, 'the very purposes' of the Society were 'to carry out the objects of a trades' union'. Since 'many' of its rules were illegal, the Society itself must also be illegal.[143]

Although it was unsuccessful, Mellish's strategy was sensible. In *Hilton*, the Court had considered the enforceability of a short-term, explicitly contractual arrangement with a clearly-defined purpose. *Hornby* involved the holistic assessment of an ongoing concern with multiple purposes, some apparently admirable and others objectionable. It was not a foregone conclusion that *Hilton* must govern *Hornby*. Indeed, Cockburn CJ accepted the principle of Mellish's argument, and later courts would evade *Hornby* through variations on this theme.[144] The difficulty for Mellish was that contracts in restraint of trade were still the only game in town: he had no alternative analysis of unions that could capture their other key qualities.[145]

As we have seen, however, the courts did not treat union agreements in the same way as other contracts in restraint of trade. Patrick Atiyah argued that this was to be expected, since unions posed a greater threat to free trade than any other restraint encountered by the courts.[146] However, the analysis in *Hilton* and *Hornby* was qualitatively different from the norm, insofar as most of the judges did not identify any public policy reasons to enforce the bond, even the importance of freedom of contract. Why, then, did the courts' understanding of free trade and freedom of contract leave no room for the operation of unions?

[140] *Hornby* (n 37) 155–56.
[141] ibid 158–60.
[142] ibid 157–58.
[143] ibid 158–59.
[144] See, eg, *Swaine v Wilson* (1889) 24 QBD 252 (CA).
[145] J Orth, 'English Combination Acts of the Eighteenth Century' (1987) 5 *Law and History Review* 175, 209; Orth (n 35) 23. The complexity of such associations would defy legal categorisation for decades: see Kahn-Freund (n 5) 196–201.
[146] Atiyah (n 9) 410.

We have seen that the restraint of trade doctrine required judges to make political decisions about the kind of freedom that was valuable in the marketplace. *Hilton* and *Hornby* demonstrate that the courts did not see unions as an expression of freedom, but as a threat to it on a number of levels. First, unions could undermine the freedom of employers. Sir William Erle, who dissented in *Hilton* and later headed a Royal Commission on trade unions,[147] wrote that it would 'infringe the right of the employer to a free course for the supply of labour' if his employees were persuaded to stop their work.[148] Others dismissed such concerns, reasoning that the laws of political economy would render unions harmless to employers.[149]

Judges were more concerned with the threat that unions posed to the freedom of their members.[150] Erle went so far as to compare union agreements to contracts of slavery and *Hilton v Eckersley* to *Somersett's Case*:[151]

> A person can neither alienate for a time his freedom to dispose of his own labour or his own capital according to his own will (see *Hilton v Eckersley*, 6 Ell&Bl 47), nor alienate such freedom generally and make himself a slave (see the argument of Hargrave in the Negro Somersett's Case, 20 State Trials, 23); it follows that he cannot transfer it to the governing body of a union.[152]

In *Hilton*, the judges repeatedly warned that workers were enslaving themselves to tyrannical unions. For Crompton J, a combination would only be acceptable 'if every party can withdraw from the association at his free will and pleasure'; otherwise, 'no workman would be able to free himself from the tyranny of [its] dictation'.[153] Alderson B described how a union member was 'oppressed by a majority of his fellow workmen'.[154] Similarly, the magistrates in *Hornby* found that one object of the Society was 'to prevent [members] from exercising their own judgment in matters connected with their occupation',[155] while Cockburn CJ explained that the purpose of a union was 'controlling the whole body, and getting the dominion over their actions'.[156]

Similar objections to unions were raised by James Booth in his report for Erle's Royal Commission.[157] He too invoked the 'habitual tyranny practised by the majority over the minority in the union'.[158] There was, he explained, a 'wide

[147] See section VI below.
[148] Erle (n 25) 21–22. See also Lobban (n 112) 213.
[149] Lobban (n 112) 215–16.
[150] Erle (n 25) 19.
[151] (1772) Lofft 1.
[152] Erle (n 25) 24–25.
[153] *Hilton* (n 41) 55–56.
[154] ibid 76.
[155] 'The Bradford Boiler Makers' Society and Their Treasurer' (n 22).
[156] *Hornby v Close* (1867) 10 Cox CC 393 (QB) 398.
[157] Curthoys (n 6) 97.
[158] *Eleventh and Final Report of the Royal Commissioners Appointed to Inquire Into the Organization and Rules of Trades Unions and Other Associations, Vol I*, vol 31 (Parliamentary Papers 1868-69) cxviii.

difference' between workers who happened to act in spontaneous combination and those who entered a 'permanent association' and sought 'to settle, by a kind of mock legislation … the policy of a trade', binding themselves to act 'whatever may be their individual opinion at the time when the case arises'.[159] He concluded that 'workmen should not be allowed to bind themselves for the future, so as to give up their right of judging and acting as they think fit'.[160] Echoing earlier warnings about contracts in restraint of trade, he prophesied that the result of combinations would be unemployment and poverty, the loss of skill and industry, and the downfall of the nation.[161]

Why were these lawyers so opposed to workers binding themselves for the future, when, as Pollock pointed out, this is the effect of any contract? Their objection was based on their individualist conception of freedom, which made room for contracts, but not combinations. It was what Mindy Chen-Wishart describes as the freedom of the 'Super-Detached Man', a 'rationally self-interested' figure who 'exists without connection with others'.[162] It was therefore a remarkably fragile kind of freedom, which was threatened simply by committing oneself to a collective. Agreeing to combine with others was a surrender of one's liberty unless one had the right to leave at any moment. As Michael Klarman puts it, these judges 'sanctified individual free will to such an extent that effective trade unionism, premised largely on collective action, was rendered virtually impossible'.[163]

Third, the courts were concerned about the threat posed by unions to non-members. They had some reason for this: in October 1866, for example, unionists in Sheffield had blown up the house of a fellow worker.[164] Even less serious incidents, however, could attract criminal sanctions. Discussing pickets in *R v Druitt* (1867), Bramwell B held that it would be a criminal conspiracy against an individual's 'liberty of mind and freedom of will' if others did anything 'unpleasant or annoying' to him, such as watching him or giving him 'black looks'.[165] As Bramwell B explained, 'everybody knows that the total aggregate happiness of mankind is increased by every man being left to the unbiased, unfettered determination of his own free will and judgment as to how he will employ his industry'. This would be threatened if he had to worry about picketers watching him while he went about his business.[166] For Stephen, this went much too far,[167]

[159] ibid cvi.
[160] ibid cvii.
[161] ibid cvii–cxi.
[162] M Chen-Wishart, 'Undue Influence: Vindicating Relationships of Influence' (2006) 59 *Current Legal Problems* 231, 240.
[163] MJ Klarman, 'The Judges Versus the Unions: The Development of British Labor Law, 1867–1913' (1989) 75 *Virginia Law Review* 1487, 1559.
[164] Orth (n 35) 134.
[165] *R v Druitt* (1867) 10 Cox CC 592, 601–02.
[166] 'The Tailors' Strike' *Times* (24 August 1867) 11.
[167] Stephen (n 101) 222.

but *Druitt* was applauded by Erle,[168] and described by AV Dicey as the logical conclusion of 'Benthamite faith in individual freedom'.[169]

Criminal cases like *Druitt* were 'close conceptual bedfellows' with the contract cases.[170] Again, the courts' individualist conception of freedom led them to value only the right of each individual to make their own decisions. Trade unions acted unlawfully when they interfered with this right by picketing.[171] However, the decision to join a union was not itself a valid exercise of freedom – it was like enslaving oneself to a collective. Thus, the common law's two objections to restraints on trade obtained: unions were a threat to the public interest, and injurious to their members.

This analysis enabled the courts to overlook the differences between workers' and employers' combinations, and to present *Hornby* as the precise analogue of *Hilton*. Erle explained that 'competition between classes' was largely irrelevant to the law of trade unions, because union members primarily sought 'to restrain others of the same class from direct competition with themselves'.[172] Similarly, in *Druitt*, Sjt Ballantine rejected the argument that the workers' strike was part of the 'contest between capital and labour',[173] observing that a union affected other workers 'to a far greater extent than it ever could affect the masters'.[174]

Of course, as Erle recognised, there were 'more frequent proceedings against working men than against employers'. Erle attributed this to the fact that workers acted more often 'in concert', since they had more interests in common, were a 'more numerous class', and were in 'closer companionship in factories and the like'.[175] He did not mention that workers had to act collectively to have any bargaining power vis-à-vis their employer.[176] By focusing on competition within, rather than between, classes, the courts could neatly elide the inequality of bargaining power that existed between workers and employers. They focused on the legal freedom of individual workers to make their own bargains, and disregarded their lack of social freedom to resist oppressive contracts.[177] Thus, the courts could compare union agreements to contracts of slavery, while campaigners argued that factory workers were really enslaved by their lack of

[168] Curthoys (n 6) 83.

[169] AV Dicey, *Lectures on the Relation Between Law and Public Opinion in England During the Nineteenth Century*, 2nd edn (London, Macmillan, 1914) 200–01. Bramwell was a strong supporter of laissez faire politics: see Atiyah (n 9) 374–75.

[170] Lobban (n 112) 232.

[171] Orth (n 35) 100.

[172] Erle (n 25) 19.

[173] *R v Druitt, Lawrence* (n 165) 596.

[174] ibid 594.

[175] Erle (n 25) 37.

[176] See Davies and Freedland (n 109) 17–18.

[177] ibid 24–25; see JM Ludlow, *The Master Engineers and Their Workmen* (London, John James Bezer, 1852) 31–32.

bargaining power and miserable working conditions.[178] The law regarded any kind of employment contract as a valuable exercise of freedom,[179] as long as it could not be characterised as 'servile'.[180] Even exploitative sweatshop contracts were not necessarily exempt: as Erle protested, 'labour of the brain' might be 'immeasurably more severe' than physical labour, which was, in many cases, 'a grand boon'.[181]

VI. AFTERMATH

Unions, then, were a threat to free trade, and their formation was contrary to public policy. For the courts, this was business as usual. Yet *Hornby*'s claim to landmark status rests primarily on its aftermath: it prompted immediate uproar and swift Parliamentary intervention. Ironically, it was this intervention that cemented *Hornby* into the law when it might naturally have eroded away.

Many unions were panicked by *Hornby*.[182] Some had trusted in an 1851 opinion by Alexander Cockburn, then attorney-general; he had reassured the Amalgamated Society of Engineers that its rules were not illegal, evidently meaning that they were not criminal.[183] Unions seem to have understood by this that their rules were not illegal under the 1855 Act, and *Hilton* did not alert them to their error.[184] Those who had mistakenly relied on Cockburn's opinion were indignant that he himself had 'allowed a trade-society to be plundered' through some legal 'technicalities'.[185] Their confusion was understandable. The fact that unions had been decriminalised but not legalised left them in an awkward limbo,[186] and the descriptor 'illegal' was unhelpfully ambiguous.[187]

Other unions were less concerned – indeed, they welcomed the guarantee that the courts would keep out of their affairs.[188] Admittedly, they regretted that they were excluded from the 1855 Act, leaving them 'at the mercy of their whole army of branch secretaries and treasurers, any one of whom might embezzle the funds with impunity'.[189] Even so, *Hornby* only affected

[178] Searle (n 60) 64–66. Harrison compared the impact of *Hornby* on unionists to that of *Dred Scott* on abolitionists: Harrison (n 3).
[179] Erle (n 25) 46–47.
[180] Pollock (n 52) 291.
[181] Erle (n 25) 18.
[182] McIlroy (n 1) 34–35.
[183] Curthoys (n 6) 48; McIlroy (n 1) 33.
[184] Curthoys (n 6) 61–62.
[185] G Howell, *The Conflicts of Capital and Labour* (London, Chatto & Windus, 1878) 142.
[186] Erle (n 25) 74.
[187] Pollock (n 52) 218–19.
[188] Kahn-Freund (n 5) 193. On this outlook, see generally AD Flanders, 'The Tradition of Voluntarism' (1974) 12 *British Journal of Industrial Relations* 352. I am grateful to Alan Bogg for this reference.
[189] Webb and Webb (n 2) 246.

the position of the 26 trade unions who had successfully deposited their rules with the Registrar.[190] Thousands of others had their rules rejected, or did not even make the attempt.[191]

Nevertheless, *Hornby* was destined to become a *cause célèbre*, partly as a result of its timing. A Royal Commission on Trades Unions, chaired by Erle, had been planned in the wake of the 'Sheffield outrages'. *Hornby* was handed down in January 1867, just weeks before the Commission was announced.[192] *R v Druitt*, which followed in August, led unionists to suspect a campaign of 'judicial aggressions' against them.[193] These cases strengthened the hand of the 'Junta' of union leaders who were working with the Commission towards political reform.[194] While the conservative press gloated over *Hornby*,[195] many sympathised with the plight of 'responsible' unions.[196]

The courts, meanwhile, seemed bemused by the outcry: unions, they pointed out, were still protected by the general criminal law, even if its processes were unwieldy. In *R v Dodd*,[197] Lush J lamented 'the entirely mistaken view which has got into the public mind' about *Hornby*. 'All that the court held', he explained, somewhat disingenuously, was that 'the society was not a friendly society … the case decided nothing more'.[198] While his conciliatory tone was a relief to unions,[199] it was left to Parliament to tweak the law. In 1868, Russell Gurney's Act solved one problem, establishing that a member of an unincorporated association could be convicted of embezzling its property.[200] The time-limited Trades Unions Funds Protection Act 1869, meanwhile, provided that a society would not be deemed to have illegal purposes under the 1855 Act simply because it had rules in restraint of trade.[201]

More extensive reforms followed when the Royal Commission reported. The Commission's influential minority report argued that unions should be afforded legal status despite their illegal purposes,[202] and the Trade Union Act 1871 was introduced to square this circle. The Act defined unions in the language of *Hilton* and *Hornby*: a trade union was a combination that would be unlawful at common law 'by reason of some one or more of its purposes being in restraint

[190] Curthoys (n 6) 70.
[191] ibid 62; McIlroy (n 1) 24–26.
[192] Curthoys (n 6) 65–68.
[193] Orth (n 35) 134.
[194] McIlroy (n 1) 42–43; W Cornish et al, *Law and Society in England 1750–1950* 2nd edn (Oxford, Hart Publishing, 2019) 304–05.
[195] Curthoys (n 6) 70.
[196] McIlroy (n 1) 41–42.
[197] *R v Dodd* (1868) 18 LT 89.
[198] ibid 90.
[199] Curthoys (n 6) 70.
[200] 31 & 32 Vic c 116, s 1; see *R v Blackburn* (1868) 11 Cox CC 157.
[201] 32 & 33 Vic c 61, s 1; see *R v Stainer* (1870) 11 Cox CC 483 (Court for Crown Cases Reserved).
[202] 'Royal Commission on Trade Unions and Employers' Associations 1965–1968' (Stationery Office, 1968) Cmnd 3623 xxx.

of trade'. Indeed, unions were so closely identified with restraints on trade that a proviso had to clarify that other such contracts were not trade unions.[203] The Act then provided that 'the purposes of any trade union shall not, by reason merely that they are in restraint of trade, be unlawful so as to render void or voidable any agreement or trust',[204] though union rules remained unenforceable.[205] Meanwhile, registered unions were granted the power to take legal action to defend their funds in the same way as friendly societies.[206]

These statutes accepted the analysis of *Hilton* and *Hornby*, but tinkered with its consequences.[207] The 1871 Act was described in Parliament as doing 'away altogether with the restraint of trade doctrine',[208] but in fact, it did nothing so radical. The legislation proceeded circuitously, by means of carve-outs and fictions, and left the common law illegality of unions undisturbed. Unions were merely granted some new statutory powers, enabling them to escape the consequences of their common law position.

The common law, however, was still evolving: as Percy Winfield observed, decisions on restraint of trade soon become 'museums of fossil economic theories'.[209] Even before the 1871 Act was passed, the courts were beating a retreat from *Hilton* and *Hornby*, perhaps because of the Royal Commission's unexpectedly positive reports.[210] *Farrer v Close*,[211] for example, involved one William Close and his theft from the Bradford branch of the Amalgamated Society of Carpenters and Joiners.[212] This Society had framed its rules with more circumspection than the Boilermakers,[213] but Cockburn CJ and Mellor J were determined to drag it into the scope of *Hornby* regardless. Hannen and Hayes JJ, however, strongly defended the Society's 'praiseworthy character'.[214] It might encourage strikes, said Hannen J, but while this was obviously not in the interest of employers, it was not necessarily 'opposed to the welfare of the community at large'.[215] A few months later, the common serjeant praised unions for their 'acts of providence which were a credit to so many of the working classes in this country'.[216] Implacable judicial hostility to unions was rapidly fading away.

Statute law did not stand still either. The Royal Commission had been convinced that all trade unions had the purpose of unlawfully restraining

[203] 34 & 35 Vic c 31, s 23.
[204] ibid s 3.
[205] ibid s 4.
[206] ibid s 9.
[207] Orth (n 35) 104, 138.
[208] HL Deb 1 May 1871, vol 205, col 1917.
[209] PH Winfield, 'Public Policy in the Common Law' (1928) 42 *Harvard Law Review* 76, 94.
[210] Kahn-Freund (n 5) 198.
[211] *Farrer* (n 44).
[212] The similarity to *Hornby v Close* is coincidental: Curthoys (n 6) 112.
[213] *Farrer* (n 44) 606–07.
[214] ibid 610.
[215] ibid 613.
[216] *R v Blackburn* (n 200) 161.

trade, but this assumption turned out to be inaccurate.[217] The Trade Union (Amendment) Act 1876 thus altered the statutory definition, providing that a union could also be a body that was not in restraint of trade at common law.[218] In a series of scraps around the turn of the century, unions strove to establish their own common law illegality in order to avoid coming under legal obligations to their members. The courts took an increasingly liberal approach to the restraint of trade doctrine, drawing fine distinctions between the rules of the Boilermakers' Society and those of later unions.[219] In an attempt to blunt this attack, unions took to proclaiming their commitment to illegal restraint of trade front and centre in their rules.[220] The case law was turned on its head.

A further consequence of *Hornby* was undone much later. Under section 4 of the 1871 Act, union rules remained unenforceable. The courts gradually chipped away at this section until, in 1968, the Donovan Report recommended its repeal, arguing that there was 'no compelling reason today why legal contracts entered into by trade unions should be placed on a different footing from other contracts as regards enforceability'.[221] The repeal was accomplished by the Industrial Relations Act 1971.[222] Today, neither the purposes nor the rules of unions are unlawful on account of *Hornby*.

Hornby, however, remains good law. Indeed, it is baked into the legislation. The provision defanging *Hornby* is still in place; it is now section 11 of the Trade Union and Labour Relations (Consolidation) Act 1992, which provides that the rules and purposes of a union are not unlawful merely because they are in restraint of trade. Almost invisibly, *Hornby* and the restraint of trade doctrine underlie trade union law today.

This legislative shell occasionally cracks open, exposing *Hornby* to the light. In November 1993, for example, it was held that prison officers were not 'workers' and that the Prison Officers' Association was outside the scope of the 1992 Act.[223] This meant that, lacking the protection of section 11, the Association's rules were caught by *Hornby* and were illegal as a contract in restraint of trade. In *Boddington v Lawton*,[224] the Association urged the Court to reconsider *Hornby*: 'society has changed since the last century, and the objectives of a law abiding trade union should no longer be regarded as contrary to the public interest'.[225] Nicholls VC, however, held that the removal of *Hornby* 'bristle[d] with difficulties'.[226] It had been followed since 1867 'in decisions too numerous

[217] 'Royal Commission on Trade Unions and Employers' Associations 1965–1968' (n 202) 205.
[218] 39 & 40 Vic c 22, s 16.
[219] See generally Kahn-Freund (n 5).
[220] ibid 203.
[221] 'Royal Commission on Trade Unions and Employers' Associations 1965–1968' (n 202) 217–18.
[222] s 169, sch 9.
[223] *Boddington v Lawton* [1994] ICR 478 (Ch) 481–82. The 1992 Act was extended to prison officers by s 126 of the Criminal Justice and Public Order Act 1994.
[224] *Boddington* (n 223).
[225] ibid 486.
[226] ibid.

to mention', and 'it would be most undesirable for judges now to hold that, to reflect changes in social conditions, the common law in this field has developed and is now to the contrary effect of what has been established and acted on for so many years'.[227] Moreover, *Hornby* was 'the footing' of the relevant legislation. When Parliament had had its say on the matter, it would be 'ill-advised' for the courts 'to attempt to re-assess the requirements of public interest' in a field of 'keen, sometimes bitter, political debate'.[228]

The argument that public policy doctrines should not reflect changes in social conditions does not hold much water, insofar as this is precisely what they do and have always done.[229] To describe *Hornby* as 'the footing' of the legislation is also somewhat misleading. It is true that the statutes have been premised on the assumption that *Hornby* is good law, but their effect is precisely to ensure that *Hornby* has no practical significance. The difficulty is that *Hornby* falls between two stools: Parliament has not overturned it, but has left the courts unable to reconsider it. Conceptions of trade and the public interest have certainly moved on since 1867.[230] Left to its own devices, the common law would likely have evolved until unions were no longer seen as restraints on trade; it is only Parliament's half-hearted intervention that has given *Hornby* its strange afterlife.

VII. CONCLUSION

Hornby v Close is a peculiar kind of landmark case. It turned on the interpretation of an obscure statute, but had enormous political ramifications; it laid down no new law, but caused widespread outrage; its consequences were immediately reversed, but it remains the foundation of the law. *Hornby* was a product of its historical moment, now preserved in statutory amber. The restraint of trade doctrine is premised on the idea that trade is necessarily good, but the law's understanding of what trade is good must constantly evolve. *Hilton* and *Hornby* exemplify the ideals of mid-Victorian individualism, which sought to secure individuals' freedom of contract but overlooked their social unfreedom and despised collective bargaining. *Hornby* was partly responsible for turning the tide of public and judicial opinion in a different direction. Ironically, the very outcry against it ensured that it would be quarantined from ordinary legal development, and secured its survival as the basis of the law today.

[227] ibid 487.
[228] ibid.
[229] Winfield (n 209) 94–95.
[230] In particular, it has been suggested that *Hornby* is not compatible with the ECHR right to freedom of association: see A Emir, *Selwyn's Law of Employment*, 21st edn (Oxford, Oxford University Press, 2020) 568.

What, finally, of our *dramatis personae*? Charles Close continued to live in Bradford and to work as a boilermaker;[231] he died in 1889.[232] The Boilermakers' Society, always striving for respectability, was the third trade union to register under the 1871 Act.[233] It was later amalgamated into (and provides the 'B' of) the general trade union GMB.[234] Nathaniel Eckersley twice sat as a Conservative MP. The Eckersley Mills complex was a prominent landmark of Wigan Pier for decades, but, when the mills closed in 1972, the site fell into disrepair. Many of its buildings were demolished while this chapter was being written;[235] *Hilton* and *Hornby* are set to outlive them.

[231] 1881 census record, 122 Grafton Street, Horton, Bradford, Yorkshire (RG11/4458), f 121v, p 12.
[232] England and Wales Civil Death Registration Index 1889, Q4, p 62.
[233] Mortimer (n 13) 78.
[234] 'The History of GMB' www.gmb.org.uk/history (accessed 18 February 2022).
[235] 'Anger as Derelict but Historic Wigan Pier Mill Buildings Are Torn Down' *Wigan Today* (20 May 2021), www.wigantoday.net/news/people/anger-as-derelict-but-historic-wigan-pier-mill-buildings-are-torn-down-3243690 (accessed 18 February 2022).

3

Devonald v Rosser and Sons *(1906)*: *Avoiding One-Sidedness in Contracts for Personal Performance of Work*

ASTRID SANDERS

I. INTRODUCTION

DEVONALD V ROSSER is one of the older cases to be discussed in this volume; however, it is a case with perhaps surprising continued contemporary relevance.[1] For instance, *Devonald* is sometimes cited for a 'general rule' against no 'lay-off' without pay (unless the contract provides otherwise).[2] As but one example, the latter would have been potentially relevant, were it not for statute 'overtaking',[3] even recently when businesses were closed due to Covid-19 related 'lockdowns'.[4] On the other hand, a 'lockdown' might be thought to be more similar to the shortage of supply example in *Devonald* rather than the lack of orders in *Devonald* itself. *Devonald* is also cited for various other different propositions, again with contemporary relevance: including a so-called 'right to work' (at least for some), a 'right to pay', a founding case on 'custom and practice' in the employment context, as an authority for the employee's right to payment being contingent upon 'ready and willingness' to work (compared to actual performance) and, finally, as a case on avoiding unfairness or one-sidedness in the contract of employment. This is even though the decision itself is only 18 pages long, with the judgment by the Court of Appeal only six pages long. This chapter traces the various different

[1] *Devonald v Rosser and Sons* [1906] 2 KB 728 (CA). The author dedicates this chapter to the memory of Roger Sanders.

[2] D Brodie, *The Contract of Employment* (Edinburgh, Green, 2008) para 11.17.

[3] ACL Davies, 'Getting More Than You Bargained for? Rethinking the Meaning of "Work" in Employment Law' (2017) 46 *ILJ* 477, 486. See, also, M Freedland, *The Personal Employment Contract* (Oxford, Oxford University Press, 2005) 134: '… the subject of statutory regulation.'

[4] Coronavirus Job Retention Scheme. (Statutory provision on 'lay-offs' and short-time working more generally: ss 147–154 of the Employment Rights Act 1996.)

implications of *Devonald* as they have evolved in modern case law, to argue that *Devonald*'s legacy should be a judicial desire to mitigate one-sidedness in contracts for personal performance of work.

When giving a historical account, commenting on *Devonald*, Deakin and Wilkinson draw attention to *Devonald* as being unusual for its time, when surrounded by seemingly a sea of, often, less worker friendly judgments.[5] For example, the infamous doctrine of common employment was still applicable, whereby employers were absolved of vicarious liability for torts committed by a fellow worker against another, on the basis of an implied term in the contract of service.[6] Indeed, *Devonald* in this respect can be contrasted with another well-known case of that era: *Addis v Gramophone Co Ltd*.[7]

II. THE FACTS AND OUTCOME

The claim in *Devonald* was brought by Daniel Devonald, a 'rollerman' who had been employed at the defendant tinplate manufacturers, Rosser and Sons, in South Wales for a number of years at the turn of the twentieth century. Transcripts of cross-examination indicate that while Devonald had worked for the defendants for 13 years, he had worked 'in the trade' for 30 years.[8] The facts of the case were that there had been a downturn in trade for the defendants, so that it would have been unprofitable for the employers to remain open at that time. The defendants accordingly closed their tinplate business for a number of weeks. Mr Devonald was a 'piece worker', which meant that he 'received wages pro rata according to the number of boxes turned out in a day'.[9] In other words, if he was given no work to do, he would not be remunerated as he was paid according to the amount of output he produced.[10] On 20 July 1903, the defendants shut down their works. However, they did not give the contractually required 28 days' notice to Mr Devonald to terminate his contract until 3 August 1903; hence there was an additional two weeks of no work. Nor, more importantly, did the employers wait until the end of the notice period before closing the tinplate

[5] S Deakin and F Wilkinson, *The Law of the Labour Market: Industrialization, Employment, and Legal Evolution* (Oxford, Oxford University Press, 2005) 85: 'As a result, the progress made in the *Devonald* case towards contractualising the employment relationship was not continued very far during this period', with reference, eg, to *Marshall v English Electric Co Ltd* [1945] 1 All ER 653 (CA). On 'lay-off' see, eg, *Browning v Crumlin Valley Colleries Ltd* [1926] 1 KB 522 (KB). For a notable exception, see *Hanley v Pease and Partners Ltd* [1915] 1 KB 698 (DC) (as discussed below, see the text accompanying n 168).

[6] *Priestley v Fowler* (1837) 3 M & W 1.

[7] Re the various limitations on damages in *Addis v Gramophone Co Ltd* [1909] AC 488 (HL).

[8] 'Tin-Plate Trade' *Evening Express and Evening Mail* (Wales, 25 May 1905) 2.

[9] *Devonald* (n 1) 730.

[10] ibid (Jelf J): 'The rates of payment were fixed, and could not be altered by the defendants without the consent of the masters' association to which the defendants belonged.'

works.[11] In total, the period of no work and no pay amounted to six weeks, under which Mr Devonald remained under contract to the defendants, however earned no wages. Mr Devonald's argument was that it was a breach of contract by his employers not to provide him with a reasonable amount of work over the six weeks and he claimed damages amounting to the wages he would have earned over the six weeks of missed work.[12] Interestingly, newspaper accounts report that Devonald and the other laid off workmen subsequently returned to work for the defendants.[13]

The judge at first instance in *Devonald*, Jelf J, himself described the case as a 'test case'.[14] *Devonald* is similarly described by newspaper accounts at the time, simultaneously being shortened simply to the 'Cilfrew case' or the 'tinplate case'.[15] One newspaper account describes that the 'contracts of employment between plaintiff and defendants ... were similar to those in force in the whole of the tin-plate trade in South Wales'.[16] Not only was Devonald's contract similar to those of other tinplate workers, it appears equally that the employer's practice was widespread.[17] The employer in this instance had shut down their works, seemingly on little to no notice for the workmen, when there was a lack of orders and trading conditions were poor.[18] While it was this practice that the plaintiff wished to challenge; as will be discussed below, for the purposes of the claim, Devonald had to argue there was no 'custom', as legally recognised, to shut down, with no notice and no pay for the workmen, for want of remunerative orders. Both because the practice was widespread and because Devonald's contract was representative of contracts in the industry generally, *Devonald* accordingly raised a question 'affecting hundreds of men in South Wales'.[19] It is also widely noted that an unusually large number of witnesses appeared. The case had been transferred from the County Court to the King's Bench Division of the High Court, due to its

[11] 'Tin-Plate Trade' (n 8) 2: 'Plaintiff said they would have had no claim but for the notice which the defendants put up on August 3 after the men left.'

[12] Devonald did not make a claim in debt. See, eg, ACL Davies, *Employment Law* (London, Pearson, 2015) 232: 'the employer's duty to pay can be enforced in two ways at common law: through the action for an agreed sum or through an action for damages'.

[13] 'Tin-Plate Trade' (n 8) 2: 'Witness and other men worked at the harvest in July while the works were shut, and when they re-opened all the men went back.' See similar statements in 'Devonald', *The Times* (London, 7 June 1905) 5.

[14] *Devonald* (n 1) 729.

[15] Eg, 'Alleged Custom to Shut Down Works' *The Economist* (21 July 1906) 212; 'Devonald' (n 13); 'Tin-Plate Trade' (n 8); 'Cilfrew Judgment: Appeal Pending' *The Cambrian* (16 June 1905) 8.

[16] 'Tin-Plate Trade' (n 8).

[17] Eg, P Jenkins, *Twenty by Fourteen: A History of the South Wales Tinplate Industry, 1700–1961* (Llandysul, Gomer Press, 1995) 212: 'Since the Cilfrew case was just another example of what was a common practice within the trade.'

[18] ibid 210: 'workers frequently found themselves dismissed with but a few hours notice'.

[19] 'Tin-Plate Trade' (n 8).

perceived importance.[20] Even before judgment was given, the scene was hence set for a landmark case.[21]

To add to the legal commentary, the wider literature on the iron and steel industry notes the broader trade union context to the case. First, one Daniel Devonald was a 'works representative' (which is not clear from the case report alone).[22] Indeed, the broader trade union context altogether is not clear from the case report.[23] While the case is named after Devonald as claimant, the wider literature describes the case as brought by the Steel Smelters Union.[24] This union backing and support to Devonald does not come across from the case report. Second, Sir Arthur Pugh states that the situation at Cilfrew previously had been referred to the 'Tinplates Dispute Board'.[25] The picture presented by Pugh is that the hope had been to progress Devonald's case as a test claim, with all the various different unions working together.[26] However, matters entirely broke down.[27] As a result, the Steel Smelters Union decided to proceed alone.[28] Indeed, this was apparently the second attempt at litigation on similar facts by the Steel Smelters Union.[29] Pugh notes that because of the (different) employer's success in the first litigation, the practice of laying off workers with little to no notice, if anything, had increased subsequently.[30] On Devonald's case specifically, Jenkins notes that 'officials of the trade union were unbending in their opinion' and 'expressed an intention of seeking a remedy even if it meant expensive litigation to test the case at the highest level of jurisdiction'.[31] In comparison, 'the owners of the Works submitted what they believed to be a strong case'.[32] However, it was Devonald and the trade union's claim which

[20] Jenkins (n 17). The case was presumably not transferred because of its financial value: Devonald was ultimately awarded £14 in damages.

[21] Eg, A Pugh, *Men of Steel: Chronicle of Eighty-eight Years of Trade Unionism in the British Iron and Steel Industry* (London, Iron and Steel Trades Confederation, 1951) 137: 'As the case affected practically all the men in the tinplate trade it aroused considerable interest in South Wales.'

[22] ibid.

[23] See the text accompanying n 130.

[24] Eg, Jenkins (n 17) 211–12: 'What the Union viewed as unlawful frustration'; 'the Union expressed an intention of seeking a remedy'.

[25] Pugh (n 21) 133–34.

[26] ibid 133, eg, 'with a view to all the unions co-operating to fight the case'. Pugh lists the different unions as the Steel Smelters Union, the Tin and Sheet Millmen, the Dockers, Gasworkers and Labourers, and the Welsh Artisans.

[27] ibid 134 (so much so that Pugh notes that subsequently various unions left the Tinplate Disputes Board, seemingly as a direct result).

[28] ibid: 'The union decided to go ahead with the Cilfrew action on its own responsibility'.

[29] Jenkins (n 17) 210: 'This practice had been challenged by the Steel Smelters Union as early as 1893'.

[30] Pugh (n 21) 133: 'This had a tendency to increase following the adverse decision in the action taken by the union against the Morriston and Midland Tinplate Co.'

[31] Jenkins (n 24).

[32] ibid 212. Interestingly Pugh (n 21) 138 said: 'Having heard arguments of the appellants' counsel, the Lord Chief Justice, without calling upon counsel for the respondents ....'

ultimately prevailed, both before Jelf J and then subsequently upheld by the Court of Appeal.[33]

It was held that Rosser and Sons were indeed in breach of contract to Daniel Devonald by not providing him with the opportunity to work and earn wages over the six weeks of shutdown, until his notice period expired. Devonald was awarded damages for six weeks of lost earnings, based on his average earnings previously.[34]

Jelf J opened his judgment at first instance by stating that the onus was on Devonald to establish a contractual right to be provided with work. The claim would immediately fail unless Mr Devonald could do this.[35] If Devonald succeeded in that respect, then the onus would fall on the employers to show a custom and practice 'cutting down' that prima facie right.[36] Jelf J's judgment is significant, on the first question, for stating that Devonald succeeded both on authority but also in principle.[37] Jelf J opined that it would be 'strange if such a right is not implied; for otherwise the bargain is of a very one-sided character. The workman must be at the beck and call of the master whenever required to do so, and yet he cannot, though ready and willing to earn his pay, earn a single penny unless the master chooses'.[38] The implications of this part of Jelf J's judgment will be discussed further below.

Jelf J then proceeded to the second stage, which was to decide whether the employer could rely on the custom and practice they asserted. They asserted a custom and practice to be able to shut their works without pay, whether for a want of orders or whether through a breakdown of machinery or shortage of supplies. Jelf J at this stage seemed to use two criteria: notoriety and reasonableness.[39] The employer's alleged custom failed on both grounds. Memorably on the latter, Jelf J stated: 'and I am of the opinion that the custom set up by the defendant would not be reasonable. It would place the men at the mercy of the masters as to the occasions when, for their own convenience, and looking to their own interests, the masters might think fit to stop the work.'[40]

Accordingly, Devonald succeeded: first, as there was an implied contractual right to provide Devonald, as a piece worker, with a reasonable amount of work

[33] Pugh (n 21) 138: 'For the union it was a decisive victory!'

[34] *Devonald* (n 1) 735 (Jelf J): 'I can think of no better mode of assessing what would have been a reasonable amount of work, and therefore a reasonable amount of pay, than to take the average wages earned by the plaintiff for some time preceding the stoppage. This was agreed to be about 2l. 6s. 8d. per week, making 14l. for the six weeks, and I give judgment for the plaintiff for that amount, with costs on the High Court scale.'

[35] *Devonald* (n 1) 730: 'If he failed in making out that prima facie case he failed altogether ....'

[36] ibid.

[37] ibid 732: 'I am of opinion, therefore, both upon principle and authority ....'

[38] ibid 731.

[39] ibid 733–34.

[40] ibid 734.

while the contract subsisted and, second, because the employer had not proved a custom or practice incorporated into the contract which would cut down that implied agreement.

The Court of Appeal upheld the decision of Jelf J at first instance.[41] The judgment on appeal is noticeably short. Three brief judgments were provided. Two of the members of the Court of Appeal separately described Jelf J's judgment as 'perfectly right'.[42] For completeness, it should, however, be observed that there are some slight differences in the judgment of the Court of Appeal as compared to that of Jelf J.

First, one difference in the Court of Appeal is that each of the judgments referred also to the general contractual authority of *The Moorcock* at what has been described here as the first stage.[43] The Court of Appeal in *Devonald* conceptualised whether there was agreement to provide work on the basis of whether this was a term implied in fact for this particular contract. In other words, the Court of Appeal likely would not have envisaged that the term implied here would be generalised afterwards.[44] Second, Lord Alverstone CJ noted that he interpreted some of the older cases slightly differently from Jelf J, although this did not change the outcome.[45] Third, similar to how the Court of Appeal utilised *The Moorcock* on the question of implied agreement, when deciding if the employer's alleged custom was made out, Farwell LJ appeared to draw upon general contractual authorities by asserting specifically a three-fold test for custom and practice: reasonableness, certainty and notoriety.[46]

There are certainly memorable passages in the judgments in *Devonald*, both by Jelf J and by the Court of Appeal. One of those memorable passages by Jelf J was already included above.[47] Freedland, for example, singles out a different passage by Farwell LJ in *Devonald*, describing this as illustrating a principle of mutuality or reciprocity:[48] 'We must bear in mind that we have to regard the matter from the point of view not only of the master, but of the workman.'[49]

There appears a similar sentiment in Lord Alverstone CJ's statement:

> What, then, is the obligation of the employers under such a contract as the present? On the one hand we must consider the matter from the point of view of the employers

[41] See n 33.

[42] *Devonald* (n 1) 739, 745.

[43] *The Moorcock* (1889) 14 PD 64 (CA). Farwell LJ quoted Bowen LJ without expressly citing *The Moorcock*.

[44] Eg, *Geys v Société Générale London Branch* [2012] UKSC 63, [2013] IRLR 122 [55] on two different types of implied term. On latter type, eg, *Wilson & Clyde Coal Co Ltd v English* [1938] AC 57 (HL) was in 1937.

[45] *Devonald* (n 1) 741.

[46] ibid 743. Lord Alverstone CJ referred, similarly to Jelf J, rather to *Reg v Stoke-upon-Trent* (1843) 5 QB 303 (QB). On the three-fold general contractual test, see, eg, H Beale (ed), *Chitty on Contracts*, 34th edn, (London, Sweet & Maxwell, 2021) para 16–035.

[47] See the text accompanying n 38.

[48] Freedland (n 3) 137 (and generally 134–37).

[49] *Devonald* (n 1) 743.

> who I agree will under ordinary circumstances desire to carry on their works at a profit, though not necessarily at a profit in every week, for it is matter of common knowledge that masters have frequently to run their mills for weeks and months together at a loss in order to keep their business together and in hopes of better times. On the other hand, we have to consider the position of the workman. The workman has to live; and the effect of the defendants' contention is that if the master at any time found that his works were being carried on at a loss, he might at once close down his works and cease to employ his men, who, even if they gave notice to quit the employment, would be bound to the master for a period of at least twenty-eight days during which time they would be unable to earn any wages at all. I agree with Jelf J. that that is an unreasonable contention from the workman's point of view.[50]

Freedland goes on to state that this principle of mutuality or reciprocity is not necessarily always followed in subsequent cases.[51] On the theme of mutuality in particular, Deakin and Wilkinson note the different use of older cases on 'mutuality' in *Devonald*:

> In upholding the claim, the Court of Appeal applied the principle of the parties' mutual obligations under the contract, which it had previously used to support claims for breach of contract by commission agents and other higher status employees. It also relied on the nineteenth century cases on mutuality, which, shorn of their significance as means of invoking the Master and Servant Acts, could now be used for the benefit of the employee.[52]

The tension in the principle of mutuality, generally, in the employment context is well documented.[53] On the one hand, the principle of mutuality assisted the workman in *Devonald*. In the other direction, mutuality can also work against workers, as in the older cases referred to by Deakin and Wilkinson but,[54] moreover, also in cases at the highest appellate level much more recently where, infamously, mutuality of obligation has been used as an exclusionary device to prevent a finding of employee (and possibly also statutory worker) status.[55]

The 'test case' of *Devonald* was hence won by the claimant (and trade union); perhaps, as suggested above, contrary to expectations. Brodie cites *Devonald* as authority for what he calls the 'general rule' that employees, generally, are entitled to be paid during a lay off unless the contract states otherwise.[56] The key word here would appear to be 'general'. The Court of Appeal in *Devonald*

[50] ibid 740.

[51] Eg, Freedland (n 3) 135.

[52] Deakin and Wilkinson (n 5) 81.

[53] Eg, N Countouris, 'Uses and Misuses of "Mutuality of Obligations" and the Autonomy of Labour Law' in A Bogg, C Costello, ACL Davies and J Prassl (eds), *The Autonomy of Labour Law* (Oxford, Hart, 2015).

[54] Eg, the seemingly factually similar case of *R v Welch* (1853) 2 E&B 357 (Lord Campbell CJ): 'the magistrates have jurisdiction'.

[55] Eg, *O'Kelly v Trusthouse Forte Plc* [1983] IRLR 369 (CA); *Carmichael v National Power Plc* [2000] IRLR 43 (HL). On application, or not, to statutory workers see, eg, *Secretary of State for Justice v Windle* [2016] EWCA Civ 459, [2016] IRLR 628.

[56] Brodie (n 2).

emphasised the 'obligation is [not] an absolute one to find work at all events': the obligation would not apply where there was a 'breakdown of machinery [or] want of water and materials'.[57] This was the reference to 'shortage of supply' above.[58] Brodie summarises the distinction as between matters which are within the employer's control, the employer's fault or the employer's responsibility (to which the 'general rule' applies), compared to matters not in the employer's control or not the employer's fault.[59] Brodie also notes that this distinction is not necessarily always easy to draw.[60] He suggests that *Devonald* was prescient by invoking modern concepts of risk allocation: 'such a role is now seen as a key function of the law of contract'.[61]

The language in the judgment in *Devonald* suggests a vulnerability or precarity on the part of the claimant. One final point is the interesting observation by Deakin and Wilkinson:

> Rollermen were skilled workers who were in the position of intermediate contractors, employing their own underhands; they were paid a tonnage rate and so were technically piece workers who could not claim wages due as earned if no work was actually done.[62]

Hence, while Jelf J referred to the one-sidedness of the contract and the rollermen as at the 'beck and call' of the master, Daniel Devonald was himself a skilled worker and, on Deakin and Wilkinson's characterisation, was likely himself also an employer.[63]

III. THE IMPLICATIONS OF *DEVONALD*

As stated above, *Devonald* is variously cited as establishing a number of different propositions. This chapter will focus on three implications of *Devonald*: first, that *Devonald* is authority for the employer's obligation to provide work at least for some working persons; second, *Devonald* stated a test for when 'custom and practice' will be contractually incorporated in the employment context; and,

[57] *Devonald* (n 1) 740.
[58] Eg, Brodie (n 2) para 11.18.
[59] ibid para 11.19.
[60] Eg, ibid: 'A difficulty particular to the employer in question, might be thought to present very different issues to, for example, those caused by a national oil-tanker drivers strike.' See, also, 'Devonald' (n 13) on *Devonald* itself: 'They said that these events were outside the control of the masters, but it was impossible to draw a distinction between shortage of materials and shortage of orders.'
[61] Brodie (n 2) para 11.19. See, also, *Devonald* (n 1) 742 (Sir Gorell Barnes): 'It seems, therefore, that the question which really has to be considered is how far that general and necessary implication in such a contract is qualified by considerations as to who takes any particular risks which may affect the continuance of the work.'
[62] Deakin and Wilkinson (n 5) 81.
[63] *Devonald* (n 1) 731.

third, *Devonald*'s potentially wider significance if it is an authority suggesting judges will or should avoid 'one-sidedness' in the contract of employment or in contracts for personal performance of work more generally.[64]

A. Obligation to Provide Work?

Devonald is invoked as an authority for an employer's obligation to provide a reasonable amount of work for piece workers or workers who earn payment via commission.[65] On this account, piece workers and commission workers are thought to be different, on the grounds that payment for these workers is wholly contingent upon the amount of tasks performed. There are indeed specific rules for 'output workers' today in the national minimum wage regulations.[66] On the other hand, immediately this distinction is not entirely convincing. Most obviously, conventionally, a zero hours worker will only be entitled to pay for shifts performed;[67] yet it would not be 'orthodox', to quote the Court of Appeal more recently, to state that they also have a right to be provided with a reasonable amount of work.[68] This leads into one of the more general observations of this chapter: namely, that the modern logical implications of *Devonald* may not have been followed through. If the response to the latter is that *Devonald* was different because the workman in *Devonald* was under contract to remain available to the employer until his notice expired, when a zero hours worker may be under no obligation to remain available, there might however be two responses.[69]

First, newspaper accounts at the time observe that in cross-examination, Mr Devonald stated that he had indeed worked elsewhere during the six weeks, as a harvester.[70] It was hence not the case that he was unable to work at all during those six weeks, contrary to suggestions at points in the judgments.[71] Presumably he was required to return to Rosser and Sons if work were to

[64] Devonald is described in the case as a 'workman'. See, the statutory definition of 'workman' at the Employers and Workmen Act 1875, s 10.

[65] *Langston v AUEW (No 2)* [1974] IRLR 182 (NIRC) 187 (Sir John Donaldson): 'Similarly, the consideration in a commission or piece work contract of employment is the express obligation to pay an agreed rate for work done plus the implied obligation to provide a reasonable amount of work: see *Devonald v Rosser & Sons*.'

[66] National Minimum Wage Regulations 2015, ch 4.

[67] Statutory definition of a 'zero hours contract' at the Employment Rights Act 1996, s 27A.

[68] *Burn v Alder Hey Children's NHS Trust* [2021] EWCA Civ 1791, [2022] ICR 492 [35] (in a different context, as discussed below).

[69] Eg, H Collins, KD Ewing and A McColgan, *Labour Law*, 2nd edn (Cambridge, Cambridge University Press, 2019) 265: 'This result was achieved in part by regarding the contract of employment as a time-service contract, despite the payment mechanism of piece-rates, by referring to them specifying a contractual notice period.'

[70] 'Tin-Plate Trade' (n 8).

[71] Eg, *Devonald* (n 1) 740 (Lord Alverstone CJ): 'who, even if they gave notice to quit the employment, would be bound to the master for a period of at least twenty-eight days during which time they would be *unable to earn any wages at all*' (emphasis added).

become available there, but while work was not available from Rosser and Sons, Devonald (and the other laid off workmen) worked elsewhere. Devonald in this respect seems more similar to a modern zero hours worker, taking shifts as and when available, even if this means from multiple employers.

Second, if the main differentiating feature between *Devonald* and a modern zero hours worker is that a zero hours worker may not be required to remain available (unlike in *Devonald*), the more recent authorities may start to indicate that a more generous approach should be taken when deciding if a zero hours worker is realistically to be described as required to work.[72] The latter point will be discussed more below.[73] Hence potentially more zero hours workers might be considered equivalent to the situation in *Devonald*, contrary to the 'orthodoxy'. In turn, if there is an equivalence between the situation in *Devonald* and at least some zero hours work, this might suggest that employers should be obliged to provide a reasonable amount of work also to some zero hours workers, in the same way that the defendants in *Devonald* were required to make a reasonable amount of work available to Mr Devonald. It might even be suggested that this would be the obvious translation of *Devonald* in the modern setting. However, as will be seen immediately below, this is not the direction, generally, in which case law on the employer's obligation to provide work has developed.[74] Indeed, although Devonald himself contractually had to remain available, a possible third factor is that in subsequent jurisprudence, when a right to work for piece workers and commissioned based workers is frequently asserted, these cases do not always add the caveat that the piece worker must be required to be available.[75] Nor do these subsequent cases state that the piece worker must have a contractual notice period, if that is another differentiating feature.[76] Later cases, more simply, seem to treat the implied term of fact in *Devonald* itself as an implied term of law for piece workers generally.[77]

Case law suggests two main categories when a right to work will today be recognised. First, as above, there is such a right for piece workers and commission-based workers. Second, there are cases where a right to work is recognised because of the importance specifically of performing the task (eg, 'theatrical engagements') or for maintenance of the employee's skills.[78] The more recent decisions on an employer's obligation to provide work have developed rather in the second category, specifically in the context of highly skilled professional workers. The Court of Appeal in *William Hill Organisation Ltd v Tucker* held that the employer there was obliged not only to provide the employee with pay

[72] Eg, *Addison Lee Ltd v Lange* [2019] ICR 637 (EAT) (appeal refused: [2021] EWCA Civ 954).
[73] See discussion in the text accompanying n 115.
[74] *cf*, eg, *Wilson v Circular Distributors Ltd* [2006] IRLR 38 (EAT).
[75] Eg, *Langston* (n 65). See, also *William Hill Organisation Ltd v Tucker* [1998] IRLR 313 (CA) [16].
[76] See Collins, Ewing and McColgan (n 69).
[77] See discussion in the text accompanying n 43.
[78] *Tucker* (n 75).

but also to provide the employee with the opportunity to work, in the context of an employee placed on so-called 'garden leave'. This was because the employee in that instance was employed in a 'specific and unique post', with skills that would atrophy if they were not used.[79] In comparison, the principle in *William Hill* was held not to be satisfied more recently, for example, in *Christie v Carmichael* when the claimant was employed by a firm of chartered accountants as a senior client relationship manager.[80] According to Lady Smith, the duties involved in his post were not unique and there was nothing in the facts to point to a risk that the claimant would become deskilled as a result of not exercising his skills over the period of 'garden leave'.[81] Seemingly, being employed as a 'generalist tax advisor' was not sufficiently skilled or unique for these purposes.

This points towards a potential irony in the subsequent application of *Devonald*. If a piece worker generally is thought potentially to be a more vulnerable category of worker,[82] the subsequent cases on an employer's obligation to provide work develop the right to work for the generally less vulnerable category of professional employees.

B. Custom and Practice

In the subsequent jurisprudence, *Devonald* seems to be most often cited as an authority for the test of custom and practice in the employment context; namely when custom and practice, not expressly included in the contract of employment, becomes legally binding. Farwell LJ stated the threshold for custom and practice to be incorporated in the contract of employment was the trio of reasonableness, notoriety and certainty.[83] Notoriety here appears to refer to the need for general awareness.[84] To refer to the Privy Council in the wider commercial contractual context, the test would seem to be whether an outsider making enquiries would not fail to discover the asserted custom and practice.[85]

The threshold of reasonable, certain and notorious for the incorporation of custom and practice derives from the general contractual context, although it

[79] ibid [21].

[80] *Christie v Carmichael* [2010] IRLR 1016 (EAT).

[81] ibid [50].

[82] Eg, separate discussion of 'piece rates' in M Taylor, *Good Work: The Taylor Review of Modern Working Practices* (2017) assets.publishing.service.gov.uk/government/uploads/system/uploads/attachment_data/file/627671/good-work-taylor-review-modern-working-practices-rg.pdf (accessed 8 April 2022).

[83] *Devonald* (n 1) 743.

[84] Eg, *Garratt v Mirror Group Newspaper Ltd* [2011] EWCA Civ 425, [2011] IRLR 591 [43].

[85] Eg, *Kum v Wah Tat Bank Ltd* [1971] 1 Lloyd's Rep 439 (PC). (In *Devonald* (n 1) 741 (Lord Alverstone CJ): 'I may say that I have always understood that a custom cannot be read into a written contract unless, to use the language of Lord Denman CJ in *Reg v Stoke-upon-Trent*, it is "so universal that no workman could be supposed to have entered into" the "service without looking to it as part of the contract."')

should be noted that in more recent cases, the wording in commercial contract cases appears to have changed instead to invariable, certain and notorious.[86] The concept of 'reasonableness', in these commercial contract cases, looks to have been dropped.

The next question is how the test for custom and practice has developed specifically in the employment context.[87] Some of the more recent cases apply the test initially from *Devonald*;[88] in other cases, there is discussion as to whether there might now be different tests for establishing industry custom as opposed to incorporating the custom and practice of a single employer.[89] *Devonald* would apply to the former group of cases. On the other hand, even in a case on alleged single employer custom, the Employment Appeal Tribunal in *Solectron Scotland Ltd v Roper* applied *Devonald*.[90] The leading authority, however, today on single employer custom and practice is the restatement by the Court of Appeal in *Park Cakes Ltd v Shumba*.[91] Underhill LJ there sidelined *Devonald* as 'concerned with rather different issues' and chose not to 'review' *Devonald* further.[92] This suggests today a declining role for *Devonald* as an authority on custom and practice in the employment context: first, if there are now less cases on alleged industry custom (as compared to cases on alleged single employer custom) and, second, in light of the treatment of *Devonald* in *Shumba*.[93]

Notwithstanding the latter, in a previous effort by the Court of Appeal to restate the law in this area, the treatment of 'reasonableness' for these purposes was interesting in *Garratt v Mirror Group Newspapers Ltd*.[94] On the one hand, Lord Justice Leveson referred to reasonableness as 'possibly going somewhat further'.[95] On the other hand, it may 'equally need no more than a consideration of the other factors'.[96] The 'other factors' in that instance were, for example, how long the alleged custom had been followed and how consistently it had been applied; which seems somewhat different to the investigation of reasonableness

[86] Eg, *Crema v Cenkos Securities Plc* [2010] EWCA Civ 1444, [2011] 1 WLR 2066.
[87] Eg, *Sagar v H Ridehalgh and Son Ltd* [1931] 1 Ch 310 (CA).
[88] Eg, *Solectron Scotland Ltd v Roper* [2004] IRLR 4 (EAT).
[89] Eg, suggestion in *Garratt* (n 84) [26].
[90] *Solectron* (n 88) [22]–[24].
[91] *Park Cakes Ltd v Shumba* [2013] EWCA Civ 974, [2013] IRLR 800.
[92] ibid [26].
[93] Brodie (n 2) para 15.02: 'However, employment cases of this type would appear to be less common nowadays.'
[94] *Garratt* (n 84) [35] (Leveson LJ): 'I prefer to focus on the broader question of what was agreed between the employers and the employees (as a group), either expressly or by clear implication because, in reality, the factors mentioned by Peter Gibson LJ to which I have referred all go to that issue.' Compare to test latterly in *Shumba* (n 91) [35] (Underhill LJ): 'Taking that approach, the essential question in a case of the present kind must be whether, by his conduct in making available a particular benefit to employees over a period, in the context of all the surrounding circumstances, the employer has evinced to the relevant employees an intention that they should enjoy that benefit as of right.'
[95] *Garratt* (n 84) [35].
[96] ibid.

back in *Devonald* itself.[97] In *Devonald*, for Jelf J, the alleged custom and practice was not reasonable because it 'would place the men at the mercy of the masters as to the occasions when, for their own convenience, and looking to their own interests, the masters might think it fit to stop the work'.[98] For Farwell LJ, it would be neither reasonable nor certain, 'because it is precarious, depending on the will of the master'.[99]

C. Avoiding One-Sidedness in Contracts of Employment (or Worker Contracts)

It is submitted that this is the most important implication of the judgment in *Devonald*. The language in this respect in *Devonald* is striking:

> Apart from authority, it would be strange if such a right is not implied; for otherwise the bargain is of a very one-sided character. The workman must be at the beck and call of the master whenever required to do so, and yet he cannot, though ready and willing to work and to earn his pay, earn a single penny unless the master chooses; and this state of things may go on for a period of nearly two months ... It would, I think, require some very clear and binding decisions to induce any fair-minded tribunal to accept this view of the law.[100]
>
> ...
>
> We must bear in mind that we have to regard the matter from the point of view not only of the master, but of the workman. Both master and workman have to make their living. The master makes his living by realizing a profit; the workman makes his by his wages. The master's profits are ascertained as an ordinary rule de anno in annum. But the workman has to live de die in diem, and his wages presumably do not leave a large scope for saving for a future day when no employment is forthcoming.[101]

A similar passage by Lord Alverstone CJ was included above.[102]

The concern by Jelf J to avoid one-sidedness led Jelf J and then the Court of Appeal to imply agreement by the employer to provide a reasonable amount of work to Mr Devonald until the expiration of his notice period. Freedland describes this as the operation of a principle of mutuality or reciprocity in contracts for personal employment.[103] The language here would be striking at

[97] Eg, with reference to *Albion Automotive Ltd v Walker* [2002] EWCA Civ 946 [15] (but also [18]).
[98] *Devonald* (n 1) 734.
[99] ibid 743 (echoed verbatim in *Solectron* (n 88) [24]).
[100] ibid 731 (Jelf J).
[101] ibid 743 (Farwell LJ).
[102] ibid 740.
[103] Eg, Freedland (n 3) 136–37: 'There are instances where the principle of mutuality or reciprocity has been applied in exactly that way. Perhaps the best illustration of all occurs in the case of *Devonald v Rosser & Sons* ...'.

any time, but is surely even more striking when taking into account the age of the case. For example, this is long before Edmund Davies LJ in 1974 telling the judiciary not to refer to older cases applying 'what would today be regarded as almost an attitude of Czar-serf'.[104]

As stated above, *Devonald* has been cited frequently subsequently in cases on custom and practice, plus in cases alleging a right to work. However, it was also memorably utilised in the very different context of *Nethermere (St Neots) Ltd v Gardiner*.[105] In the words of Lord Justice Stephenson in the Court of Appeal in 1984, 'I think that means evidence at least of an obligation to accept work offered by the company, and on the authority of *Devonald v Rosser* the obligation to accept piecework would imply an obligation to offer it.'[106]

This was in the context of a discussion of the 'irreducible minimum of obligation on each side' for there to be a contract of employment.[107] The two claimants in *Nethermere* were casual homeworkers. *Nethermere* is, of course, a well-known case in its own right: the employer's argument was that the claimants could not bring statutory claims for unfair dismissal because, the employer argued, they were not working under contracts of employment. The decision of the Court of Appeal in *Nethermere* was admittedly split and stated to be close to the borderline.[108] Nevertheless, the Court of Appeal there found that the claimants were indeed employees: memorably, even though the relationship had started off on an informal basis, the regular giving and taking of work had 'hardened', or crystallised, from a matter of convenience into a matter of binding legal obligation.[109] This meant then that there was the necessary 'mutuality of obligation' in order to constitute a contract of employment, with later cases confirming that mutuality of obligation is a necessary ingredient for a contract of employment.[110] Mutuality of obligation here is construed as the ongoing promise by an employer to provide work in return for the ongoing promise by an employee to perform work, if the argument is for a single contract.[111]

However, the more specific point for present purposes is the use of *Devonald* in *Nethermere*. *Devonald* in *Nethermere* was authority for the reading in of a matching obligation where there is otherwise a one-sided commitment in the

[104] *P D Wilson v M Racher* [1974] IRLR 114 (NIRC) [5].

[105] *Nethermere (St Neots) Ltd v Gardiner* [1984] IRLR 240 (CA).

[106] ibid [28].

[107] ibid [22].

[108] ibid [28] (Stephenson LJ): 'I agree that the evidence of these obligations is tenuous, so tenuous that the Industrial Tribunal's decision comes dangerously near the ill-defined boundary which separates the grey area of possible reasonable decisions from the jurisdiction of an appeal court to declare the decision wrong and put it right.'

[109] ibid.

[110] See n 55.

[111] Eg, *Carmichael* (n 55) [18]. On the difference between singular and successive contracts, see, eg, the difference between the Employment Appeal Tribunal and the Court of Appeal in *O'Kelly* (n 51). On this, see ch 8 in this volume. See, also, the same chapter for discussion of mutuality of obligation generally.

contract of employment. In Stephenson LJ's example in *Nethermere*, if there is a promise by the worker to accept work, this should be matched by implying a corollary promise by the employer to offer work. While conceivably implying reciprocal promises could add to the employee or worker's burden, it is likely that this would more often operate to the employee or worker's advantage: similarly to how recognition of the implied term of mutual trust and confidence, although which is 'mutual', tends to be regarded as an employee-protective implied term.[112]

More specifically, the example in *Nethermere* might seem to resurrect the idea, discussed above, that employers should also have an obligation to provide casual or zero hours workers with a reasonable amount of work if workers are required to remain available. On the other hand, this was situated, however, in a discussion in *Nethermere* about the prior question of employment status (*Nethermere*) rather than about the consequences of employment status once employment status is established (*Devonald*). The tensions in the concept of mutuality in the employment context were noted above. One of these tensions is that the concept is, problematically, used in very different contexts even within the employment sphere: being used both as a test for employee status but also, as in *Devonald*, when determining the consequences of employment status.[113]

In the more recent cases, it certainly seems that courts and tribunals are latterly interpreting an obligation to accept work more broadly. This is to be welcomed, in comparison to the formalistic approach taken by the House of Lords to this question previously in *O'Kelly v Trusthouse Forte Plc*: the latter which is the subject of a different chapter in this volume and to which the reader is directed.[114] For example, the Employment Appeal Tribunal recently in *Addison Lee Ltd v Lange* referred, amongst others, to the driver's required expenditure on the car for work purposes, meaning drivers had no realistic obligation but to accept work.[115] This was a more 'realistic' approach, to use the vernacular in this area.[116] Courts and employment tribunals may also appear to be taking a more realistic approach to the 'crystallisation' question from *Nethermere*.[117]

While theoretically the example in *Nethermere* using *Devonald* might help a zero hours worker argue also for a right to a reasonable amount of work, the example itself and the more recent cases on a broader interpretation of an

[112] Eg, *Malik v BCCI SA* [1997] IRLR 462 (HL) [55]. *cf* Brodie (n 2) paras 6.05–6.09 on sometimes the difficulties of identifying reciprocal obligations in the employment context.

[113] See Countouris (n 53).

[114] See ch 8 in this volume.

[115] *Lange* (n 72) [63] (and [60]).

[116] With reference initially to *Autoclenz Ltd v Belcher* [2011] UKSC 41, [2011] IRLR 820 [34]–[35].

[117] Eg, *St Ives Plymouth Ltd v Haggerty* (EAT, 22 May 2008) [28]–[29]. *cf*, eg, *Knight v Fairway & Kenwood Service Ltd* (EAT, 10 July 2012) [16]–[17].

obligation to accept work tend more to occur in cases about prior establishing employment status, whether as an employee or a worker. As another example, in *Wilson v Circular Distributors Ltd*, when the Employment Appeal Tribunal implied an obligation on that particular employer to provide work when work was available, this was not in a case challenging the amount of work as breach of contract but was rather a claimant asserting employee status so that he could bring an unfair dismissal claim.[118] Similarly in the *Addison Lee* example noted above, a broad interpretation of the obligation to accept work was taken there when discussing if the claimant was a statutory worker eligible to bring a working time claim.[119] While then *Devonald* might in theory assist a zero hours worker to argue for a right to a reasonable amount of work, at least current usage in cases suggests that *Devonald* would be more likely to assist the casual or zero hours worker when making a claim for a particular employment status so that they can bring a statutory claim such as for unfair dismissal in *Nethermere* or in *Wilson*,[120] or under the Working Time Regulations 1998 in *Lange*.[121] However, even then, there are limits to the assistance which *Devonald* alone can provide in this respect: for instance, where, even taking the aforementioned 'realistic' approach, there is still no obligation on the zero hour contract worker to accept work. A broader discussion of the issues involving zero hours work goes beyond the scope of this chapter.[122]

The other point to note is Freedland's observation that the 'logic of *Devonald*', contrary to the above, rather than assisting casual workers, could potentially hinder casual workers if seeking employee status.[123] As interpreted by judges subsequently, the logic of *Devonald* may be to suggest that matching promises, to provide work and to perform work, are necessary to constitute a contract of service. If those matching promises cannot be found, the claimant is not an employee. Freedland attributes the outcome in *Carmichael v National Power Plc* to the House of Lords' interpretation of the logic of *Devonald*.[124]

The response here is two-fold: first, there is again the general point about difficulty in the concept of mutuality in the employment context. One timely question is whether the Supreme Court's decision more recently in *Uber BV v Aslam* might possibly obviate the mutuality requirement for employment

[118] *Wilson* (n 74).

[119] *Lange* (n 72).

[120] Employment Rights Act 1996, s 94(1).

[121] Working Time Regulations 1998, reg 2(1).

[122] Eg, A Adams, M Freedland and J Adams-Prassl, 'The "Zero-Hours Contract": Regulating Casual Work, or Legitimating Precarity?' [2015] *Giornale di Diritto del Lavoro e di Relazioni Industriali* 529.

[123] Freedland (n 3) 477–78 ('logic' at 478).

[124] ibid 478: 'However, in recent cases culminating in the decision of the House of Lords in *Carmichael v National Power plc*, the courts have in effect accepted the logic of *Devonald v Rosser* and have applied it to the effect that a casual or "as required" worker cannot be regarded as having a continuing contract of employment which subsists through periods off work as well as through periods at work.'

status.[125] Lord Leggatt in *Uber* memorably stated that the 'primary question', in relation to employment classification if bringing a statutory claim is 'one of statutory interpretation, not contractual interpretation'.[126] Mutuality is a contractual concept. On the other hand, the signs in the most immediate case law may not be the most promising in this regard, with the Court of Appeal in another case, even on employment classification, finding *Uber* not to be relevant, for example, as there was a substitution clause in this later case and not in *Uber*.[127]

Second, the House of Lords in *Carmichael* would appear to have turned the logic of *Devonald* on its head. The wider literature on the workings of the tinplate industry notes that lay-off without notice and without pay was widespread at the time of *Devonald*: possibly 'a common feature when trading conditions slackened'.[128] Plenty of representatives from the tinplate industry appeared at the court to testify in favour of this custom, albeit Devonald and his witnesses argued there was a difference between a recognised custom to close for 'breakage, repairs and want of water or coal' whilst 'absolutely [denying] the right to shut down for want of remunerative orders'.[129] Indeed, this is the only reference in the entire case report even indirectly to the Steel Smelters Union: 'for the plaintiff, a number of witnesses, including workmen, secretaries of workmen's associations, and others likely to know of the alleged custom if existed' testified.[130] Moreover, Devonald himself in cross-examination apparently conceded that he had been laid off previously without pay.[131] It would have been very easy for Jelf J and the Court of Appeal to rule with the defendants;[132] however, as has been discussed here, they did not.[133] It would have been extremely easy, or even likely, for them to find the employer's alleged custom established; but possibly also easy for them to find there was no implied agreement to provide work on the facts, particularly if Devonald himself had previously accepted lay off without pay.[134] The real logic of *Devonald* was to use concepts of mutuality,

[125] *Uber BV v Aslam* [2021] UKSC 5, [2021] IRLR 407.

[126] ibid [69].

[127] *Independent Workers of Great Britain v Central Arbitration Committee* [2021] EWCA Civ 952, [2021] IRLR 796 [84] (Underhill LJ): 'Equally importantly, however, there was no issue about personal service: Uber did not rely on any substitution clause … Second, the question of how that analysis would apply on the facts of the present case, as found by the CAC, does not seem to me straightforward.'

[128] See Jenkins (n 17) 210.

[129] *Devonald* (n 1) 734 (Jelf J).

[130] ibid.

[131] 'Tin-Plate Trade' (n 8): 'Sometimes the works had been stopped and no reason was given, and then the men received no notice or payment.'

[132] Eg, Pugh (n 21) 125: 'So the secretary remarked: "It would appear that High Court or Low Court the judges have an animus against trade unions …".'

[133] For example, on the criteria of 'certainty', Lord Alverstone CJ referred to 'the closing of the works is a matter that depends entirely upon the will of the employer', see *Devonald* (n 1) 741.

[134] *cf* Pugh (n 21) 125: 'Many of the legal fraternity thought the men's side had made out an unanswerable case ….'

reciprocity and corollaries to read in a matching obligation to assist the worker in a very 'one-sided' situation; not to use the apparent absence of mutuality or reciprocity to deny employment status when individuals are bringing claims for the most basic of statutory employment rights.[135]

With reference to the suggestion in *Devonald* to avoid 'one-sidedness' in contracts of service, this author elsewhere has previously argued for an implied term of fairness to be recognised henceforth in contracts of employment, as an implied term to be read as a default into all contracts of employment and work.[136] The argument was that such an implied term was already latent. *Devonald* was one of the sources used to make that argument.[137]

A suggested implied term of fairness in the contract of employment was discussed more recently once again by the Court of Appeal in *Burn v Alder Hey Children's NHS Foundation Trust*.[138] In the words of Underhill LJ:

> There may not on the orthodox view be a general implied duty on an employer to act fairly in all contexts; but such a term is very readily implied in the context of disciplinary processes – see para. 114 of the judgment of Simler J in *Chakrabarty v Ipswich Hospital NHS Trust*.[139]

Similarly, Singh LJ said: 'For my part, I can well understand why the law does not imply a general obligation to act fairly into a contract of employment.'[140]

While Singh LJ was more tentative in this respect than Underhill LJ,[141] Underhill LJ does, however, seem expressly to recognise a duty of procedural fairness in contracts of employment or an implied term to act fairly during disciplinary procedures.[142] For both Lords Justices, this is stated conceptually to be separate from the well-established existing implied term, in employment contracts, of mutual trust and confidence.[143] The reasoning, however, is admittedly brief.[144]

[135] The claim in *Carmichael* (n 55) was for a statement of employment particulars (now, Employment Rights Act 1996, Part I).

[136] A Sanders, 'Fairness in the Contract of Employment' (2017) 46 *ILJ* 508.

[137] ibid 538.

[138] *Burn* (n 68). See, also, beforehand *IBM UK Holdings Ltd v Dalgleish* [2017] EWCA Civ 1212, [2018] IRLR 4 (partially summarised in *Smo v Hywel Dda University Health Board* [2021] IRLR 273 (EAT) [205]).

[139] *Burn* (n 68) [35] (the reference to *Chakrabarty* is [2014] EWHC 2735 (QB), [2014] Med LR 379).

[140] *Burn* (n 68) [46].

[141] ibid [48] (Singh LJ): 'I would prefer to leave this important issue of principle open for a future case, in which it may be necessary to decide the point, but it does not appear to me that there would be a legal impediment to such an implied term … In my view, if the law were to imply a term into the contract of employment that disciplinary processes must be conducted fairly, that would be a short step which builds on *Braganza*.'

[142] ibid [35] ('such a term is readily implied in the context of disciplinary processes'), [42] ('the duty of procedural fairness to which I refer at para 35 above').

[143] ibid [42], [47]. See, also, *Malik* (n 112).

[144] In comparison notably to *IBM* (n 138): the judgment in the *Industrial Relations Law Reports* is 56 pages long.

While the tentative recognition of an implied term of procedural fairness is a welcome addition to the corpus of employers' implied obligations in the contract of employment, the reasons for rejecting a substantive version of fairness are not the most convincing. Singh LJ suggests a requirement of substantive fairness in the contract of employment would 'cut across' statutory unfair dismissal law.[145] Two responses can be given. First, procedural fairness is also an aspect of the statutory law of unfair dismissal, if not the most important aspect.[146] Second, not all cases where an implied term of fairness might be argued will be dismissal or discipline cases.[147] On the other hand, in relation to this second point, the Court of Appeal in *Burn* perhaps only intended its comments to be directed to dismissal and discipline cases.[148] Against that, the language used is at times more general;[149] moreover, Singh LJ bases this implied term rather on *Braganza v BP Shipping Ltd*, the latter which evidently was not a dismissal or discipline case.[150] Nevertheless, even if that was the intention, it would not seem sensible to silo off dismissal and discipline cases. For example, even the more reticent jurisprudence on bonuses acknowledges the importance of procedural fairness.[151] However, this is to digress from the broader point.

If only a procedural version of fairness is recognised as opposed to also a substantive version, or if this implied term only extends to disciplinary procedures, as important as fairness is in the latter context; this potentially leaves untouched substantively 'very one-sided' contracts as in *Devonald*. Presumably the workman in *Devonald* would have preferred recognition of an implied agreement to provide a reasonable amount of work, as occurred, rather than the reading in of an internal grievance procedure for him to challenge the unreasonable allocation of work.

In another more recent case, *Agbeze v Barnet Enfield and Haringey Mental Health NHS Trust*, *Devonald* was cited for the following proposition: '*Devonald v Rosser* itself, she submitted, could be seen as an illustration of the court stepping in to protect a vulnerable worker.'[152] This author, as well as other employment law scholars would seemingly agree.[153] Auerbach J's disappointing response in the Employment Appeal Tribunal was as follows:

> I turn to the general authorities on contractual implied terms. *Devonald v Rosser* was concerned with whether the lack of any work for the employees to do excused the

[145] *Burn* (n 68) [46].

[146] Eg, *W Devis & Sons Ltd v RA Atkins* [1977] IRLR 314 (HL) [24] (Viscount Dilhorne): 'Para. 6(8) appears to me to direct the Tribunal to focus its attention on the conduct of the employer and not on whether the employee in fact suffered any injustice.'

[147] Eg, bonus cases as discussed at Sanders (n 136) 522–27.

[148] Eg, the text accompanying n 139.

[149] Eg, the text accompanying n 140 and the broader reference to procedural fairness at n 142.

[150] *Burn* (n 68) [48]. See, also, *Braganza v BP Shipping Ltd* [2015] UKSC 17, [2015] IRLR 487.

[151] Eg, *Commerzbank AG v Keen* [2006] EWCA Civ 1536, [2007] IRLR 132 [44]–[45].

[152] *Agbeze v Barnet Enfield and Haringey Mental Health NHS Trust* [2022] IRLR 115 (EAT) [30] (Auerbach J).

[153] Eg, Davies (n 3) 486: 'Other examples arise where the courts have been more obviously influenced by a concern for the fair treatment of employees', followed by discussion of *Devonald*.

> employer from its obligation to pay wages, and, specifically, whether there was in fact, in that case, a custom and practice of a sort that could give rise to an implied term to that effect. I do not think that anything in that decision assists the present claimant's case for an implied term conferring a positive right on him, such as is contended for in this case.[154]

This leads to a brief discussion of *Agbeze* to conclude, as in some ways a twenty-first century example of the precarity evident in *Devonald*. Precarity is used in this sense to refer to the otherwise 'very one-sided' nature of the agreement in *Devonald*.

D. A Modern Example of *Devonald*?

The claimant in *Agbeze v Barnet* was a so-called 'bank worker', employed as a health care assistant by the defendant Trust.[155] He would appear to have been a zero hours worker. His contract specifically stated there was no obligation on the trust to offer him any work nor on him to accept any work, and there would be no regular hours. The claimant in *Agbeze* was suspended for some three months, during a disciplinary investigation. The situation seems similar to *Devonald* in the sense that the claimant argued that he could not work elsewhere, in similar employment, for the three months. Seemingly, no other Trust would employ him while he was under investigation.[156] *Agbeze* however is obviously very different from *Devonald* in other key respects: there were entirely different reasons for the lay off in *Devonald*.[157] There is no reference to *Agbeze* as a test case or the involvement of a large number of witnesses across the industry. There is no reference to a trade union in *Agbeze*.

The disappointing feature of *Agbeze* is, first, the seeming lack of substantive engagement with the reasoning by the Supreme Court in *Uber BV v Aslam*.[158] The Supreme Court in *Uber* confirmed and extended a purposive approach to matters of employment status, with Lord Leggatt memorably referring to the undoubted purpose of employment legislation as to protect workers.[159] This approach surely should not stop at employment classification.[160] There is little point in using a purposive approach to classify employment status then not also to deploy a purposive approach to the interpretation of substantive legislation. In *Agbeze*, a purposive approach might suggest a different, less formalistic reading of wages 'properly payable' in section 13(3) of the Employment Rights

[154] *Agbeze* (n 152) [68] (Auerbach J).
[155] ibid. Eg, also, earlier: *Clark v Oxfordshire Health Authority* [1998] IRLR 125 (CA).
[156] *Agbeze* (n 152) [26].
[157] Although it was a disciplinary investigation in *Agbeze* (n 152) [29] (Auerbach J): 'based on a suspicion that was subsequently found to be unfounded'.
[158] *Uber* (n 125).
[159] ibid [71].
[160] *cf Agbeze* (n 152) [75].

Act 1996.[161] In the same way that contract was not key to matters of employment status classification in *Uber*, contract may not have needed to be key to the interpretation of section 13(3) of the Employment Rights Act 1996.[162]

Second, in *Agbeze*, if the claimant truly was not able to work for the three or so months while an investigation was carried out, this is potentially another example of the aforementioned 'one sidedness' noted, but moreover mitigated, in *Devonald*. In order to avoid one-sidedness, there was surely basis, on the grounds of mutuality or reciprocity, to imply a term in *Agbeze* that the disciplinary procedure would be conducted without undue delay.[163] Indeed, such is arguably already required by existing cases. In 1995, the Employment Appeal Tribunal in *W A Goold (Pearmak) Ltd v McConnell* found 'an implied term in the contract of employment that the employers would reasonably and promptly afford a reasonable opportunity to their employees to obtain redress of any grievance they may have'.[164] The key word there for present purposes would be 'promptly'. A requirement to act promptly would also presumably be part of a potential new implied term of procedural fairness as tentatively recognised subsequently in *Burn*.[165]

Third, the Employment Appeal Tribunal in *Agbeze* rejected the suggestion for a general implied term (or a 'so-called "class" or "category" implied term') for statutory workers that suspension will be with pay unless the worker's contract states otherwise.[166] Auerbach J chose to distinguish between two types of contracts of work, at common law, agreeing:

> There is a fundamental difference between a contract the basic architecture of which was of that sort, and a conventional employment contract, which itself provided for guaranteed and required work and hours, and correspondingly guaranteed and required pay, so long as the employee was ready, willing and able to work.[167]

In comparison, in *Hanley v Pease and Partners Ltd* in 1915,[168] indeed which is categorised as the partner case to *Devonald* by Deakin and Wilkinson and by

[161] Eg, traditionally, *New Century Cleaning Co Ltd v Church* [2000] IRLR 27 (CA).

[162] *Uber* (n 125) [69] on which see, eg, A Bogg and Michael Ford QC, 'The Death of Contract in Determining Employment Status' (2021) 137 *LQR* 392.

[163] *Agbeze* (n 152) [26] (Auerbach J): 'the suspension in his case, of several months, could not be described as brief'. Counsel for Agbeze also cited 'para 8 of the ACAS Code' (at [23]): 'this period should be as brief as possible'. *cf Agbeze* (n 152) [40]. However statutory workers also have a statutory right to accompaniment at formal disciplinary and grievance procedures under the Employment Relations Act 1999, s 10.

[164] *W A Goold (Pearmak) Ltd v McConnell* [1995] IRLR 516 (EAT) (Morison J).

[165] *Burn* (n 68) [35]. Eg, also, *Chakrabarty* (n 139) [114] (Simler J): 'without unjustified delay'. Once again, the statutory right to accompaniment at formal disciplinary and grievance procedures also applies to statutory workers.

[166] *Agbeze* (n 152) [77]. On the other hand, Auerbach J did seem to recognise that the implied term of mutual trust and confidence would be applicable: ref to 'all working relationships'. *cf*, eg, previously *Bedfordshire County Council v Fitzpatrick Contractors Ltd* (1998) 62 Con LR 64 (QB) 72 (with reference to eligibility of employees only to bring statutory unfair dismissal claims).

[167] *Agbeze* (n 152) [54].

[168] *Hanley* (n 5).

Deakin and Morris, it was held there is no implied right to suspend without pay.[169]

Agbeze differentiated between 'zero hour or bank type contracts' (where the employer could suspend without pay) and 'conventional employee' examples (where the employer cannot suspend without pay, unless there is an express term otherwise).[170] Notably, however, the workman in *Hanley* (where the claim succeeded) was a 'cokeman', different to the professional employee counterexamples discussed in *Agbeze*.[171] Against this, even if it is relevant that there was express reference in *Hanley* to there being a 'continuing' contract, recent case law developments as noted above might support the finding of a continuing contract for casual or zero hours workers in a broader range of circumstances.[172] In comparison to *Agbeze* (2021), the Court of Appeal in *Devonald* (1906) had stated: 'No distinction in principle can be drawn between wages by time and wages by piece.'[173]

IV. CONCLUSION

Devonald is a landmark case for various reasons, but two will be highlighted in this concluding section. First, *Devonald* is noted as an authority for a number of widely different propositions: a right to pay, the employer's obligation to provide work (at least for some employees), protection against lay-off, an authority on what triggers the employee's entitlement to pay, an early modern case on the importance of reciprocity in the contract of employment; as well as an authority for the more technical point as to when custom and practice in the employment context will become legally binding. Strikingly as a much older authority in the employment context, it has endured.[174]

Second, *Devonald* is a remarkable decision for its time. The Court of Appeal implied a contractual right to be provided with a reasonable amount of work to a piece worker, at a time when lay off without pay was widespread in that industry. Initially this was regarded as an implied term in fact but subsequent cases treat this as an implied term of law for piece workers.[175] In comparison, more recently, when it was suggested to the Employment Appeal Tribunal that there

[169] Eg, Freedland (n 3) 475.

[170] Eg, *Agbeze* (n 152) [54]–[55], [77]. For 'conventional employees', in *Agbeze*, this is not via a separate implied term but rather by construing the wage-work bargain: eg, *Agbeze* (n 152) [66].

[171] Examples discussed in *Agbeze* (n 152): senior capacity energy purchasing manager in *Kent County Council v Knowles* (EAT, 9 March 2012) [2] and consultant anaesthetist in *North West Anglia NHS Foundation Trust v Gregg* [2019] EWCA Civ 387, [2019] IRLR 570.

[172] *Hanley* (n 5) 705.

[173] *Devonald* (n 1) 739 (Lord Alverstone CJ). See, also, *Miles v Wakefield Metropolitan District Council* [1987] IRLR 193 (HL) [15].

[174] See, eg, *Wilson* (n 104). Also compare the reception of *Devonald* to the reception of *Addis* (n 7): eg, *Johnson v Unisys Ltd* [2001] UKHL 13, [2001] IRLR 279 [3]–[4].

[175] See discussion in the text accompanying n 77.

should be recognised a far less wide-ranging implied term that zero hour workers be paid during a disciplinary suspension, the Employment Appeal Tribunal refused, stating that to imply such a term would materially change the nature of the contract.[176] Jelf J and the Court of Appeal in 1906 were concerned with mitigating the otherwise 'one sidedness' of the claimant's contract of service, even while the Employers and Workmen Act 1875 was still in use.[177] The Court was concerned that 'all' the risk should not be placed on the workman (unless the contract expressly stated otherwise) and accordingly an implied agreement to provide work was found. By contrast, in that same recent Employment Appeal Tribunal judgment (*Agbeze*), the Employment Appeal Tribunal discussed *Devonald* in a decision recognising two types of contract of work at common law, but at the same time was seemingly content, unlike *Devonald*, with one of those two types of contract placing all the risk on the worker. While one legacy of *Devonald* may, counterintuitively, have been partially to contribute to restrictive decisions on mutuality of obligation, this is to misunderstand *Devonald* by subsequent judges.[178] *Devonald* itself did not use the absence of a matching obligation in an exclusionary fashion to deny employment status but instead to imply a matching obligation where that is possible, in *Devonald* itself positively to provide the workman in that instance with a right to work, perhaps contrary to the odds.[179]

The real legacy of *Devonald* should be the recognition of the words and principle: 'apart from authority, it would be strange if such a right is not implied; for otherwise the bargain is of a very one-sided character'.[180] Devonald, and his trade union, brought a test claim, successfully, on behalf of hundreds of workmen at the turn of the twentieth century.[181] It would be hoped that the desire to avoid 'one-sidedness' would guide developments in the future, judicial and statutory, to the benefit of all workers and employees.

[176] *Agbeze* (n 152) [77].

[177] Eg, S Deakin and GS Morris, *Labour Law*, 6th edn (Oxford, Hart, 2012) para 1.17: 'Under section 3(3) of the Employers and Workmen Act 1875 the court had the power in effect to order specific performance against an employee who was in breach of contract, a right not available under the general law of contract either at that time or since.'

[178] See n 123.

[179] Although the Steel Smelters Union was sure that it had a strong case, see discussion in the text accompanying n 128.

[180] *Devonald* (n 1) 731.

[181] Pugh (n 21) 138: 'It had a salutary effect upon those South Wales employers who had been too ready to take a one-sided view of the contract of notice as between themselves and their work-people.'

4

Financing the Parliamentary Representation of Labour: Amalgamated Society of Railway Servants v Osborne

DAVID CABRELLI*

I. INTRODUCTION

IN THE AUTUMN of 1907, the secretary of the Walthamstow branch of the Amalgamated Society of Railway Servants ('ASRS') raised legal proceedings against the ASRS challenging the fact that part of the union dues he had paid to the ASRS had been compulsorily applied to fund prospective Labour Party candidates seeking representation in Parliament. As a supporter of the Liberal Party and no friend of what he called 'the Socialists', Mr Walter Osborne took great exception to this enforced political levy and the ASRS's administration of a political fund.[1] The basis for Osborne's disquiet rested in the ASRS's rulebook. This had been amended in 1903 and 1905 to confer a power on the trade union to apply a portion of members' dues towards political purposes in funding Parliamentary representation for Labour Party members.[2] Osborne also had a much broader concern about this development. His anxiety was that the ASRS and other trade unions had been distracted from their original industrial objectives, and diverted towards what he considered an illegitimate focus on securing political representation and influence in Parliament. Osborne found

* I would like to thank the editors for their valuable insights and suggestions. Of course, all inaccuracies, errors, etc, remain my own.

[1] For a full account from Osborne's perspective, see WV Osborne, *My Case* (London, E Nash, 1910) and WV Osborne, *Sane Trade Unionism* (London, Collins, 1913) 128ff. See also MJ Klarman, '*Osborne*: A Judgment Gone Too Far?' (1988) 103 *The English Historical Review* 21, 25.

[2] Technically, during the 1903–1905 period, the relevant organisation was the Labour Representation Committee ('LRC'), which was the forerunner of the Labour Party established in 1906.

this development lamentable, as it was his firm view that party politics ought to be kept strictly outside of the business of trade unions since their true, proper, functions were at once economic and industrial.[3]

Osborne's claim that sought to challenge the compulsory political levy was unsuccessful in the Chancery division. Mr Justice Neville followed the precedent of *Steele v South Wales Miners' Federation*[4] to dismiss Osborne's case. Osborne appealed to the Court of Appeal, changing his arguments slightly, and in the autumn of 1909, he was successful.[5] The ASRS appealed to the House of Lords who upheld the decision of the Court of Appeal.[6] From the textual definition of a trade union in the Trade Union Acts 1871 and 1876, the majority of the Law Lords saw no reason to infer a power enabling trade unions to ingather, administer, and hold funds for political purposes. Taking that premise to its logical conclusion, any provision in a trade union's rulebook that permitted it to administer a political fund for the purposes of securing the parliamentary representation of independent candidates or the candidates of an affiliated political party (such as the LRC/Labour), was held to be illegal on the basis that it was ultra vires.

In this chapter, the discussion starts by positioning the *Osborne* decision in its historical context. Section III turns to a dissection of the speeches of the Law Lords, including an analysis of the role of the ultra vires doctrine in the decision. In section IV, the post-*Osborne* legislative history is charted, particularly in terms of the subsequent initiatives of the Liberal Party administration. As part of that process, the Liberal Government's motives behind the passing of the Trade Union Act 1913 will be considered. Sections V and VI devote their attention to *Osborne*'s legacy for the regulation of the funding of political parties in the UK and Labour Law more broadly as a discipline. At this juncture, the discussion makes the point that the subject matter of the decision is not some arcane or stale historical aside, but of continuing contemporary relevance in light of recurring debates about the financing of parliamentary parties whose purpose is the promotion of the economic interests of working people.[7] Indeed, the broader significance and originality of this chapter lies in the extent to which it reminds labour lawyers of the ongoing significance of the rules governing

[3] Osborne, *Sane Trade Unionism* (n 1) 129.

[4] *Steele v South Wales Miners' Federation* [1907] 1 KB 361 (KBD).

[5] *Osborne v Amalgamated Society of Railway Servants (No 1)* [1909] 1 Ch 163 (CA).

[6] *Osborne v Amalgamated Society of Railway Servants (No 1)* [1910] AC 87 (HL).

[7] The voluminous body of work that has been produced by Ewing on the subject of political funding is a testament to this proposition: KD Ewing, *Trade Unions, the Labour Party and the Law: A Study of the Trade Union Act 1913* (Edinburgh, Edinburgh University Press, 1982); KD Ewing, 'The Trade Union Question' in KD Ewing, J Rowbottom and J Tham (eds), *The Funding of Political Parties: Where Now?* (London, Routledge, 2012) 54, 56–57; KD Ewing, *The Funding of Political Parties in Britain* (Cambridge, Cambridge University Press, 1987); KD Ewing, *The Cost of Democracy* (Oxford, Hart Publishing, 2007) 64–67; KD Ewing and S Issacharoff, *Party Funding and Campaign Financing in International Perspective* (Oxford, Hart Publishing, 2006); KD Ewing, 'Trade Union Political Funds: The 1913 Act Revised' (1984) 13 *ILJ* 227.

trade union contributions to the Labour Party, which historically has made a seminal contribution towards cementing employment protection rights into place in legislation. Section VII concludes.

II. SOME HISTORICAL BACKGROUND

It has been estimated that the candidacy of approximately 70 per cent of all Labour Party MPs had been sponsored by the trade unions in the general election of 1906 that immediately preceded the *Osborne* litigation.[8] In that general election, the Labour Party succeeded in returning 29 MPs to Parliament. The figure of 70 per cent rose to 95 per cent in the subsequent two general elections of 1910, with Labour securing 40 and 42 parliamentary seats respectively.[9] That increase in trade union support for Labour Party candidates was not particularly surprising considering the events of 1903 to 1905. Osborne's own personal account of the goings on at the Walthamstow branch of the ASRS charts how the LRC – the forerunner of the Labour Party – had taken widespread action throughout the country to procure that the rulebooks of several affiliated trade unions, including the ASRS, be modified to provide for the imposition of a political levy on their members.[10] This was intended to furnish financial support to its sponsored candidates who were running for, or had been elected to, Parliament. Before the rulebook changes, trade union spending on parliamentary representation had been restricted to the support of independent candidates, rather than those affiliated to any one political party.[11] The rulebook modifications represented a singling out of the Labour Party as the sole worthy recipients of political finance from the trade unions. What ensued was a war of attrition of sorts between those members and officials of the ASRS who were sympathetic to the LRC's goal of securing a stable funding source for parliamentary representation and those with strong connections to the Liberal Party who resisted what they considered to be the unwarranted infiltration of the LRC/Labour Party and 'socialists' into the business of 'their' trade union.[12] This internal struggle in the machinations of the ASRS lasted for around three years, centring around somewhat arcane, internal ASRS procedures, with Osborne and others seeking discontinuation of the political levy, ultimately to no avail. By 1906, it had

[8] K Coates and T Topham, *Trade Unions in Britain* (Nottingham, Spokesman, 1980) 304–05.

[9] ibid.

[10] Osborne, *Sane Trade Unionism* (n 1) 110–28. See also the account in WB Gwyn, *Democracy and the Cost of Politics in Britain* (London, Athlone Press, 1962) 163–70, 180–83. At that time, in terms of the Labour Party constitution, only affiliated trade unions were members: individual membership of the Party was not permitted until 1918.

[11] See Klarman (n 1) 21.

[12] Throughout the late Victorian and early Edwardian eras, there had been very strong links between the trade unions and the Liberal Party: see Ewing, *Trade Unions, the Labour Party and the Law: A Study of the Trade Union Act 1913* (n 7) 12–15; Klarman (n 1) 30–33.

become clear to Osborne and his supporters that they were on the losing side of the internal debate, and at that point, Osborne realised that recourse to the law would be a last, but necessary, resort.[13]

The ASRS obtained legal opinions from leading counsel, which were particularly sanguine about its prospects of success in defending any legal action challenging the political levy.[14] This glowing appraisal rested largely on the authority of *Steele v South Wales Miners' Federation*.[15] *Steele* had been decided in early 1907, with the King's Bench ruling that a political levy imposed on trade union members was lawful since its rulebook provided for the maintenance of a political fund. Mr Justices Darling and Phillimore ruled that it was not ultra vires of the objects of the trade union since the levy had been approved implicitly by a majority of its members in a ballot who had sanctioned the political fund.[16] In fact, Gwyn notes how *Steele* was 'believed by nearly everyone [at that time] to have completely settled the legality of trade union political levies'.[17] Nevertheless, undeterred, Osborne was determined to raise the matter afresh in the courts. He busily set about securing funding for his litigation. Pelling notes how he issued a call in the *Daily Express* newspaper to like-minded anti-socialists to help fund his case, which eventually extended to him writing letters to *The Times* newspaper.[18] Sympathetic trade unionists from all over the UK sent money to help finance his case and he was also the recipient of pro bono legal advice from supportive anti-socialist solicitors. Nevertheless, the suspicion that he had been clandestinely backed by capitalist interests to constrain the growth of the fledgling Labour Party was never far away and could not be so easily dispelled.[19]

When the case reached the High Court, Mr Justice Neville was of the view that the primary consideration animating the dispute was democratic in nature and followed *Steele*.[20] In other words, that if the administration of a political fund had been approved by a majority of ASRS's members, then the substance of the issue of the collection of the political levy was one that was outside the scope of juridical scrutiny: it was not for the judiciary to interfere, no matter how unsavoury they found the matter. As such, it was held that the political levy was within the powers of the trade union where the majority of the members supported this.[21] Osborne appealed to the Court of Appeal, and in doing so, adapted his strategy by arguing the much broader point that *all* trade union spending on Parliamentary representation – rather than solely Labour Party

[13] See Osborne, *My Case* (n 1) 60; Gwyn (n 10) 182; Klarman (n 1) 26.

[14] See H Pelling, 'The Politics of the Osborne Judgment' (1983) 25 *The Historical Journal* 889, 891.

[15] *Steele* (n 4).

[16] ibid 368, 370–71 (Darling and Phillimore JJ).

[17] Gwyn (n 10) 181.

[18] See Pelling (n 14) 892–93; Gwyn (n 10) 182.

[19] Gwyn (n 10) 182; P S Bagwell, *The Railwaymen* (London, Allen & Unwin, 1963) 253–54.

[20] *Osborne v Amalgamated Society of Railway Servants* 77 LJ Ch 763 (Ch). For a comprehensive account of the litigation in the courts, see Gwyn (n 10) 183–91.

[21] *Osborne* (n 20) 765.

representation – was unlawful as ultra vires the powers of trade unions and that it was irrelevant what the majority of members had agreed in their rulebook.[22] The Court of Appeal agreed and overruled *Steele*. Rather than emphasise or dissect the democratic credentials of ASRS's decision to incorporate the political levy or maintain the political fund in terms of its rulebook, instead, it decided that the definition of a trade union in the Trade Union Acts of 1871 and 1876 was paramount. And, of material importance to the Master of the Rolls and the Lord Justices was the fact that that statutory definition did not contain provision for a political fund or parliamentary representation. Instead, it held that Parliament had intended for the statutory definition to be exhaustive, which precluded the rulebooks of trade unions from charging their members sums to afford financial support to the candidates of any political party (including the Labour Party) seeking election to Parliament.[23] To that extent, the question was one of ultra vires in the sense that bodies such as trade unions who owed, and attributed, their existence to statutory authority could only exercise powers for the limited purposes and objects specified in the relevant legislation. Having reached that point, the scene was set for the ASRS to appeal the Court of Appeal's judgment to the House of Lords.

III. THE DECISION OF THE HOUSE OF LORDS

The legal issues on which the speeches of the Law Lords centred in *Osborne* were twofold: first, *vires* and second, that of *constitutionality*.[24] The vires matter related to whether the ASRS had exceeded its powers in providing for a political levy in its rulebook insofar as it was a power that no trade union enjoyed as a quasi-corporate entity recognised by statutory authority under the Trade Union Acts of 1871 and 1876.[25] Meanwhile, the constitutionality issue concerned the legality of provisions in the ASRS's rulebook (and other trade unions) that enjoined MPs funded by the political levy (charged to, and paid by, trade union members) and elected to Parliament to adhere to the Labour Party whip at all times. Osborne argued that this injunction restricted the freedom of individual conscience of MPs, and that accordingly, it was unconstitutional.

The main speech that covered whether the ASRS's rulebook was ultra vires was given by Lord Atkinson.[26] His Lordship focused on the statutory definition

[22] Klarman (n 1) 28–29; Osborne, *My Case* (n 1) 29.

[23] Interestingly, in *Steele*, unlike the Court of Appeal, Mr Justice Darling had interpreted the statutory definition as being broad enough to cover political objects, funds and levies: see *Steele* (n 4) 367.

[24] See W Cornish and others, *Law and Society in England 1750–1950*, 2nd edn (Oxford, Hart Publishing, 2019) 327–28; WM Geldart, *The Present Law of Trade Disputes and Trade Unions* (Oxford, Oxford University Press, 1914) 56–61.

[25] For contemporary commentary on the case, see WM Geldart, 'Trade Unions and Parliamentary Representation' (1910) 20 *The Economic Journal* 480.

[26] See *Osborne* (n 6) 102–05.

in section 16 of the Trade Union Act 1876, which provided that a trade union was

> any combination, whether temporary or permanent, for regulating the relations between workmen and masters, or between workmen and workmen, or between masters and masters, or for imposing restrictive conditions on the conduct of any trade or business, whether such combination would or would not, if the [1876 Act] had not been passed, have been deemed to have been an unlawful combination by reason of some one or more of its purposes being in restraint of trade ....

In his Lordship's opinion, that definition was intended to be comprehensive, setting parameters around what a trade union could lawfully do. The collection of a political levy from members, and the maintenance of a political fund for parliamentary representation in accordance with the trade union's rulebook was not specifically included in that definition. As such, these were activities or processes that were auxiliary or collateral to, and fell outside, the purposes of trade unions definitively articulated in the legislation. For that reason, he ruled that trade unions had no power to collect and administer any funds for political objectives, since Parliament had set statutory limitations on the activities of trade unions. Both the Earl of Halsbury and Lord Macnaghten agreed with Lord Atkinson on this point.[27] On that basis, ASRS's rulebook was held to be unenforceable and the collection of the political levy from members could be restrained lawfully by injunction. Effectively, the democratic implications of the judgment were sidelined, in the sense that its adverse consequences for internal union democracy were ignored.[28]

Lord Shaw looked beyond the vires point, to focus on the question of the constitutionality of the declaration in the ASRS's rulebook that Labour Party MPs would be bound to follow the whip. In his view, this provision was contrary to public policy; that is to say, the application of the political levy and fund towards the financial support of Labour Party MPs – who would have to forego both their own personal liberty and the exercise of personal judgment on matters put to a parliamentary vote – was a provision that was contrary to public policy.[29] The justification for this finding lay in the adverse impact that this process would have on the constituents of those Labour MPs, who his Lordship opined would be disenfranchised, and the fact that the interests of

[27] ibid 93, 97. However, Lord Hereford disagreed with, and Lord Shaw hesitated to accept, this interpretation of the import of the language in the statute: ibid 98–99, 107–08.

[28] Kahn-Freund described *Osborne* as a 'decision [that] could not stand' for it fundamentally interfered with basic democratic principles, ie that the trade unions and their members should be entitled to financially support any organisation that they may desire, without legal sanction: see P Davies and M Freedland (eds), *Kahn-Freund's Labour and the Law* (London, Stevens & Sons, 1983) 247. For that reason, the decision is said to have led to an 'outcry': Lord Wedderburn, *The Worker and the Law: Text and Materials*, 3rd edn (London, Penguin Books, 1986) 760; Ewing, *Trade Unions, the Labour Party and the Law: A Study of the Trade Union Act 1913* (n 7) 38–56.

[29] For extensive discussion of this issue, see Geldart (n 24) 56–61.

those who paid the MPs would dictate how they voted, converting them into paid delegates. Lord Hereford agreed with Lord Shaw's analysis.[30]

The speeches of the Law Lords who invoked the vires point to reject the ASRS's arguments, raise a pertinent question. And that is whether it was ever justifiable or appropriate for the Law Lords to harness a doctrine derived from company law (based on the 'state concession' theory of the corporation) to regulate the affairs of a non-corporate, albeit quasi-corporate, body, such as a trade union?[31] The state concession theory holds that corporate status is a kind of gift or licence from the state, which is contingent on powers being exercised by the corporate body within the scope and limits set by the concession, ie the relevant objectives of that corporation. This point is significant for two reasons. First, by recognising the purchase and relevance of the state concession theory, the decision of the House of Lords in *Osborne* goes entirely against the grain of contemporary thinking. As noted by Bogg, the ruling 'collective laissez-faire' theory of British Labour Law of the time,[32] perceived trade unions in terms of the 'realist' theory of the corporation.[33] This philosophy directed that trade unions were treated as quasi-separate legal personalities by the law in order to reflect the social reality of matters, rather than as some kind of fiction under the state concession approach. Considered against that benchmark, with its emphasis on the state setting legislative limits and parameters on trade union powers, the *Osborne* decision looks somewhat anomalous. The second reason for its importance lies in the fact that since the Trade Union Acts 1871 and 1876,

[30] *Osborne* (n 6) 99. The other Law Lords expressed no opinion on this constitutionality/public policy issue.

[31] On the nature of the 'state concession' theory, see CA Coke, *Corporation, Trust and Company* (Cambridge, MA, Harvard University Press, 1951) 67–69; J Dewey, 'The Historic Background of Corporate Legal Personality' (1926) 35 *Yale Law Journal* 655, 666–69; PG Mahoney, 'Contract or Concession? An Essay on the History of Corporate Law' (2000) 34 *Georgia Law Review* 873; FW Maitland, 'The Corporation Sole' in D Runciman and M Ryan (eds), *Maitland: Trust and Corporation* (Cambridge, Cambridge University Press, 2003) 9; BR Cheffins, *The Trajectory of (Corporate Law) Scholarship* (Cambridge, Cambridge University Press, 2004) 39; SM Watson, 'The Corporate Legal Person' (2019) 19 *Journal of Corporate Law Studies* 137, 142–45; J Hardman, 'Looking Beyond Separate Legal Personality or How Many Titles have Rangers Won?' [2022] *Juridical Review* 1, 4–8.

[32] On the subject of 'collective laissez-faire', see O Kahn-Freund, 'Labour Law' in M Ginsberg (ed), *Law and Opinion in England in the 20th Century* (London, Stevens, 1959); O Kahn-Freund, 'Legal Framework' in A Flanders and H Clegg (eds), *The System of Industrial Relations in Great Britain* (Basil Blackwell, Oxford, 1954) 42, 53, 58; O Kahn-Freund, 'Collective Agreements' (1941) 4 *Modern Law Review* 225, 226–27; O Kahn-Freund, 'The Shifting Frontiers of the Law: Law and Custom in Labour Relations' (1969) 22 *Current Legal Problems* 1; O Kahn-Freund, 'Collective Agreements under War Legislation' (1943) 6 *Modern Law Review* 112; O Kahn-Freund, 'Intergroup Conflicts and their Settlement' in O Kahn-Freund (ed), *Selected Writings* (London, Steven & Sons, 1978) 41; P Davies and M Freedland (eds), *Kahn-Freund's Labour and the Law* (London, Stevens, 1983). For commentary, see S Deakin and F Wilkinson, 'The Evolution of Collective Laissez-Faire' (2004) 17 *Historical Studies in Industrial Relations* 1; K Ewing, 'The State and Industrial Relations: "Collective Laissez-Faire" Revisited' (1998) 5 *Historical Studies in Industrial Relations* 1.

[33] A Bogg, *The Democratic Aspects of Trade Union Recognition* (Oxford, Hart Publishing, 2009) 10–11, 13–15.

trade unions and their activities have been lawful, clothing them with a quasi-corporate status.[34] From that position, a number of powers, immunities, and privileges were bestowed on registered trade unions, such as the power of the trustees of the union to hold property. Seen from that perspective, an analogy was drawn between a registered trade union and a joint stock company that becomes an incorporated body via registration. This point is explicitly reflected in the speech of the Earl of Halsbury, who equated a 'corporation and a combination'.[35] At the time, it was trite law that statutorily registered companies were bound by the ultra vires doctrine, and the leading case was *Ashbury Railway Carriage & Iron Co Ltd v Riche*.[36] In this decision, the House of Lords had ruled that statutory corporations incorporated under the Companies Act 1862 could not carry out any activities that fell outside the general objects specified in their memorandum of association.[37] In that sense, anything that was not expressly or implicitly authorised was proscribed and the majority or unanimous consent of the company's members could neither cure any such activity nor convert it into acts that were intra vires.[38] This was rooted in the argument that the 1862 Act conferred powers and privileges on statutory corporations and as such, were subject to qualified limitations. In the same way, the Law Lords reasoned that the key point for resolution in *Osborne* was whether the Trade Union Acts 1871 and 1876 – conferring certain benefits on trade unions that also stemmed from registration – should also be subject to similar limits. The majority of the Law Lords ruled that they undoubtedly ought to be and that provision for a parliamentary fund fell outside those limits, since what was not within the terms of the statute, was implicitly proscribed.

In the view of Lord Wedderburn, the answer to the question posed above is that it was an illegitimate exercise of judicial authority for the Law Lords to adopt such a *statutory incarnation* of the ultra vires doctrine to strike down the political levy in the ASRS's rulebook.[39] In essence, the majority of the Law Lords tested the legality of the political levy against the statutory definition of a trade union, rather than the activities that were authorised and permitted under the union's rulebook. As such, by failing to approach the *Osborne* case through a contractual lens and instead by adopting a statutory analysis, the decision goes against the grain of the times, with its espousal of the 'freedom of contract' ideology. Furthermore, arguably, the Law Lords misconstrued the

[34] To that extent, it did not confer corporate status on trade unions, who were not (nor continue to be) created by statute.

[35] *Osborne* (n 6) 93. On how the Earl of Halsbury took the Trade Union Acts 1871 and 1876 as quasi-charters of incorporation for trade unions, which triggered the application of the ultra vires doctrine, see HH Slesser, *The Law Relating to Trade Unions* (London, Allen & Unwin, 1921) 86.

[36] *Ashbury Railway Carriage & Iron Co Ltd v Riche* (1874–75) LR 7 HL 653 (HL).

[37] This rule stemmed from a similar adoption of the ultra vires doctrine in the case of chartered corporations, both of which were applications of the state concession theory: see LCB Gower, *The Principles of Modern Company Law*, 2nd edn (London, Steven & Sons, 1957) 78–79.

[38] ibid 78–85.

[39] Lord Wedderburn (n 28) 759–60.

basis of the *Ashbury v Riche* decision, since in that case, the issue was whether the activities of the railway company exceeded the objects narrated in its memorandum of association – which is the functional equivalent of a union's rulebook or constitution – rather than the definition of a commercial company in the Companies Act 1862. It was on this point that Wedderburn was scathing of the approach taken by the Law Lords in *Osborne*. His claim was that the proper application of that doctrine would have entailed an assessment of the political activities of the union (in prescribing the political levy) against the objects laid down in its rulebook, ie whether it included a political element. If that had been the approach adopted in the case, the ASRS would have successfully defended Osborne's legal action. Instead, the notion that the trade union movement had a political dimension was rejected and the provisions of the ASRS's rulebook enjoining its members to lay out expenditure towards the subsidisation of a funding scheme for parliamentary representation was held to be invalid.

One of the surprising features of the judgments of the Law Lords in *Osborne* was their *ex facie* failure to engage with any of the political consequences of their decision. Although there is no contemporary evidence, one gains the impression that the Lords might even have been staggered had an outside observer pointed these out to them at the time. Unless the Lords were living as hermits in a cave, they would surely have been aware that Labour was a nascent political party, who in light of the growing sympathy of the enfranchised (male members of the) working classes towards its objectives, had the potential to break through as a major force in Parliament. And to achieve that objective, they needed a stable source of funding. Instead, the questions the Law Lords addressed in the case were reduced to quaint doctrinal niceties and articulated in starkly legalistic terms. The primary consideration of the Law Lords in the case was to invoke a purely legal doctrine which masked its much more heightened political ramifications. And the odd thing about their approach is that even the Lord Chancellor, Lord Loreburn – who as Lord Chancellor could hear cases presented to the House of Lords, but had sat out the *Osborne* case – expressed strong reservations about the soundness of the juridical basis of the decision: his Lordship remarked that 'it was incontestable that until 1909 the doctrine laid down in the *Osborne* case had never been asserted by any court of law'.[40] Indeed, Ewing has noted with astonishment how 'there was no recognition that the decision had profound implications for the survival of a political party …'.[41] It is as if the Court of Appeal and the Law Lords acted instrumentally, ie that they had already decided the issue based on its adverse consequences for the funding of the Labour Party, and invoked what they considered to be the most appropriate legal doctrine available in their toolkit to reach the desired result. Indeed, Klarman has suggested that there were ulterior motives for the decision of the House of Lords. In particular, there is an undercurrent that it was illegitimate for

[40] TNA, CAB 37/103/44.
[41] Ewing, *The Cost of Democracy* (n 7) 64.

individual trade union members (some of whom sympathised with the Liberal Party) to be forced to support political opponents with whom they disagreed via the political levy and fund.[42]

In the final analysis, the judgments of the Law Lords were largely reflective of the contemporary received judicial perception of trade unions as somewhat suspect bodies.[43] To the extent that they interfered with lawful trade, the judiciary sympathised with the view that they carried out activities of dubious import. Unsurprisingly, these sentiments translated into a decision that held that any statutory powers, immunities, rights or entitlements that they had must be strictly construed and limited. The immediate to medium-term effects of the House of Lords' decision were far-reaching. In the next section, we turn to consider some of these deep-seated consequences.

IV. THE PRACTICAL EFFECT OF *OSBORNE*

As noted by McKibbin, subsequent to the judgment of the House of Lords, trade union members who were sympathetic to, or members of, the Liberal Party 'enthusiastically [took legal action to have] their unions enjoined' where the rulebook provided for the collection of a political levy and maintenance of a political fund.[44] Likewise, voluntary contributions made by trade union members to a union's political fund were challenged frequently, and subjected by the courts to exacting requirements.[45] However, paradoxically, it has also been claimed that the *Osborne* decision 'infuriated the Liberals'.[46] Whatever the immediate reaction of the Liberal Government and its party members, what is beyond doubt is that the *Osborne* decision was one of the two most important labour law decisions in the first decade of the twentieth century. The other was *Taff Vale*.[47] Like *Taff Vale*, which resulted in the passing of the Trade Disputes Act 1906, the political response to *Osborne* was also statutory, in the guise of the Trade Union Act 1913. This is one of the three vital and enduring implications

[42] MJ Klarman, 'Parliamentary Reversal of the *Osborne* Judgment' (1989) 32 *Historical Journal* 893, 893. The protection of the dissenting minority was also an article of faith for the Liberal Government in passing the Trade Union Act 1913.

[43] ACL Davies, 'Judicial Self-Restraint in Labour Law' (2009) 38 *ILJ* 278, 287–88; H Arthurs, 'The Constitutionalization of Employment Relations: Multiple Models, Pernicious Problems' (2010) 19 *Social & Legal Studies* 403, 405–06.

[44] R McKibbin, *The Evolution of the Labour Party 1910–1924* (Oxford, Oxford University Press, 1974) 86. See also the discussion in Ewing, *The Funding of Political Parties in Britain* (n 7) 49–50; Klarman (n 42) 914, 920–21 (charting the extent of the financial problems for trade unions that *Osborne* caused). For the lengths that Liberal and Conservative trade union minorities took to support litigation that sought injunctions, see Gwyn (n 10) 190; S Webb and B Webb, *The History of Trade Unionism* (London, Longmans, 1920) 631.

[45] Ewing, *Trade Unions, the Labour Party and the Law: A Study of the Trade Union Act 1913* (n 7) 40.

[46] Cornish and others (n 24) 80.

[47] *Taff Vale Railway Co v Amalgamated Society of Railway Servants* [1901] AC 426 (HL).

of the *Osborne* judgment, ie the statutory prescription of a conditional licence of sorts on trade union funding for political parties. Notably, however, its consequences were not completely reversed by the Liberal Government of the time.[48] Instead, having introduced legislation in 1911 providing for the payment of MPs salaries, in 1913,[49] the Liberal Government made the levying of funds from trade union members for political purposes subject to a selection of carefully controlled conditions.[50] As noted by Davies and Freedland:

> [The Trade Union Act 1913] provided that 'political' expenditure by trade unions had to be made from a fund separate from the general funds of the union, that a political fund could be established only if a majority of the members of the union in a secret ballot approved of [the adoption of political objects in its rulebook], that any individual member of the union was to be free not to contribute to the political fund, and that he or she was not to be discriminated against in other areas of union activity on account of the decision not to contribute to the political fund.[51]

Interestingly, in terms of the 1913 Act, there was no requirement for a trade union to renew the ballot after a particular period of time had elapsed, eg five years, ten years, etc. In other words, once a ballot was taken resulting in a majority vote, there was no need for continuing collective consent by review or renewal of that vote on a periodic basis: more later on the importance of this point. Finally, the right to complain of discrimination where the statutory rules on the maintenance of a political fund were breached, or a member opted out of the political fund contribution was vested in the Chief Registrar of Friendly Societies, which is now a jurisdiction of the Certification Officer.[52]

Turning to the second vital consequence, *Osborne* galvanised the trade unions throughout the UK. By ruling that the collection of a political levy and maintenance of a political fund were invariably beyond the powers of trade unions because such practices exceeded the legislative definition of a trade union, and irrespective of the content of their rulebooks/constitutions (or whether a majority of the members had approved them), the judiciary 'unified, rather than ruptured, the trade union movement'.[53] In essence, by confining the lawful activities of trade unions to the statutory definition in the 1871 and 1876 Acts, *Osborne* meant that anything falling outside that scope – including financial contributions to trade councils, attendance at the trade unions congress, friendly society benefits, spending on education and support grants to union

[48] Cornish and others (n 24) 80.

[49] See the commentary in Klarman (n 42) 905.

[50] For a full analysis of the legislation, see Klarman (n 42) 893 and Ewing, *The Funding of Political Parties in Britain* (n 7) 50.

[51] P Davies and M Freedland, *Labour Legislation and Public Policy* (Oxford, Clarendon Press, 1993) 23. See also the discussion in the Donovan Commission: Report of the Royal Commission on Trade Unions and Employers' Associations 1965–1968 (London, HMSO, Cmnd 3623) paras 912–27.

[52] Section 80 of the Trade Union and Labour Relations (Consolidation) Act 1992 ('1992 Act').

[53] Klarman (n 1) 21 and 33. Klarman's principal claim is that by proscribing all trade union spending on *any* parliamentary representation, the decision in *Osborne* exceeded Osborne's intentions, which had been to prevent spending on Labour Party candidates and MPs only.

strikers – were unlawful.[54] This led to a sort of legal paralysis for the trade unions in terms of their understanding of what they could safely do within the boundaries of the law and a general sense of injustice.[55] The effect was to bring trade unions – and the unions and the Labour Party – much closer together with a common unity of purpose, entirely focused on reversing the effect of the judgment. And this culminated in the passage of the Trade Union Act 1913.

The final significant implication of *Osborne* was financial in nature.[56] It has always been the case that the majority of the Labour Party's annual income has consisted of trade union affiliation fees.[57] Owing to the *Osborne* judgment, 16 Labour MPs lost their salaries, 'debilitat[ing] the new Labour Party in the elections of 1910'.[58] In this way, the judgment in *Osborne* has been cast as one that almost bankrupted, or radically depleted the finances of, the Labour Party on the eve of the two 1910 general elections.[59] However, some scholars have doubted whether this picture is wholly accurate. For example, McKibbin describes how the *Osborne* judgment did not impede the Labour Party in its efforts to sponsor and finance its election candidates, since despite it, 'the Party's electoral finances were, on the whole, sufficient [and e]ach candidate endorsed was assured of adequate funds'.[60] McKibbin goes on to conclude that the Labour Party 'got around Osborne', primarily for two reasons: first, by dint of the fact that the Party decided to drop the number of candidates it put up for election in the second general election of 1910 in December; and second, owing to there being no post-1910 general election until 1918.[61] To that extent, the Party was able to ride out the threat to its finances between 1909 and 1913 until the introduction of the 1913 Act, which enabled it to swell its coffers, buoyed by the positive volume of endorsements it received from trade union members to the reinstatement of political levies.

In this way, if the famous historian AJP Taylor's remarks are correct that the Trade Union Act 1913 had been 'designed to cripple the Labour Party', then tested against that yardstick of an objective, subsequent history has taught us that it was a failure.[62] As noted by Thorpe:

> Many Liberals hoped these complexities would stymie Labour, but in fact, the Act was to prove a blessing in disguise … most of the ballots went in favour of establishing

[54] See the discussion in Klarman (n 1) 34–35.

[55] ibid 37–38.

[56] Gwyn referred to *Osborne* as having created a 'financial crisis' for the Labour Party: Gwyn (n 10) 205 and Ewing have referred to the judgment as having 'effectively [held] the Labour Party [to be] unlawful': KD Ewing, 'The Importance of Trade Union Political Voice' in A Bogg and T Novitz (eds), *Voices at Work* (Oxford, Oxford University Press, 2014) 282.

[57] Ewing, *The Funding of Political Parties in Britain* (n 7) 55.

[58] Lord Wedderburn (n 28) 760.

[59] Pelling (n 14) 899; E McGaughey, *A Casebook on Labour Law* (Oxford, Hart Publishing, 2018) 337; Klarman (n 42) 919–20.

[60] McKibbin (n 44) 18 and 72.

[61] ibid 21.

[62] AJP Taylor, *English History 1914–1945* (Oxford, Oxford University Press, 1965) 114. For scepticism that this was the Liberal Government's intention, see Pelling (n 14) 909.

> political funds … and, finally, there was little else that the political fund money could be spent on except the Labour Party, giving [it] a firmer base of income and budgeting than ever before.[63]

As such, an enduring question is why the Liberal Party ultimately signed its own death warrant by devising the legislative scheme enshrined in the Trade Union Act 1913 to enable trade unions to set up political funds favouring Labour? After all, the fortunes of the Labour Party were revitalised by the 1913 Act, to the extent that they would go on to eclipse the Liberal Party in the 1923 general election; and the Liberals would never recover.

One compelling and plausible explanation is that the Liberal Party had to commit to legislation overturning *Osborne* as a trade-off for the support of Labour Party MPs to sustain a majority government after the 1910 general elections. However, this remains a theory, since it is entirely unverifiable in the absence of any substantiating primary sources.[64] Another suggestion is that the Liberals feared that the failure to reverse the *Osborne* judgment would lead to heightened trade union militancy and greater penetration of 'socialistic tendencies'.[65] It has also been claimed that the era was a particular 'time of strong combination[s] of capital' and as such, some kind of reversal of the judgment was essential.[66] Whatever the reasons of the Liberal Government, it is somewhat ironic that the Labour Party opposed many of the provisions of the Trade Union Bill during its passage through the House of Commons. At that time, it was unclear to the Party whether members of trade unions would be positively enthusiastic about the approval of any rule legitimising the contributions towards a political fund or whether they would exercise their right to opt out. Of course, with hindsight, we now know that the Labour Party had nothing to be concerned about. But that was not necessarily obvious at the time.

V. *OSBORNE'S* LEGACY FOR THE REGULATION OF POLITICAL FUNDING OF THE LABOUR PARTY

Ewing famously described the immediate legislative response to the *Osborne* case – the 1913 Act – as a 'fragile settlement'.[67] It left both the Labour and Conservative Parties dissatisfied. The primary source of that dissatisfaction was the statutory provision on the ability of trade union members to opt out of making contributions via the political levy to the trade union's political fund. On the one hand, the Labour Party objected on the general principle that

[63] A Thorpe, *A History of the British Labour Party*, 4th edn (London, Palgrave, 2015) 29.

[64] Ewing, *Trade Unions, the Labour Party and the Law: A Study of the Trade Union Act 1913* (n 7) 40; Gwyn (n 10) 197–98; RP Arnot, *The Miners: Years of Struggle* (London, Allen & Unwin Ltd, 1953) 135–36. See also Klarman (n 42) 915–16.

[65] Ewing, *Trade Unions, the Labour Party and the Law: A Study of the Trade Union Act 1913* (n 7) 41.

[66] ibid 41.

[67] ibid 50.

'majority rule' should apply in the same way as it did to shareholders in a registered company. Its argument ran that it was unconscionable that individual trade union members could contract out of making a payment.[68] There was also the anxiety that it would give rise to the free-rider problem, whereby contracted-out members would benefit from the activities of Labour Party MPs affiliated to the trade union even though they had paid none of the dues.[69] Another explanation for the Labour Party's hostility to the opt-out was their claim that if an individual member objected to the ingathering of the levy, he or she could simply leave the union. Of course, in the context of the operation of the 'closed shop' at that time, this could be cast as a red herring of an argument, which is exactly what the Home Secretary, Winston Churchill, said in the House of Commons.[70] If an employee voiced his/her dissent to the levy and fund by leaving the trade union, the operation of the 'closed shop' potentially meant career suicide.[71]

On the other hand, of course, the Conservative Party had a problem with the opt-out for reasons which were ideological and completely opposite to those of Labour. Protecting the dissenting trade union member was an everlasting anxiety for the Conservatives, in the sense that they fundamentally disagreed with the emphasis on individual contracting-out of the collection of the political levy. Clinging to lofty principles that extolled the liberty of the trade union member to be free from having to subscribe to political agendas, albeit, in reality motivated by a thinly concealed desire to strike the Labour Party in the pocket, the Conservative Party campaigned to replace the contracting-out rule with a freedom to contract-in. In the eyes of the Conservative Party, this would transform the rights of the dissenting trade union member, who would otherwise be 'certain to be hounded out of his union by his fellow members'.[72]

When the Conservative Party formed a government in 1924 under Stanley Baldwin, partially as a response to the General Strike of 1926, it introduced a Bill to Parliament amending the provisions of the Trade Union Act 1913. Section 4 of the Trade Disputes and Trade Union Act 1927 regulated the political funds of trade unions and reversed the right of members to contract-out with a right to contract into the contribution of the political levy.[73] The trade unions and the Labour Party were obviously concerned about this legislative change. It was felt that active coaxing would be needed to ensure that trade union members – the majority of whom were considered to be generally apathetic – opted into paying

[68] Klarman (n 42) 895–96.

[69] Ewing, *Trade Unions, the Labour Party and the Law: A Study of the Trade Union Act 1913* (n 7) 44.

[70] 26 HC Deb, 30 May 1911, vol 26, col 1017. See also Gwyn (n 10) 200.

[71] The 'closed shop' is a practice where employers undertake to dismiss any employees who have left a recognised trade union pursuant to a 'union labour only' arrangement agreed with that union. This can be distinguished from the pre-entry closed shop where membership of a trade union is a precondition to accessing employment with a particular employer or industry.

[72] Gwyn (n 10) 200.

[73] For detailed consideration of the 1927 Act, see A Williamson, 'The Trade Disputes and Trade Unions Act 1927 Reconsidered' (2016) 37 *Historical Studies in Industrial Relations* 33; D Brodie, *A History of British Labour Law* (Oxford, Hart, 2005) 190–98.

the levy. It has been claimed that such attempts to persuade members to opt-in were unsuccessful, as the 'effect of opting-in was a substantial drop in contributions to political funds'.[74] However, this account has been disputed. Ewing has noted how the Labour Party's income fell by roughly a third between 1926 and 1929 and the percentage of trade unionists contributing to the political levy fell from 75 per cent in 1925 to 48 per cent in 1936, but that it weathered the storm by collecting additional sums from affiliated trade unions and raising the political levy.[75] In this way, the Conservative Party's attempt to break the Labour Party by paralysing it financially did not work. Nevertheless, it imbued the Labour Party with a deep sense of resentment and injustice.

This wound festered until 1945, when the Labour Party finally secured a majority government.[76] In terms of the Trade Disputes and Trade Union Act 1946, section 4 of the Trade Disputes and Trade Union Act 1927 was repealed and the original position restored, ie the trade union member's exemption right reverted back from contracting-in to contracting-out. It is particularly noteworthy that the Labour Party did not take the opportunity to repeal the exemption altogether. This might seem surprising in light of its original critique of the 1913 Act that all trade union members should be bound by the decision of the majority to pay a political levy and maintain a political fund. However, Ewing explains that by 1936 – perhaps as an implicit recognition of the validity of the point about the 'closed shop' – the Labour Party had 'accepted contracting out as a reasonable compromise'.[77] And it was that way – a contracting-out regime – that matters largely remained until the recent coming into force of the Trade Union Act 2016.[78] The effect of the 2016 Act has been to flip back the regulatory scheme to an opt-in requirement.[79] This was something of 'unfinished business' for the Conservative Party and came into force on 1 March 2018 for new trade union members, having been passed by Parliament with a majority of Conservative MPs.[80] The member's opt-in notice may be delivered by post or hand or by using email or other electronic means that the union has informed

[74] D Pyper, *Trade Union Political Funds and Levy* (House of Commons Library Briefing Paper No 00593, 8 August 2013) 4 researchbriefings.files.parliament.uk/documents/SN00593/SN00593.pdf (accessed 14 April 2022).

[75] Ewing, *Trade Unions, the Labour Party and the Law: A Study of the Trade Union Act 1913* (n 7) 62; Ewing, *The Funding of Political Parties in Britain* (n 7) 51.

[76] The Labour Party formed minority governments in 1923 and 1929, but had insufficient parliamentary support to pass the requisite legislation reversing the provisions of section 4 of the Trade Disputes and Trade Union Act 1927: for discussion, see Ewing, *Trade Unions, the Labour Party and the Law: A Study of the Trade Union Act 1913* (n 7) 62–65.

[77] Ewing, *Trade Unions, the Labour Party and the Law: A Study of the Trade Union Act 1913* (n 7) 66.

[78] Although the Conservative Government toyed with the idea of reinstating contracting-in in 1984, the Trade Union Act 1984 stopped short of doing so: see Ewing, 'Trade Union Political Funds: The 1913 Act Revised' (n 7) 242; Ewing, *The Funding of Political Parties in Britain* (n 7) 69–72.

[79] See ss 84, 84A and 85 of the 1992 Act. See also DBEIS, *Trade Union Political Funds* (London, National Archives, 2018) 9–11 assets.publishing.service.gov.uk/government/uploads/system/uploads/attachment_data/file/683245/trade-union-political-funds-guidance.pdfZ:\Word Folders\Landmark Cases on Labour Law\trade-union-political-funds-guidance.pdf (accessed 14 April 2022).

[80] Ewing, *The Funding of Political Parties in Britain* (n 7) 69.

members they can use. The member of the trade union may also serve a withdrawal notice in respect of his or her prior opt-in.[81]

What is ironic about this recent legislative activity is that there is arguably no longer any justificatory foundation for any form of opt-out or opt-in. That is to say that the 'closed shop' is no longer lawful in the UK. And it is on the existence of the 'closed shop' that the current scheme hinges. Since 1990, if a trade union member is dismissed by his employer for not being a member of a recognised trade union, that is treated as an automatically unfair dismissal in terms of sections 152(1)(c) and 153 of the 1992 Act. Seen from this angle, if a trade union member has no desire to contribute to the political levy, he or she can simply leave the trade union without fear of victimisation. The question of signing an opt-out or opt-in or a withdrawal notice to an opt-in, is a red herring and entirely irrelevant. In the final analysis, there is no suggestion of any employees being compelled to support (financially or otherwise) any political party against their own will.[82]

A second reason for Ewing describing the 1913 Act as a 'fragile settlement'[83] relates to the provisions mandating the disclosure to trade union members of their entitlement to exempt themselves from contributing to the union's political fund. At the time the 1913 Act was passed, the Conservative Party was particularly critical of the relevant statutory procedures. Section 5 of the 1913 Act prescribed that any trade union member was to be given notice that he or she had '... a right to be exempt from contributing to the political fund of the union, and that a form of exemption notice can be obtained' from any branch or head office of the trade union or the Certification Officer. Over time, the Conservative Party complained consistently about these information provisions, arguing that it was overly challenging for trade union members to discover that they had the right to contract out. It was also alleged that illegitimate pressure had regularly been brought to bear on members not to contract out.[84] These alleged abuses gave rise to the concern that there was inadequate transparency surrounding notices to trade union members and ultimately, became the focus of the Conservative Government's attention in section 11 of the Trade Union Act 2016.[85] Having switched the format to one of contracting-in from contracting-out, there is no longer any statutory requirement in the 1992 Act for a trade union to notify a

[81] Section 84(2) of the 1992 Act.

[82] See the discussion in Ewing, 'The Trade Union Question' (n 7) 54, 72. The position probably has more to do with the anticipated effects of opt-in from nudge behavioural economics – the endowment effect means that opt-in arrangements lead to much lower levels of participation than opt-out arrangements.

[83] Ewing, *Trade Unions, the Labour Party and the Law: A Study of the Trade Union Act 1913* (n 7) 50.

[84] For the palpable lack of evidence for these allegations, see the Donovan Commission: Report of the Royal Commission on Trade Unions and Employers' Associations 1965–1968 (London, HMSO, Cmnd 3623) para 923. See also the discussion in Ewing, *Trade Unions, the Labour Party and the Law: A Study of the Trade Union Act 1913* (n 7) 59–60.

[85] On the lack of transparency ground, see HL Deb, 16 March 2016, vol 769, cols 1889–91 (Baroness Neville-Rolfe).

member about his/her right to serve an exemption notice. Instead, the disclosure provisions are concentrated on withdrawal notices, to the extent that the union has an obligation to supply members on an annual basis with information about their right to withdraw their opt-in notice.[86]

A third rationale for the proposition that the terms of the 1913 Act were fragile in nature centres around the absence of any process for the renewal of the trade union ballot approving the political levy contribution and political fund. To recap, in order to be lawfully established, the ballot had to be secret and the provisions demanded majority approval of the trade union members. The 1913 Act prescribed that this approval had no expiry period and there was no requirement for its renewal. However, that changed with the passing of the 'ten-year' rule in section 12 of the Trade Union Act 1984 by the Conservative Government.[87] This modification was justified by the government on the basis that it would further the democratisation of trade unions.[88] However, contemporary accounts were critical of this statutory change. Concerns were expressed that some trade unions would decide to remove their political objects and affiliation with the Labour Party.[89] However, this did not happen in practice, with renewals being processed relatively smoothly by the trade unions.[90] In addition, the 1984 Act extended the definition of 'political objects', ie the nature of the activities of the trade unions that a political fund would support. Ultimately, this backfired on the Conservative Government as it incentivised unaffiliated trade unions to establish political funds and levies in support of the Labour Party.[91]

VI. *OSBORNE'S* LEGACY FOR LABOUR LAW

Having considered *Osborne*'s consequences for the funding of political parties, it is necessary to address its wider implications for labour law. It is undoubtedly the case that there have been a multitude of short-term, medium-term, and long-term consequences, but here, the discussion is restricted to two of the most material. Both stem from the forging of ever-closer links between the trade unions and the Labour Party that is largely attributable to the shock caused by the *Osborne* decision. At the outset, it should be reiterated that the effect of *Osborne* was to energise the trade union movement, and ultimately meld it together with the labour movement at the expense of the Liberals. As such, although something of a fringe party at the time of *Osborne*, the significance of this point lies in the influential role that the Labour Party subsequently went

[86] See s 84A of the 1992 Act.

[87] Ewing, 'Trade Union Political Funds: The 1913 Act Revised' (n 7); P Dorey, 'Weakening the Trade Unions, One Step at a Time: The Thatcher Governments' Strategy for the Reform of Trade-Union Law, 1979–1984' (2016) 37 *Historical Studies in Industrial Relations* 169, 188–89.

[88] *Democracy In Trade Unions*, Cmnd, 8778 (1983) paras 80–84.

[89] Ewing, *The Funding of Political Parties in Britain* (n 7) 64–71.

[90] Ewing, 'The Trade Union Question' (n 7) 57.

[91] ibid 58.

on to play in UK politics. From the period from 1945 to the present day, for a total of 30 years, the Labour Party has formed the British Government. And the Governments of Atlee, Wilson, and Callaghan from 1945 to 1950, 1964 to 1970 and 1974 to 1979 are associated with the provision of ongoing auxiliary support for the system of 'collective laissez-faire', whereby the trade unions and employers would set terms and conditions of employment via annual collective bargaining rounds, culminating in collective agreements. As such, during this era of 'collective laissez-faire', the Labour Party was particularly important for collective labour law – and it is this, which is the first of the aforementioned enduring material implications of *Osborne*. Ewing has illustrated how one of the primary functions of a trade union is close governmental engagement, to the extent that trade unions lobby the relevant Ministers of State for legislation sympathetic to the needs of working people and are closely 'involved in the development, implementation and delivery of government policy'.[92] During the period from 1945 to the early 1980s, the vast majority of terms and conditions of employment of working people were governed by the content of collective agreements, rather than their individual employment contracts. For that reason, the edifice of 'collective laissez-faire' was of signal importance for the norms, rules and conventions governing labour relations and laws. Collective laissez-faire was accompanied by a policy of 'legal abstentionism', whereby, although by no means irrelevant, individual employment laws were of more marginal materiality than the content of collective agreements, since there was no such thing as a statutory framework of substantive rules governing terms and conditions of employment that supplemented those agreed by the parties themselves.

The second material implication of the *Osborne* judgment closely related to the intimate relationship between the trade unions and the Labour Party – namely juridification of individual employment rights via statutory intervention – is a by-product of the evolution in the industrial relations landscape from the 1960s.[93] As the system of collective laissez-faire began to retreat during the period from the late 1960s to mid-1980s, a vacuum emerged in respect of the principal source of the terms and conditions of employees. And this gap was plugged by statutory employment protection rights. The Labour Party played a crucial part in this development. For example, during Wilson's first Government, something slightly unusual occurred. Legislation directly conferring legal rights on individual employees was passed in the guise of the Redundancy Payments Act 1965 and the Equal Pay Act 1970. At that time, these provisions were something of an aberration as the collective laissez-faire regime had not yet completely collapsed. However, over the course of time, statutory intervention grew exponentially and occupied the territory vacated by collective bargaining. The end result has been a Labour Party that has been principally responsible for the

[92] K Ewing, 'The Function of Trade Unions' (2005) 34 *ILJ* 1, 5.

[93] J Fudge, 'Labour as a "Fictive Commodity"' in G Davidov and B Langille (eds), *The Idea of Labour Law* (Oxford, Oxford University Press, 2011) 124; M O'Sullivan, T Turner and J Wallace, 'Is Individual Employment Law Displacing the Role of Trade Unions?' (2015) 44 *ILJ* 222, 223–26.

burgeoning of statutory employment protection. Of course, a counterfactual question that may be posed is whether the current body and incarnation of statutory employment rights would have been the same had the Labour Party been unable to secure for itself a stable post-*Osborne* funding source. Unfortunately, this is something that we will never know and can only offer conjecture about. But at the very least, what we do know is that Labour Governments have made a seminal contribution to labour law in the UK, by introducing a wider range of employment entitlements, from maternity leave/pay, paternity leave/pay and the protection of fixed-term and part-time workers, to the national minimum wage, paid annual leave and restrictions on working time.

A final observation that ought to be made, concerns how *Osborne* might be approached today if it were to be adjudicated by a court. What is particularly striking about the decision is how its effect was to ride roughshod over the freedoms of the workers who had voluntarily decided to apply a portion of their union dues towards the funding of political representation. To that extent, there is a strong case for the proposition that the freedom of association and expression of those workers was completely set aside, which raises a question regarding whether an infringement of Articles 10 and 11 of the European Convention on Human Rights would be treated as the relevant legal issue today. Of course, the legal discourse of freedom of association and expression had no purchase or relevance in *Osborne* at all, as well as in respect of its subsequent reception in the legal system. This leads us on to question the pressures at work in the evolution in the mores and approaches society considers to be the most pressing labour law infractions, and particularly how cases are argued before, and adjudicated by, the courts.

VII. CONCLUSION

In 1910 in the *Osborne* case, the judiciary held that sums deducted from trade union members for any political purposes, and for the trade union to administer a political fund, were unlawful. The decision was underpinned by a judicial mindset borne of the Victorian era that unions were considered to be purely economic and industrial entities that had absolutely no part to play in politics. How times have changed. In his seminal article, 'The Function of Trade Unions', Ewing cites the governmental function as one of the central purposes of a trade union in the UK.[94] This entails the close involvement of trade unions in governmental policymaking and the shaping of legislation protective of workers. Contemporary lawyers, politicians, policy-makers and the general public would perceive such a statement to be relatively uncontroversial. Seen from that angle, the received juridical understanding of trade unions, their objectives and position in influencing labour laws has come a very far long way indeed since 1910.

[94] Ewing (n 92).

5

Rookes' Tale

RODERICK BAGSHAW

I. INTRODUCTION

When Douglas Rookes resigned from his trade union, the Association of Engineering and Shipbuilding Draughtsmen (AESD),[1] in November 1955, he was employed by the British Overseas Airways Corporation (BOAC), a state corporation, in its Design Office at London Airport (Heathrow).[2] The local leadership of the AESD treated his resignation as significant, in part because BOAC had accepted that if any shop achieved 100 per cent union membership then they would not disrupt that state of affairs by introducing a non-union recruit and this level had been reached in the Design Office in 1951.[3] After a workplace vote on Tuesday 10 January 1956,

[1] The union became the Draughtsmens' and Allied Technicians' Association (DATA) in 1960 (the Executive Committee having failed to get the required two-thirds majority in favour of the change at the annual conference in 1957), and Rookes refers to it as DATA in his book about the case: D Rookes, *Conspiracy* (London, Johnson, 1966).

[2] The Lord Chancellor, who – as Gerald Gardiner QC – had represented the defendants during the appellate litigation, provided an explanation for Rookes' resignation when, as Lord Chancellor, he was seeking to secure the passage of the Trade Disputes Bill 1965 through the House of Lords, to mitigate the effects of the House of Lords' decision in *Rookes v Barnard* [1964] AC 1129 (HL): HL Deb 2 August 1965, vol 269, cols 37–38: in brief, the Design Office, which was on the top floor of a new building (almost certainly the Queen's Building, opened 1955), was too hot in the summer and too cold in the winter, and the union had not backed Rookes' proposal of threatening industrial action to stimulate BOAC into resolving these problems. But the notion that the dispute originated with the union's *reluctance* to threaten a strike may be too neat; the General Secretary's contemporary account went no further than claiming that Rookes was in a minority seeking 'more direct action' on complaints about the building (GH Doughty, *Keep the Unions Free: A Statement on the Rookes v Barnard Case by the Draughtsmen's and Allied Technicians' Association* (Surrey, Richmond, 1964) 5), and Rookes described even this as 'a malicious distortion of the truth that cannot be substantiated' (Rookes (n 1) 9): he attributed his resignation to general disillusionment with the union's Executive, which he perceived to be preoccupied with enhancing its power within BOAC.

[3] The '100 per cent membership agreement' was oral and not intended to be legally binding. It specifically provided that, although the employer would not introduce a non-unionist into a 100% shop, a member could resign from the union without losing his employment: *Rookes* (n 2) 1133.

the three defendants, Barnard, Fistal and Silverthorne, respectively two elected representatives (the chairman of the local Branch and the Shop Steward) and a permanent official (the Divisional Organiser), delivered an ultimatum to BOAC: 'We, the members of the AESD, inform BOAC that if the non-unionist Mr D.E. Rookes is not removed from the Design Office by 4.0 pm on Friday 13 January 1956, a withdrawal of labour of all AESD membership will take place.'[4] In fact, the prospects for BOAC were more severe; a mass meeting of the other unions at the airport had agreed to support the AESD by going on strike on Monday 16 January if the AESD went out.[5] The Design Office strike would have been 'unconstitutional': there was a 1949 agreement between the union and BOAC that there would be no strikes or lock-outs and that disputes would instead be dealt with through an arbitration procedure: importantly, during the litigation it was conceded that the undertaking not to strike had become a term of each employee's contract.[6] Moreover, the proposed strike would have started before the expiration of the seven days' notice the employees had to give to terminate their contracts.[7] In the event, however, no strike took place; on the Friday morning BOAC suspended Rookes on full pay, then, two months later, exercised its liberty to dismiss him, with notice.

Eight years later, in late January 1964, the House of Lords reversed the Court of Appeal and unanimously restored Sachs J's decision, reached following a jury trial, that Rookes had been a victim of a tort committed by the three defendants, and that their acts were protected by neither section 1 nor section 3 of the Trade Disputes Act 1906; the defendants' success was limited to an order for a retrial as to the appropriate sum of damages.[8] The defendants were held liable because they had been parties to a conspiracy to use unlawful acts to injure Rookes, and had each made threats to BOAC to advance that conspiracy.[9] Crucially, the Court held that the threats were unlawful acts because they constituted the tort of three-party intimidation, which requires a defendant to injure a claimant by making a threat of an unlawful act to a third party, with the intention of coercing that third party into acting in a way that injures the claimant. That conclusion caused immediate controversy because the threat that the defendants

[4] *Rookes* (n 2) 1166; Rookes (n 1) 75.

[5] Rookes (n 1) 79.

[6] *Rookes* (n 2) 1166.

[7] In any case, the employees probably did not intend to terminate their contracts.

[8] The jury had awarded £7,500, without making clear what portion, if any, was exemplary or punitive. Rookes complained that his lawyers subsequently pressurised him into accepting a payment into court of £4,000 (partly, perhaps, to reduce the risk of costs falling on the Legal Aid fund) rather than proceeding with a retrial: Rookes (n 1) 148–150. The union could not be held vicariously liable (Trade Disputes Act 1906, s 4) and its rules precluded it from paying the damages from its funds; but it made a benevolent grant to each of the defendants and organised an appeal for donations; a further collection raised £16,000 towards the costs, principally from other unions: T Foley, *A Most Formidable Union: The History of DATA and TASS* (London, MSF, 1992) 27–28.

[9] This formulation of the tort follows the answers that the jury gave to the questions that Sachs J left to it: quoted by Lord Reid in *Rookes* (n 2) 1165.

had made to BOAC was that its employees who were union members would strike, and before the case it had been widely assumed that no civil liability would be incurred by defendants who organised a strike 'in contemplation or furtherance of a trade dispute'.[10] In this case, however, the strike would have involved each striker breaking their contract of employment, both because of the incorporated 'no strike' agreement and because less than a week's notice had been given, and the characterisation of the proposed strike as involving a co-ordinated breaking of contracts was pivotal: the House of Lords held that it was the furtherance of the conspiracy against Rookes by threats to break contracts that made it tortious, and took it outside the immunities conferred by the 1906 Act.[11] The *New Statesman* rapidly summarised what had occurred: 'The Lords first of all extended an obscure and unfamiliar civil wrong, and then decided that the 1906 Act gives no protection against it.'[12] More divisively, the union's General Secretary complained: 'The Judges have insisted on discovering a new liability in order to evade that for which the statute was passed.'[13] With the advantage of historical perspective, but without a direct allegation of judicial agency, Professors Davies and Freedland wrote:

> The case [...] was the labour law *cause célèbre* of the 1960s in which the House of Lords encroached upon the assumption, crucial to the whole structure of collective *laissez-faire*, that the Trade Disputes Act 1906 had been intended to exclude economic tort law from the whole field of industrial disputes and should be construed accordingly.[14]

[10] In *Stratford v Lindley* [1965] AC 269 (HL), which was decided by the House of Lords six months after *Rookes*, two of the Lords chose to express their opinions that section 3 would still protect a union official who, in the context of a trade dispute, threatened an employer that he or she would induce the employees to break their contacts and strike: ibid 336 (Lord Pearce), 337 (Lord Upjohn), 340 (Lord Donovan, who does not make clear whether his opinion related to the effect of section 3 or the scope of the underlying tort).

[11] In the aftermath of the decision particular controversy surrounded the position of Silverthorne, the Union's Divisional Organiser, who was not an employee of BOAC and consequently could not have threatened to break any contract that *he* had with BOAC. But, leaving aside the 1906 Act, it seems Silverthorne could have been liable either on the basis of joint liability for intimidation or for committing unlawful means conspiracy: this was the view of Lord Devlin, *Rookes* (n 2) 1210: 'the only action against him is conspiracy or joint intimidation'. Turning to the statutory immunity, there is no strong reason for believing that section 1 of the Trade Disputes Act 1906 was intended to limit liability for either joint tortfeasance or *unlawful means* conspiracy.

[12] 'A Legal Correspondent' *New Statesman* (London, 24 January 1964).

[13] Doughty (n 2) 10. This view was not the most extreme: eg, F Hilson told the conference of the Clerical and Administrative Workers' Union: 'In my opinion, this particular judgment of the House of Lords has been directed not so much on points of law but on points of Tory Party policy'; part of a 'cool, calculated plot to destroy the trade union movement': *The Guardian* (London, 30 March 1964) 2: quoted by RB Stevens, 'The Role of a Final Appeal Court in a Democracy: The House of Lords Today' (1965) 28 *MLR* 509, 529, in support of the proposition that '[a]fter *Rookes v Barnard* and *Stratford v Lindley* ... many unions were convinced that the law lords were setting out to legislate judicially against the unions.'

[14] P Davies and M Freedland, *Labour Legislation and Public Policy: A Contemporary History* (Oxford, Clarendon Press, 1993) 244–45.

The legitimacy of the House of Lords' decision in *Rookes* has divided academic lawyers since 1964,[15] with the split largely tracking whether the author's primary research interest was labour law or tort law. Thus, from the tort law side, JA Weir commended 'the central message of *Rookes*, that it is a tort intentionally to hurt another by means of an impermissible act' as 'an extremely important and beneficial contribution to the development of the law'.[16] Whilst from the labour law side, Roger Rideout saw the decision as 'an incontrovertible example … of judicial reversal of the protective intent of the legislature',[17] opining, of *Rookes* and *Stratford v Lindley*:[18]

> Trade unionists may trace their descent through a long series of adverse judicial decisions even unto the Tolpuddle martyrs and conclude that it is high time that the courts decided to come to terms with them, as has happened with the welfare state, and agree that the liberty of the individual must on occasion be subordinated to the welfare of the group.[19]

Seeing *Rookes* defended by tort lawyers, amongst others, Professor Wedderburn complained that it was

> no great pleasure to watch experienced lawyers, many exulting, even heedless, often angry at criticism, anxious to paper over any cracks in the judicial edifice, rarely conscious of their own social policy assumptions, but confident of their 'objectivity' with all the security which only that unselfconscious enthusiasm can bring, hasten like their forebears, the jurists of 1901 and 1910, to the support of judicial interventions in labour law which not merely are novel, even questionable, law, but may prove even more disastrous than their predecessors of the *Quinn*, *Taff Vale* and *Osborne* decade, both for industrial relations and for the common law itself.[20]

But, despite the hedonic risk, my goal in this chapter is to present the mythopoeic decision in *Rookes* as simultaneously a product of legitimate judicial reasoning *and* problematic from the perspective of labour relations.

[15] Divisions about the appropriate outcome appeared before the case reached the House of Lords: in the Court of Appeal (*Rookes v Barnard* [1963] 1 QB 623 (CA) 652, 657) the appellants 'adopted' the arguments in the casenote written by KW Wedderburn, 'The Right to Threaten Strikes' (1961) 24 *MLR* 572, whilst the respondents 'adopted' those of CJ Hamson, 'A Note on *Rookes v Barnard*' (1961) 19 *CLJ* 189. Jack Hamson had taught Bill Wedderburn contract and tort at Cambridge (B Hepple, 'Bill Wedderburn in Conversation with Bob Hepple' (2015) 44 *Industrial Law Journal* 430), and had provided comments on his casenote, including the opinion, which Wedderburn underlined and notated with an exclamation mark, that his trouble in accepting Hamson's general propositions about intimidation may have resulted from the 'irrelevant passions' aroused by *Rookes* being a trade dispute case: Papers of Professor Kenneth William (Bill) Wedderburn, Lord Wedderburn of Charlton, MRC 972/1/9/30.

[16] JA Weir, 'Chaos or Cosmos? *Rookes*, *Stratford* and the Economic Torts' [1964] *CLJ* 225, 233.

[17] RW Rideout, 'The Future of Trade Union Law' [1965] *Current Legal Problems* 110, 117.

[18] *Stratford v Lindley* (n 10). The case involved an interlocutory injunction that had been granted against trade union officers a fortnight after the House of Lords' decision in *Rookes*. The House of Lords re-imposed the injunction, though a majority expressed opinions about the limited relevance of *Rookes* to a claim brought by an employer whose employees proposed to strike.

[19] RW Rideout, *Trade Unions: Some Social and Legal Problems* (London, Tavistock Publications, 1964) 53.

[20] KW Wedderburn, 'Stratford and Son Ltd v Lindley' (1965) 28 *MLR* 205, 213.

II. THE LEGAL REASONING

The substantive issue before the House of Lords[21] can be divided into three elements: (1) Did a tort of three-party intimidation exist? (2) If so, could it be committed by a threat to break a contract? (3) If so, did the circumstances in which the defendants conspired to injure Douglas Rookes through the commission of this tort fall outside the protection conferred by section 1 and section 3 of the Trade Disputes Act 1906?

A. Did A Tort of Three-Party Intimidation Exist?

The first question was the least controversial from the perspective of orthodox judicial reasoning. Although the Court of Appeal had overturned Sachs J's decision in favour of Rookes, it had accepted the existence of a tort, which could properly be called 'three-party intimidation'.[22] In the House of Lords, Rookes' counsel, Samuel Silkin QC[23] and Alan de Piro, formulated it thus: 'the defendant, intending to cause harm to the plaintiff, coerces T, a third party, to do that harm to the plaintiff by the threat that, if T does not do it, acts will be done to the detriment of T which would be wrongful as against T'. Such a wrong was labelled 'intimidation' in Salmond's textbook, and Lord Devlin required 'no further authorities or reasons'.[24] Gerald Gardiner QC, the defendants' counsel before the Court of Appeal and House of Lords, complained that this tort was 'to a large extent invented by Salmond',[25] but this is potentially misleading; most contemporary textbooks accepted that it was actionable to use threats of violence to scare off those intending on trading with a claimant even if they did not label the tort 'intimidation'. Indeed, when George Woodcock, the TUC's General Secretary, denounced the refusal of the Douglas-Home Government to pass legislation reversing *Rookes*, his objection was that the House of Lords had 'held that a threat to break an individual contract to achieve an end was the equivalent of a threat to "bash a man's face to pulp"',[26] rather than that it had conjured up a novel tort.

[21] This chapter does not discuss the remedial issue: whether Sachs J misdirected the jury as to when it might be appropriate to award exemplary or punitive damages.

[22] In *Rookes* (n 2) 1205–06, Lord Devlin accepted that there were two forms of the tort of intimidation. 'Two-party intimidation' will be committed by a defendant who intentionally causes loss to the claimant by making a threat of the sort 'unless you act in this way (that will cause you loss), I will do this unlawful act', which coerces the claimant into acting in the required way and suffering loss. The case, however, involved the second form: 'three-party intimidation'.

[23] Samuel Silkin QC was elected as MP for Dulwich, representing the Labour Party, in October 1964, and subsequently served as Attorney General from 1974 until 1979. After securing his seat, he sought, and received, Rookes' permission to withdraw from the case, anticipating that he would have to vote in favour of legislation reversing the decision: Rookes (n 1) 144.

[24] Lord Devlin relied on the contemporary edition of J Salmond and RFV Heuston, *Salmond on the Law of Torts*, 13th edn (London, Sweet & Maxwell, 1961) 697, but the same passage was in the first edition (J Salmond, *The Law of Torts* (London, Stevens & Haynes, 1907) 439–40.

[25] *Rookes* (n 2) 1141.

[26] 'Demand for Change in the Law on Strikes' *The Guardian* (London, 11 September 1964) 2.

B. Trade Disputes Act 1906, section 3

The conclusion that it was tortious to get an employee dismissed by threatening his or her employer with violence was crucial in tipping the third issue, the availability of a statutory defence, against the defendants. This was because several of the constructions of section 3 of the Trade Disputes Act 1906 put forward on their behalf would have extended the defence to protect such threats, and, as Lord Devlin said:

> The Act was no doubt intended to give immunity for all forms of peaceful persuasion, but I am sure – and Lord Loreburn LC in the passage I have cited from *Conway v Wade* says as much[27] – that it was not intended to give protection from violent persuasion. I do not think it would be right so to construe it. It would mean that under the licence of a trade dispute one man could force another out of his job by threats of violence ….[28]

To explain in detail why it was difficult to interpret section 3 so as to protect intimidation by means of threats of breaking contracts without also protecting intimidation by threats of violence it is necessary to turn to the wording of the legislation. Section 3 states:

> An act done by a person in contemplation or furtherance of a trade dispute shall not be actionable on the ground only that it induces some other person to break a contract of employment or that it is an interference with the trade, business, or employment of some other person, or with the right of some other person to dispose of his capital or his labour as he wills.

To ensure that section 3 did not protect *using violence* to persuade someone to break a contract or *using violence* to interfere with another's trade, business or employment it was necessary to interpret 'shall not be actionable on the ground only that' as effective to *exclude* from the immunity situations where *violence* was used to induce a breach of contract or to generate the interference; to achieve this, 'on the ground *only* that' was read as excluding situations where *other crimes or torts* had been used to bring about the breaking of the contract or the interference; and, once use of *other torts* fell outside the immunity, the obvious consequence was that any *tortious intimidation* that induced a breach of contract or – more relevantly to Rookes' claim – any *tortious intimidation* that interfered with another's employment, also fell outside the immunity.[29]

[27] *Conway v Wade* [1909] AC 495 (HL) 511. Lord Loreburn LC was Lord Chancellor when the Trade Disputes Act 1906 was enacted.

[28] *Rookes* (n 2) 1220.

[29] The most awkward case for this construction of section 3 involved interference by intimidation where the intimidation involved a threat to induce a breach of an employment contract, since here the 'other tort' (taking the case outside the 'interference' limb of the immunity) would involve a threat to commit a tort (inducing breach) that would have been within the first limb of the immunity. Lord Devlin clearly assumed that a threat to *induce* a breach of an employment contract in a trade dispute context would have been protected by section 3 (*Rookes* (n 2) 1206).

Thus, on this construction, the question whether section 3 protected the defendants turned on whether the threats made by the defendants had amounted to *tortious intimidation*, the second element in the case. To put the same point in reverse, once the House of Lords decided that second element against the defendants – which they did – then to interpret section 3 as protecting the defendants' actions would have been contrary to the intention of the 1906 Parliament, since the protection would have inevitably extended to intimidation by violence:[30] the provision contained no wording that would permit a distinction between violent tortious interference and non-violent tortious interference.[31]

C. Trade Disputes Act 1906, section 1

The tortious nature of *violent* intimidation was not the key, however, to establishing that the defendants were not protected by section 1 of the Trade Disputes Act 1906. But here the defendants' submission that their situation fell within the provision relied on a highly contestable construction of section 1, which read: 'An act done in pursuance of an agreement or combination by two or more persons shall, if done in contemplation or furtherance of a trade dispute, not be actionable unless the act, if done without any such agreement or combination, would be actionable.'

The argument on behalf of Rookes was that, when the trade dispute condition is met, this provision prevents liability for *types of tort* that require an allegation of conspiracy, in particular liability for *simple*, *Quinn v Leathem*,[32]

[30] Lord Evershed, who came closest to supporting the defendants' reading of section 3 (*Rookes* (n 2) 1190–96) sought to explain away the difficulty of a broader construction of section 3 protecting intimidation by *violence* by suggesting that in cases where there was violence a claimant *might* be able to sue for injury to his or her health, rather than just the 'interference ... with employment' that the statute protects. But this solution could not have helped an employee who was lawfully dismissed by an employer who had been threatened with violence.

[31] In the Court of Appeal, *Rookes* (n 15) 685, Donovan LJ held (and Sellers LJ agreed, 675) that section 3 protected a defendant from liability for interference by a breach of contract, or a threat to break a contract, but perhaps not by 'violence, threats, molestation, and such acts as would justify a binding over to keep the peace'. He did not explain, however, how Parliament's use of the word 'interference' communicated such a distinction; relying instead on a general conviction that Parliament intended to protect some form of unobjectionable but 'unlawful' behaviour. The alternative view, supported by Pearson LJ, 692, was that the protection for 'interference' was intended to prevent resuscitation of the broad liability that had appealed to the dissenting minority in *Allen v Flood* [1898] AC 1 (HL), so would not protect any form of intimidation that was tortious at common law, 688. This was also the understanding of the intention behind section 3 that prevailed in the House of Lords: *Rookes* (n 2) 1177–78 (Lord Reid); 1203 (Lord Hodson); 1216–18 (Lord Devlin); 1236–38 (Lord Pearce).

[32] [1901] AC 495 (HL). It is not clear what the House of Lords, in 1901, believed itself to be deciding. By the time of the decision in *Rookes*, however, it was accepted that it had held that a defendant who had participated in a conspiracy with the predominant purpose of causing harm to a claimant could be held liable, even if he or she had used no independently-unlawful means, but that a defendant could not be held liable in such circumstances if he or she was not a conspirator. Simple conspiracy is now generally known as 'lawful means conspiracy', in order to distinguish it from

conspiracy;[33] since intimidation is a type of tort that does not require an allegation of conspiracy, section 1 could not protect defendants who had combined to commit intimidation or had formed a conspiracy to pursue their goals by intimidation, if the second issue (the possibility of committing intimidation by a threat to break a contract) was decided against them.

The defendants' rival submission was that section 1 required a focus on whether the 'act' they were alleged to have committed could – on the facts – have amounted to an actionable tort in the absence of 'agreement or combination'. They submitted that, in the circumstances of London Airport in 1956, the threats to break employment contracts only became effective to coerce BOAC because all the union's members in the Design Office had resolved to act together; an ineffective threat, such as Barnard or Fistal threatening to break his employment contract, would have caused no damage to Rookes, so could not have led to a claim; thus, the 'act' that the defendants had performed could not have been actionable in the absence of 'agreement or combination'. In other words, the defendants' construction focused on whether a conspiracy was essential to making their acts damaging, and hence tortious, *as a matter of fact*, rather than on whether the type of act they were alleged to have conspired to use to injure the claimant was one which could be *actionable as a matter of law* if a single defendant had performed it.

On this point, the House of Lords held unanimously that section 1 did not protect the defendants' actions, though their explanations diverged. Lord Devlin held that section 1 would not protect a participant in a conspiracy to cause harm by intimidation if *the nature* of the tort of intimidation is such that it is a tort that can, as a matter of law, be committed by a single individual,[34] which seems consistent with the briefer explanations of Lord Hodson and Lord Pearce.[35] Lord Reid reached a similar conclusion by holding that to apply section 1 it was necessary for a court to identify what the defendants had done in fact, then describe the nearest equivalent act that an individual *could have* done, then consider whether this alternative act would have been actionable.[36] By contrast, Lord Evershed determined that the threats *in fact* made by each defendant had

'unlawful means conspiracy': see the joint judgment of Lord Sumption and Lord Lloyd-Jones in *JSC BTA Bank v Ablyazov (No 14)* [2018] UKSC 19, [2020] AC 727 [8].

[33] The opinion that the purpose of section 1 was to protect defendants against claims for simple conspiracy was most clearly accepted in *Rookes* (n 2) 1204, 1210–12 (Lord Devlin), 1235 (Lord Pearce); 1202 (Lord Hodson rejected the defendants' submissions directly without explaining the intended effect of the provision). The way in which the other form of tortious conspiracy – 'unlawful means conspiracy' – has developed since *Rookes* means that the modern form of the section 1 immunity, found in s 219(2) of the Trade Union and Labour Relations (Consolidation) Act 1992, ought to cover some instances of 'unlawful means conspiracy', but no case to confirm this has been litigated.

[34] *Rookes* (n 2) 1211.

[35] ibid 1202, 1235. Neither Lord Hodson nor Lord Pearce felt it necessary to assess what made the threats effective, consequently we may infer that they agreed that the scope of section 1 depended on the *legal nature* of the means that the conspiracy was alleged to have employed.

[36] *Rookes* (n 2) 1171.

real and coercive force.[37] Setting aside these differences, there were persuasive reasons for not adopting the defendants' construction of section 1; it would require courts to make counterfactual assessments of what pressure would have been sufficient to tip the third party into submission and would have had the strange effect of granting immunity to conspirators who coerce by co-ordinated threats of minor acts of violence or vandalism (if the third party would have been sufficiently resilient to stand up to one person threatening such acts).

In the aftermath of the case, Professor Wedderburn continued to press the defendants' construction, raising the ingenious argument that Parliament in 1906 could not have intended the provision to protect defendants against liability for lawful means conspiracy since that tort's requirement of a 'predominant purpose of injuring the claimant' would in any case be sufficient to prevent defendants from establishing that their acts were 'done in contemplation or furtherance of a trade dispute'.[38] But most proposals for legislation to reverse the decision in *Rookes* envisaged extending the scope of section 3.[39] And when the provision corresponding to section 1 was re-enacted in a broader form in 1974, after the brief reign of the National Industrial Relations Court, the legislature did not rephrase the provision to try to secure the defendants' construction.[40]

D. Could Three-Party Intimidation Be Committed by A Threat to Break a Contract?

The analysis so far has identified the second element in the case before the House of Lords – the question whether the tort of three-party intimidation could be committed by a threat to break a contract, as opposed to by a threat of violence,

[37] ibid 1189.

[38] KW Wedderburn, 'Intimidation and the Right to Strike' (1964) 27 *MLR* 257, 271–72. Other casenotes supported the House of Lords' approach to section 1: eg, CJ Hamson, 'A Further Note on *Rookes v Barnard*' [1964] *CLJ* 159, 172, opining that 'only Lord Devlin experienced any real difficulty as to section 1' and suggesting that he made 'heavier weather … of it than the occasion really warranted'.

[39] See 'TUC Discuss *Rookes* Case with Counsel' *The Times* (London, 21 April 1964) 6, reporting that the TUC had discussed the *Rookes* case with Sir Frank Soskice QC (then the Shadow Home Secretary, and chair of a Labour Party working party on the case; previously, Solicitor General, and briefly Attorney General, in the Attlee government) and Godfray le Quesne QC. The former recommended legislation to insert 14 words into section 3, between the parts of that section removing liability for inducing a breach of contract and interference: 'or that it constitutes or involves intimidation by a threat to break a contract', and this was supported by the TUC's Finance and General Purposes Committee: Trades Union Congress (TUC), *Annual Report 1964*, 355. When the issue was eventually addressed by section 1 of the Trade Disputes Act 1965, this followed the pattern of section 3, but expressly removed liability for three types of threats.

[40] Trade Union and Labour Relations Act 1974, ss 13(3) and 13(4) ensured that a conspiracy to break contracts would not be actionable provided that the contracts were broken 'in contemplation or furtherance of a trade dispute'. The Donovan Commission had recommended such a change: *Royal Commission on Trade Unions and Employers' Associations 1965–1968 (Chmn: Lord Donovan)* (Cmnd 3623, 1968) para 854.

or a threat to commit a tort or a crime – as pivotal to the defensibility of the overall outcome; it was also the element on which the defendants had primarily succeeded in the Court of Appeal.[41] At this point, my attempt to present the Lords' decision as proceeding from legitimate judicial reasoning will benefit from separation of a formal and a pragmatic perspective.

From a formal perspective, the primary difficulty for the defendants was that the House of Lords in *Allen v Flood*[42] decided to structure the general economic torts around a catalogue of prohibited means ('unlawful means') rather than evaluation of the parties' motives; a court would not rule on the merits of a dispute, but could hold that prohibited means had been deployed.[43] For this form of judicial abstentionism to work, the catalogue of prohibited means had to reflect what was already unlawful as a result of some other body of law,[44] rather than being bespoke for the industrial arena; a bespoke list could have been supplemented by the judiciary and would have introduced additional uncertainty.[45] Against this benchmark,[46] it was difficult for the defendants to present breaking a contract as 'lawful', as opposed to being 'unlawful':[47] *inducing* an employee to break a contract of employment was an actionable wrong,[48] and

[41] As noted above, n 31, two members of the Court of Appeal held that *if* they were wrong about the scope of the tort of intimidation then section 3 would nonetheless have protected the defendants.

[42] *Allen v Flood* (n 31).

[43] In *Quinn* (n 32) the House of Lords had adopted a different approach to assessment of the legality of a conspiracy to injure, but this had been defused by section 1 of the 1906 Act and the decision of the House of Lords in *Crofter Hand Woven Harris Tweed Co Ltd v Veitch* [1942] AC 435 (HL).

[44] Leaving aside the question of breaches of contract, at the time it seemed likely that the catalogue would cover torts and crimes: Lord Devlin recorded that it was 'not … disputed' that a threat of a crime would be an unlawful threat for the purposes of the tort of intimidation (*Rookes* (n 2) 1207). In the light of the subsequent decision of the House of Lords as to the scope of 'unlawful means' for the purposes of the tort of causing loss by unlawful means (see *OBG Ltd v Allan* [2007] UKHL 21, [2008] 1 AC 1 [57] (Lord Hoffmann)), which excludes crimes, this point might now be more contentious.

[45] Since *Rookes*, influential figures such as Lord Hoffmann and Hazel Carty have recommended that the catalogue of prohibited means used by the general economic torts should be both non-bespoke and 'minimalist'. Their minimalist agenda has advantages in terms of predictability – a reduced likelihood of defendants accidentally straying into liability – and legitimacy – minimalism leaves the courts responsible only for policing what is *obviously* unacceptable, with any more intrusive regulation, where choices about where to draw the lines will be more contentious, falling to Parliament, or perhaps to an expert executive body like the Competition and Markets Authority.

[46] The defendants' counsel at first instance, J Thompson QC, submitted (*Rookes* (n 15) 632) that all torts were 'unlawful' and that a line should be drawn between torts and breaches of contract; before the House of Lords, C Duncan QC's submissions, as reported in the Appeal Cases, sought to confine the tort to threats of violence (*Rookes* (n 2) 1145), though Lord Reid (at 1167) understood the defendants to be relying on a distinction between threats to commit a tort and threats to break a contract.

[47] As Sachs J put it, in his judgment at first instance, *Rookes* (n 15) 633: 'It seems difficult successfully to argue that a breach of contract is something that is lawful.' In the Court of Appeal (ibid 664) Sellers LJ appeared sympathetic to a contrary view, suggesting that breaking a contract is 'not forbidden by law' and would not be described as 'unlawful' or 'illegal' in ordinary language, though it is not wholly clear in the passage when he is summarising submissions and when he is expressing his own opinions.

[48] *Glamorgan Coal Co Ltd v South Wales Miners' Federation* [1905] AC 239 (HL).

only protected from liability by section 3 of the Trade Disputes Act 1906 when done 'in contemplation or furtherance of a trade dispute'; moreover, nothing in the 1906 legislation removed the notional liability of employees who broke their contracts (even when participating in such a dispute).[49] The 1906 Royal Commission on Trade Disputes and Trade Combinations, that preceded the legislation, had only proposed that an Act should be passed to declare 'strikes for whatever purposes (including sympathetic or secondary strikes), apart from crime *or breach of contract*, legal …' and to declare that 'to persuade to strike, ie to desist from working, *apart from breach of contract*, is not illegal'.[50]

How then, from a formal perspective, could the defendants hope to undermine the proposition that it is unlawful to break a binding contractual promise? Three lines of argument were deployed: obligations to avoid committing torts and crimes are general, whilst contractual obligations are voluntarily assumed between specific parties; allowing a third party to a contract to rely on the unlawfulness of a threat to break it would be inconsistent with the doctrine of privity; and, breaking a contract is less serious than committing a crime or a tort, indeed a contract-breaker can sometimes be blameless.[51]

The House of Lords was not convinced; each line was vulnerable to counter-arguments, and collectively they were insufficient to undermine the attractions of the 'natural line' between 'what is lawful and unlawful as against the party threatened'.[52] The weakness in the privity argument, for example, was that allowing Rookes to identify a threat of a breach of contract as an 'unlawful' method of coercing BOAC, would not involve his being allowed to *enforce* a contract that he was not a party to, any more than allowing him to identify as 'unlawful' a threat to smash the Design Office windows would have involved allocating him a right of property in the building.[53] Similarly, the fact that contracts are 'voluntary', cannot determine whether – after one has been made – threatening to break it is a 'lawful' method of putting pressure on a party who is in a position to cause loss

[49] *Denaby & Cadeby Main Collieries Ltd v Yorkshire Miners' Association* [1906] AC 384 (HL). In this case Lord Loreburn LC (at 387) drew a clear distinction between the miners' liberty to terminate their contracts with 14 days' notice and the immediate cessation of work that occurred, which amounted to a breach of contract: one of the reasons why the union defendant succeeded in the case was because *it* had drawn the same distinction, instructing its members to return to work, hold a ballot, and then – if the result favoured resumption of the strike – work out their 14 days.

[50] *Report of the Royal Commission on Trade Disputes and Trade Combinations* (Cd. 2825, 1906), majority report, para 66 (emphasis added). See also Sir Godfery Lushington's minority report, p. 77, agreeing with these two proposals.

[51] The idea that a party to a contract is only obliged to perform *or* pay damages was also mentioned, though the defendants' threat was not accompanied by an indication of willingness to pay BOAC for any losses it might suffer as a result of the envisaged strike!

[52] *Rookes* (n 2) 1207.

[53] Tort duties are subject to an equivalent of the contractual privity rule – only the person to whom the tortious duty is owed can claim for the damage they have suffered as a result of a breach; the contractual rule is simply more visible, perhaps because it sometimes thwarts the intentions of contracting parties. Further, as Lord Devlin pointed out, Rookes could hardly be said to have been seeking to sue on his former colleagues' breaches of their contracts of employment since BOAC's capitulation had prevented these contracts from being broken: *Rookes* (n 2) 1208.

to a claimant; owning a Design Office is similarly 'voluntary', but no one would suggest that BOAC's free choice to build one should make a threat to break its windows a 'lawful' tactic in a dispute. Turning to the question whether threatening to break contracts is a trivial form of wrong-doing, the difficulty for the defendants was that, as they intended, it was a form of wrong that BOAC took very seriously, and was willing to dismiss a long-serving employee to avoid.[54] Moreover, as Tony Weir pointed out, the possibility of *innocent* breaches of contract was of marginal relevance since the tort requires a *threat* to be made with the *intention* of causing harm to a claimant.[55]

The real force of the defendants' submission that the tort of intimidation should not be extended to threats to break contracts relied on a pragmatic perspective relating to *contracts of employment*:[56] by the middle of the twentieth century,[57] a threat of a strike would frequently be a threat that employment contracts would be broken, so a decision that the tort of intimidation could be committed by making such a threat would severely impinge on the usual practices of trade union representatives and officials.[58] Thus, in the Court of

[54] In any case, the generalisation that *all* crimes are serious is doubtful, given how many forms of behaviour have been designated as criminal by primary or secondary legislation. Partly for this reason, it is now clear that all crimes are *not* 'unlawful means' for the purposes of the general economic torts: see *OBG* (n 44).

[55] JA Weir, 'Chaos or Cosmos? *Rookes*, *Stratford* and the Economic Torts' [1964] *CLJ* 225, 230. Similarly, *Rookes* (n 2) 1208 (Lord Devlin).

[56] Supporters of the outcome in *Rookes* frequently pointed to hypothetical cases involving *different sorts of contract*: for example, Lord Pearce raised the prospect of an essential supplier threatening to withhold supplies from a manufacturer in breach of contract: *Rookes* (n 2) 1234. A further non-labour example involved tenants coercing a landlord by means of a co-ordinated rent-strike: in July 1961, 600 tenants had threatened a rent strike to try to coerce Smethwick Council into not renting a flat in the Price Street re-development to a Pakistani family: *The Guardian* (London, 24 July 1961) front page. (The Council held firm, and at the end of the week sent notices to quit to the 64 tenants who were still withholding their rent.)

[57] I have failed to locate firm evidence about what proportion of the labour force in each decade had employment contracts *formally* lasting more than one day. In the leading case of *Allen v Flood* (n 31), the ironworkers and shipwrights were apparently employed on day-to-day terms where a fresh contract was made at the yard gate each morning; but for miners longer notice terms were usual: for example, in *Glamorgan Coal Co Ltd v South Wales Miners' Federation* [1903] 1 KB 118 (KBD) (which reached the House of Lords: n 48) termination of the contracts required a month's notice by either party, which could only be given on the first of each month.) In the second reading debate for what became the Contracts of Employment Act 1963, the Minister of Labour, John Hare, stated that an entitlement to a week's notice of termination of employment had only become generally established during, or shortly after, the Second World War and that notice terms had not subsequently improved for the great majority of the country's 15 million manual workers: HC Deb 14 February 1963, vol 671, cols 1505–06. Some of his critics observed that in construction and shipbuilding short engagements were still so prevalent that such workers would not qualify for the minimum notice that the legislation stipulated (which required 26 weeks of continuous service).

[58] Even Lord Wedderburn, one of the strongest critics of *Rookes*, offers some support for the opinion that the main problem was the unpalatable conclusion reached rather than use of illegitimate methods to get there: 'The Law Lords' judgments in *Rookes* created new principles out of old; but their *methods* were within the traditional reasoning of the common law' (KW Wedderburn, *The Worker and the Law*, 3rd edn (Harmondsworth, Penguin,1986) 45 (emphasis in the original). His next sentence, however, returns to the indictment: 'This is the way judicial social policy is expressed.'

Appeal, Donovan LJ noted that '[t]here can be few strikes which do not involve a breach of contract by the strikers', then reasoned that: (1) an actual breach of contract by a striker could not amount to 'unlawful means' for the purposes of the economic torts, since to hold otherwise would mean that almost all strikes would have been tortious through being unlawful means conspiracies, but without anyone noticing this; and (2) it could make no sense to hold that a threat to breach could be unlawful if an actual breach was not.[59] In the House of Lords, Lord Devlin similarly isolated the pragmatic argument: '... the strike weapon is now so generally sanctioned that it cannot really be regarded as an unlawful weapon of intimidation; and so there must be something wrong with a conclusion that treats it as such'.[60] But he went on to identify the weakness in such a chain of reasoning: the post-1906 rarity of actions against workers for breaking their contracts, or for participating in conspiracies to break their contracts, could be explained by the practical reasons employers had for not pursuing such claims rather than by a premise that the workers had acted *lawfully*.

Should the House of Lords have accepted the pragmatic case and held that threatening to break a *contract of employment* was not a threat of an 'unlawful act' such as could ground a claim for three-party intimidation? The question when a court can legitimately rely on arguments of public policy to reject a conclusion justified by formal reasoning from principle was, and remains, controversial. In the circumstances of Rookes' claim the case for relying on such arguments was relatively strong, since their conclusion was consistent with a widespread *assumption* as to what the 1906 Act had been designed to achieve.[61] Significantly, however, Lord Devlin's overt reason for rejecting the pragmatic case did not involve espousing formalist puritanism; he could see no route to accommodating the pragmatic concern without creating a zone of immunity broader than its legitimate rationale: '... your Lordships can, in my opinion, give effect to it only if you are prepared either to hobble the common law in all classes of disputes lest its range is too wide to suit industrial disputes or to give the statute a wider scope than it was ever intended to have'.[62] The second part of this sentence, invoking the intended breadth of the statute, refers to the problem, noted above, of a broad interpretation of the second limb in section 3 – sufficient to meet a pragmatic need to immunise intimidation *by threats of breaking employment contracts* leading to interference with employment – inevitably extending protection to the use of threats of violence to achieve

[59] *Rookes* (n 15) 682–84.
[60] *Rookes* (n 2) 1218.
[61] As noted above, the 1906 Act conferred immunity on procuring a breach of contract, but preserved liability for actually breaking a contract: thus it could be argued that threatening to break a contract should be protected, alongside procuring, because both were acts likely to be taken in organising a strike, and the legislature had sought to protect those who organised strikes, or that threatening to break a contract should be treated as unlawful, just as an actual breach by a striker remained unlawful.
[62] *Rookes* (n 2) 1218.

similar goals: '... your Lordships cannot construe the Act to give protection in the case of a threat of a breach of contract unless you also make it wide enough to protect the threatener of physical violence'.[63] But Lord Devlin provided a less clear explanation of the 'hobbling' he was referring to in the first part of his sentence: the next two paragraphs do not elaborate on a distinction between 'all classes of disputes' and 'industrial disputes' but simply illustrate how compelling a threat to strike may be. The distinction, however, suggests that he believed that it would be impossible[64] for the *general common law of tort* to incorporate a 'trade dispute' condition, or to develop a special rule for contracts of employment: consequently, if *general tort law* held that it was not tortious to threaten to break a contract, or to make a threat to a *purely* economic interest,[65] the conclusion would: (i) protect defendant employees (such as those in *Rookes*) from liability even when they were *not* acting in contemplation or furtherance of a trade dispute; and (ii) protect other classes of defendants who might be in a position to coerce by threatening to break different types of contracts, such as vital suppliers or purchasers essential for a business's cash flow.[66] Importantly, Lord Devlin did not reject the *rational* force of the pragmatic case:

> The essence of the difficulty lies in the fact that in determining what constitutes the tort of intimidation your Lordships have drawn the dividing line not between physical and economic coercion but between lawful and unlawful coercion. For the universal purposes of the common law, I am sure that that is the right, natural and logical line. For the purpose of the limited field of industrial disputes which is controlled by statute and where much that is in principle unlawful is already tolerated, it may be that pragmatically and on grounds of policy the line should be drawn between physical and economic pressure. But that is for Parliament to decide.[67]

[63] ibid 1220.

[64] A Bogg, 'Common Law and Statute in the Law of Employment' (2016) 69 *Current Legal Problems* 67, 88, identifies *Rookes* as involving 'something of a constitutional revolt by the judges in developing the economic torts in defiance of legislative policy'. He suggests that (at 89) 'legislative policy' should have led the Court to hold that the tort of intimidation could not be committed by threats to break contracts, but does not discuss whether it also authorised incorporating a 'trade dispute' condition into the common law tort.

[65] In a post-judicial lecture in 1977, Lord Devlin treated *Rookes* as involving the question whether it was satisfactory for the tort of intimidation to be confined to *physical* threats, or should be extended to *economic* ones, and associated it with the House of Lords' decision in *Hedley Byrne v Heller* [1964] AC 465 (HL), which held that the tort of negligence could accommodate duties to protect claimants against economic risks as well as physical ones: P Devlin, *The Judge* (Oxford, Oxford University Press, 1981) 94–95 (By coincidence, in *Hedley Byrne*, it was Gerald Gardiner QC who persuaded the Court to demolish a rigid physical / economic distinction, though the claim of the party who he represented was rejected.)

[66] The power of classes of defendants *other than* employees to coerce by means of threats to break contracts is illustrated through the case law on economic duress.

[67] *Rookes* (n 2) 1220. Lord Devlin completed the paragraph by making reference to Lord Macnaghten's 'clear warning ... against the interference of the courts in matters of policy in this branch of the law' in *Vacher & Sons Ltd v London Society of Compositors* [1913] AC 107 (HL) 118. For those that agree with the assessment of Professor Bob Simpson, that '[t]here is no clearer illustration [than *Rookes*] of judicial construction of legislation so as to preclude it from impacting on judicial extension of common law liability', the citation of this warning must seem an outrageous act of hypocrisy: R Simpson, 'Trade Disputes Legislation and the Economic Torts' in TT Arvind and J Steele (eds), *Tort Law and the Legislature* (Oxford, Hart, 2013) 118.

It is, of course, impossible to be sure that the rejection of the pragmatic case was not influenced by a lack of judicial sympathy for trade unionists, in particular those who promoted 'unconstitutional strikes' at short notice. At the same time, however, it would be rash to insist that *Rookes* was the source of either the idea that breaking a contract of employment is no different from breaking other types of contract or the idea that there is a general (for Lord Devlin, 'universal') common law of torts, rather than a special version for industrial disputes. Professor Bogg has observed that, for labour lawyers with functionalist sympathies, the common law has appeared to be 'a highly regressive and anti-democratic impediment to progressive social and economic change'.[68] But an alternative impression is that the common law judges have striven to provide only rudimentary *general* default rules, channelling contentious social and economic reallocation into the democratic legislative process. On this view by refusing to incorporate – into the general common law – the *choices* that the 1906 Parliament *could* have made the House of Lords was not defying legislative choices, or even indicating opposition to such *possible* choices, but simply inviting the legislature to confirm that: 'in contemplation or furtherance of a trade dispute' it is lawful for a person intentionally to cause loss to another by making threats of a sort that it would *generally* be unlawful to carry out in pursuing their ends. No doubt a preference for general rules reflects a choice about values, and any selection of default rules will be to the advantage of some people rather than others: the common law cannot claim to be neutral. But there is an important gulf between the allegation that *Rookes* exemplifies the common law's *hostility* to collective action by employees, and the demurrer that the common law's *preference for generality* led to a decision that had unexpected and unwelcome effects for ordinary trade union activity. That said, the judges who rejected the pragmatic case may not have understood the effects that their decision was likely to have for trade unionists; certainly, as I will discuss under the next heading, the political actors who had to respond to *Rookes* found it difficult to agree what it had decided, and how far this would impinge on legitimate trade union activities.

III. THE AFTERMATH

To this point, my analysis of the judicial reasoning in *Rookes* has proposed that: (1) the interpretation of the Trade Disputes Act 1906 was plausible and defensible; (2) the understanding of the tort of three-party intimidation was one that could be derived using defensible methods of formal reasoning; but (3) it was

[68] Bogg (n 64) 69. Professor Bogg contrasts this negative view with the notion that 'the common law embodied the public reason of the political community, the community's norms refined through incremental historical development in the common law courts'. But this formulation is unhelpfully broad; it can cover both Whiggish delusions about the common law's normative perfection and the more moderate view that it represents a bona fide attempt to identify generally-tolerable, generally-applicable *default* rules.

more contentious to reject the pragmatic argument – that such an understanding of the tort should be rejected because it would unduly (and unexpectedly) impinge on the usual practices of trade union representatives and officials – though to accommodate it the judges would have had to limit the scope of the tort in cases not arising from trade disputes (or not involving employment contracts) or accepted a variegated (non-universal) law of torts. In this section, I intend reviewing the aftermath of the decision, focusing on the responses of the government and the trade union movement. For convenience, I have divided the assessment between the first 12 months after their Lordships' decision and the longer term.

A. The First Twelve Months

The House of Lords' decision was published on 21 January 1964 and the Bill which became the Trade Disputes Act 1965, creating a statutory immunity to cover the facts of similar cases, was presented to Parliament on 2 February 1965.[69] Between these events, a General Election on 15 October 1964 ended 13 years of government by the Conservative Party.[70] Significantly, the Conservative administration's failure to propose legislation in early 1964 did not stem from its enthusiasm for the new legal restraints on trade union activity;[71] rather the government initially doubted the strength of the pragmatic case for immediate legislation to reverse the decision, sought to postpone the question of reform until after a broader enquiry, and hesitated because of anxiety that introducing even a short Bill, such as what the Trades Union Congress [TUC] proposed, would provide backbenchers with 'the opportunity to propose other difficult and controversial changes in the law'.[72]

[69] The Act received Royal Assent on 5 August 1965. During its legislative passage one of the main points of controversy concerned whether it could be given retrospective effect. Eventually, claimants were allowed six months to institute any claim based on a tort committed before it received Royal Assent: Trade Disputes Act 1965, s 1(2).

[70] Given the slender overall majority that the Labour Party achieved, a mere four seats, it is arguable that the way in which the government of Alec Douglas-Home responded to *Rookes* made a difference to the outcome. C Wrigley, 'Trade Unions and the 1964 General Election' (2007) 21 *Contemporary British History* 325, 326, claims that *Rookes* helped to mobilise trade unionists to vote Labour in 1964. Douglas-Home apparently attributed more significance to a press story that he had become Prime Minister through the machinations of a 'magic circle' of Old Etonians: V Bogdanor, 'The Spectator Book Review that Brought Down Macmillan's Government' *The Spectator* (London, 18 January 2014).

[71] In May 1961 Macmillan's Cabinet had discussed and approved a Memorandum produced by the then Minister of Labour, John Hare, which insisted that '[l]egislation against strikes is not a practical proposition', and identified the weaknesses of the most popular proposals. It noted that the trade union movement was 'undoubtedly a stabilising influence in the country', that its co-operation was essential to improving industrial relations, and that '[o]ur object should always be to strengthen and stimulate the responsible elements': Memorandum, CAB 129/105/14; Cabinet conclusions, CAB 128/35/28.

[72] Minister of Labour's Memorandum for the Cabinet, 'Trade Unions and the Law' (16 June 1964) para 7: CAB 129/118/19. At the time that the question of the government's response first arose,

Sir Denis Barnes, who was Deputy Permanent Secretary in the Ministry of Labour at the time, wrote, in a book co-authored with Eileen Reid, that: 'Woodcock [– the General Secretary of the TUC –] pressed Joseph Godber, Minister of Labour since October 1963, for a Bill to restore the protection the unions thought they had, offering in return to accept the appointment of a Royal Commission.'[73] But whilst Woodcock certainly sought such legislation from June 1964,[74] there is less evidence in the Ministry of Labour's files to support the suggestion that a Royal Commission would have been acceptable to the TUC. Shortly after the decision, on 7 February 1964, The Prime Minister asked ministers to urgently consider the appointment of a Royal Commission, but Godber's response, on 10 February, was that this would be 'bitterly resented by the trade unions', and his more detailed advice was that it would be difficult to secure a balanced composition for such a commission before the election, and that the trade unions might not co-operate.[75] On 4 March, he circulated a memorandum to the Cabinet, having consulted trade union opinion, in which he reported that it would be impossible, at that point in time, to secure the co-operation of the TUC in setting up a Royal Commission;[76] Cabinet authorised him to state to the House of Commons that the government thought that an inquiry to review 'the law affecting trade unions and employers' associations … should be undertaken early in the life of the next Parliament'.[77]

The government's early response to *Rookes* was significantly influenced by uncertainty as to how far the decision would impinge on ordinary trade union activities. Henry Huxham, the solicitor within the Ministry of Labour,

February–March 1964, the Cabinet was contemplating a summer election, and this may have affected assessment of the practicality of trying to pass legislation in the remainder of the session: CAB 195/24/12 (Chief Whip).

[73] D Barnes and E Reid, *Governments and Trade Unions: The British Experience 1964–79* (London, Heinemann Educational, 1980) 42–43.

[74] A deputation from the TUC met the Minister of Labour on 11 June 1964 and pressed for legislation. The Minister's Memorandum for the Cabinet, above n 72, following this meeting, conceded that the state of the law was 'unsatisfactory', but reported (para 5) that he had told the deputation that it 'was unrealistic … to assume that we could legislate on this point in the short remaining lifetime of the present Parliament or in advance of clarification of the extent of the liability of trade union officials by the House of Lords in the case of *Stratford v Lindley*'.

[75] LAB 43/416. It is not clear from the file what precipitated the Prime Minister's interest in the prospects of a Royal Commission. The Cabinet, on 13 February, was informed that two groups of private members were considering putting down motions calling for inquiries following *Rookes*, but the Ministry of Labour's file also contains the results of a Gallup Poll on trade union reform that had been commissioned and circulated by the Freedom Group.

[76] CAB 129/117/12. A note on the file in the Ministry of Labour reports that an official, probably [the author's initials are unclear] Sir James Dunnett, the Permanent Secretary, had informally met George Woodcock, General Secretary of the TUC, on 5 February and asked him what line the TUC was going to take about *Rookes*. Woodcock replied that they were taking advice, and that '[h]e himself was not disposed to get too excited about it at this stage.' Woodcock also asked about the prospect of a Royal Commission, indicating that he was not opposed to the idea, but was concerned about the burden that it might impose on TUC officials: LAB 10/2075

[77] HC Deb 19 March 1964, vol 691, cols 1598–1602. On the same day, Godfray Le Quesne QC provided an opinion on the effects of *Rookes* to the TUC, and WH Thompson sent GH Doughty, the General Secretary of DATA (see n 1), the opinion that he had obtained from Gerald Gardiner QC.

circulated a note 10 days after the decision was published, which used language echoing Gerald Gardiner QC's submissions: the decision had driven 'a coach and four through the Trade Disputes Act 1906' and '[removed] from the trade unions and their members the protection which the Trade Disputes Act 1906 had hitherto been thought to give them if there is in existence a trade dispute'.[78] The Lord Chancellor, Viscount Dilhorne, was unconvinced. He wrote to Godber: 'I regret that I am not able to agree with the views expressed in the note';[79] and sent a stronger reaction to the Attorney General: 'The solicitor to the Ministry of Labour's note on this case appears to me entirely misconceived',[80] receiving the lawyerly reply 'I think that substantially I agree with all you say.'[81] The Law Officers' formal Opinion on the effects of the decision, which was completed the next month, provided a measured assessment of its practical consequences, predicting – plausibly – that '[t]he effect of the decision is … unlikely to provide employers with any additional legal weapons against their employees' and opining – less plausibly – that the effect of the 1906 Act was neither 'defeated nor diminished'.[82]

The impression conveyed by the Law Officers' Opinion – that an immediate legislative reversal was not required – was consistent with the strategy of proposing no legislation until after a broader inquiry, to commence 'early in the life of the next Parliament'.[83] But this strategy, and the Ministerial statement that announced it, had in fact been refined through detailed debate in Cabinet before the Opinion was available. On 4 March, Godber had provided a Memorandum for his colleagues that argued that there was a strong case on the merits for a general inquiry into trade union law and practice, and although the government had been resisting pressure from its supporters for such an inquiry for several years, so that suddenly to set one up towards the end of a Parliament would expose the government to the charge that it was 'actuated by merely political motives', on the other side, it would be difficult to do nothing, particularly when the government was about to publish a White Paper on monopolies and restrictive practices, and delaying any announcement until a manifesto would risk a last minute negative reaction.[84]

The 4 March Memorandum also disclosed that Godber believed that the TUC had not yet secured a formal Opinion on the effects of *Rookes*.

[78] There are copies of Huxham's note, dated 31 January 1964, in several government files, eg, LCO2/ 8139.

[79] Lord Chancellor to Minister of Labour, 19 February 1964: LCO2/ 8139.

[80] The Lord Chancellor expressed this view in a document he described as an aide memoire of his own opinions, but shared with the Attorney General, who was engaged in preparing formal advice: 18 February 1964: LCO2/ 8139.

[81] Attorney General to Lord Chancellor, 24 February 1964: LCO2/ 8139.

[82] There are copies of the opinion, dated 11 March 1964, in several government files, eg, LAB10/ 2178.

[83] Above, n 77.

[84] CAB 129/117/12. The Cabinet did not reach a conclusion on the strategy at the meeting when this memorandum was discussed, and a revised memorandum was produced for the next meeting.

When the TUC did receive one, two weeks later, from Godfray Le Quesne QC,[85] it provided a temperate assessment: '[it] still remains unlikely that unions will find in practice that there has been any change of any consequence'. But on 21 April 1964, *The Times* reported that Le Quesne QC and Sir Frank Soskice QC, Chair of a Labour Party working party on the issue, had met with the TUC, and recommended immediate legislation: 'In any effort to enforce a closed shop policy there is likely to be one or more persons in the position of Rookes, and liability may arise as a result of official as well as wild-cat strikes.'[86] Thereafter, it appears that the TUC began to press the Government for an immediate legislative response.[87]

Three issues clouded early assessments of the effects of *Rookes* on trade union activity. First, it was unclear how frequently workplace disputes involved *threats* to strike. One view was that every strike involved an implied threat that it would continue if the strikers' demands were not met; but at the other extreme, it was – perhaps optimistically – suggested that the new tort liability might be avoided by going no further than 'passing on information', or merely 'predicting' what might occur in the future, as opposed to making *threats*.

The second source of doubts related to the proportion of strikes that might involve the *breaking* of contracts. There was a widespread belief that striking after giving the notice necessary to terminate a contract was different from an immediate walkout, and this led to uncertainty as to whether the outcome in *Rookes* had only been reached because the threatened strike had been too precipitate, or whether it had depended on the presence of the 'no strike' agreement.[88] At the same time, however, there was a tension between the belief that strikes after notice were lawful and the difficulty that the most convincing theory to explain this, that a strike after notice was lawful because it took effect as a voluntary termination of each employee's contract, did not correspond to the strikers' understanding: in giving notice most strikers did not think that they were 'asking for their cards'.[89]

[85] A copy of an Opinion signed by him and dated 19 March 1964 is present in one of the Ministry of Labour's files: LAB 10/2178. It appears to be the same opinion as the TUC published as a pamphlet in September: *Rookes v Barnard: Opinion of Leading Counsel* (London, Trades Union Congress, 1964).

[86] *The Times*, (London, 21 April 1964) 6.

[87] In a Memorandum prepared for the Cabinet, dated 28 April, the minister set out options for the government's line *if* the TUC should ask for immediate legislation to 'cancel' *Rookes*. But this Memorandum does not appear to have been discussed by the Cabinet. By the end of May the TUC had asked for the meeting that took place on June 11, and at which they pressed for legislation; the Cabinet then discussed (and rejected) this request on 18 June.

[88] In the Court of Appeal, Rookes' counsel had submitted that his action 'would have foundered in limine' if the defendants had given appropriate notice: *Rookes* (n 15) 647. Before the House of Lords, they submitted that the no-strike agreement overrode the provisions relating to notice so that even a strike with notice would have been unlawful: *Rookes* (n 2) 1146.

[89] The government's Official Committee on Trade Unions and the Law, which had reported shortly before *Rookes*, issued a Supplementary Report in June 1964. It noted (para 11) that strikers would frequently not want to terminate their contracts of employment because this could lead to a loss of superannuation and pension rights, but that the recently passed Contracts of Employment Act 1963

The third issue was the question of how many people might want to make use of any extended opportunity to bring claims. The lawyers generally advised that most *employers* would not seek to sue their employees for having *threatened* to break their contracts of employment, just as they had usually not taken the opportunity to sue them for having actually broken their contracts during a strike. Thus, the main challenge was to identify the categories of claimants *other than employers* that *Rookes* might have created. On this, some of the trade union assessments overstated the dangers by overlooking the fact that for a claim for three-party intimidation to succeed a claimant would have to prove that the defendant made the threats with the *intention* of causing it harm.[90] The government's lawyers identified three principal situations where an *intention* to harm a third party might most frequently be found: where action was taken against a non-unionist to enforce a closed shop, where secondary action was being taken against an employer's supplier or customer, and where action was being taken against another union as a result of a demarcation dispute, but there was no clear data as to what proportion of strikes involved one of these three dimensions.[91]

When Godber met a deputation from the TUC's General Purposes Committee on 11 June 1964, he consciously chose not to concede that immediate legislation was necessary; instead, having heard Woodcock's complaint that 'the judgment had created an impossible situation for the unions and was inhibiting trade union officials from discharging their proper functions', he pressed for details of the practical difficulties that the case was allegedly causing. Reporting back to the Cabinet, Godber stated that legislation in the current session was 'out of the question'; since the TUC's proposed amendment to the Trade Disputes Act 1906 would have been 'unacceptable to backbenchers',[92] and introducing

provided that there could only be 'continuity of employment' (for the purposes of calculating what rights an employee had acquired) through a strike *without* a breach of contract.

[90] For example, a pamphlet published by the Labour Research Department: OH Parsons, 'The Meaning of *Rookes v Barnard*' (London, LRD, 1964) 15, claimed that a trade union official who threatened a strike could be sued 'by anyone who can be reasonably foreseen to be a loser by his action, notably the employer'.

[91] JA Lincoln, *Journey to Coercion: From Tolpuddle to Rookes v Barnard* (London, Institute of Economic Affairs, 1964), quoted a Ministry of Labour publication as the source for his claim that 50% of strikes concerned not matters of wages, hours and working conditions but issues such as the 'closed shop'. The Supplementary Report of the Official Committee on Trade Unions and the Law (June 1964) distinguished between 'official' and 'unofficial' strikes; suggesting that the decision would have relatively little practical effect on unofficial strikes, which were generally aimed at the employer (para 17) but might have a more significant effect on official action where the goal was to enforce a 'closed shop' or strike a secondary target. The absence of data may reflect absence of a consistent pattern of disputes – for example, more than seven times as many employees stopped work in 1962 than in 1963; ironically, given the timing of the decision in *Rookes*, fewer working days were lost to strikes in 1963 than in any year between 1952 and 1991.

[92] Although the TUC's proposed amendment would have gone no further than reversing *Rookes* with respect to threats to break contracts in furtherance or contemplation of a trade dispute, there was a concern that it could be presented as an instance of trade union officials being placed 'above the law'. A series of cases where claimants, such as Rookes, had lost work after leaving (or being expelled from) a trade union, had gained public attention and sympathy in the previous decade, and

legislation would present an opportunity for backbenchers to propose controversial changes; in other words, the minister was concerned that an attempt to reverse *Rookes* would enable backbenchers to press for more repressive, and divisive, measures. With Cabinet's sanction, he wrote to Woodcock refusing to put forward the legislation sought, but offering to set up the broader inquiry immediately (rather than 'early in the life of the next Parliament'), with a request for it to give prior consideration to the issues raised by *Rookes*. But the Cabinet Secretary's note of the meeting suggests that Godber did not expect his offer to be accepted.[93]

The TUC's reply sought a discussion between legal advisers to try to establish why the sides had different views about the effects of *Rookes*. It also requested a further meeting, which took place on 20 July 1964, but was similarly unsuccessful. At the July meeting, Godber drew attention to the absence of evidence that *Rookes* had generated new litigation, and attached significance to the prospect of the pending decision in *Stratford v Lindley* clarifying matters,[94] whilst the minister's legal adviser insisted that *Rookes* only changed the law in situations where a no strike clause had been incorporated into the individual contracts of the employees.

The *uncertainty* as to what the case had decided was an important argument in favour of the TUC's opinion that legislation to reverse *Rookes* was immediately necessary. At the 11 June meeting, the deputation pressed the points that the decision was having a psychological impact on trade union work and that the uncertainty of trade union officials as to what was now illegal was encouraging unofficial stoppages.[95] In the Memorandum in which Godber reported this meeting to Cabinet he repeated these points and conceded that it was now 'undeniable' that the present state of the law was 'unsatisfactory'.[96] He attached a Report compiled by officials, which complained that *Rookes* raised 'complex and bewildering issues of law', and had enhanced the significance of the divergence between when lawyers would identify a breach of an employment contract and the view of when strikes were unlawful 'established by the accepted code of industrial behaviour'. Whilst Godber made no similar concessions in the

the case for designing legislation specifically to permit trade unions to continue to take such action was not regarded as strong.

[93] CAB 195/24/12, item 8. At Cabinet, the Lord Chancellor (Dilhorne) pointed out that there would be little advantage in starting the inquiry early since it would take months; Godber agreed and said he made the offer to 'embarrass' the TUC.

[94] The decision of the House of Lords in *Stratford* (n 10) was published eight days after the July meeting: it did not clarify what *Rookes* had decided, though three of the Law Lords offered opinions as to what it had *not* decided. Lord Donovan (at 339) noted that counsel for the trade union defendants had invited the Lords to reach its decision about the law swiftly so that electors in the anticipated General Election could cast their votes on the basis of how each party planned to amend it by legislation.

[95] The deputation reported its meeting to the TUC's Finance and General Purposes Committee on 22 June: Modern Records Centre, 292B/42.26.

[96] CAB 129/118/19.

July meeting, and his subsequent speeches continued to claim that the effects of *Rookes* had been exaggerated, he also described the government's differences with the TUC as 'mainly to what timing and approach to adopt' in re-examining the law.[97] A fortnight before the general election he prepared a draft Memorandum for Cabinet, for use if he remained in office, in which he envisaged further meetings with the TUC 'to produce an agreed statement of the legal and practical results of the judgment and of any uncertainties that may still remain' and to agree 'what, if any, immediate and interim action ought to be taken'.[98]

After the election it fell to Godber's successor as Minister of Labour, Ray Gunter, to co-ordinate the passage of the legislation necessary to reverse *Rookes*. He told Cabinet, in a Memorandum that he prepared for its meeting on 18 December 1964, that he recommended a brief and simple Bill to reverse *Rookes*,[99] alongside a more general inquiry, and intended to have discussions with the TUC and British Employers' Confederation before the Bill was published, but the TUC's Finance and General Purposes Committee had debated the proposal earlier in the week.[100] The TUC eventually decided to support the legislation, resisting pressure from DATA and the Watermen to demand broader protections.[101]

B. The Longer Term

The experience of the half century following *Rookes* makes it difficult to maintain that the House of Lords should have recognised an irresistible case for ensuring a freedom from tort liability as broad as the defendants' expectations: if the Parliament of 1906 had been asked about the legality of threats to break contracts of employment it might well have broadened its drafting of section 3, but by January 1964 the state of the tide was less clear. Paul Smith has described

[97] On 22 August 1964, Godber devoted six pages to *Rookes* in his ten-page speech to the South-Eastern Provincial Area Young Conservative Council Half-Yearly Meeting. He appeared on television during the TUC Conference, undertaking that if the report of the general inquiry that he had promised showed a need for legislation 'we shall act on this promptly and expeditiously'.

[98] Ministry of Labour's files, draft dated 29.9.64, LAB 10/2178 [3].

[99] On 4 November 1964, the day of the Queen's Speech, which promised a Bill 'to give workers and their representatives the protection necessary for freedom of industrial negotiation', civil servants in the Ministry of Labour had met in the Secretary's Room, and decided that the Bill that Sir Frank Soskice QC (the newly appointed Home Secretary) had recommended to the TUC in April was too broad, and immunity should only be granted to threats to break (and to procure the breach of) *contracts of employment*, rather than contracts generally: the Trade Disputes Act 1965, s 1(1) coincided with this decision: LAB 10/2303.

[100] Gunter's memorandum to the Cabinet, 15.12.64: CAB 129/119/29.

[101] DATA had been at the heart of *Rookes*, and the Watermen (Watermen, Lightermen, Tugmen and Bargemen's Union) at the heart of *Stratford* (n 10): they sought legislation to abolish the tort of intimidation, remove the trade dispute condition from section 3 of the 1906 Act, and extend the protection of section 1 to conspiracies to break contracts.

Rookes as 'a harbinger of a new judicial activism'.[102] But it would be difficult to portray the *judiciary* as spearheading the process of revising the legal regulation of trade disputes. In terms of the goals that strikes and threats of strikes could be used to pursue, in 1980, legislation removed the protection from liability from most industrial action aimed at secondary targets, and imposed restrictions on the actions that could be taken to compel union membership; by the end of 1992, the protection from liability for industrial action aimed at enforcing 'closed shops' had been removed. Alongside this, the possibility of general trade union liability had been resurrected, as the underpinning to making the trade dispute immunities conditional on compliance with rules on ballots and notice. The process by which freedom from the economic torts has been eroded by legislation has not been simple and linear; there were, for example, some extensions of immunities in 1974 and 1976. But the longer-term direction of legislative policy has been relatively consistent, and it would seem implausible to claim that it was precipitated, accelerated, or amplified by the decision in *Rookes*.

IV. CONCLUSION: *ROOKES* AS A LANDMARK CASE

Rookes gained extraordinary attention in the trade union movement and in the general press, in part because it seemed to fit within two *popular* narratives: class-biased judges defying democracy to crush the power of workers acting collectively, or trade union officials ruthlessly crushing free thinkers whilst claiming to be 'above the law'. This chapter has submitted that Douglas Rookes' victory turned on more mundane legal arguments: interpretation of the words enacted by the 1906 Parliament and consideration of what concepts could properly be incorporated into a general common law tort. Subsequent scholars have noted that the case provides a vantage point for surveying the tendency of common law methods to thwart expedient public policies, and invites investigation of the ideologies that underpin those methods;[103] but these broader questions were not the reason that the judgment provoked a Resolution at the TUC's Blackpool Congress[104] or that Rookes' story was published in *The Sunday Telegraph*.[105]

[102] P Smith, 'The Law Behind the Law: *Rookes v Barnard* [1964], the Common Law and the Right to Strike' (2017) 38 *Historical Studies in Industrial Relations* 37, 38.

[103] Bogg (n 64).

[104] The Resolution stated that 'Congress views with concern the judgment of the House of Lords in the *Rookes v Barnard* case' and called on all affiliated unions 'to assist the General Council's efforts to obtain a change in legislation'.

[105] 'One Man's Fight for a Right' *The Sunday Telegraph* (London, 26 June 1964) 17.

6

Grunwick Processing Laboratories Ltd v ACAS: *The Social Contract, Trade Union Recognition, and the Rule of Law*

KD EWING

I. INTRODUCTION

Mrs Jayaben Desai is a hero of the British labour movement. Born in Gujarat in 1933, she settled in Tanganyika (later Zanzibar), where she 'enjoyed a comfortable lifestyle'.[1] Expelled with many other East African Asians, Mrs Desai arrived in North London with her family, taking up part-time employment initially as a 'sewing machinist in a Harlesden sweatshop'.[2] In 1974 she moved to Grunwick, a medium-sized company in north-west London that processed photographs. In the days before iPhones, people who liked to take photographs had cameras which had to be loaded with film. The films had to be developed and printed in a market dominated by big companies such as Kodak and Ilford. Grunwick was a player in this market, and operated largely on a mail order basis: photographers would send their film to the company for processing and return by post. The operation was staffed by a workforce of about 500, many of whom like Jayaben Desai were of Indian descent evicted from their homes in East Africa before arriving in north-west London. Desai shot to prominence as the leader of a strike at Grunwick in 1976, and was celebrated posthumously as 'one courageous woman' who 'inspired all who heard her', whose 'nationwide tour encouraged workers from all over Britain, outraged that the strikers had been sacked, to join the picket line outside the factory'.[3]

[1] J Dromey, 'Jayaben Desai Obituary' *The Guardian* (28 December 2010).
[2] ibid.
[3] ibid.

But before proceeding further with the *Grunwick* case and the Grunwick dispute of which the former is an integral part, it is necessary to begin briefly with the political context to both. Ostensibly, the case was about the scope of the statutory powers of the Advisory, Conciliation and Arbitration Service (ACAS) which had been established by the Labour Government elected in 1974. The legislation in question was part of the Social Contract between the Labour Party and the TUC, which was included in the Labour Party's election manifesto in February 1974,[4] having been 'discussed at length and agreed with the TUC and which must take its place as a central feature of the new economic policy of a Labour Government'.[5] Re-affirming its commitment in October 1974, the Labour Party made clear not only that the Social Contract 'between the Labour Government and the trade unions' was at 'the heart of the manifesto', but that

> [t]he Social Contract is no mere paper agreement approved by politicians and trade unions. It is not concerned solely or even primarily with wages. It covers the whole range of national policies. It is the agreed basis upon which the Labour Party and the trade unions define their common purpose.[6]

Key elements of the Social Contract included 'the fairer sharing of the nation's wealth', 'the restoration of voluntary collective bargaining', and a desire 'to make industry democratic – to develop joint control and action by management and workers across the whole range of industry, commerce and the public services'.[7]

By these proposals, trade unions would be brought into not only the government of industry but also into the government of the country, in a way that was to rub up against constitutional principle, notably the sovereignty of Parliament.[8] That said, the Grunwick dispute was also to raise the profile of the rule of law, another of the three great British constitutional principles,[9] at a time when coincidentally the latter was beginning to attract detailed academic interest about its scope and content.[10] There were, however, two rule of law debates taking place: one was the debate about the rule of law as a political doctrine as Tony Bradley

[4] Labour Party, *Let us Work Together – Labour's Way Out of the Crisis* (February 1974).
[5] ibid.
[6] Labour Party, *Britain Will Win with Labour* (October 1974).
[7] ibid. Proposals on industrial relations based on 'strong trade union organisation and widening the scope of collective bargaining' would involve 'new rights for workers', 'new rights to unions in collective bargaining, including new safeguards for peaceful picketing', and 'a key role for the new Conciliation and Arbitration Service in helping to get rid of low pay'. Notably in light of current debates, another concern was employment agencies and precarious workers: 'Measures will also be taken to tackle the evils created by private employment agencies and to deal with abuses of labour-only contracting.'
[8] This is an issue explored in KD Ewing, 'The Politics of the British Constitution' [2000] *PL* 405.
[9] The third (and often overlooked) for those who have forgotten their constitutional law being ministerial responsibility.
[10] Notably J Raz, 'The Rule of Law and its Virtue' (1977) 93 *LQR* 195.

referred to it,[11] a debate about whether it was a necessary feature of the rule of law that it should include protection for human rights.[12] That was not the principle concern in the Grunwick dispute, though important elements of it did emerge.[13] The rule of law debate in the Grunwick dispute was thus principally about something much more basic and perhaps even visceral, namely the scope and content of the rule of law as a principle of legality. This debate was becoming more urgent because of new forms of government emerging in the UK under the Social Contract, and new challenges to which constitutional principle would have to adapt if the latter were to succeed.

For some politicians the position was clear and unequivocal: 'The coercive combinations of the trade unions' had 'corroded the constitution': 'Gang warfare has taken over and challenges not only the rule of law, but democracy itself.'[14] Heady stuff, and not lightly to be dismissed. But Grunwick was not just about postal boycotts and mass picketing. Apart from questions about who was responsible for the breakdown of law and order, there were a number of other questions to emerge about the nature of the rule of law as a principle of legality, Grunwick revealing real tension between the rigid and formal demands of the liberal constitution on the one hand, and the more expansive and flexible (but no less principled) approach to the nature of law and its enforcement embraced by the social democratic constitution on the other. In exploring this tension in the pages that follow, section II is devoted to an account of the Grunwick dispute, followed in section III by an account of the *Grunwick* case. The lasting significance of the *Grunwick* case for labour law is addressed in section III, while section IV considers the broader constitutional implications of the Grunwick dispute of which, as already indicated, the former was a prominent part. The chapter concludes with some general reflections in section VI.

[11] ECS Wade and GG Phillips, *Constitutional and Administrative Law*, 9th edn by A W Bradley (London, Longman, 1977) ch 6.

[12] This is a debate that was taking place at the same time as the Grunwick dispute was live, and was considered at a Cabinet meeting in early 1977. The government was not in favour of strengthening this dimension of the rule of law: TNA, CAB 128/62, Cabinet Conclusions, 27 January 1977: 'Much of the pressure for human rights legislation came from right wing elements in society who saw it as a means of erecting a judicial barrier against the powers of Parliament and against social reform of the kind to which the Government was committed. The language of the European Convention was very imprecise and its interpretation would leave a wide degree of judicial discretion in determining politically sensitive issues. It was alleged by the proponents of human rights legislation that our existing law was in many respects inadequate to protect the rights of the individual; but if there were defects in the law, they could be remedied by specific legislation.' This is a position that would have been vindicated by some at the time by the decision in *Young, James and Webster v United Kingdom* (1981) 4 EHRR 38.

[13] Report of a Court of Inquiry under the Rt Hon Lord Justice Scarman OBE into a Dispute Between Grunwick Processing Laboratories Ltd and Members of the Association of Professional, Executive, Clerical and Computer Staff, Cmnd 6922, 1977 (hereafter Scarman Report or Scarman), paras 56–57.

[14] HC Deb, 30 June 1977, vol 934, col 568 (Ronald Bell).

II. THE GRUNWICK DISPUTE

A. The Strike and its Objectives

The dispute is said to have started on Friday 20 August 1976 when Devshi Bhudia was dismissed following a dispute with his supervisor.[15] Various sources claim that the action was premeditated, Mr Bhudia having already obtained a job elsewhere. In a separate spontaneous incident later that afternoon, Jayaben Desai and her son Sunil walked out following a dispute about the need to complete some jobs in order to catch the weekend post. Following a heated exchange, Mrs Desai 'asked for her cards and walked out',[16] to be met on the street by Mr Bhudia and some colleagues who were still milling around. On the following Monday, a number of others walked out on strike, with the numbers on strike rising eventually to 137 out of a total workforce of 490, the 137 said to include 91 full-time staff, the others being students. Also on the Monday, there was a 'violent scene' outside the workplace as the strikers sought to persuade those still working to join the strike.[17] An attempt was made by some of the strikers forcibly to enter the premises and windows were broken, the strikers dispersing after the police had been called.

None of the strikers at this stage was a union member, and in the week beginning 23 August contact was made with both APEX (which accepted the strikers into membership) and the Brent Trades Council (of which Jack Dromey was the secretary, and which together with APEX 'exercised great influence upon the strikers').[18] On 27 August, Len Gristey, the senior London organiser of APEX approached the company with a request for recognition and for a meeting to discuss a recognition and procedure agreement. Before receiving a reply from the company, APEX declared the strike official to enable those taking part to receive strike pay, this to take effect on 1 September. In the meantime, the company took legal advice and on 2 September it sent dismissal notices to all the strikers, writing subsequently to APEX indicating that it would 'not be recognising the union so long as there was no evidence that its staff wanted union representation',[19] making clear that the company would exclude the views of the strikers from further consideration on the ground that they were no longer employees. There was no meeting between the company and the union thereafter.

[15] The following account draws mainly from the Scarman Report (n 13), as well as P Elias, B Napier and P Wallington, *Labour Law: Cases and Materials* (London, Butterworths, 1980) 29–59 and J Rogaly, *Grunwick* (Harmondsworth, Penguin, 1977). The latter was published before the House of Lords decision, and the former shortly after the decision was reported. A rather different account of the origins of the dispute is to be found in *Grunwick Processing Laboratories Ltd v ACAS* [1978] AC 665 (HL).

[16] Scarman Report (n 13) para 14. For a fuller account of what was said, see B Bell and S Mahmood, 'What Did the 'Strikers in Saris' Achieve?' *BBC News* (16 November 2016).

[17] Scarman Report (n 13) para 15.

[18] ibid, para 19.

[19] ibid, para 24.

At this stage the union had two objectives: reinstatement of the strikers, and recognition for bargaining purposes. But faced with the employer's response, APEX felt that it had no alternative but to secure the support of the wider trade union movement which at the time 'it was perfectly entitled to do'.[20] In the meantime, and as the dispute entered this new phase, ACAS had offered to assist by way of conciliation, but four offers of assistance between 31 August and 30 September were declined by the company. Adopting a more formal approach, on 15 October APEX made a recognition application under section 11 of the Employment Protection Act 1975, by which a recognition issue could be referred to ACAS, which would then be required legally to conduct an inquiry under the statutory procedure and prepare a report, and if appropriate make a recommendation that the union should be recognised. However, there was a disagreement about which workers were to be included in the recognition application, the company resisting ACAS' demand to include the strikers, on the basis that they were no longer in its employment.

Until this latter disagreement could be resolved, the company refused to provide ACAS with access to the existing workforce, or details of their names and addresses so that they might be contacted. By 20 December, ACAS was not willing to wait any longer, taking the view that 'the interests of good industrial relations required that the recognition issue be resolved as expeditiously as was reasonably and properly practicable'.[21] ACAS proceeded thereafter without the assistance of the company, and sought the views of the strikers about the recognition issue, but not the views of the existing workforce. Before it issued its report, however, the decisions were announced in the unfair dismissal applications that had been brought by 59 of the strikers. On 2 March 1977, the industrial tribunal dismissed the claims for reinstatement or compensation, vindicating the legal advice received by the company that it would be protected from unfair dismissal liability if it dismissed all the strikers, even though it may have been prepared to countenance the return of some of them.[22]

Just over a week later (10 March), ACAS published its report recommending that the union should be recognised for weekly paid staff at its two establishments in Brent, north west London. Although ACAS regretted the lack of

[20] ibid, para 25. However, steps taken by postal workers to black Grunwick's mail were called off following the threat of prosecution. It had been established in a separate dispute involving the blacking of mail to South Africa that a postal boycott could be an offence under the Post Office Act 1953, s 58: *Gouriet v UPW* [1978] AC 435 (HL). The House of Lords decision in *Gouriet* was made on 27 July 1977 with obvious implications for the Grunwick dispute. See GS Morris, *Strikes in Essential Services* (London, Mansell, 1986) 18–19. In his Obituary of Jayaben Desai, Dromey (n 1) wrote that the 'decision of postmen at the local sorting office in Cricklewood to black the firm's mail almost won the dispute for the strikers', and that 'when blacking of the sorting office was called off', following the legal challenge 'defeat stared the dismayed strikers in the face'.

[21] ACAS, APEX and Grunwick Processing Laboratories Ltd, *ACAS Recognition Report No 19* (March 1977) para 19.

[22] Scarman Report (n 13) para 23.

cooperation by the company, it nevertheless felt obliged to proceed in light of the facts and opinions available to it:

> We have concluded from our inquiries that the union recruited a considerable number of the company's employees into membership at an early stage of the dispute and that a considerable number of these individuals had retained their union membership at the time of our opinion survey four months later. In our view it would be in the interests of good industrial relations for properly constituted collective bargaining arrangements to be established at the company.[23]

This was a bold position for ACAS to have taken, though it was based on the virtually unanimous views of about a third of the workers ACAS deemed to be relevant for the purposes of the application. Nevertheless, it was also one that was to be contested, with a writ being issued to challenge the recommendation on 5 April 1977.

B. Mass Picketing and Employer Resistance

It was not until 12 July 1977 that Lord Chief Justice Widgery issued his decision to reject the challenge on the ground that the legislation was to be read in such a way that ACAS was required to make inquiries of the workers to whom the issue relates, but only to the extent that was 'reasonably practicable to do so'.[24] This is what ACAS had done. That said, between the issuing of the writ on 5 April, and the decision on 12 July, matters were to take a darker turn, as the dispute entered another new phase. This was a phase in which the union sought to intensify the action by broadening the appeal to the wider trade union movement – seeking further assistance from the UPW by blacking Grunwick's mail, and inviting all trade unionists to join a mass picket of Grunwick's premises. This led to the Post Office closing the Cricklewood sorting office, 'thereby depriving a sizeable area of NW London of postal services for some time'.[25] But although following *Gouriet v UPW* the blacking was said to be illegal,[26] the Attorney General nevertheless refused consent to a prosecution.[27]

So far as the mass picketing is concerned, this had started on 13 June 1977 and continued for several weeks. The picketing was 'marked on occasions by scenes of violence which have shocked the nation', which it was said helped to

[23] *ACAS Recognition Report No 19* (n 21) para 25.

[24] '*Grunwick Processing Laboratories Ltd v ACAS*' *The Times* (13 July 1977).

[25] Scarman Report (n 13) para 37. On which, see *Harold Stephen & Co Ltd v Post Office* [1978] 1 All ER 939 (CA).

[26] For the Court of Appeal decision, see *Gouriet v UPW* [1977] 2 WLR 310 (CA); for the House of Lords decision, see *Gouriet* (n 20). The case concerned the postal boycott by Post Office staff of mail for South Africa, which raised questions of liability under the Post Office Act 1953, s 58.

[27] HC Deb, 30 June 1977, vol 934, cols 569–632. The Attorney General cited the Shawcross doctrine, whereby prosecutions should only be brought where it was in the public interest to do so. On the Shawcross doctrine, see n (99).

convince 'public opinion' that the country was watching an industrial dispute develop into unacceptable social strife'.[28] As subsequently acknowledged by Len Gristey, there have been 'very few strikes in this country which match the history of the Grunwick strike', and 'very few have had the examples of violence on the picket line which have existed during the course of this dispute'.[29] On the first day of the mass picket alone, it is claimed that up to 700 pickets attended, and that 84 people were arrested. The picketing was heavily policed throughout, with more police officers than pickets present on some days. There were allegations of violence on both sides,[30] with the deployment of the Special Patrol Group on the police side reflecting the emerging para-militarisation of the police at the time.[31]

The developing situation alarmed both the TUC and especially the government, occupying much of the time of two ministers. The first was the Home Secretary (Merlyn Rees) concerned about the public order situation, and the other was the Employment Secretary (Albert Booth) anxious for a settlement. But talks on 23 June 1977 and possibly thereafter between Booth and the Grunwick management led by Mr George Ward appeared to break down: 'all along Mr Ward was saying, in essence, that he would abide by what the law told him, and no more, while Mr Booth was saying that the law itself was not a sufficient mechanism for the maintenance of good industrial relations'.[32] In the same week, the Home Secretary chaired the first meeting of an ad hoc Cabinet Committee appointed to oversee the day-to-day handling of the dispute,[33] and also in the same week the Committee heard that 'the troubles outside Grunwick were giving the Metropolitan Police greater difficulty than any mass picket in their experience. It seemed to be getting out of hand'.[34] By the end of the week plans were set in train to establish a Court of Inquiry.

The picketing was widely criticised, including by Lord Denning, the Master of the Rolls, in a speech delivered on 28 June 1977.[35] Two days later (though not because of Lord Denning's intervention), Lord Scarman was appointed by Booth under the Industrial Courts Act 1919 to chair a Court of Inquiry to inquire into the dispute and to report. Lord Scarman was joined by Pat Lowry

[28] Scarman Report (n 13) para 38.

[29] Rogaly (n 15) 126.

[30] Roy Lewis described the policing as 'forceful' and 'uncompromising': R Lewis, 'Picketing' in R Lewis (ed), *Labour Law in Britain* (Oxford, Basil Blackwell, 1986) ch 7.

[31] See T Bunyan, *The History and Practice of the Political Police in Britain* (London, Quartet Books, 1977) 93–98. Other controversial policing events at this time in which the SPG was deployed include an anti-racism demonstration against the National Front on 23 April 1979, after which Blair Peach, an activist, died following a blow to the head.

[32] Rogaly (n 15) 107.

[33] ibid 97.

[34] ibid 104.

[35] ibid 128. Lord Denning referred to the 'intimidation and violence' which were 'contrary to the law of the land', and 'should be condemned by every responsible citizen'. Denning's speech was ventilated in the House of Commons two days later, providing ammunition for those politicians critical of the trade unions: HC Deb, 30 June 1977, vol 934, col 588 (Derek Walker-Smith).

(formerly Engineering Employers' Federation, by now British Leyland),[36] and Terry Parry (General Secretary of the Fire Brigades Union), the Court of Inquiry meeting for the first time on 5 July 1977. The mass picketing nevertheless continued, culminating in a mass demonstration on 11 July 1977, attended by an estimated 18,000 people.[37] According to the Home Secretary, by 14 July 1977, 377 people had been arrested and 243 police officers had been injured since 13 June 1977.[38] Following the event on 11 July 1977, the picketing was scaled back, the High Court deciding on the following day in favour of ACAS. On 29 July 1977, however, the High Court decision was reversed by the Court of Appeal led by Lord Denning who appears not to have been embarrassed by his public intervention in the dispute four weeks earlier.

ACAS decided immediately to appeal to the House of Lords. In the meantime, however, the Scarman report was published on 25 August 1977, taking a completely different view from the Court of Appeal on the question of recognition. Apart from recommending the reinstatement of the strikers, the Scarman Report also expressed the view that 'union representation, if properly encouraged and responsibly exercised, could in the future help the company as well as its employees'.[39] Grunwick responded in a long and powerful repudiation by saying that it would recognise APEX for 'the existing workforce' if 'the House of Lords overturns the judgment of the Court of Appeal', but that it would not 'under any circumstances' reinstate 'those who were very properly dismissed'.[40] The House of Lords upheld the Court of Appeal, and 'with the movement around the dispute wound down', there were 'no avenues left' for the strikers, who 'conceded defeat on 14 July 1978', after 'a second bitter winter on the picket line'.[41] In securing a notable victory, Grunwick had conducted itself in accordance with the law: it did no more and no less than the law required.

III. THE *GRUNWICK* CASE

A. Running with the Grain in the High Court

The importance of the *Grunwick* case to the Grunwick dispute is perhaps obvious, though defeat for ACAS would have implications extending beyond

[36] Lowry was to become chairman of ACAS in 1981. He was knighted in 1985. For a sympathetic obituary see G Goodman, 'Britain's Industrial Peacemaker' *The Guardian* (5 June 2001). Parry had been General Secretary of the FBU, and led them during a bitter national strike in 1977 and 1978. He had been made CBE in June 1977.

[37] Rogaly (n 15) 182

[38] HC Deb, 14 July 1977, vol 935, cols 759–60.

[39] Scarman Report (n 13) para 73.

[40] Grunwick Processing Laboratories, 'Statement in Response to Scarman Report' *The Times* (1 September 1977) (published as an appendix to Rogaly (n 15)). The company also made clear that it would not 'submit and give another hostage to an iniquitous tyranny'.

[41] Dromey (n 1). According to Elias, Napier and Wallington (n 15) 57 (writing virtually contemporaneously), ACAS 'resumed attempts to secure a conciliated settlement, or the co-operation of Grunwick in balloting the workforce', but 'failed in both'.

this single dispute, and potentially would deliver a fatal blow to the recognition legislation itself. The recognition procedure in the Employment Protection Act 1975 was the second such procedure, the first having been introduced by the Industrial Relations Act 1971, which had been repealed in 1974.[42] The procedure in the 1975 Act was designed to implement the recommendations of the Donovan Commission made eight years earlier, though it was to be barely more successful than the one it replaced.[43] Under the 1975 Act, a trade union could refer a recognition issue to ACAS, if unable to obtain recognition from an employer voluntarily. On receipt of a complaint, ACAS was required to examine the issue, consult all parties who it considered would be affected by the outcome of the reference, and make such inquiries as it thought fit. As pointed out by Lord Diplock in the House of Lords, 'this involves a threefold process, (1) examination, (2) consultation and (3) inquiry'.[44]

The *Grunwick* case was thus concerned with a different legality question from the law and order issues that at least superficially dominated the Grunwick dispute: public bodies must act within the scope of their statutory powers, the courts additionally suspicious of wide discretion and anxious to impose some limits.[45] But this in turn gave to the courts a wide discretion as to how to apply loose and evolving principles of judicial review to resolve any dispute before them. They could approach the matter by giving a wide and generous interpretation to the legislation conferring discretion on bodies such as ACAS; or they could adopt a narrow and 'legalistic' approach to hold such bodies under tight control, because of the perceived far-reaching consequences of the powers vested in them. Neither approach is demanded on any principled application of the rule of law; either is permissible, though the method chosen is obviously likely to affect the outcome of any particular case. This was clearly highlighted by the different approaches of the Lord Chief Justice on the one hand, and the Court of Appeal and subsequently the House of Lords on the other.

It is notable that the Lord Chief Justice started from the position that 'where a body such as ACAS was given such discretion as was contained in sections 12 and 14 [of the Employment Protection Act 1975], its conclusions could not be questioned by the courts unless it had misdirected itself'. And in order to show a misdirection, it would be necessary to show 'either (a) that no reasonable body

[42] See B Weekes, M Mellish, L Dickens and J Lloyd, *Industrial Relations and the Limits of Law* (Oxford, Basil Blackwell, 1975).

[43] See Royal Commission on Trade Unions and Employers' Associations, 1965–1968, Chairman Lord Donovan, Report, Cmnd 3623, 1968, the importance of which was highlighted by Lord Scarman in *UKAPE v ACAS* [1980] ICR 201 (HL).

[44] *Grunwick Processing Laboratories Ltd v ACAS* [1978] AC 655 (HL) 687. So far as the last of the third stage is concerned, Lord Diplock also pointed out that there was 'no requirement as to the scope or the nature of the inquiries which ACAS must undertake or as to the manner of conducting them' (ibid).

[45] See *Padfield v Minister of Agriculture, Fisheries and Food* [1968] AC 997 (HL). This reflects in part Dicey's conception of the rule of law which eschews 'wide discretionary authority on the part of the government', and presumably government agencies (albeit that empowered by legislation ACAS was nevertheless independent of government).

properly instructed could have reached the conclusion in question, or (b) that in reaching its conclusion the body took into account factors which were irrelevant or failed to take into account matters that were relevant', citing *Associated Provincial Picture Houses Ltd v Wednesbury Co*.[46] Although these remarks were made in the context of a preliminary point that proved to be unimportant, it nevertheless informed the way in which the Lord Chief Justice disposed of the two defining legal questions in the case: the first was whether ACAS was entitled to consult the strikers who had been dismissed, and the second was whether ACAS was entitled to proceed without having consulted the vast bulk of the workforce who had not joined the strike and who continued to work.

As to the first question, Lord Widgery was in no doubt that under the statutory definition of worker (in section 126 of the Employment Protection Act 1975), the dismissed strikers were workers, and that under sections 11–16 of the Employment Protection Act 1975, they were 'workers to whom the issue relates'. ACAS was thus entitled to ascertain their views, a position which the Court of Appeal by a majority accepted, as did the House of Lords unanimously. This seemed fairly straightforward. So was the answer to the second question. The ACAS report had had given a full account of the reasons for failing to seek the views of the non-striking workforce, and in the circumstances Lord Widgery 'did not see what else ACAS could do', also suggesting that Grunwick may have been misguided in failing to co-operate with ACAS. Had they handed over the information, ACAS would have attempted to discover the opinion of the two-thirds of the employees who stayed at work, noting that it was at least possible that the result would have favoured the company, 'perhaps heavily', the Lord Chief Justice referring earlier in his judgment to a MORI opinion poll commissioned by the company indicating resistance to unionisation.

As pointed out subsequently by Scarman, the company had thus done 'what ACAS had not been able to do',[47] the opinion poll revealing that 216 (86.4 per cent) 'want things left as they are'.[48] But the report was ignored by Lord Widgery because it had not been made available to ACAS, and could not have affected the legality of its decision. So having decided not to wait any longer for Grunwick to deliver the lists, ACAS then had a duty to look for other ways of testing worker opinion. According to the ACAS report, it could not do so without the company's co-operation, and it was not for Lord Widgery to 'ventilate his own ideas of what was possible', or 'to criticise ACAS for not attempting to have a mass meeting or the like'. Notably, nor did the Lord Chief Justice wish to criticise the company management who 'though occasionally misguided', had shown great determination in the face of severe problems'. It was at this point that Lord Widgery agreed with ACAS' submission that the obligation to canvass opinion under the 1975 Act was qualified by such words as 'so far as reasonably practicable'.

[46] *Associated Provincial Picture Houses Ltd v Wednesbury Co* [1948] 1 KB 223 (CA).
[47] Scarman Report (n 13) para 34.
[48] ibid.

B. Running against the Grain in the Court of Appeal and House of Lords

Lord Widgery is of course infamous for other reasons,[49] which perhaps makes his purposive and extremely constructive judgment all the more surprising. This was an interpretive approach and an outcome that might be said to run with the grain of the emerging new constitutional order, even if it is an order with which the Lord Chief Justice might be presumed not to have supported. As such it nevertheless contrasted sharply with the narrow and 'legalistic' approach of the Court of Appeal and the House of Lords,[50] with Lord Denning in the Court of Appeal in particular standing firm in protection of the old constitutional order.[51] So far as the Court of Appeal decision on 29 July 1977 is concerned, Lord Denning was moved by the claim that the legislation 'makes great powers available to trade unions', enabling them to 'bring immense pressure on an employer who does not wish to recognize a trade union'.[52] Not only that: 'The union can go to ACAS and get a recommendation for recognition and thence to the [CAC] and get an award', by means of which 'there can be inserted in every man's contract terms and conditions to which neither he nor his employers have agreed'.[53]

Lord Denning was to continue by saying that 'such an interference of individual liberty could hardly be tolerated in a free society unless there were safeguards against abuse', with the result that the legislation was to be construed in favour of individuals and not in favour of the union in this case.[54] Although the House of Lords was not as explicit,[55] the same approach is to be detected for the same reasons, Lord Diplock highlighting the importance and impact of a recognition award, with a trade union claiming the power to act on behalf of employees 'upon a whole range of matters affecting their employment', and thus a large

[49] See C Gearty, 'The Cost of Human Rights: English Judges and the Northern Irish Troubles' (1994) 47 *Current Legal Problems* 19.

[50] 'Legalism' is charged by Simpson: RC Simpson, 'Judicial Control of ACAS' (1979) 8 *ILJ* 69, which also highlights the 'individualistic' approach. Also, R Lewis and B Simpson, *Striking a Balance? – Employment Law after the 1980 Act* (Oxford, Martin Robertson, 1981) 142. See R Townsend-Smith, 'Trade Union Recognition Legislation – Britain and America Compared' (1981) 1 *Legal Studies* 190.

[51] Lord Denning was joined by Browne and Geoffrey Lane LJJ, who each gave concurring judgments.

[52] *Grunwick* (n 44) 661.

[53] ibid. Under the Employment Protection Act 1975, s 16, the remedy for a failure to comply with an ACAS recognition recommendation was the variation of contractual terms by the CAC, a body created by the 1975 Act. Lord Denning cited strong criticism of this procedure by Browne Wilkinson J in *Powley v ACAS* [1978] ICR 123 (Ch), which Lord Diplock repudiated in the House of Lords, though Lord Salmon agreed. However, this was not a novel power, which had previously been exercised by a CAC predecessor body, the Industrial Disputes Tribunal having similar powers under the Industrial Disputes Order 1951. A similar power was also created to enforce the disclosure of information obligations introduced by the Employment Protection Act 1975, ss 17–21, and is still with us, though never used to my knowledge. Wages Councils effectively had a similar power.

[54] *Grunwick* (n 44) 661.

[55] The leading speech was delivered by Lord Diplock, with whom Lords Edmund Davies and Fraser concurred. Lords Salmon and Keith delivered concurring speeches.

part of their daily lives'.[56] True, in the House of Lords speeches there was some moderation not only of language, but also of the intensity of judicial scrutiny to which ACAS was to be subjected. Nevertheless, the House of Lords was just as clear as the Court of Appeal on the central question whether those workers who were still working should have been consulted, falling back on the express terms of section 14 of the Employment Protection Act 1975: ACAS 'shall ascertain the opinion of workers to whom the issue relates by any means it thinks fit'.

It begins with the use of 'shall': according to Lord Diplock, 'this expression appearing in a statute is used as a term of art to impose a duty to do what is prescribed, not a discretion to do it or not according to whether it is reasonably practicable to do it, or to do something like it instead'.[57] This disposed of the Widgery point, which according to Lord Diplock did 'too great violence to the express words', thereby raising questions about the views of which workers had to be ascertained.[58] Here Lord Diplock pulled back from Lord Denning's position which appeared to insist that all workers had to be involved, to a position which required ACAS to seek the views more broadly of the workforce as a whole, and where there was a conflict of opinion, to take into account the views held by different groups of workers.[59] So far as the means adopted to ascertain the views of these workers was concerned, it was for ACAS not the courts to decide the most convenient way for carrying out the duty, whether it be by ballot, meetings, interviews, inference, or otherwise, or by a combination of all or some of these.[60]

It is also for ACAS to decide how much weight ought to be given to the views of workers when making its recommendation. However, what ACAS was not permitted to do was to 'make *any* recommendation for recognition so long as it [remained] in ignorance of the opinions held by the majority of the workforce or of what may be conflicting opinions held by any group among them of significant size'.[61] Notably, Lord Diplock did not insist that the views of those crossing the picket lines would necessarily have been decisive: but they did have to be considered. He suggested that it had been possible for ACAS to infer from the conduct of those workers in continuing to run the gauntlet of the picketing that the opinions of most of them would be adverse to being represented by APEX.[62] Rather implausibly, however, he also suggested that if ACAS

> had thought fit to draw that inference but had nevertheless recommended APEX for recognition despite the adverse opinion of a majority of workers to whom the recognition issue relates, and had given the reasons for such recommendation it may be that the High Court would have had no jurisdiction to interfere.[63]

[56] *Grunwick* (n 44) 691.
[57] ibid 690.
[58] ibid 692.
[59] ibid.
[60] ibid 693.
[61] ibid 693–94 (Lord Diplock).
[62] ibid 694.
[63] ibid.

According to Lord Diplock any such decision would have been within the wide discretion conferred by ACAS unless in light of the reasons given it could be attacked on one of the *Wednesbury* grounds. This left finally the argument that the company should not be allowed to benefit from its failure to co-operate as a result of which ACAS had been unable to perform its duty. But reverting to a very formal legalistic position, Lord Diplock pointed out that 'Grunwick have done nothing unlawful'. Under the 1975 Act, the employer was under no duty to co-operate with ACAS, no matter how 'sensible' it may have been to do so. The only obligation on the company under the Act was to notify the results of a recognition ballot to the workforce: any additional obligation would require fresh legislation.[64] Resisting the claim that the court should refuse to grant a remedy despite the ultra vires nature of the report, Lord Diplock did so on the ground that it would be open to any of the workers affected by the recommendation to seek a remedy to annul the report. In that case 'there would be no possible ground' for a court 'to exercise a discretion to refuse it'.[65]

IV. THE LEGACY OF THE *GRUNWICK* CASE AND LABOUR LAW

A. Repeal of the Employment Protection Act 1975, sections 11–16

Grunwick was one of a number of judicial decisions within a few years of the 1975 Act's implementation that disarmed ACAS, contributing to a feeling that they (ACAS) would be better off without the statutory procedure. This is evident in the well-known letter the Service's then Chairman (Jim Mortimer) wrote to the new Secretary of State for Employment in the Thatcher Government (Jim Prior) in September 1979, asserting that 'in light of the increasing difficulties which [ACAS] is encountering it cannot satisfactorily operate the statutory recognition procedures as they stand'.[66] This dramatic claim was informed not only by the *Grunwick* decision, though it was part of it. According to Mr Mortimer:

> The *Grunwick* case established that the Service has a mandatory duty to ascertain the opinion of workers to whom a recognition issue relates. The statute provides for no discretion, so that even where an employer or a union refuses co-operation, the Service is left with a duty it cannot perform. The procedures are therefore statutorily

[64] Employment Protection Act 1975, s 14(6).

[65] *Grunwick* (n 44) 695.

[66] Jim Mortimer to James Prior, 29 June 1979, published as an appendix to the Department of Employment, Working Paper on the Trade Union Recognition Provisions of the Employment Protection Act 1975 [nd] (hereinafter 'Mortimer to Prior'). For discussion of the letter, see P Davies and M Freedland, *Labour Law Text and Materials*, 2nd edn, (London, Weidenfeld and Nicolson, 1984) 202–04. Note that in March 1977, Mr Prior had urged Grunwick to accept the ACAS recommendation. Some of his Conservative colleagues – notably Sir Keith Joseph six months later – took a different view (Rogaly (n 15) 78).

> binding on ACAS whilst leaving employers and unions free to cooperate with the Service on a voluntary basis. In some cases this has left ACAS being unable to report under section 12 of the Act.[67]

In relation to the last point, Mr Mortimer referred to the *Grunwick* case, but notably to only one other example (*Michelin*). According to Davies and Freedland, however, 'by the end of 1979 the Service estimated that in over one quarter of the cases then being handled full cooperation was not forthcoming'.[68]

Also notably, Mr Mortimer did not call for the legislation to be amended to deal with the *Grunwick* problem, as had been proposed in a number of Private Member's Bills.[69] One of the Bills would have allowed ACAS to make an award without ascertaining the views of workers whose details were withheld by the employer, and would have entrenched the Widgery CJ test that ACAS was required to do only that which was reasonably practicable. But the moment for that had passed: *Grunwick* was only part of the problem of judicial interference which had provoked the ACAS Council, while there was also a feeling that problems were embedded in the legislation itself, with Mr Mortimer claiming that some of the duties imposed on ACAS by the 1975 Act generally were 'not necessarily compatible with its duty to promote the improvement of industrial relations'.[70] He gave the example of the duty 'to pursue and complete any reference made to it in respect of any group of workers that a trade union cares to define', with which ACAS 'has no discretion not to proceed however much it believes its intervention would be harmful'.[71]

Here Mr Mortimer cited 'competitive claims by unions which the Act appears to have encouraged'.[72] More explicitly, he complained that ACAS' 'ability to exercise its own judgments in recognition matters has always been circumscribed by the legislation', with its discretion 'further limited by the decisions of the courts which have made it progressively more difficult for the Council to exercise its industrial relations judgment in reaching decisions on recognition issues'.[73]

[67] Mortimer to Prior (n 66) 3.

[68] O Kahn Freund, *Labour and the Law* (3rd edn by P Davies and M Freedland, London, Stevens, 1983) 100. They also wrote that in 11 cases including *Grunwick*, ACAS was unable to ascertain the opinions of the affected workers and so were unable to make a recommendation (ibid). See also L Dickens and G Bain, 'A Duty to Bargain? Union Recognition and Information Disclosure' in R Lewis (ed), *Labour Law in Britain* (Oxford, Basil Blackwell, 1986) 88.

[69] On the Private Members' Bills, see Elias, Napier and Wallington (n 15) 57.

[70] Mortimer to Prior (n 66) 3. See also W McCarthy, *Freedom at Work: Towards the Reform of Tory Employment Laws* (London, Fabian Society, 1985) 28–29, where there is a strong criticism of the weaknesses of the Employment Protection Act 1975, ss 11–16. This is interesting and begs the question about who was advising the people who drafted the legislation, given that ACAS had been formed by prerogative in 1974 in advance of the 1975 Act and might have been expected to have been consulted about the procedures.

[71] Mortimer to Prior (n 66) 3.

[72] ibid.

[73] ibid 5. Davies and Freedland (n 66) 204 point to an element of contradiction in Mr Mortimer's letter: the courts had restricted ACAS' discretion, but Parliament had not done enough to define its powers.

This was not to say that ACAS proposed to give up on union recognition disputes, with the strong implication that sections 11–16 of the 1975 Act were useless, accompanied by an equally strong implication that recognition disputes would be better dealt with under the general powers of ACAS. Crucially, these were underpinned by a statutory duty on the part of ACAS to promote collective bargaining,[74] a duty that was unconstrained in the manner of sections 11–16, and which appeared to allow the Service to exercise greater flexibility in carrying out its duties, this flexibility being required if ACAS was to 'function properly'.[75]

That apart, the data provided by Mr Mortimer suggested that ACAS thought the statutory procedure was more trouble than it was worth. True, eighty per cent of applications under the statutory procedure led to a conciliated outcome, without the need for a report issued under section 12 of the Employment Protection Act 1975. However, 'considerably more recognition issues were referred to the Service' under the general powers of ACAS in section 2 of the Employment Protection Act 1975. In just over three years since the statutory recognition scheme was introduced, only 10,000 workers obtained the benefits of recognition as a result of the recognition procedure going its full distance.[76] To what seems like a clear request – or in the words of Wedderburn 'an invitation' – from ACAS to repeal the offending provisions of the 1975 Act,[77] the government responded in a Working Paper to express its 'considerable concern' about the impact of the recognition procedure on the impartiality of ACAS, and to accept that there is now 'an urgent need' for the procedures to be changed 'in view of the problems encountered in their operation'.[78] This was not of course to imply any criticism of the courts for having helped to create the mess.[79]

The Working Paper was a prelude to repeal, with the Employment Act 1980 providing a vehicle for this purpose, the government accepting that 'it would be better to rely on the ability of ACAS to help settle recognition disputes through the provision of voluntary conciliation and advice, as happens in most cases at present'.[80] The repeal of the 1975 Act's recognition provisions was not due only to the *Grunwick* decision, but it is clear that the decision contributed to ACAS' disquiet about the legal regime, and its preference to rely on its general powers with a duty to promote collective bargaining.[81] The latter plan was to be dashed,

[74] Employment Protection Act 1975, s 1(2).

[75] Mortimer to Prior (n 66) 2.

[76] ibid 1.

[77] Lord Wedderburn, 'Otto Kahn Freund and British Labour Law' in Lord Wedderburn, R Lewis and J Clark (eds), *Labour Law and Industrial Relations: Building on Kahn-Freund* (Oxford, Oxford University Press, 1983) 187.

[78] Department of Employment (n 66) 3.

[79] ibid.

[80] ibid.

[81] As pointed out by Davies and Freedland (n 66) 204, by the time the government had committed itself to remove rather than repeal the Employment Protection Act 1975, ss 11–16, the House of Lords had 'considerably relaxed the degree of judicial scrutiny to which ACAS was subject in recognition cases'. See *UKAPE v ACAS* (n 43); *EMA v ACAS* [1980] ICR 215 (HL). Along with *Grunwick*,

however, with the general duty later to be removed by the Major Government, in a new chapter of de-unionisation with which any such statutory obligation to promote collective bargaining was incompatible.[82] To the disappointment of trade unions, that duty has never been restored, though it is not clear that it would now be welcome by ACAS. The New Labour Government chose instead to introduce what was to be a third attempt at a recognition procedure, albeit one which was to be radically different from either of those which preceded it.

B. A New Legal Architecture – Schedule A1 of the Trade Union Labour Relations (Consolidation) Act 1992

The passing of the 1975 recognition procedure appears to have been largely unlamented by trade unions,[83] and indeed Wedderburn was to ask controversially: 'Did the history of this interventionist measure teach unions that they should rely upon their own strength and mistrust .... even the friendliest governments bearing such gifts?'[84] We now know that the answer is no: history was to teach a different lesson, confounding the suggestion that trade unions could operate effectively without the support of the State. Within ten years of the *Grunwick* decision, collective bargaining coverage was in freefall, and what was left of trade union industrial power was gradually being eroded by legislation. In that context, trade union 'strength' supported at best by ACAS' general powers were evidently not enough to deal with the employer who 'faced with clear workforce support for recognition' can nevertheless 'persist in denying effective representation and bargaining rights'.[85] Cue the TUC-led campaign launched in 1991 for a new and differently designed statutory recognition procedure,[86] a campaign which would eventually bear fruit in the Employment Relations Act 1999, introducing what is now the Trade Union Labour Relations (Consolidation) Act 1992 ('TULRCA 1992'), Schedule A1.[87]

both of these cases informed the content of Mr Mortimer's response. See also Lewis and Simpson (n 50) 143–47, highlighting the post *Grunwick* report role of Lord Scarman in these later two House of Lords decisions.

[82] Trade Union Reform and Employment Rights Act 1993, s 43, amending TULRCA 1992, s 209.

[83] The TUC 'raised little if any resistance' to the repeal of the Employment Protection Act 1975, ss 11–16 (Lewis and Simpson (n 50) 145).

[84] Lord Wedderburn (n 77) 187.

[85] TUC, *Trade Union Recognition – A TUC Consultative Document* (1991) 6.

[86] For the origins of the campaign, see TUC, *Employment Policy and Organisation Committee, Trade Union Recognition* (EPOC 3/1, 16 January 1991). See also TUC, *Trade Union Recognition – A TUC Consultative Document* (EPOC 3/1, 16 January 1991); subsequently TUC, *Representation at Work: A TUC Consultative Report* (1995); and TUC, *Your Voice at Work: TUC Proposals for Rights to Representation at Work* (1995). See also KD Ewing, 'Trade Union Recognition – A Framework for Discussion' (1990) 19 *ILJ* 209.

[87] For a critique, see T Novitz, 'A Revised Role for Trade Unions as Designed by New Labour: The Representation Pyramid and "Partnership"' (2002) 29 *JLS* 487.

At one level, the approach adopted by the New Labour Government has been vindicated by events: the recognition procedure introduced in 2000 has survived for 22 years at the time of writing, in contrast to the 1971 Act procedure which lasted for just over two years, and the 1975 Act procedure which lasted for just over four years. That said, the survival of the 1999 Act's procedure may be a symptom of its relative ineffectiveness.[88] New Labour rejected the idea that general powers underpinned by a focussed duty to promote collective bargaining is to be preferred to a specific power to facilitate recognition with a circumscribed discretion. In doing so it did nevertheless learn from the experience of the 1975 recognition procedure, which was to minimise the scope for judicial review by addressing the problem identified by Jim Mortimer of operating statutory procedures 'without criteria'. Although not eliminating the need for discretionary decision-making at critical stages, the new statutory procedure greatly circumscribes that discretion and contains 'criteria' in abundance in its 172 paragraphs.[89]

The influence of *Grunwick* is to be seen in other aspects of the existing procedure. Not only is discretion displaced to a large extent by rules, the administration of the legislation was given to the CAC, a quasi-judicial body, chaired by a High Court judge.[90] This too may have protected the procedure from the initially intense judicial review ACAS faced in the 1970s, despite the continued expansion of judicial review since then with the procedural reforms to Order 53 in 1979, and the introduction of the Human Rights Act 1998. The influence of *Grunwick* is to be seen further in the substance of the law, particularly in the steps taken affirmatively to answer the question posed by Davies and Freedland, who asked whether it was not 'naïve to draft recognition legislation on an assumption of goodwill?'[91] Whether the steps taken in the new procedure are sufficient to address the problem of employer hostility is of course another question, and it is arguable that if the Widgery line in *Grunwick* had held, it would have produced a better outcome than the currently under-used statutory penalties for non-cooperation, by putting pressure on employers indirectly to comply.

[88] On which see A Bogg, 'The Death of Statutory Union Recognition in the United Kingdom' (2012) 54 *JIR* 59.

[89] See DTI, *Fairness at Work* (Cm 3968, 1998) para 4.13: 'it is vital that a clear framework and process are established governing decisions on trade recognition'. Contrast the six sections of the Employment Protection Act 1975.

[90] See *R (BBC) v CAC* [2003] EWHC 1375 (Admin), [2003] ICR 1542. And although it is not an invariable rule that the High Court will not interfere, there is a general impatience with some of the challenges: *R (Cable & Wireless Services UK Ltd) v CAC* [2018] EWHC 115 (Admin), [2018] QB 1086. That said, judicial acceptance is no guarantee of legislative success: the autonomy of the CAC takes place in the context of a very different political climate and a very different legal framework.

[91] P Davies and M Freedland, *Labour Legislation and Public Policy* (Oxford, Oxford University Press, 1993), 390.

Nevertheless, paragraph 26 of the procedure introduced by the Employment Relations Act 1999 imposes a duty on the employer 'to co-operate generally, in connection with the ballot, with the union (or unions) and the person appointed to conduct the ballot'. It also imposes a duty on the employer 'to give to the union (or unions) such access to the workers constituting the bargaining unit as is reasonable to enable the union (or unions) to inform the workers of the object of the ballot and to seek their support and their opinions on the issues involved'.[92] And crucially, paragraph 26 imposes the further duty on the employer to provide the CAC with the names and addresses of the workers in the proposed bargaining unit, so that the latter can send information on behalf of the union to the workers concerned, and presumably also to ensure that the ballot is properly conducted in the sense that all those entitled to vote have an opportunity to do so.[93] Failure to comply with these duties on the part of the employer may in principle lead to the CAC making a declaration that the union is recognised for the purposes of collective bargaining.[94]

It is tempting to speculate what would have happened at Grunwick if a regime of this kind had been in place then, underpinned at the same time by the now repealed duty of ACAS to promote collective bargaining. Presumably the strikers would have counted as workers to get the claim off the ground, meeting the ten per cent admissibility threshold. There may then have been a dispute about the bargaining unit which inevitably would have included both the strikers and the non strikers, though whether it would have included everyone is impossible to say.[95] APEX was unlikely to have had majority membership so that a ballot would have been required, and may well also have been required in the interests of good industrial relations even if the union did have majority membership.[96] It would, however, have had access to the workers on the premises, which may well have been difficult for the company to contemplate in view of its belief that those currently working were not sympathetic to the union. Is it likely nevertheless that under a different legal regime, the outcome would have been the same?

V. THE LEGACY OF THE GRUNWICK DISPUTE AND CONSTITUTIONAL LAW

A. The Rule of Law

Although Grunwick was a trade dispute and is best remembered by labour lawyers, it was a dispute which produced some important constitutional insights,

[92] TULRCA 1992, Sch A1, para 26(3).
[93] ibid, para 26(4).
[94] ibid, para 27.
[95] The union was seeking recognition only for 'certain grades of weekly paid staff in the company': Scarman Report (n 13) para 25. For further detail, see *ACAS Recognition Report No 19* (n 21) para 26.
[96] TULRCA 1992, Sch A1, para 22(4)(a).

particularly in relation to the rule of law. In his masterly analysis of the rule of law as the Grunwick dispute was brewing, Tony Bradley wrote about it as a 'buttress of the democratic principle'.[97] This, however, begs questions about the nature of democracy and whether the substance of the rule of law must adapt to the nature of the democracy in question. There is a sense in the debates taking place in the heat of the Grunwick dispute that if it was to succeed, the Social Contract would require a less formal approach to legality than the liberal constitution would permit. The rule of law was used as a stick with which to beat the union, ACAS, and the government, mainly in relation to the postal boycott and the mass picketing.[98] But as the government pointed out, the rule of law does not require the law always to be enforced,[99] and as Scarman pointed out, there were more subtle rule of law issues at stake, and more subtle ways of looking at (and enriching) the rule of law as a constitutional principle.

Scarman's approach to the rule of law is to be seen in his conceptualisation of the dispute in human rights terms, an extraordinary initiative for its time, even if Scarman himself was a human rights modernist with strong (but mixed) civil liberties credentials.[100] The section of his report headed 'The Legal Aspect' begins disarmingly with the claim that had rarely if ever been made before that 'in the field of industrial relations the law has to effect a reconciliation and adjustment of a number of fundamental human rights and basic freedoms'.[101] The starting point was thus not the contract of employment, or the liberty of the individual not to have his or her contractual terms varied by a state agency, Scarman drawing attention first to the rights associated with the position of the company as they are set out in the European Convention on Human Rights (ECHR), First Protocol, Article 1 (the right to conduct a legitimate business);[102] the Universal Declaration of Human Rights (UDHR), Article 24 (the right not to join a union); and the Universal Declaration of Human Rights, Article 23 (the right to free choice of employment).[103]

[97] Wade and Phillips (n 11) ch 6.

[98] See HC Deb, 30 June 1977, vol 934, col 568.

[99] ibid, cols 683–84, citing extensively from Shawcross whose statement is at HC Deb, 29 January 1951, vol 483, cols 683–84. On 29 January 1951, the *Daily Telegraph* asked rhetorically in response to strikes alleged to be unlawful whether it was 'not in fact a basic principle of the rule of law that the operation of the law is automatic (except when the law is specifically permissive and not mandatory) where the offence is known or suspected? Is not the arbitrary implementation of the law just as offensive to the elementary motion of justice as an arbitrary law?' Shawcross replied that 'the true doctrine is that it is the duty of an Attorney-General, in deciding whether or not to authorise the prosecution, to acquaint himself with all the relevant facts, including, for instance, the effect which the prosecution, successful or unsuccessful as the case may be, would have upon public morale and order, and with any other considerations affecting public policy' (HC Deb, 29 January 1951, vol 483, col 683). See now *R (Corner House Research) v Director of Serious Fraud Office* [2008] UKHL 60, [2009] 1 AC 756.

[100] See L Scarman, *English Law – The New Dimension* (London, Stevens, 1975). But see *BBC v Hearn* [1977] ICR 685 (CA).

[101] Scarman Report (n 13) para 56.

[102] There is no such right in the First Protocol of Article 1.

[103] Scarman Report (n 13) para 56.

But Scarman also identified those rights associated with the position of the union, these being the right to freedom of association (ECHR, Article 11, and UDHR, Articles 20 and 24) (but notably not the right to strike); freedom of peaceful assembly including peaceful picketing (ECHR, Article 11, and UDHR, Article 20); and the right to just and favourable conditions of work (UDHR, Article 23, and European Social Charter 1961).[104] The reference to the Social Charter may have been its first ever judicial acknowledgement in the UK, at least in a formal setting such as a Court of Inquiry.[105] The legal framework was thus set in terms of international treaties, none of which had been incorporated into domestic law. It would be another 30 years before a senior British judge would formally acknowledge that the rule of law insisted on compliance with international law, and then in the very different context of the Iraq war.[106] But having set the scene in this way, Scarman proceeded to explain how the 'English (sic) reconciliation of these rights and freedoms has been traditionally sought through voluntary collective bargaining',[107] now supported by legislation.

The legislation in question was the Labour Government's TULRA 1974 and the Employment Protection Act 1975, 'which have themselves to be interpreted in the context of the common law – the backcloth of English law'.[108] However, in thus elevating the discussion to the high plains of international law, the parties in this dispute were starting as equals, with neither subordinate to the other, as was the case at common law. The rule of law thus enriched substantively, Scarman turned in general terms to the obligations of the parties under the law:

> The policy of the law is to exclude trade disputes – or industrial disputes, as they are more familiarly known – from judicial review by the courts, while leaving to individual workers a recourse to the courts (ie, industrial tribunals) to pursue certain individual grievances. There is substituted for judicial review of trade disputes an advisory, conciliation and arbitration process under the guidance of ACAS. The sanctions of the law (such as they are) are indirect and not those associated with the execution or enforcement of a judgment delivered by a court of law. An inevitable consequence of the system is that, where the process fails to secure agreement, industrial action is the one weapon left to resolve the dispute. Industrial action is a form of

[104] ibid, para 57. ECHR, Art 11 was later invoked by Lord Denning in *UKAPE v ACAS* [1979] ICR 303 (CA) to justify further restraints on ACAS' discretion, but his interpretation of the Convention was rejected by Lord Scarman in the appeal: *UKAPE v ACAS* (n 43). Lord Denning's position would no doubt have vindicated the position of the ECHR sceptics at the Cabinet meeting on 27 January 1977, see n 12 above.

[105] Indeed, it had been used by the European Court of Human Rights to constrain rather than expand Convention rights (*National Union of Belgian Police v Belgium* (1979–80) 1 EHRR 578). But that was to change: see *Wilson v United Kingdom* (2002) 35 EHRR 20 (on which see ch 10 in this volume); *Demir and Baycara v Turkey* (2009) 48 EHRR 54, where *National Union of Belgian Police* was formally overruled.

[106] Lord Bingham, 'The Rule of Law' [2007] 66 *CLJ* 67.

[107] Scarman Report (n 13) para 58

[108] ibid. For a nice analysis of the common law position at the time, see *RMT v Serco Ltd* [2011] EWCA Civ 226, [2011] ICR 848, para 9 (Elias LJ).

> organised self-help – eg, the lock-out, the strike, 'blacking', and the picket. And there is always a risk that self-help, if not coupled with self-restraint may end in violence. English law, if it is to work, requires of parties to an industrial dispute a modicum of self-restraint in the pursuit of their rights. Men must act reasonably within the law. The British tradition of compromise is implicit in the modern English law governing industrial relations.[109]

And by the same token: 'The efficacy of such a law depends upon goodwill. If men act unreasonably, by which we mean in obedience to the letter but not the spirit of the law, it will not work. It does not, however, follow that judicial review of trade disputes would be an effective substitute: for, whatever the sanctions imposed by law, its efficacy depends on the consent of the people.'[110] So here we have a re-conceptualisation of the rule of law, defined to mean not acting within the law, but: (i) acting reasonably within the law; (ii) acting reasonably in accordance with the spirit and policy of the law; and (as will be discussed) (iii) acting within the norms of extra-legal practices and procedures. This might perhaps be defined as a contextualised social democratic conception of the rule of law in contrast to the more de-contextualised liberal conception relied on by Grunwick and its supporters. But it is the approach perhaps unwittingly stumbled upon by Albert Booth when in responding to criticism of ACAS in the House of Commons debate on 30 June 1977 he said:

> In the debate there have been many references to the rule of law. I put it to the House that the rule of law is to be respected as much when it depends upon consent as when it is backed by criminal sanctions, and that for people to refuse to co-operate with bodies established under the law, going about their business under the law, is in a very real sense to show a contempt for the law.[111]

B. The Rule of Law Applied

A sense of what the foregoing means in practice is to be seen in Scarman's assessment of the company's attitudes to trade unionism. Although he accepted that the company recognised the right of every employee to join a union, Scarman was 'sure' that it 'does all that it can to persuade employees that they are better placed without a union'.[112] Although there was 'nothing unlawful in the company's attitude towards unionisation', Scarman did question whether 'it remains today reasonable'.[113] And in relation to the dismissal of strikers: 'Though within

[109] Scarman Report (n 13) para 58.
[110] ibid, para 72.
[111] HC Deb, 30 June 1977, vol 934, col 629 (Albert Booth, Secretary of State for Employment).
[112] Scarman Report (n 13) para 21. Compare Bell and Mahmood (n 16): 'Grunwick refused to recognize they had joined a union and refused to give them permission to do so').
[113] Lord Scarman (n 13) para 21. Indeed, this was said to be the 'fundamental question' facing the Court of Inquiry (ibid).

their rights in refusing reinstatement and in rejecting the means available of attempting a settlement of the dispute at that stage, the company, in our view, acted unreasonably, and inconsistently with the policy of the law.'[114] According to Scarman it was 'extremely rare in practice' for strikers to be dismissed', while 'by their own admission in evidence, [the company] would have been willing to take some of the strikers back', but refused to do so to avoid facing unfair dismissal proceedings by the others in which the company 'would have to show in each case that the dismissal was unfair'.[115]

On the basis of his 'analysis of the underlying causes of the strike', Scarman thought it was neither 'unfair no[r] unreasonable that a dismissed employee should have his individual case considered by a court or tribunal on its merits'.[116] Scarman continued to be guided by industrial relations practice rather than formal legality, repeating that 'in the conduct of industrial relations in this country, and no matter what the legalities are, it is the exception rather than the rule for employees who are dismissed during the course of a strike not to be re-engaged after the dispute is ended'.[117] With that in mind Scarman recommended that the company should offer to re-employ those strikers who wanted to return, and where this was not practicable because there were no vacancies, for those concerned to be made an ex gratia payment commensurate with the length of service of the individuals concerned.[118] Notable too are the consequences of failing to comply with Scarman's broader conception of the rule of law. By shielding behind the letter of the law, the company had to 'accept a measure of responsibility for prolonging, deepening, and widening the dispute'.[119]

Here Scarman was not questioning the judgment or wisdom of the company as Lords Widgery and Diplock had done; rather, he appeared to be allocating blame, despite the company having acted lawfully throughout. As a result of Grunwick's 'rejection of the advisory and conciliation processes provided by the law for the resolution of disputes',[120] the union had no option but to broaden the dispute to the wider trade union movement. Needless to say, this was a vision and an approach unequivocally repudiated by the company, which in its response to Scarman a few weeks later began by referencing what it saw as the 'philosophy that lies behind the report':

> It is not a philosophy based on malice, not upon a desire to sanctify an injustice. Put baldly, it is the philosophy of the corporate state. The report does not of course claim that English law has yet benefitted from the legislation needed to sustain a corporate state and that Grunwick are law breakers for defying such enactments.

[114] ibid, para 60.
[115] ibid, para 59.
[116] ibid.
[117] ibid, para 73.
[118] ibid.
[119] ibid, para 61.
[120] ibid.

> On the contrary, the report makes constant reference to Grunwick's scrupulous observance of the law and praises for the Company for this. But the praise is qualified by an occasional reference to the 'letter of the law', and there are several references to the 'spirit of the law', or even more vaguely to the 'policy of the law'. Grunwick is held to have behaved according to the 'letter of the law', but somehow fallen short of apprehending the niceties of the policy of the law, as the Government and powerful vested interests would wish that policy to be.[121]

Grunwick's response continued in an equally forthright manner:

> But when this 'policy of the law' is examined, it turns out to have nothing to do with law of any description and everything to do with conciliating the trade unions. It is the trade unions themselves who have most strenuously insisted that as little law as possible be applied to trade disputes. They have been unwilling to allow the law in these matters to become coherent, or to apply to a whole range of cases that are of daily occurrence in British industry. Their assumption has been that the law would compel them to honour bargains and regulate their activities in a way they find uncongenial, or adverse to their interest. Thus it is a very strange argument that arrives at the conclusion that where the law is not on the side of the trade unions, businessmen owe it to the community to interpret it as if it were.[122]

Here the company was contesting the basic premises of the Scarman report: so far as they were concerned, the rule of law means doing only what the law requires, it does not require anyone to act reasonably within the law, and it does not require anyone to act in accordance with the policy of the law (first paragraph quoted immediately above); nor does it require compliance with other non-legal normative standards such as those relating to the conduct of industrial relations (second paragraph quoted immediately above). On the contrary, the company was to insist that it had 'acted within the law, both in letter and spirit', and that it 'will not abandon its legal rights and is shocked that it should be asked to do so'.[123] In terms of contrasting approaches to the rule of law, nothing could be more stark. But it did mean that Scarman's recommendation for reinstatement was flatly rejected by the company, ostensibly on the ground that 'the existing workforce simply would not tolerate the re-employment of the strikers'. So too was the recommendation for an ex gratia payment, the company 'rejecting any such suggestion of payments to those who by their own actions terminated their employment'.

That said, Scarman did not lose sight of traditional law and order issues, and criticised the union for the mass picketing, the subsequent course of which 'greatly disturbed the nation'. He was also critical of APEX asking the UPW to black Grunwick's mail, despite the decision in *Gouriet v UPW*.[124] Thus, both the

[121] Grunwick Processing Laboratories, 'Statement in Response to Scarman Report' (n 40).
[122] ibid.
[123] ibid.
[124] (n 20).

company and the union had 'in certain respects failed to respond to the spirit of the law',[125] though in the case of the union the culpability may have gone further than that. But notably, Scarman did not criticise the Attorney General for failing to prosecute the postal workers for breach of the Post Office Act 1953, which of course is not necessarily to say that he condoned the failure. Nevertheless, Scarman's was a strikingly different vision of the rule of law than that presented by Grunwick and its supporters on the Conservative benches and in the emerging free market think-tanks at the time. These included the National Association for Freedom which is said to have done 'so much' to 'support' Grunwick.[126] The role of these organisations is a reminder that abstract debates about the soul of the rule of law may be simply proxies for more serious ideological debates taking place elsewhere.

VI. CONCLUSION

As support for the strikers dissipated, Jayaben Desai fell out with APEX; she was suspended from the union and had her strike pay withdrawn, staging (with two colleagues) a hunger strike outside Congress House. With the passage of time, she was subsequently honoured by the GMB (with which APEX merged in 1989), and Mrs Desai is now celebrated as someone who 'contributed immeasurably to increasing the level of respect shown to newly arrived immigrant workers, many of them women'.[127] By her organising, campaigning and persuasion she is credited with having 'challenged the stereotype of South Asian women as passive and obedient',[128] with inspiring 'the biggest mobilisation in British labour-movement history',[129] and with forging powerful 'civic bonds across racial difference'.[130] The last was a particularly significant achievement: as Jack Dromey pointed out shortly after Desai's death, 'only 10 years previously, dockers had marched in support of the Conservative politician Enoch Powell, and workforces had polarised along racial lines at Mansfield Hosiery Mills in Nottinghamshire and Imperial Typewriters in Leicester'.[131]

Mrs Desai's legacy is also to be seen in the way in which the law has developed. The Grunwick dispute revealed the need for formal legal protection for workers who take part in strike action, a battle which is ongoing.[132] In addition, the *Grunwick* case exposed the 'naivete' of recognition legislation which relied

[125] Scarman Report (n 13) para 64.
[126] Rogaly (n 15) 70.
[127] Dromey (n 1).
[128] S Anitha and R Pearson, 'Remembering the Grunwick Dispute' (British Library Website (nd)).
[129] Dromey (n 1).
[130] A Bogg, *The Democratic Aspects of Trade Union Recognition* (Oxford, Hart Publishing, 2009) 120.
[131] Dromey (n 1)
[132] *Mercer v Alternative Future Group Ltd* [2022] EWCA Civ 379.

on the co-operation of employers, in what the Grunwick dispute reminded us would often be hostile and confrontational environments.[133] It was probably Wapping rather than Grunwick that led directly to unfair dismissal law being changed to protect those taking part in lawful industrial action,[134] though Grunwick set in train a pattern of behaviour by employers which if not typical would nevertheless dramatically undermine the ability of workers to strike. It is worth pointing out, however, that had the present law been in force in 1976, the strikers would have been protected only if their action was endorsed by the union. But if the union were to have done so under the law as it currently stands, it would thereby have exposed itself to the risk of liability by way of injunction and damages, having declared the action official without a ballot of the workers.

Yet for all that, Grunwick was a dispute fought on the territory of contested constitutional principle in which the employer prevailed: the government found it difficult to build social democratic structures within the framework of a 'dominant [constitutional] liberal ideology'.[135] Despite the unwritten and flexible nature of the British constitution, constitutional constraints were to be as unforgiving in the United Kingdom as they had been and were again to become as a result of more formal constraints of other liberal democracies.[136] That liberal ideology in the British context was mediated through formal conceptions of the rule of law emphasising that 'within the known rules of the game the individual is free to pursue his personal ends and desires, certain that the powers of government will not be used to frustrate his efforts'.[137] This not only trumped Scarman's socialised alternative, but in the process was used as a weapon in the *Grunwick* case in relation to ACAS and the trade union recognition legislation, as well as more generally to attack the Social Contract and the institutions required to sustain it.[138]

But although the Grunwick dispute and the *Grunwick* case were contested on grounds of constitutional principle, it should not be overlooked that conflicting views of the latter were informed by politics. The Grunwick dispute ostensibly may have been a dispute provoked by working conditions at a relatively small enterprise in London, but it became in effect a dispute about competing visions of government and competing visions of the trade union role. The company and

[133] Davies and Freedland, *Labour Legislation and Public Policy* (n 91) 390.

[134] KD Ewing and BW Napier, 'The Wapping Dispute and Labour Law' [1986] 45 *CLJ* 285.

[135] See Bogg (n 132) 128. See also Ewing (n 8).

[136] Other examples of labour law being frustrated by constitutional orthodoxy include *Taff Vale Railway Co Ltd v ASRS* [1901] AC 426 (HL); *Amalgamated Society of Railway Servants v Osborne* [1910] AC 87 (HL) (on which see ch 4 in this volume); and *Roberts v Hopwood* [1925] AC 578 (HL). See further JAG Griffith, *The Politics of the Judiciary* (Glasgow, Harper Collins, 1977). Note the date of the first edition.

[137] FA Hayek, *The Road to Serfdom* (London, George Routledge & Sons Ltd, 1944), 54. See also FA Hayek, *1980s Unemployment and the Unions* (London, Institute of Economic Affairs, 1980).

[138] See CG Hanson, *Taming the Trade Unions: A Guide to the Thatcher Government's Reforms, 1980–1990* (Macmillan, 1981). Although not persuasive, this gives a good sense of the economic liberal rejection of the Social Contract.

its political supporters repudiated the 'philosophy of the corporate state' which they saw in the Scarman report.[139] The philosophy was repudiated by others as well, and was to lead to litigation on multiple fronts to challenge different aspects of the Social Contract's legislative underpinning.[140] Perhaps ironically, the Grunwick dispute ended in defeat for the trade union movement at the height of its 'power'. But perhaps even more ironically, the Grunwick dispute was a prelude to a new governing ideology in which the Social Contract was displaced along with the purpose it served, the forms of political and industrial government it nurtured, and the trade union freedoms it sought to promote.

[139] Grunwick Processing Laboratories, 'Statement in Response to Scarman Report' (n 40).

[140] See also A Moretta, *Benchmarking Workplace Rights* (PhD Thesis, University of Liverpool, 2019), particularly on the politics behind *Young v United Kingdom* (1982) 4 EHRR 38, where some new primary source material is analysed.

7

Iceland Frozen Foods Ltd v Jones (1982): *Fairness, Forty Years on*

PHILIPPA COLLINS

I. INTRODUCTION

A LAWYER WITH even a passing knowledge of British labour law would not be surprised to find *Iceland Frozen Food v Jones*[1] on a list of landmark cases. The principles set out in its leading passage guide Employment Tribunals on how to approach a central jurisdiction that they exercise over employment relationships: the right not to be unfairly dismissed. A tribunal's assessment of the fairness of a dismissal is a pivotal moment in such a claim. According to section 98(4) of the Employment Rights Act 1996 (ERA), where we find the current iteration of the fairness test, the question of whether a dismissal is fair or unfair depends on whether the employer acted reasonably or unreasonably in treating the reason that they have put before the Tribunal as a sufficient reason for dismissing the employee. In addition, fairness shall be determined in accordance with the equity and substantial merits of the case. The interpretation of this provision, and the way it is applied by the tribunals, is a powerful factor in establishing the standard to which an employee's right against unfair dismissal is guaranteed.

Despite its practical significance, one would have difficulty claiming that *Iceland Frozen Foods* deserves the mantle of a landmark on the sole grounds of its originality. Much of the work had been done by its forbearers, such as the Court of Appeal's decision in *British Leyland v Swift*.[2] Rather, *Iceland*'s position amongst the landmarks of the labour law has been attained as a result of the clear and concise articulation by Mr Justice Browne-Wilkinson (as he then was) of a set of principles that still guide tribunal judges in their navigation of questions of fairness forty years on. Through a complex terrain of differing judicial

[1] *Iceland Frozen Food Ltd v Jones* [1983] ICR 17 (EAT).
[2] *British Leyland (UK) Ltd v Swift* [1981] IRLR 91 (CA).

approaches and wildly divergent interpretations of the statutory phrasing, his reasoning charted a precise course of compromise. I shall not seek to improve upon the passage itself:

> We consider that the authorities establish that in law the correct approach for the industrial tribunal to adopt in answering the question posed by section 57(3) of the Act of 1978 is as follows: (1) the starting point should always be the words of section 57(3) themselves; (2) in applying the section an industrial tribunal must consider the reasonableness of the employer's conduct, not simply whether they (the members of the industrial tribunal) consider the dismissal to be fair; (3) in judging the reasonableness of the employer's conduct an industrial tribunal must not substitute its decision as to what was the right course to adopt for that of the employer; (4) in many, though not all, cases there is a band of reasonable responses to the employee's conduct within which one employer might reasonably take one view, another quite reasonably take another; (5) the function of the industrial tribunal, as an industrial jury, is to determine whether in the particular circumstance of each case the decision to dismiss the employee fell within the band of reasonable responses which a reasonable employer might have adopted. If the dismissal falls within the band the dismissal is fair: if the dismissal falls outside the band it is unfair.[3]

In this extract, we find a pair of principles. First, the prohibition of the substitution mindset, set out at (2) and (3), prevents tribunal members from basing their decision solely on their own perception of the fairness of the employer's actions. The fairness of a dismissal must be judged from the perspective of what a reasonable employer would have done. Second, we see from (4) and (5) that the tribunal should not assess a dismissal's fairness by asking simply whether the dismissal was reasonable or unreasonable. Rather, tribunal members must bear in mind the existence of a band of reasonable responses open to the employer in the circumstances of each case. Only dismissals outside this band or range of reasonable responses (RORR) should be held to be unfair. The relationship between this pair of principles and the statement at (1), that we must start with the words of the statute, is just one source of controversy about *Iceland Frozen Foods* to which we shall return.

The chapter is structured as follows. We begin well before Mr Jones' brief period of employment with Iceland with an account of the origins of the right not to be unfairly dismissed and its key elements. After outlining the dispute between Mr Jones and his employer, we shall investigate the case-law leading up to the Employment Appeal Tribunal's decision, which demonstrates that there were several directions of travel open to the courts with regard to the interpretation and application of the fairness standard. *Iceland Frozen Foods* represents an attempt to strike a middle ground between a *Wednesbury*-style perversity standard and a straightforward application of the reasonableness test and section V outlines possible explanations and motivations behind the 'range' test.

[3] *Iceland* (n 1) 24–25.

The critiques of the principles laid down in *Iceland* will be introduced and they are grouped into three broad categories of concern. First, directed at the combination of the RORR test and the prohibition of the substitution mindset, comes their results in practice, particularly the limitations that they place on the Employment Tribunals' capacity to articulate clear standards of reasonable behaviour to employers and the downwards pressure upon those standards that is generated if they are applied rigidly. Second, we turn to the relationship between the RORR test and a perversity standard: the two can be distinguished in theory but for some periods of time may have elided in practice. In this section, the uneven prospects of successful appeals, as between employees and employers, will be discussed. The third area to probe is the assertion that the RORR test amounts to an unjustified gloss on the legislation that undermines the capacity of the law of unfair dismissal to achieve its objectives, as well as the additional aim of giving further effect to the human rights of employees as required by the Human Rights Act 1998.

In the final section, we move to the most contemporary discussions regarding the principles set out in *Iceland*. The decisions of the Employment Tribunal (ET)[4] and the Employment Appeal Tribunal[5] in *Hammersmith & Fulham v Keable* will be used to demonstrate how the approach to the question of a dismissal's fairness has adjusted its course in recent years. The ET showed concern that an employee must not be dismissed for conduct connected to the exercise of their rights to freedom of expression and to association. The EAT took a restrained approach to the analysis of the ET's judgment, avoiding pitfalls such as 'over-analysis' and 'being hyper-critical' that the Court of Appeal has recently cautioned against.[6] The shift in tack on questions of issues of fundamental rights and the scope of the appellate tribunals' jurisdiction gives hope that the balance between employee's and employer's rights and interests, sought by Browne-Wilkinson J in *Iceland*, can be achieved. In the concluding section, the incorporation of a concern for the proportionality of a decision to dismiss will be recommended.

II. THE ORIGINS AND DESIGN OF THE LAW OF UNFAIR DISMISSAL

Throughout the early twentieth century,[7] collective bargaining was central to the regulation of work. State intervention was limited to providing the framework through which agreement could be reached by employers and unions and guaranteeing a floor of basic rights for workers on topics such as safety, wages,

[4] *Keable v LB of Hammersmith & Fulham* (ET, 26 June 2019).
[5] *LB of Hammersmith & Fulham v Keable* [2022] IRLR 4 (EAT).
[6] *Brent LBC v Fuller* [2011] EWCA Civ 267, [2011] ICR 806, 813.
[7] The account offered in this section draws upon P Davies and M Freedland, *Labour Legislation and Public Policy* (Oxford, Clarendon Press, 1993) particularly 194–204.

and working hours. The common law of the contract of employment permitted employers to dismiss employees for any reason or no reason at all, subject to the employee's entitlement to wages for a short notice period.[8] For any protection or a right to appeal a dismissal, workers relied upon procedures agreed between employers and unions, but their coverage was far from universal. Combined with the lack of individual rights against unjust dismissals, workers used strikes as a tool to challenge their employer's use of discipline.

In the same period, the International Labour Organisation (ILO) produced a Recommendation on the Termination of Employment that applied to 'all categories of workers'.[9] The Recommendation created two categories of reason for dismissal – valid (eg conduct) and invalid (eg union membership, discriminatory reasons) – and it gave workers a right to appeal an unjustifiable termination, either internally in accordance with a company's procedures or to a court or arbitrator.[10] The UK accepted the ILO Recommendation, but there was concern for the rights of those outside the coverage of any collective procedures.[11] In addition, the Donovan Commission observed that some of the industrial action caused by employers' disciplinary decisions could have been averted if workers had access to an impartial decision-maker that could rule on the justification of a dismissal.[12] The Commission reported its view that it was 'urgently necessary' for workers to be given improved, statutory protection against unfair dismissals.[13] The Industrial Relations Act 1971 gave effect to that recommendation. The Act introduced a form of job security protection heavily influenced by the ILO's Recommendation.[14]

Although the 1971 Act was short-lived and many of its other provisions were not re-introduced, the law of unfair dismissal endured. The right not to be unfairly dismissed retains the same structure as when it was first enacted, which can be examined in five stages. A potential claimant first must demonstrate their eligibility to make a claim. The claim must be presented to the Employment Tribunal within three months of the effective date of termination and the individual must be accepted by the tribunal as an employee under a contract of employment.[15] In most cases, the employee must satisfy a qualifying period of continuous service under section 108, which – had it been set at the current

[8] *Malloch v Aberdeen Corporation* [1971] 1 WLR 1578 (HL) 1581 (Lord Reid) and 1593 (Lord Guest).

[9] International Labour Organisation Termination of Employment Recommendation, No 119 (1963) [18].

[10] ibid [2], [3], and [4].

[11] Royal Commission on Trade Unions and Employers' Associations 1965–1968, *Report* (Cmnd 3623, 1968) [525].

[12] ibid [528].

[13] ibid [529].

[14] See Davies and Freedland (n 7) 195; Royal Commission on Trade Unions and Employers' Associations (n 11) [545].

[15] Employment Rights Act 1996 (ERA 1996), ss 111(2), 94 and 230.

two-year period in 1980 – would have excluded Mr Jones from making his claim. The second stage, under sections 95 and 97, is to isolate the occurrence of a dismissal and determine the effective date of termination.

The third and fourth stages relate to the reason relied upon by the employer for the dismissal and the fairness of that reason. The employer must show the principal reason for the dismissal. The 'potentially fair reasons' for a dismissal are the employee's capability or qualifications, their conduct, a redundancy, the contravention of a statutory duty, or 'some other substantial reason' of a kind that justifies the dismissal of the employee.[16] The employee can contest the reason put forward by the employer. They may introduce evidence of an automatically unfair reason for dismissal; for example that they were dismissed for blowing the whistle or asserting their statutory employment rights, because of an employer's use of a blacklist, or on the grounds of their trade union membership or activities.[17] If the judge is satisfied on an assessment of all the evidence that either the employer failed to meet their burden of showing a potentially fair reason or had in fact dismissed for an automatically unfair reason, then the dismissal must be held to be unfair.

Where the employer has produced a potentially fair reason for dismissal, the standard of fairness tests the employer's reliance upon that reason in the circumstances of the case. Did the employer act reasonably or unreasonably in treating, for example, the employee's conduct as a sufficient reason to dismiss? The guidance in *Iceland Frozen Foods* is applicable here. The starting points must be the words of the statute, but in applying them to the case, the tribunal must avoid the substitution mindset and take into account the RORR open to a reasonable employer in that particular situation. Only dismissals that fall outside that range should be considered unfair. In misconduct cases, guidance from another prominent case decided shortly before *Iceland* (but interestingly not cited in it) – *British Home Stores v Burchell*[18] – must also be applied. *Burchell* asks whether the employer had a genuine belief in the misconduct; whether they possessed reasonable grounds to sustain that belief and whether that belief was formed on the basis of reasonable investigations.[19] More generally, the courts have been clear that a reasonable dismissal, in most circumstances, can only occur after a fair procedure has been followed.[20] Good industrial practice regarding procedures leading to dismissals has been set out in various codes, most recently the Advisory, Conciliation and Arbitration Service's Code of Practice on

[16] ERA 1996, s 98(1)–(2).

[17] See ERA 1996, ss 98B–105; Trade Union and Labour Relations (Consolidation) Act 1992, ss 152, 153, 238 and 238A.

[18] *British Home Stores v Burchell* [1978] IRLR 379 (EAT).

[19] ibid 380.

[20] See *W Devis & Sons Ltd v Atkins* [1977] AC 931 (HL) [35]; *Polkey v AE Dayton Services Ltd* [1988] AC 344 (HL) 357–58 (Lord Mackay), 364 (Lord Bridge).

Disciplinary and Grievance Procedures, which applies to dismissals for conduct and poor performance.[21]

The final stage is awarding a remedy to a successful claimant. The employee may express a desire to be re-employed by their old employer and the tribunal must take that into account, along with whether it is practicable for the employer to comply.[22] Perhaps because employees are reluctant to return to an employer that has treated them unfairly and also employers are likely to resist an order for re-employment, such orders are rare.[23] The remedy for an unfair dismissal is likely to be compensation, consisting of the basic award and the compensatory award. The basic award is calculated by a statutory formula according to the employee's length of service, their age, and their weekly pay.[24] The tribunal sets the compensatory award at such an amount as it considers 'just and equitable in all the circumstances' under section 123 and it includes financial losses that flow from the dismissal. Both components can be reduced on a number of grounds and are subject to statutory limits. For example, the compensatory award cannot exceed the lower of 52 weeks of the claimant's pay or £93,878.[25]

III. MR JONES' DISMISSAL BEFORE THE INDUSTRIAL TRIBUNAL

Mr Jones was a nightshift foreman at an Iceland warehouse.[26] Having worked in this position for a little over a year, Mr Jones was dismissed summarily. Two causes prompted his manager's decision to dismiss Mr Jones after his shift on 1 July 1981. First, the warehouse and neighbouring offices had not been adequately secured between the end of the nightshift at 6 am and the arrival of the day shift at around 7.30 am. Second, the distribution manager found that the number of items loaded onto trucks by the nightshift team was substantially less than was usual. The manager surmised that the workers had engaged in a 'go-slow' because, if the required items were not loaded by the end of shift, the workers would continue to work and thereby receive overtime payments. Mr Jones was summoned to a meeting before the start of his next shift on the grounds that securing the building was his responsibility and he had potentially participated in what appeared to be a 'go-slow'. The meeting between Mr Jones

[21] Advisory, Conciliation and Arbitration Service, *Code of Practice on Disciplinary and Grievance Procedures* (TSO, 2015) www.acas.org.uk/acas-code-of-practice-for-disciplinary-and-grievance-procedures/html (accessed 8 March 2022).

[22] ERA 1996, ss 112 and 116.

[23] See J Howe, 'Why Do So Few Employees Return to their Jobs? In Pursuit of a Right to Work Following Unfair Dismissal' in V Mantouvalou (ed), *The Right to Work: Legal and Philosophical Perspectives* (Oxford, Hart Publishing, 2014) 258.

[24] ERA 1996, s 119.

[25] ERA 1996, s 124(1ZA) and the Schedule of The Employment Rights (Increase of Limits) Order 2022.

[26] The facts and account of the Industrial Tribunal's decision are drawn from the EAT's judgment: *Iceland* (n 1) 18–21.

and his manager lasted around 10 minutes and he was dismissed without notice at its conclusion.

Mr Jones brought a claim for unfair dismissal to the Industrial Tribunal. The Tribunal concluded that his dismissal was indeed unfair and awarded him £1,719 in compensation, a figure reached after a 40 per cent deduction for Mr Jones' contributory fault. The reason for the dismissal was held to be the security failure and the manager's belief that Mr Jones had either encouraged or permitted the 'go-slow' to occur. The tribunal then addressed the substantive and procedural fairness of the dismissal separately. With regard to the substantive reason for the dismissal, the tribunal did not regard the issues – either separately or taken together – as sufficiently serious to make the decision to dismiss reasonable.[27] The first was a simple mistake and the second was not considered to be a reasonable basis to dismiss Mr Jones in the circumstances. He had previously been reprimanded for being too harsh with his shift of workers and the Tribunal surmised that this may have explained his lack of interference on the night of the 'go-slow'.

On the procedural point, the Industrial Tribunal found further evidence of unfairness. There was a contractual right to be accompanied by a representative that had been breached. Overall, the decision was taken very hastily. It appeared to the Tribunal that the employee's explanation was not heard; that case being that the workers were seeking to gain a bonus that was on offer for careful loading, which had slowed the pace of work. This latter point was doubted by the Employment Appeal Tribunal on the basis that both the manager and the employee gave evidence that the explanation had been given during the meeting. Before remitting the case to a different tribunal, the Employment Appeal Tribunal did however query that '[i]t may not have been fair, and we say no more than that, to have dismissed the employee with the haste which was shown in this case without giving him an opportunity to have a representative there.'[28]

IV. THE NAVIGATION TOWARDS A LANDMARK: FAIRNESS BEFORE *ICELAND FROZEN FOODS*

When we look back at the central passage of *Iceland*, it can be with a sense of inevitability: the RORR test and the prohibition of the substitution mindset were an irresistible direction of travel for the fairness standard. The actual picture, however, is more complex, with distinct strands of case-law setting out contrasting approaches to the interpretation of the statute and the application of the fairness standard. The four positions outlined here provide context to the decision of the Employment Appeal Tribunal in *Iceland*.

[27] *Iceland* (n 1) 20.
[28] ibid 26.

A good example of the initial approach of Industrial Tribunals to their jurisdiction over unfair dismissals is *Clarkson v Brown Muff & Co Ltd*.[29] An employee was dismissed summarily after taking an unauthorised absence and answering dishonestly when asked later about the length of his absence. The Industrial Tribunal stated boldly: 'We do not think that [this instance of misconduct] has merited dismissal at all.'[30] Summary dismissal was therefore out of the question – the most appropriate sanction would have been a warning – and the dismissal was held to be unfair. This style of reasoning can be found in other cases,[31] and received support at appellate level. In *Hilti v Windridge*,[32] the Industrial Tribunal held that the employee's dismissal for dishonesty in gaining commission from outside their sales region, after 11 years of good service, was unfair. A suspension or the refusal of pay increases would have been warranted in this case. When the employer appealed to the National Industrial Relations Court (the predecessor to the Employment Appeal Tribunal), it refused to intervene. As the Court understood it, 'the question of whether or not a dismissal is unfair is one for the discretion of the Tribunal', even in cases such as *Hilti* where 'different views might be taken in assessing whether or not it justified dismissal'.[33]

Reported only three years after *Hilti*, the decision in *Vickers Ltd v Smith*[34] falls at the opposite end of the spectrum, both in terms of the standard of review to be applied *and* the role of the Tribunal in that process. In an appeal on the fairness of a selection for redundancy, the Employment Appeal Tribunal indicated that the Industrial Tribunal's error lay

> ... in failing to appreciate that not only was it necessary to arrive at the conclusion that the decision of the management was wrong, but that it was necessary to go a stage further, if they thought that the management's decision was wrong, and to ask themselves the question whether it was *so wrong, that no sensible or reasonable management could have arrived at the decision at which the management arrived in deciding who should be selected* ... for redundancy.[35]

The *Vickers* approach, setting a higher threshold before a decision would be held to be fair and seeming to limit the Tribunal's role dramatically, was met with swift resistance. In cases such as *Wells v Derwent Plastics Ltd*[36] and *Earl of Bradford v Jowett (No 2)*,[37] Bristow J led the Employment Appeal Tribunal's censure of the addition of judicial interpretation to a provision that 'could not

[29] [1974] IRLR 66 (IT).
[30] ibid 67.
[31] Eg, *Ramroop v Goldman Ltd* [1974] IRLR 313 (IT); *Frame v McKean & Graham* [1974] IRLR 179 (IT); *Blanchard v DRE Holdings* (1971) Ltd [1974] IRLR 266 (IT).
[32] *Hilti v Windridge* (IT, 22 August 1973).
[33] *Hilti v Windridge* [1974] IRLR 53 (NIRC) 54.
[34] *Vickers Ltd v Smith* [1977] IRLR 11 (EAT).
[35] ibid 12 (emphasis added).
[36] *Wells v Derwent Plastics Ltd* [1978] ICR 424 (EAT).
[37] *Earl of Bradford v Jowett (No 2)* [1978] IRLR 16 (EAT).

well be plainer'.[38] Tribunals, the Employment Appeal Tribunal argued, should not be criticised for a failure to apply the *Vickers* formulation but could draw on it as guidance if appropriate. The Industrial Tribunal in *Iceland* falls into line with *Wells/Jowett*. The Tribunal points out that adherence to *Vickers* would result in a 'very much reduced' success rate for claimants in unfair dismissal as only in very few conduct dismissals would the Tribunal be able to say that *no* reasonable employer would have dismissed.[39]

Throughout this tussle between the *Vickers* and the *Wells/Jowett* perspective, a final approach cuts through in cases such as *NC Watling v Richardson*,[40] *Rolls-Royce v Walpole*,[41] and *British Leyland v Swift*.[42] The decisions in *Watling* and *Walpole* emphasised that employers may respond in different ways to the same situation and that there will be a range of responses that can be considered reasonable. This line of reasoning was adopted by the CA in *British Leyland v Swift*,[43] a misconduct case related to the fraudulent misuse of a tax disc, who stated that:

> The correct test is: Was it reasonable for the employers to dismiss him? If no reasonable employer would have dismissed him, then the dismissal was unfair. But if a reasonable employer might reasonably have dismissed him, then the dismissal was fair.[44]

The second debate, regarding the role of the Tribunal members' subjective view of whether dismissal was the right course of action, was resolved less conspicuously. By the time *Watling* was reported in 1978, the substitution mindset was viewed as 'heretical'. The fairness of a dismissal must be judged against an objective standard, not 'by the hunch of the particular Industrial Tribunal'.[45]

The central passage of the Employment Appeal Tribunal's decision in *Iceland* has already been reproduced. Browne-Wilkinson J draws together key principles that emerged over the course of an unsettled period of decisions, during which the first instance and appellate tribunals grappled with the nature of their own role as well as the proper interpretation of the statutory phrasing. The judgment combines an emphasis on applying the statutory phrasing with the prohibition of the substitution mindset and a reminder of the existence of a 'band of reasonable responses' in most cases. The latter two aspects put the Industrial Tribunal's findings in jeopardy. The Tribunal's unadorned application of the statutory language, without reference to a RORR, amounted to a misdirection.[46] The case was remitted to a differently constituted tribunal for a rehearing.

[38] *Wells* (n 36) 428; *Jowett* (n 37) 17–18.
[39] *Iceland* (n 1) 21.
[40] *NC Watling v Richardson* [1978] IRLR 255 (EAT).
[41] *Rolls-Royce v Walpole* [1980] IRLR 343 (EAT).
[42] *British Leyland v Swift* (n 2).
[43] ibid.
[44] ibid [11].
[45] ibid.
[46] *Iceland* (n 1) 26.

V. THE RATIONALE FOR THE 'RANGE' TEST

Having charted the course taken by the cases, it is opportune to consider *why* the courts adopted the approach set out in *Iceland Frozen Foods*. On the prohibition of the substitution mindset, the tribunal in *Watling* pointed to a concern that the views of Tribunal members regarding a particular case may be 'whimsical or eccentric'.[47] Although some variation between the views of different Employment Tribunals was accepted,[48] asking what the reasonable employer would have done in the relevant circumstances rather than whether the Employment Tribunal considers the dismissal fair reduces the scope for inconsistencies within the jurisdiction of unfair dismissal.[49] An objective approach, in alignment with the statute's reference to reasonableness, must be preferred.

Turning to the RORR test, we enter contested territory. The judicial explanation of the 'range' is pinned on the idea that – in most cases – one clear, 'correct' response to the situation is unlikely to emerge. An employer must be able to select between a range of possibilities, as long as they are reasonable. Where one employer might elect to dismiss an employee upon an allegation of theft, for example, another employer may give them a written warning and a second chance.[50] When the interpretation of section 98(4) has been questioned in the years since,[51] courts affirming the RORR test have not added much of substance to its defence. In the 2000 decision in *Post Office v Foley*,[52] the Court of Appeal refuted the criticisms that had been levelled against the consequences of the RORR test and stated that *Iceland Frozen Foods* remained authoritative on the interpretation of the provisions, given the lack of parliamentary intervention.

Mark Freedland argued that the courts were seeking a 'golden mean', in relation to their judicial-review-like function in unfair dismissal law.[53] The courts, in using the RORR test, sought to avoid the usurpation of the initial decision-maker (the employer), whilst ensuring that the new controls placed on those decisions were in fact imposed.[54] Other scholars have been more sceptical, hypothesising that other, unexpressed concerns or ideals have motivated the courts in their adoption and affirmation of the RORR test over the decades. For example, instrumental concerns, such as an anxiety regarding opening the floodgates and generating an unmanageable tribunal workload, have been postulated.[55]

[47] *Watling* (n 40) 257.

[48] See *Bessenden Properties Ltd v Corness* [1974] IRLR 338 (CA) [18].

[49] See *Brent* (n 6) 812.

[50] See *Swift* (n 2) 93 (Ackner LJ); *Walpole* (n 41) 346; *Watling* (n 40) 257.

[51] See *Haddon v Van Der Bergh Foods Ltd* [1999] ICR 1150 (EAT) (Morison J).

[52] *HSBC Bank plc v Madden* [2000] ICR 1283 (CA).

[53] M Freedland and H Collins, 'Finding the Right Direction for the "Industrial Jury"' (2000) 29 *ILJ* 288, 291.

[54] ibid 292.

[55] S Anderman, 'Termination of Employment: Whose Property Rights?' in C Barnard, S Deakin and GS Morris (eds), *The Future of Labour Law: Liber Amicorum Bob Hepple QC* (Oxford, Hart Publishing, 2004) 103.

Unease about the role of Tribunals in reviewing decisions of managers who understand the organisation and its needs, particularly where the substance of the decision is concerned, have been raised.[56] It must be added, however, that such reasons for Employment Tribunals exercising deference to employers have been questioned strongly by ACL Davies, particularly given that employers are under no general obligation to deploy their expertise for anything other than their own interests.[57]

On a normative level, commentators such as Steven Anderman and Hugh Collins argue that the application of the RORR permitted judges to preserve the employer's managerial prerogative to the greatest degree possible.[58] Hugh Collins suggested that, although the law of unfair dismissal was intended to disrupt the common law values of privacy, neutrality and equality between the parties, they have been reasserted through the statutory interpretation adopted.[59] The courts, via the RORR test, declined the statute's invitation to reign in the autonomy of employers in disciplinary matters, creating a 'presumption of fairness and an excuse for non-intervention' and legitimating a 'strong conception of managerial prerogative'.[60]

VI. THE FAIRNESS STANDARD IN ACTION

As a well-established landmark, it would be impossible to map the effects and analysis of *Iceland* comprehensively in a single chapter. Indeed, the approach to questions of fairness has gone through distinctive phases,[61] the most recent of which will be elaborated upon in the final section below. My focus here is on the enduring criticisms of the operation of the 'range' test and the prohibition of the substitution mindset. Some of the critiques are not targeted at the *Iceland* principles, but rather the route taken in the case-law in the years since.

A consistent point of criticism is the move from fairness as a standard of behaviour determined by tribunals and expected of employers to a standard that reflects the potential responses of a range of reasonable employers.[62] On a straightforward reasonableness standard, the tribunal could hold that the employer's decision to dismiss the employee was unreasonable without relying

[56] P Elias, 'Fairness in Unfair Dismissal: Trends and Tensions' (1981) 10 *ILJ* 201, 211; H Collins, 'Capitalist Discipline and Corporatist Law – Part I' (1982) 11 *ILJ* 78, 88.

[57] ACL Davies, 'Judicial Self-restraint in Labour Law' (2009) 38 *ILJ* 278, 294.

[58] Anderman (n 55) 107, 114; Collins (n 56); H Collins, 'Capitalist Discipline and Corporatist Law – Part II' (1982) 11 *ILJ* 170.

[59] H Collins, *Justice in Dismissal: The Law of Termination of Employment* (Oxford, Oxford University Press, 1992) 32–40.

[60] ibid 39; Collins (n 58) 177.

[61] See T Brodtkorb, 'Judicial Reform of Unfair Dismissal Law: Recent Developments in the Range of Reasonable Responses' (2014) 25 *King's Law Journal* 201.

[62] Collins (n 59) 38.

on the subjective opinion of its members and whilst acknowledging that several reasonable options were available to the employer. However, a tribunal that wishes to indicate that one particular response would have been most appropriate (and thereby guide the actions of employers in the future) would run a risk of either falling foul of the *range* of reasonable responses test or, depending on the phrasing used by the tribunal, the prohibition of the substitution mindset. The principles set out in *Iceland Frozen Foods* make it more difficult for tribunals to articulate clear guidance on how employers should respond to particular circumstances, thereby curbing the capacity of unfair dismissal law to establish firm standards of good industrial practice.

Further, Hugh Collins argued persuasively that, by denying the application of a fixed standard of reasonableness, the RORR legitimates a wider range of disciplinary actions.[63] Rather than encouraging convergence upon the reasonable responses in the middle of the spectrum, the RORR can be taken to mean only that unreasonable responses at its limits must be avoided.[64] Once a permissible reason for dismissal has been established and a fair procedure followed, a strict application of the RORR standard makes a finding of unfairness very unlikely.[65] This is so even if there are factors that the Tribunal may have weighed in the employee's favour, such as a long period of good service or evidence that a less severe measure could have served the business' needs, because pointing out the relevance of these considerations may open a tribunal up to a challenge on the basis of the substitution mindset.

Moreover, the RORR test has been argued to create a downwards pressure on the standards expected of employers.[66] Dismissal is the most severe option available to employers, and each defendant need only convince the tribunal that other, reasonable employers would have adopted that same course of action. For example, in *Haddon v van der Bergh Foods*,[67] the employee was dismissed for failing to return to his shift after a company awards ceremony. Mr Haddon had been invited to the ceremony to celebrate 15 years of service to the company. He had been instructed to go back to work but decided not to do so as he had consumed alcohol at the event. *Obiter*, the Employment Tribunal expressed its view that dismissal was not justified here: 'Most people would regard [the dismissal] as harsh in the extreme' and '[i]t was a decision that many reasonable employers would not have taken.'[68] Nevertheless, the Tribunal considered itself

[63] ibid; A Baker, 'The 'Range of Reasonable Responses' Test: A Poor Substitution for the Statutory Language' (2021) 50 *ILJ* 226, 245–47.

[64] Collins (n 59) 39; A Freer, 'The Range of Reasonable Responses Test – From Guidelines to Statute' (1998) 27 *ILJ* 335, 340–41.

[65] Freedland and Collins (n 53) 294.

[66] M Bennett, 'Interpreting Unfair Dismissal and Redundancy Payments Law: The Judicial Reluctance to Disapprove Employer Decisions to Dismiss' (2002) 23 *Statute Law Review* 135, 142; P Collins, 'The Inadequate Protection of Human Rights in Unfair Dismissal Law' (2018) 47 *ILJ* 504, 524; Baker (n 63) 247.

[67] *Haddon v van der Bergh Foods* (n 51).

[68] ibid 1153–54.

bound to find that the dismissal was fair under the statute: the instruction itself could not be said to be unreasonable nor could it be said that no reasonable employer would have dismissed Mr Haddon.[69] The Employment Tribunal decision in *Haddon* demonstrates Anderman's critique that, rather than requiring employers to meet a general standard of equity or reasonableness, the RORR 'requires tribunals to adjust their standards to the lower reaches of existing standards of reasonableness in industry'.[70]

VII. THE PERVERSITY QUESTION AND THE PROBLEM OF APPEALS

The Employment Appeal Tribunal's decision in *Haddon*, like *Iceland Frozen Foods*, is a notable moment in the history of the fairness standard. In it, Morison J (then President of the Employment Appeal Tribunal) set out a forceful critique of the established approach to interpreting section 98(4):

> The mantra 'the band or range of reasonable responses' is not helpful because it has led tribunals into applying what amounts to a perversity test, which, as is clear from *Iceland Frozen Foods Ltd v Jones* ... itself, was not its purpose.[71]

The relationship between a perversity standard and the 'range' test is far from clear, even within the *Iceland* decision itself. Browne-Wilkinson J states at once that *Vickers* is 'entirely accurate in law' but also that 'tribunals would do well not to direct themselves by reference to it' and a standard close to perversity 'is not the law'.[72] Mr Justice Lindsay, for the Employment Appeal Tribunal in *Madden*,[73] pointed out the logical flaw in this series of statements. He also observed that the Court in *Iceland* did not set out the precise mistake involved in seeing the RORR test as leading to a perversity argument or something akin to it, despite the importance of the distinction drawn between the two standards in the decision itself.

Observers have also discussed the relationship between the *Vickers* formulation ('no sensible/reasonable employer would made this decision') and a perversity or *Wednesbury* unreasonableness standard usually associated with public law.[74] Andy Freer argued that the only real difference between *Vickers* and *Iceland* is what they describe: the former focuses on decisions beyond the RORR, whereas the latter describes and assesses whether the decision falls within the RORR.[75] David Cabrelli, in contrast, resists the conflation of the

[69] ibid.
[70] S Anderman, 'Recent Cases – Unfair Dismissal' (1977) 6 *ILJ* 110, 112–13.
[71] *Haddon* (n 51) 1160 (emphasis added).
[72] *Iceland* (n 1) 25.
[73] See *Midland Bank plc v Madden* [2000] 2 All ER 741 (EAT) 755.
[74] Freer (n 64) 336; Elias (n 56) 205–06; Freedland and Collins (n 53) 294.
[75] Freer (n 64) 340.

RORR test with a perversity standard.[76] He argues that the burden upon an employee would be more onerous if the employee were required to demonstrate that no reasonable employer would have dismissed them than where a tribunal considers a range of reasonable responses. The 'point of demarcation' is different, and less exacting, under the latter approach.[77]

I argue that this difference of opinion can be explained by the effect of the potential for an appeal against a tribunal's decision. The *Iceland* principles are conceptually distinct from a perversity standard but, in periods during which the appeal tribunals are particularly active in overturning Employment Tribunal decisions on fairness, the two standards may elide in their application. An appeal can only be lodged for an error of law. However, as observed by Patrick Elias writing extra-judicially, if an Employment Tribunal has found a dismissal to be unfair but the Employment Appeal Tribunal perceives it to be within the RORR, 'the very fact that there is a disagreement between the two tribunals itself suggests that the employer's original decision to dismiss was one which a reasonable employer might adopt'.[78] Thus, in an attempt to avoid having their decision overturned, tribunals may begin to find unfairness only in cases where the employer has flagrantly breached procedural principles or the dismissal lacked any foundation in a fair reason. If this kind of approach takes hold within the tribunal system, then it is easy to see how the theoretical distinction between the *Iceland* interpretation and a perversity/irrationality standard could collapse in practice.

This point about the relationship between the Employment Tribunal and the appeal courts leads to one final consequence of the *Iceland* approach to fairness: the asymmetry in opportunities to overturn a tribunal's decision. If the Employment Tribunal finds that a dismissal is fair, the employee must allege an error of law, such as a misdirection as to the correct test or the possibility that no reasonable tribunal would have reached that decision. They cannot rely on the substitution mindset argument: the Tribunal has found in favour of the employer, so fault cannot be found on the ground that it has impermissibly asserted its own view.[79] In addition, because the first instance tribunal has found the dismissal to be fair, it is very difficult for an Employment Appeal Tribunal that would have considered the dismissal to be unreasonable to overturn that decision.[80] An Employment Judge has, by that point, accepted the dismissal as within the RORR and, as mentioned above, that is strong evidence that the dismissal can be regarded as fair. This conundrum for the employee is what Freer called 'a "double" perversity test': a decision applying a perversity standard must be shown to be perverse.[81]

[76] D Cabrelli, 'The Hierarchy of Differing Behavioural Standards of Review in Labour Law' (2011) 40 *ILJ* 146.
[77] ibid 157.
[78] Elias (n 56) 207.
[79] Brodtkorb (n 61) 210.
[80] Elias (n 56) 207.
[81] Freer (n 64) 345.

Take the opposite starting point, an Employment Tribunal holds that the dismissal is unfair, and the employer has two potential routes to argue the decision was in error. If the tribunal references their own views as to the reasonableness of the dismissal without plainly also examining the perspective of the reasonable employer, the argument can be that they have fallen into the substitution mindset.[82] For example, in *Madden*, Mr Madden worked in a bank and was investigated after it was alleged that he had fraudulently used customers' credit cards. The tribunal found his dismissal to be unfair on the grounds that the investigation was inadequate. The Court of Appeal, on the other hand, held that the investigations were reasonable and the tribunal had fallen into the substitution mindset.[83] The employer could also seek to convince an appeal tribunal that the dismissal can be regarded as reasonable in the circumstances, thereby creating a difference of opinion between the tribunals and leading to the conclusion that the dismissal was within the RORR. If the appeal tribunals exercise their jurisdiction eagerly, the ultimate result of a succession of appeals is likely to err with whichever court is willing to accept harsher sanctions or more minimal investigations.

VIII. THE RIGHT NOT TO BE UNFAIRLY DISMISSED, THE STATUTORY PURPOSE, AND THE RORR TEST

An additional layer of discussion of the RORR test, as set out in *Iceland Frozen Foods*, regards its relationship to the statutory phrasing, the legislative intent, and the overarching aim of the law of unfair dismissal. The appraisal can be constructed on three levels. First, as mentioned in section VI above, the *Iceland* guidance diverges from the statutory formulation of straightforward reasonableness, thereby widening the class of employers' responses that are accepted as fair under the statute and diminishing the standard to which the employee's right to challenge an unfair dismissal is guaranteed. The divergence between the statutory phrasing and its interpretation has led to a second set of criticisms on the basis that the RORR particularly amounts to a judicial gloss on the law that is not justified in the light of the clarity of the statutory provisions. At a more abstract level, commentators question whether the RORR test runs contrary to parliamentary intention in introducing the law of unfair dismissal and the overarching purpose of the right itself.

The statutory phrase, in all versions after 1978, directs Tribunals to consider whether 'the employer acted reasonably or unreasonably' in treating the reason relied upon as sufficient to dismiss.[84] Although Browne-Wilkinson J was keen to emphasise that 'the starting point should always be the words of section 57(3) themselves',[85] the RORR test has been criticised as an unjustified judicial gloss

[82] Baker (n 63) 248; Brodtkorb (n 61) 207–09.
[83] *Madden* (n 52) 560.
[84] Employment Protection (Consolidation) Act 1978, s 57.
[85] *Iceland* (n 1) 24.

on the statute. In cases decided before and indeed after *Iceland*, dissenting judicial voices have argued that the statutory phrasing is plain and unambiguous.[86] In 1985, Dillon LJ criticised the 'over-sophistication' of the standard of fairness that had occurred in the preceding cases.[87] Morison J, in *Haddon*, argued that the 'obvious statements' that flow from the statute – that the Tribunal should not use only their own perception of what should have been done and that in some cases there are multiple responses that are reasonable – do not include the 'range' test.[88] Tribunal judges, he recommended, should return to the task of applying the words of the statute without embellishment.[89]

Meanwhile, scholars have argued that the RORR test amounts to nothing short of judicial legislation. With regard to the CA's reassertion of the RORR test after Morison's attack in *Haddon*,[90] Steven Anderman argued that '[t]he inability of judges to see that the current interpretation of section 98(4) *is* a form of judicial legislation is evidence of their underlying assumptions about exclusive employer property rights in the contract of employment.'[91] Despite the passing of time in which Parliament could have overturned it, as the authors of Deakin and Morris astutely observe, 'it remains the case that there is nothing in section 98 to indicate that Parliament intended a "band of reasonableness" test to be applied by employment tribunals'.[92]

One's perspective on the charge that the *Iceland* principles deviate from, or prevent the full achievement of, the purpose of the statute depends upon the interpretation taken of that purpose. Viewed as a means to incentivise and formalise workplace-level disciplinary procedures, the law has been effective and *Iceland* is not problematic.[93] The RORR test, however, stands at odds with a more ambitious view of the aims of the law of unfair dismissal. Hugh Collins, in his seminal study in 1992, argued that that the law of unfair dismissal forms part of the wider pursuit of a just workplace.[94] The employer's discretionary powers are subjected to standards 'which constrain the rational pursuit of business objectives by the need to protect the individual employee's autonomy and dignity in the workplace'.[95]

How do the principles of *Iceland* stand up to scrutiny against the objective of achieving justice and upholding the autonomy and dignity of employees in dismissal? The 'range' test reinforces a need for rationality, but its application has also limited the tribunals' capacity to pursue procedural and particularly

[86] See n 38.
[87] *Gilham v Kent County Council (No 2)* [1985] ICR 233 (CA) 244.
[88] *Haddon* (n 51) 1160.
[89] ibid 1160–61.
[90] See *Madden* (n 52).
[91] Anderman (n 55) 127.
[92] Z Adams and others, *Deakin and Morris' Labour Law*, 7th edn, (Oxford, Hart Publishing, 2021) 490.
[93] ibid 559; Collins (n 56) 83, 87–88.
[94] Collins (n 59) 272.
[95] ibid.

substantive ideals of justice in dismissal. Collins has suggested an alternative to the RORR test that would imitate a different standard associated with administrative law: rather than perversity, tribunals should consider whether a dismissal was proportionate.[96] The decision-maker would be required to produce a legitimate objective that they sought to achieve in exercising their disciplinary power and a tribunal would ask whether this aim was in fact being pursued, and whether it was being pursued in a necessary and proportionate manner. The employer's needs, such as efficient production or protection of company property, would be balanced against the employee's right not to be unfairly dismissed.[97] The employee's dignity and autonomy can thereby be respected, by ensuring that they only lose their job, and its associated values and benefits, where it was necessary in the circumstances.

The proportionality/necessity standard, or the lack thereof, has been most discussed in relation to a subset of unfair dismissal cases: those where the rights of the European Convention on Human Rights are engaged by the circumstances or reason for dismissal. Section 3 of the Human Rights Act 1998 places an obligation upon courts to read and give effect to legislation in a way that is compatible with the rights contained in the Convention. A *reading* of the fairness standard that takes account of the employee's fundamental rights, such as the right to respect for private life or to freedom of expression, was achieved in short order by the Court of Appeal in *X v Y*.[98] The Court held that the breadth and flexibility of section 98's concepts – fairness, reasonableness, etc – could be used to ensure that Tribunals can achieve an interpretation of unfair dismissal law, and a result in the case before them, that is compatible with the Convention.[99]

Whether the fairness standard is consistently applied in a fashion that *gives full effect* to a dismissed employee's Convention rights, however, has been questioned. Elsewhere I have argued that Employment Tribunal judgments frequently neglect to mention interferences with an employee's fundamental rights that have occurred by reason of, or in the procedure leading to, their dismissal.[100] For example, in *Gibbins v British Council*,[101] an employee was dismissed for sharing an offensive post on Facebook regarding the Royal family. Ms Gibbins was using Facebook in her private capacity, outside of working time, and the content of the post was connected to her Republican views. Thus, her dismissal in response to this conduct could be seen as an infringement on her right to freedom of expression and to thought and belief, as well as an interference with her right to respect for her private life. In discussing her unfair dismissal claim, however, the Tribunal did not reference any of the fundamental rights that may have been

[96] Freedland and Collins (n 53) 296.
[97] ibid.
[98] *X v Y* [2004] EWCA Civ 662, [2004] ICR 1634.
[99] ibid [59].
[100] Collins (n 66) 520–22.
[101] *Gibbins v British Council* (ET, 11 July 2017).

engaged by the facts of the case.[102] If the employee's arguments do enough to raise their Convention rights to the attention of the court, the consideration of them is often cursory and leaves the conclusion that the tribunal would otherwise have reached untouched.[103] Where the dismissal of an employee is concerned, the Convention's rights and freedoms are not reliably given their fullest effect.

IX. *HAMMERSMITH V KEABLE*: A CONTEMPORARY APPROACH TO FAIRNESS

Looking at a recent case, such as *Keable*,[104] permits us to move beyond the pessimistic outlook that has mired the fairness standard to-date. After years of criticism based on the failure to incorporate the employee's fundamental rights satisfactorily, there is some hope that section 98(4) can perform this additional function successfully. In addition, the role of the appeal courts with regard to questions of fairness has come full circle. Patrick Elias noted, around the time that *Iceland* was decided, that the Court of Appeal was keen to emphasise that Industrial Tribunals were intended to be a quick, informal way to resolve disputes and that scrutinising their decisions too closely would undermine this policy.[105] The approach of the appeal courts has waxed and waned in terms of the degree of intervention with tribunal decision-making.[106] The period following *Madden*[107] was a high watermark, whereas the more recent era of Court of Appeal and Employment Appeal Tribunal decisions return to a more circumspect approach.

Hammersmith v Keable illustrates both directions of travel. Mr Keable worked for the Borough Council for 17 years and had a good record of service. In 2018, he attended a demonstration with Enough is Enough, a group concerned with anti-Semitism in the Labour Party. Mr Keable spoke at the rally and got into a discussion about the role of anti-Semitism in the Holocaust, which was filmed and posted on Twitter by a BBC Newsnight journalist. A local MP also wrote on Twitter, naming Mr Keable as the person in the video and calling on local Labour leaders to investigate. Mr Keable was suspended during an investigation and later dismissed. The reason for his dismissal was that the exchange had been widely circulated and caused offence, which had brought the Council into disrepute. The Council accepted Mr Keable's explanation of his comments and there was discussion of his right to freedom of expression throughout the process, as well as in the decisions of the courts.

[102] ibid [134]–[141].
[103] Collins (n 66) 522–26; P Collins, 'Square Peg vs a Round Hole? The Necessity of a Bill of Rights for Workers' (2020) 11 *European Labour Law Journal* 199, 215–16.
[104] *Keable* (n 5).
[105] Elias (n 56) 209.
[106] See Brodtkorb (n 61).
[107] *Madden* (n 52).

The Employment Tribunal found the dismissal was procedurally and substantively unfair. On procedure, the Employment Judge held that the precise statements relied on by the Council had changed during the course of the disciplinary process, meaning that Mr Keable was not given the chance to respond to the specific comments and their interpretation before his dismissal. Neither was the claimant permitted to comment upon whether he would heed a warning, as a sanction alternative to dismissal. The Tribunal further concluded that it was 'well beyond the range of reasonable responses of a reasonable employer' to dismiss Mr Keable given that it was undisputed that: 'the claimant made the comments outside of work and in his private capacity; he did not publish the comments, nor were they found to be discriminatory, unlawful, threatening or obscene'.[108] On any reasonable view, his culpability was 'extremely limited'[109] and it was a first offence after 17 years of diligent service. After repeating the need to avoid substituting one's own view for that of the employer and drawing on prior decisions referencing the right to freedom of speech of employees, the judge concluded that the dismissal was unfair. The Council was ordered to reinstate Mr Keable.

Given the strength of the Employment Tribunal's findings on a variety of aspects of unfairness, an appeal was not surprising. On their liability, the Council's main argument was that the judge had fallen into the error of substitution and that she had impermissibly relied upon case law that was not put to the parties in argument.[110] The Employment Appeal Tribunal found against the Council on both points. On the procedural aspects that led to the Employment Tribunal's conclusion of unfairness, the Employment Appeal Tribunal defended its findings. For example, the Tribunal had set out matters that Mr Keable could have raised, had he been aware of the interpretation of his comments that the employer had adopted. This detail could have been seen as a form of substitution, but the Employment Appeal Tribunal rejected this suggestion: the judge was 'illustrating why it is not a meaningless requirement to provide an opportunity for comment'.[111]

The Employment Appeal Tribunal's response to the substitution argument reflects the court's wider approach to its review of the Tribunal's reasoning in *Keable*. Although the Employment Appeal Tribunal acknowledged that the Employment Tribunal's points could have been better expressed on occasion,[112] there is no sense that the appeal tribunal was going over the first instance decision with a fine toothcomb. The Employment Appeal Tribunal emphasised the need to take a 'fair reading of the Reasons as a whole' and read particular statements 'in context', not focusing unduly on single sentences in order to find an

[108] *Keable* (n 4) [167].
[109] ibid.
[110] *Keable* (n 5) [52] and [59].
[111] ibid [89].
[112] ibid [87], [89].

error of law.[113] This less minute scrutiny of Employment Tribunal decisions is in line with a collection of Court of Appeal decisions.[114] In *Newbound v Thames Water*, for example, the Court of Appeal reminded Employment Appeal Tribunals that 'the band [of reasonable responses] is not infinitely wide' and tribunals must be able to apply the statutory test of reasonableness without the accusation of substitution.[115]

Similarly, in *Brent LBC v Fuller*, the Court of Appeal steered Employment Appeal Tribunals towards checking that the law is correctly stated and is in fact applied by the Employment Tribunal, but avoid a reading 'so fussy that it produces pernickety critiques'.[116] Lord Justice Mummery reiterated the division of responsibilities between employer, Employment Tribunal and appeal tribunals. Employers make the decision whether or not to dismiss the employee. Employment Tribunals find the facts and apply an objective test of fairness: 'As appellate tribunals and courts are confined to questions of law they must not, in the absence of an error of law (including perversity), take over the tribunal's role as an "industrial jury" with a fund of relevant and diverse specialist expertise.'[117]

The emphasis upon the role of the Employment Tribunal as an 'industrial jury' is particularly interesting, given that many unfair dismissal cases are now heard by an Employment Judge sitting alone.[118] The absence of the perspective of wing members informing the Tribunal's view of the reasonableness of the employer's actions could have been taken as a reason to reassert the breadth of the RORR and for Employment Appeal Tribunals to intervene more readily. It appears, however, from both *Newbound* and *Brent* that the appellate courts instead show regard for the knowledge and insights of expert Employment judges who consider unfair dismissal complaints regularly and hear the evidence first-hand. The entreaty to appellate tribunals to exercise their jurisdiction cautiously will, it is hoped, embolden tribunals in placing limits on the RORR and enhance the standard to which the right not to be unfairly dismissed is guaranteed.

Hammersmith v Keable also shows significant progress in the use of unfair dismissal law as a mechanism for the protection of the employee's other fundamental rights. The Employment Judge showed great concern that the employer's decision to dismiss failed to respect Mr Keable's right to attend protests in his own time and to express his opinions. The judge argued that 'there is a very great risk of dismissal to any person who expresses their lawful political views outside the workplace' if a dismissal such as this, where the employee had exercised their rights to freedom of expression and assembly lawfully and their comments were

[113] ibid [89], [95].

[114] See also *Bowater v Northwest London Hospitals NHS Trust* [2011] EWCA Civ 63, [2011] IRLR 331, 335–36; *Newbound v Thames Water Utilities Ltd* [2015] EWCA Civ 677, [2015] IRLR 734; *DPP Law Ltd v Greenberg* [2021] EWCA Civ 672, [2021] IRLR 1016, 1024 onwards.

[115] *Newbound* (n 114) 743.

[116] ibid 813.

[117] *Brent* (n 6) 810.

[118] See The Employment Tribunals Act 1996 (Tribunal Composition) Order 2012.

circulated without their consent, was considered to be within the RORR.[119] Whilst the employer launched a range of appeals against the decision on liability and remedies, there was no appeal against the Tribunal's conclusion that the dismissal was substantively unfair.[120] The *Keable* decision demonstrates that the law of unfair dismissal can be applied in a manner that protects the Convention rights of the employee.

X. CONCLUDING REMARKS: THE FUTURE OF *ICELAND FROZEN FOODS*

Where next for this much-maligned, but certainly still upright, landmark? It might be said that the centrality of the 'range' test is in decline. Of the RORR, Mummery LJ stated in *Brent*: 'That favourite form of words is not statutory or mandatory. Its appearance in most tribunal judgments on unfair dismissal is a reassurance of objectivity.'[121] In addition, we have seen the courts begin to give due regard to the Convention rights of employees. This consideration is currently limited to cases where the reason for the dismissal amounts to a direct interference with an individual's fundamental rights, rather than other types of infringements such as investigations that intrude into employee's private lives. But, taken to its fullest conclusion, a rights-centred analysis of dismissals would also lead to the Employment Tribunal evaluating the necessity or proportionality of a dismissal, including the question of whether a less severe sanction would have served the employer's aims equally. Distinct regard for this factor would amount to a major departure for the standard of fairness, distancing it further from the principles as set out by Browne-Wilkinson J in *Iceland*.

Further, in her concurring opinion in the 2018 case of *Reilly v Sandwell MBC*,[122] Lady Hale appeared to invite discussion of the future of section 98(4) ERA 1996 before the UK Supreme Court. On one hand, many with experience of the law of unfair dismissal, she observed, may consider that the current interpretation of section 98(4) 'does not lead to injustice in practice'.[123] On the other, her Ladyship acknowledged the dissenting judicial voices, such as Morison J in *Haddon*,[124] that have criticised the law as it stands. Although there have been calls for a judicial re-interpretation of section 98(4), Lady Hale argued that destabilising the law after 40 years would be irresponsible, absent a 'very good reason' to do so.[125] Can such a pressing reason to change the course of the fairness standard be found?

[119] *Keable* (n 4) [175].
[120] *Keable* (n 5) [92].
[121] *Brent* (n 6) 809.
[122] *Reilly v Sandwell Metropolitan Borough Council* [2018] UKSC 16, [2018] IRLR 558, 562.
[123] ibid.
[124] *Haddon* (n 51).
[125] *Reilly* (n 122) 662.

It may be that, in the light of the recent reminders of the scope of the appellate jurisdiction, we find ourselves in an era where the force of several critiques of the *Iceland* formulation fades. Above, the perceived imbalance between employer and employee protection within the standard of fairness was connected to the employer's opportunity to appeal to the Employment Appeal Tribunal. The prospect of such an appeal being successful, I argued, was one reason why the RORR test has moved closer, in practice, to operating as a perversity standard. If appellate tribunals adopt a 'benevolent reading' of Employment Tribunal judgments, the likelihood of a successful appeal diminishes and first instance Tribunals can be more confident in finding that a dismissal lies beyond the limits of the RORR.

One might ask where faults can still be found in the interpretation of the fairness test. As observed in section VIII, the reading of section 98(4) has been argued to run contrary to the purpose of the law of unfair dismissal, particularly when that purpose is interpreted ambitiously. Upholding the dignity and autonomy of an employee in circumstances of dismissal, for example, requires searching scrutiny and clear benchmarks, particularly regarding substantive fairness, to be set by tribunals. Whilst the *Keable* decision indicates progress on this score, a sense of proportionality remains steadfastly absent from tribunals' considerations. Establishing whether the dismissal was a proportionate response is essential to give effect to the employee's Convention rights and it has also been suggested a standard of scrutiny that would better realise justice in all types of dismissal.[126]

The framework of proportionality gives a structure through which the rights and interests of both parties can be balanced. The employee's right to challenge an unfair dismissal, their rights to a due process and, in some cases, to the lawful exercise of other fundamental rights can be weighed against the employer's pursuit of their legitimate aims, such as the need to enforce reasonable disciplinary rules or make changes that ensure the company's continued viability. Such an analysis would ensure that a termination of employment is only deployed where necessary to achieve the employer's aims. Dismissal is removed as an option in some cases where it would be disproportionate, but there remains a 'range of reasonable responses' open to employers beyond that 'red line' in terms of substantive and procedural decision-making. It is not a wild leap, given the malleability of the statutory phrasing, that this approach could be adopted through a judicial articulation regarding the correct approach to section 98(4). *Iceland*'s twinset of principles would become a trio: the avoidance of the substitution mindset, the permissibility of a 'range of reasonable responses', and the need for a dismissal to represent a proportionate response.

[126] Freedland and Collins (n 53) 296.

8

O'Kelly v Trusthouse Forte PLC: *A Landmark of Legalism*

ACL DAVIES

I. INTRODUCTION

THE TERM 'LANDMARK case' is commonly used to denote a decision marking a turning-point in the development of the law on a particular topic. In some ways, it is difficult to single out any decision on employment status as a landmark because there are so many of them, and because they all turn to some extent on their own facts and circumstances. Indeed, it is arguable that many scholars (me included) sometimes fall into a trap of attributing greater precedential value to these decisions than they truly deserve. However, *O'Kelly v Trusthouse Forte* does seem to fit the idea of a landmark case.[1] Strictly speaking, I would argue that *Nethermere* is primarily responsible for the emergence of mutuality of obligation as part of the 'test' for employee status.[2] But this would not necessarily have been quite so problematic without two further developments for which *O'Kelly* is largely responsible: the application of mutuality of obligation in a strict, legalistic and ultimately employer-friendly manner, and the emergence of the idea that a casual worker who does not have mutuality of obligation might not even be an employee during the wage-work bargain. While the law shows promising signs of freeing itself of the first of these developments, the second continues to cast a long shadow.[3]

[1] *O'Kelly v Trusthouse Forte Plc* [1984] QB 90 (CA). This chapter deals with developments to 14 March 2022.

[2] *Nethermere (St Neots) Ltd v Gardiner* [1984] ICR 612 (CA). See also N Countouris, 'Uses and Misuses of "Mutuality of Obligations" and the Autonomy of Labour Law' in A Bogg, C Costello, ACL Davies and J Prassl (eds), *The Autonomy of Labour Law* (Oxford, Hart Publishing, 2015) 176–79. The underlying conceptual analysis of course originates in MR Freedland, *The Contract of Employment* (Oxford, Clarendon Press, 1976).

[3] An expression also used in relation to *O'Kelly* by S Fredman, 'Labour Law in Flux: the Changing Composition of the Workforce' (1997) 26 *ILJ* 337, 347.

In this contribution, I re-examine the factual and legal background to the case, and carefully analyse the decisions of the Industrial Tribunal, the Employment Appeal Tribunal and the Court of Appeal. This is a worthwhile exercise in relation to a case which is so very well-known because of the risk that familiarity leads us to overlook important details. I then examine the two main 'landmark' elements of the case – the treatment of mutuality of obligation and employment status within the wage-work bargain – considering their impact on the subsequent development of the case-law and their status today, particularly in the light of the Supreme Court's decision in *Uber*.[4]

II. OVERVIEW

Mr O'Kelly, Mr Pearman and Mr Florent worked at the Grosvenor House Hotel, a luxury hotel on Park Lane in London then owned by Trusthouse Forte Plc.[5] O'Kelly and Pearman were wine butlers and Florent was a barman. The Grosvenor House did a roaring trade in special events which were run by the Banqueting Department. This employed 34 permanent staff under contracts of employment, supported by a huge number of casual workers. This latter group consisted of over 100 'regular casuals', who were given work opportunities in preference to another bigger group of 200–300 occasional workers. O'Kelly, Pearman and Florent were 'regular casuals'. Although there were wide fluctuations in the hours they worked from week to week, there were very few weeks in which they did not work at all, and many weeks in which they worked 40–50 hours. The precise working arrangements were, of course, highly relevant to the determination of their employment status and I analyse these in further detail below.

O'Kelly, Pearman and Florent were members of the Hotel Catering Workers' Union (HCWU), part of the General Municipal Boilermakers (GMB). In 1982–83, the HCWU sought recognition for the purposes of collective bargaining in respect of all workers at the Grosvenor House, and an agreement that 'regular casuals' employed in the Banqueting Department should be regarded as employees under a contract of employment.[6] The union's request for a meeting was rejected, on the basis that the company had well-established consultation procedures with its staff. This appears to have been part of a broader Trusthouse Forte Plc policy at the time of resisting unionisation through an emphasis on Staff Consultative Committees organised by management.

[4] *Uber BV v Aslam* [2021] UKSC 5, [2021] ICR 657.

[5] The facts are detailed in the decision of the Industrial Tribunal: *O'Kelly v Trusthouse Forte Plc* (Industrial Tribunal, 11 April 1983) [1]–[20].

[6] ibid [16]–[18].

In February 1983, the claimants received letters from the Conference and Banqueting Executive, a Mr Green, to the effect that it was 'unlikely that we will need to call on your services again'. This was attributed to a 're-organisation' of the Banqueting Department, but the claimants drew a different inference from this sudden change in requirements.

A. The Industrial Tribunal Decision

The case was decided in the Industrial Tribunal on 11 April 1983. Since the claimants considered that they had been dismissed on trade union grounds, they applied for interim relief under what was then section 77 of the Employment Protection (Consolidation) Act 1978 (EPCA). The employer argued that the claimants did not have the statutory right not to be unfairly dismissed because they were not employees under a contract of employment under what was then section 153(1) EPCA. By a majority, the tribunal accepted the employer's argument and dismissed the application for interim relief.

To modern eyes, one of the most striking things about the tribunal's decision is the formal nature of its reasoning. It provided a list of 'factors' relevant to the individuals' employment status, and grouped these into nine factors consistent with them being employees, four factors 'not inconsistent' with that status, and five factors inconsistent with employee status.[7] The nine employee factors included the control exercised over the claimants by the hotel management, their integration into the operations of the business, and the fact that they were just paid for work done and did not invest to make a profit. The five inconsistent factors were that the relationship was terminable without notice on either side, the claimants could refuse assignments, the hotel was under no obligation to provide work, the parties thought that they were independent contractors and it was the custom and practice of the industry that casual workers of this kind were independent contractors.

The crux of the decision lay in the second stage of reasoning, in which the tribunal decided how to weigh up the factors for and against in order to reach a decision.[8] The only case cited by the tribunal was an Employment Appeal Tribunal decision from 1980, *Addison v London Philharmonic Orchestra Ltd*.[9] The Employment Appeal Tribunal in that case had considered a list of ten factors presented by counsel and applied the well-known test from *Market Investigations*: 'is the person who has engaged himself to perform these services performing them as a person in business on his own account?'.[10] The dissenting

[7] ibid [23].
[8] ibid [22].
[9] *Addison v London Philharmonic Orchestra Ltd* [1981] ICR 261 (EAT).
[10] *Market Investigations Ltd v Minister of Social Security* [1969] 2 QB 173 (QB) 184 (Cooke J).

member found that the factors in favour of employee status far outweighed those against.[11] The majority evidently thought that a mathematical approach was inappropriate, but it is not entirely clear why they gave particular weight to some factors over others. Moreover, as Leighton pointed out at the time, there was no real effort to answer the question posed by *Market Investigations* or to explain how the different factors might be of assistance in that regard.[12]

The majority focused heavily on the absence of mutuality of obligation as 'the one important ingredient which was missing',[13] despite also noting, confusingly, that mutuality should not be treated as a decisive factor.[14] According to the tribunal, the hotel was under no obligation to offer the claimants work, and the claimants' willingness to accept work when offered stemmed from their desire to earn money rather than from a legal duty. As many commentators have pointed out, these views of the facts are open to question.[15] It was clear that a system of sanctions was in operation if the waiters turned down work, so that the arrangement on their side was held together by more than just their desire to earn money. And on the 'employer' side, while there may not have been an obligation to provide a specific amount of work and pay, it was clear that there was an obligation to offer the available work to the 'regular' casuals in preference to others. I have argued elsewhere that an obligation of this type should be sufficient for employee status.[16] More generally, the tribunal swept aside the analysis from *Airfix*,[17] which found mutuality to be established by course of dealing, and from *Nethermere* (not yet decided by the Court of Appeal at that point)[18] which played down the role of mutuality in favour of a multi-factor analysis, with no real explanation of why neither approach was applicable in the case.[19]

Importantly, the tribunal also noted that it would not be reasonable to expect a person whose 'business' consisted solely of supplying their own labour to have made a significant investment in their 'business' or to take a substantial risk of profit and loss.[20] Of course, on one view, a person who supplies their labour to a single 'customer' does take a significant risk because they have not diversified their business across different 'customers'. However, the tribunal read this factor differently to conclude that a person whose only asset was their labour, and thus whose only means of earning more money was to work more hours, could

[11] *O'Kelly* (n 5) [24].
[12] P Leighton, 'Employment Status and the "Casual" Worker: *O'Kelly v Trust House Forte plc*' (1984) 13 *ILJ* 62.
[13] *O'Kelly* (n 5) [25].
[14] ibid [26].
[15] See, eg, Leighton (n 12) 65; Fredman (n 3) 347.
[16] ACL Davies, 'The Contract for Intermittent Employment' (2007) 36 *ILJ* 102.
[17] *Airfix Footwear Ltd v Cope* [1978] IRLR 396 (EAT).
[18] *Nethermere (St Neots) Ltd v Gardiner* [1983] IRLR 103 (EAT).
[19] *O'Kelly* (n 5) [26].
[20] ibid [24].

still count as running their own business. Arguably, rather than applying the business test, this approach subverts it completely by taking away some of the key indicators of running a business: having assets and customers, and taking a risk of profit and loss that goes beyond just deciding to work more or fewer hours oneself. We have had to wait until the Supreme Court's decision in *Uber* for judicial recognition of how questionable this analysis is.[21]

Finally, the tribunal reinforced its conclusion on the claimants' status by noting that they had accepted that they were independent contractors (not least because the trade union official who had approached management about the claimants' employment status had (unfortunately) said they were seeking a 'change'[22]) and that this reflected industry norms.[23] While the tribunal was concerned not to make a decision with 'damaging repercussions' for the hotel sector, the obvious problem with this aspect of the decision is that custom and practice, however widespread, may not be legally accurate, an issue which is for the tribunal to determine.[24] Indeed, particular customs may have arisen because, for example, they are convenient for employers and are not easy for low-paid, precarious workers to contest.

The tribunal thus concluded, by a majority, that the waiters were not employees and were not eligible for interim relief. It is important to note that, on any sensible reading of the judgment, the tribunal did not clearly separate out the question of the waiters' status during the wage-work bargain from the question of mutual obligations giving rise to a 'global' or 'umbrella' contract.[25] This strategy for analysing the case only emerged at the appellate level.

B. The Employment Appeal Tribunal Decision

Because the claim took the form of an application for interim relief, the Employment Appeal Tribunal heard it on an expedited basis and gave an ex tempore judgment which (to the best of my knowledge) was not reported at the time.[26] The Employment Appeal Tribunal expressed some irritation that the need to decide preliminary points of law regarding employment status undermined the purpose of section 77.[27]

The Employment Appeal Tribunal's jurisdiction is, of course, to hear appeals on a point of law, and at the relevant time the exact scope of its jurisdiction in

[21] *Uber* (n 4) [101] (Lord Leggatt).
[22] *O'Kelly* (n 5) [17].
[23] ibid [27]–[28].
[24] ibid [28]. The Supreme Court's decision in *Uber* (n 4) [76] is based on an awareness of this risk.
[25] ibid [28].
[26] *O'Kelly v Trusthouse Forte Plc* (EAT, 11 May 1983). The transcript is available in the National Archives, J149/217.
[27] ibid 1.

employment status cases had become contested.[28] While it is tolerably clear that the definition of a contract of employment is a question of law, and the actual arrangements between the parties are a question of fact, uncertainty can arise in relation to the crucial question: the application of the definition to the facts to determine whether the claimant is an employee. The traditional view, derived from *Simmons v Heath Laundry*,[29] was that this was a 'mixed' question of fact and law, so that an appeal on a point of law would lie only if the tribunal had misdirected itself on the law or had made a decision that could be characterised as perverse.[30] However, the Court of Appeal in *Young & Woods v West* had treated employment status as a question of law,[31] and this had been followed by the Employment Appeal Tribunal in a number of subsequent cases.[32] The Employment Appeal Tribunal in *O'Kelly* regarded itself as bound by *Young & Woods*, and therefore held that it was entitled to reach its own decision on the claimants' employment status.[33]

Turning to the substance, the Employment Appeal Tribunal regarded the case as raising two questions: whether there was an 'overall' contract between the hotel and the regular casuals, and their status while actually working.[34] On the 'overall' contract question, the Employment Appeal Tribunal considered two challenges to the tribunal's decision. First, it was argued on behalf of the claimants that mutuality of obligation did exist in the relationship because of the priority given to the regular casuals by the hotel, and the obligation on them to attend for work once they had accepted an assignment. However, the Employment Appeal Tribunal refused to disturb the tribunal's ruling on this point and accepted that the relationship was held together by economic forces rather than by legal obligations.[35] The Employment Appeal Tribunal also noted that there was (in its view) no obligation to roster the regular casuals which it regarded as an insurmountable obstacle to demonstrating a promise on the part of the employer to offer work.[36]

The Employment Appeal Tribunal was more critical of the tribunal's approach to the custom and practice of the industry, and the parties' view of the nature of their agreement.[37] It held there was insufficient evidence to support the

[28] Then Employment Protection (Consolidation) Act 1978, s 136; currently Employment Tribunals Act 1996, s 21.

[29] *Simmons v Heath Laundry Co* [1910] 1 KB 543 (CA). See also *Edwards v Bairstow* [1956] AC 14 (HL).

[30] See, eg, *Construction Industry Training Board v Labour Force Ltd* [1970] 3 All ER 220 (DC); *Global Plant Ltd v Secretary of State for Health and Social Security* [1972] 1 QB 139 (QB); *Ferguson v John Dawson & Partners (Contractors) Ltd* [1976] 1 WLR 1213 (CA) 1230.

[31] *Young & Woods v West* [1980] IRLR 201 (CA) [15] (Stephenson LJ).

[32] See, eg, *Addison* (n 9); *Nethermere* (n 18).

[33] *O'Kelly* (n 26) 12.

[34] ibid 12.

[35] ibid 14–15.

[36] ibid 15.

[37] ibid 17.

tribunal's conclusions on these points and, in particular, that there was no basis for concluding that the parties had given any thought to the legal implications of the arrangements they had made. However, this made no difference to the outcome given the earlier conclusion on mutuality of obligation.

The Employment Appeal Tribunal then considered the claimants' status while working.[38] A finding that they had a series of short contracts of employment each covering a particular work engagement at the hotel, even without mutuality of obligation to tie them together, might still have paved the way for the claim of unfair dismissal on trade union grounds because it did not require any period of qualifying employment. The Employment Appeal Tribunal regarded the tribunal as having either not addressed the point at all or asserted that the individual contracts were contracts for services without giving any reasons for that conclusion.[39] The Employment Appeal Tribunal examined the list of factors used by the tribunal to decide the 'overall' contract question, and concluded that those used to argue that there was no 'overall' contract of employment did not apply to the individual contracts, with the result that these could be and were contracts of employment.[40] The Employment Appeal Tribunal had already ruled that the parties' intentions and the custom and practice of the industry could not be taken into account because there was no evidence to support the tribunal's conclusions, so the key factors were, of course, mutuality of obligation and the ability to terminate the arrangement on either side. In relation to the individual contracts, neither factor applied: mutuality of obligation was not relevant during an engagement, and (according to the Employment Appeal Tribunal) there was no ability to terminate the arrangement on either side once the waiter had arrived to complete an assigned shift. Therefore, the individual contracts were contracts of employment.

C. The Court of Appeal Decision

The main focus of the case in the Court of Appeal was the correct approach to be taken to appeals on a point of law, responding to an invitation from the Employment Appeal Tribunal to resolve this question. The majority held that the Employment Appeal Tribunal had been too ready to interfere in the tribunal's decision. Having cast itself into more of a reviewing role, the Court of Appeal inevitably engaged much less fully with the substantive issues of employment status in the case.

Sir John Donaldson MR and Fox LJ held that the Employment Appeal Tribunal or a higher court could only interfere with a tribunal's decision if it

[38] ibid 18–23.
[39] ibid 18. See also *O'Kelly* (n 5) [28].
[40] *O'Kelly* (n 26) 21.

could be found that the tribunal had misdirected itself in law, either expressly, in the way that the tribunal had stated the law it was applying, or by inference, from the conclusion that the tribunal had reached.[41] The latter option would require the Employment Appeal Tribunal or higher court to find that 'no reasonable tribunal, properly directing itself on the relevant questions of law, could have reached the conclusion under appeal'.[42] This restored the orthodoxy of *Edwards v Bairstow* in preference to the Employment Appeal Tribunal's reading of *Young & Woods*.[43] Ackner LJ, who had also been on the court in *Young & Woods*, continued to support the more interventionist approach of finding an error of law either where the tribunal had taken into account the wrong factors or where the tribunal had given one or more of the factors the wrong weight.[44]

In the Court of Appeal, the tribunal's finding that there was no mutuality of obligation was, again, upheld.[45] The parties' view of their own arrangements was regarded as irrelevant, because there was no ambiguity about the legal nature of the relationship and therefore no need to consider this factor.[46] The Court of Appeal did, however, question the Employment Appeal Tribunal's exclusion of custom and practice from consideration, holding that this was a legitimate factor, but it had little importance given the mutuality point.[47] The Court of Appeal's treatment of the mutuality point was relatively limited. This is not surprising, given its approach to its own jurisdiction, because it was simply in the business of assessing whether the tribunal had directed itself properly in law. Thus, to the extent that *O'Kelly* has influenced later cases on the mutuality question, it is on the basis of a relatively limited discussion at the appellate level.

On the individual contracts point, the Court of Appeal did not uphold the Employment Appeal Tribunal's conclusion but split in its approach. Ackner LJ, in the minority, would have remitted the case to the tribunal to determine whether the individual contracts should be classified as contracts of employment or contracts for services.[48] He also raised a further issue about the application of the concept of dismissal in this context.[49] Although it is not entirely clear, this seems to be the concern that, if the waiters were only employees while actually at work, the hotel would only have 'dismissed' them for the purposes of the claim had it done so in the middle of a shift. I return to this point below.

[41] *O'Kelly* (n 1) 121 (Fox LJ), 123 (Sir John Donaldson MR).
[42] ibid 123.
[43] *Edwards* (n 29); *Young* (n 31).
[44] *O'Kelly* (n 1) 111.
[45] ibid 116 (Ackner LJ), 121–22 (Fox LJ), 124 (Sir John Donaldson MR).
[46] ibid 116 (Ackner LJ).
[47] ibid 117 (Ackner LJ), 124 (Sir John Donaldson MR).
[48] ibid 118 (Ackner LJ).
[49] ibid.

Sir John Donaldson MR and Fox LJ, in the majority, took a tougher line on the individual contracts point, one which has cast a long shadow over subsequent case-law. They agreed that, if the tribunal had not decided the question, the Employment Appeal Tribunal had been wrong to reach its own conclusion and should have remitted the point to the tribunal for decision.[50] However, they were prepared to infer that the tribunal had addressed the issue through its discussion of the 'overall' contract: the fact that the waiters had no 'overall' contract meant that each individual engagement was performed on the basis of a contract for services, not a contract of employment.[51] Sir John Donaldson MR suggested that to hold otherwise would mean that any independent contractor with only one client would become an employee of that client.[52]

D. Summary

Although the two substantive issues in *O'Kelly* – mutuality of obligation and the claimants' status during the wage-work bargain – have had an important influence over subsequent cases and will form the main focus of my discussion, it is important to be clear that the judges in the Court of Appeal, and to some extent also the Employment Appeal Tribunal, were principally focused on a procedural matter: the proper scope of an appeal on a point of law in this context.

While this can be treated as an analytical question, it has strong policy overtones.[53] The majority in the Court of Appeal was concerned to minimise litigation by making it harder for people to appeal against tribunal decisions, and it is clear that there are some benefits to this, particularly if tribunals are intended to provide a quick and cheap resolution to disputes. It is also arguable that tribunals have greater expertise than the higher courts in questions they deal with regularly, such as the definition of 'employee', so it should not be assumed that the Employment Appeal Tribunal or the Court of Appeal are necessarily able to make better decisions on the matter. However, as Ackner LJ pointed out in *O'Kelly* itself, and as Leighton argued in a case note at the time, the disadvantage of giving greater scope to tribunals is the uncertainty and inconsistency that is likely to develop.[54] It was clear on the facts that Mr O'Kelly and his colleagues were among many hundreds of casual workers in one hotel, let alone across the industry as a whole, and it is not helpful if the employment status of such workers depends on which tribunal decides the case or on the tribunal's composition on a particular day. The less scope there is for the Employment Appeal Tribunal to intervene, the harder it becomes to ensure a broad consistency of approach.

[50] ibid 122 (Fox LJ), 126 (Sir John Donaldson MR).
[51] ibid 122 (Fox LJ), 125 (Sir John Donaldson MR).
[52] ibid 126.
[53] For an analytical approach, see, eg, T Endicott, 'Questions of Law' (1998) 114 *LQR* 292.
[54] *O'Kelly* (n 1) 115 (Ackner LJ). See also Leighton (n 12) 62–63.

III. 'LANDMARK' ELEMENT 1: MUTUALITY OF OBLIGATION

Probably the idea most closely associated with *O'Kelly* is the proposition that mutuality of obligation – a promise on the part of the employer to offer work in the future and a promise on the part of the employee to accept it – is a key requirement in proving the presence of a 'global' or an 'umbrella' contract of employment. In this section, I review some of the subsequent case-law and consider the role of mutuality of obligation in the law on employment status today.

A. Mutuality after *O'Kelly*

Assessing the impact of *O'Kelly* on discussions of mutuality of obligation (and employee status more generally) in later cases is not an easy task, not least because of the sheer volume of decisions involved. Moreover, it is important to recognise that the influence of any particular decision is bound to be limited, in the sense that each case turns on its own facts and circumstances, particularly given the appellate courts' reluctance to intervene. The task of the tribunal is not to identify and apply previous cases with similar-looking work relationships, but rather to direct itself appropriately as to the law and to reach a reasonable conclusion on the relationship at issue in the case. Nevertheless, we can attribute to *O'Kelly* a particularly strict approach to the definition and application of mutuality of obligation (adopted by the tribunal and upheld in the Court of Appeal) which made it harder for subsequent tribunals and courts to adopt worker-protective approaches to employment status. This became particularly pernicious when coupled with another line of case-law focusing on construing contract documents to the exclusion of other evidence of the parties' intentions.

Most cases in fact cite *Nethermere* rather than *O'Kelly* as authority for the proposition that there must be mutuality of obligation in order to give rise to a global or umbrella contract of employment.[55] The Court of Appeal handed down its judgment in *Nethermere* in May 1984, almost a year after its decision in *O'Kelly*.[56] Stephenson LJ, after quoting various passages from *Ready Mixed Concrete*,[57] stated that '[t]here must, in my judgment, be an irreducible minimum of obligation on each side to create a contract of service'.[58]

[55] *Nethermere* (n 2).

[56] Because the claimants were applying for interim relief, *O'Kelly* was heard relatively quickly in 1983 with the Court of Appeal decision being handed down in July of that year. *Nethermere* was decided in the Industrial Tribunal in October 1981.

[57] *Ready Mixed Concrete (South East) Ltd v Minister of Pensions and National Insurance* [1968] 2 QB 497 (QB).

[58] *Nethermere* (n 2) 623.

He identified the employer's obligation to provide work and pay and the employee's obligation to accept or do the work as constituting the minimum obligations in question.[59] The tribunal's ruling in *Nethermere* was ambiguously worded so that it was not entirely clear whether it had held that mutuality of obligation was not required, or that mutuality of obligation was present in the case.[60] Its decision was rescued because of its reference to the *Airfix* case, a case with similar facts in which it had been held that an ostensibly casual, piece-work relationship could become a contract of employment by course of dealing, particularly where the provision and performance of work was regular and of long duration.[61] Stephenson LJ expressed regret for his comments on the appellate jurisdiction in the *Young & Woods* case and adopted the *O'Kelly* approach instead,[62] upholding the tribunal's decision (but only by the narrowest of margins) because there was no obvious misdirection.[63] *Nethermere* was approved by the House of Lords in *Carmichael* in 1999.[64]

Both *Nethermere* and *O'Kelly* adopt quite stringent ways of defining the pair of promises required for mutuality of obligation: *Nethermere* in Stephenson LJ's discussion of the 'irreducible minimum', and *O'Kelly* in the Court of Appeal's ready acceptance of the idea that the waiters' status as 'regular casuals' counted for nothing in law. As I have argued elsewhere, the regulars' expectation that they would be given priority in the award of work and the hotel manager's use of sanctions if they turned down work could have been treated as a pair of (lesser) promises giving rise to a contract, but were instead seen as matters of practicality or economics.[65] Although this strictness is tempered to some extent by the result on the facts in *Nethermere*, the Court of Appeal's obvious doubt about the tribunal's decision meant that there was no strong encouragement to tribunals to adopt more worker-protective strategies in this context.

Nevertheless, it is possible to trace a number of subsequent decisions in which a generous approach to finding mutuality of obligation was taken. For example, in *Boyd Line v Pitts*, the claimant trawlerman had worked for the shipowner for some 30 years on a series of short-term assignments for which he was paid a wage and a share of the profits.[66] He was not paid when he was not at sea. However, it was clear that the shipowner was obliged to offer him work in preference to others, and he was expected not to accept assignments with other firms (it appeared that there was a 'no poaching' agreement between the firms)

[59] ibid.
[60] ibid 624.
[61] *Airfix Footwear Ltd v Cope* [1978] ICR 1210 (EAT).
[62] *Nethermere* (n 2) 620–22.
[63] ibid 627. See also 734–35 (Dillon LJ).
[64] *Carmichael v National Power Plc* [1999] ICR 1226 (HL) 1230 (Lord Irvine LC).
[65] Davies (n 16).
[66] *Boyd Line v Pitts* [1986] ICR 244 (EAT).

and had, in practice, never done so. This set of facts was found to give rise to a global contract. Perhaps most strikingly, the Trusthouse Forte group lost a case with very similar facts to *O'Kelly* in relation to the staff of its racecourse catering division.[67] The claimants were – as in *O'Kelly* – described as 'regular casuals', who were required to present themselves at a meeting point to be collected by a bus and taken to the relevant racecourse whenever there was a race meeting. If they were unable or unwilling to work, they had to find a substitute, and if they did not turn up for work or provide a substitute, they faced a sanction in the form of a short period of suspension. The tribunal's decision is, admittedly, very brief, but it appears that the tribunal found that they had mutuality of obligation because of the regularity and duration of their work, following *Nethermere*, and that their employee status was not defeated by the substitution option because it was very limited in practice. Most strikingly, the tribunal said: 'We feel that the decision in the *O'Kelly* case has to some extent been overtaken by the *Nethermere* case and we find that the applicants were employed ....'[68]

There was also some support at appellate level for the idea that mutuality of obligation could be fulfilled in a variety of different ways, not just in the strict *O'Kelly* sense. In *Clark*, Sir Christopher Slade said that:

> I would, for my part, accept that the mutual obligations required to found a global contract of employment need not necessarily and in every case consist of obligations to provide and perform work. To take one obvious example, an obligation by the one party to accept and do work if offered and an obligation on the other party to pay a retainer during such periods as work was not offered would in my opinion, be likely to suffice.[69]

However, this approach could not be applied in *Clark* itself in which the claimant's only suggestion of a continuing obligation between assignments as a bank nurse was to keep patient information confidential, an obligation which was found to stem from each separate assignment.

These worker-protective decisions and statements are, however, largely outweighed by cases in what we might term 'the *O'Kelly* tradition' in which a stricter approach to mutuality of obligation was preferred, leaving claimants without access to statutory employment rights. For example, in *Nicholls*, a case about homeworkers assembling bolts with parallels to *Nethermere*, it was found that the claimants were not employees, in part because of a lack of mutuality of obligation.[70] The 'employer' was not dependent on their work and was not obliged to provide any work for them to do, and they were free to turn down work in weeks when they did not want it without any sanction. In *Hellyer Brothers Ltd v McLeod*, two joined cases concerning trawlermen with similar facts to

[67] *Lawson v Ring & Brymer Ltd* (Industrial Tribunal, 18 February 1985).
[68] ibid [19].
[69] *Clark v Oxfordshire HA* [1998] IRLR 125 (CA) [41].
[70] *Nicholls v Hilti Industries Ltd* (Industrial Tribunal, 14 January 1985) [8].

Boyd Line, the claimants sought redundancy payments when their employers decided to cease fishing.[71] They had been employed over a period of many years on a series of short-term engagements each time the fishing boat put to sea. In both cases, the industrial tribunal found that mutuality of obligation could be inferred from the surrounding circumstances, but their decisions were overturned by the Employment Appeal Tribunal and Court of Appeal on the basis that there was insufficient evidence to support their conclusions.[72] In particular, it was held that although in practice the trawlermen made themselves available to the shipowner and did not work for anyone else between assignments, it could not be inferred that this was because they were under any legal obligation to be so available. They could have taken other work had they wished to do so.

With grim inevitability, the emphasis on mutuality of obligation in the strict *O'Kelly* sense created an opportunity for employers to draw up casual contracts excluding the relevant promises and thus to deny working people employee status. *Stevedoring & Haulage Services v Fuller* offers an example of this.[73] The claimants in that case were dockers who had been made redundant by their employer and subsequently 're-hired' on a casual basis. There were a number of potential indicators of employee status: they worked regularly (and did not work for any other employer), they were assigned work in preference to other casuals, they were subject to the alleged employer's detailed control, they were provided with protective clothing and training, and they were punished if they turned down shifts. However, the documents with which they had been supplied when they began work stated that they were not employees and that there was no obligation on the employer to offer work or on them to accept it. They were required to sign a statement to the effect that they understood that they were being engaged on an 'ad hoc and casual' basis. The Employment Tribunal held that the necessary pair of promises to give rise to mutuality of obligation could be implied into the parties' contract based on the way the parties had conducted themselves in practice. Although the Court of Appeal accepted that the written documents need not be treated as conclusive unless this was the parties' clear intention, following *Carmichael*,[74] the Employment Tribunal's decision was overturned on the basis that it was not legitimate to imply terms which contradicted the express terms of the contract.[75]

B. Mutuality Today

I will conclude this section by offering a few thoughts on mutuality of obligation in the current law. Space precludes a full discussion of this large and complex

[71] *Hellyer Brothers Ltd v McLeod* [1987] ICR 526 (CA).
[72] ibid 552 (Slade LJ), 560 (Gibson LJ).
[73] *Stevedoring & Haulage Services Ltd v Fuller* [2001] EWCA Civ 651, [2001] IRLR 627.
[74] *Carmichael* (n 64).
[75] *Fuller* (n 73) [10]–[11] (Tuckey LJ).

topic, but there are two important developments closely related to *O'Kelly* which are worthy of note: the courts' modern approach to contractual and statutory interpretation, and the more widespread use of the worker concept as the key to unlocking statutory employment rights.

One positive change is that it should nowadays be much harder for employers to use written contracts to deny mutuality of obligation and thus employee status. This is as a result of the *Autoclenz* decision, in which the Supreme Court recognised the importance of considering all the evidence when classifying working relationships, given the risk that contract documents drawn up by employers in a situation of unequal bargaining power might not reflect the reality of the situation.[76] The employer's attempt to create an impression of self-employment by using clauses in a written contract stating that there were no obligations to offer or accept work did not succeed in that case. The rationale for *Autoclenz* was reformulated and strengthened in the *Uber* decision, in which the Supreme Court held that tribunals should have regard both to the reality of the situation and to the worker-protective purpose of the statutory rights being claimed when deciding how to classify a work relationship.[77] This not only reinforces the requirement to look beyond any written documentation, but also encourages a greater focus on the rights at stake. Although *Uber* is concerned with the statutory 'worker' definition, the same reasoning – that the employer should not be allowed to dictate the personal scope of protective legislation – is also applicable to cases in which Parliament has invoked the common law concept of employee.[78]

Thus, in a case with similar facts to *O'Kelly*, a number of new arguments could now be made. First, and most obviously, the written documentation denying mutuality of obligation should not be treated as conclusive and is just one element of the evidence of the parties' relationship. Other employer-driven factors, such as the custom and practice of the industry, should also be disregarded or given only minimal weight. Second, attention should be paid to the statutory purpose: in this case, protecting freedom of association, a fundamental right. As Fredman has pointed out, a casual reader of the judgments in *O'Kelly* would be forgiven for not realising what was at stake for the claimants.[79] *Uber* places this centre-stage. Third, the courts should apply definitional criteria – whether statutory (for worker) or common law (for employee) – in a realistic and non-technical way.[80] For example, although a substantial element of traditional control was missing from the parties' relationship in *Uber*, in the sense that the claimants could choose when to log on and work, the Supreme Court did not

[76] *Autoclenz Ltd v Belcher* [2011] UKSC 41, [2011] ICR 1157.

[77] *Uber* (n 4) [69] and [87] (Lord Leggatt JSC).

[78] A point persuasively made by A Bogg and M Ford QC, 'The Death of Contract in Determining Employment Status' (2021) 137 *LQR* 392, 395.

[79] Fredman (n 3).

[80] *Uber* (n 4) [70].

allow this to defeat the claims and identified other forms of control instead.[81] Similarly, although mutuality of obligation in a very strict sense was missing from *O'Kelly*, another pair of promises that were present (to give priority to 'regular casuals' when offering work and to accept work when offered) could have been taken to be sufficient to establish the parties' long-term commitment to each other.

However, a potential difficulty remains. Parliament has drawn a distinction between rights for workers and employees, and rights enjoyed by employees only.[82] When interpreting the employee concept in the light of *Uber*, the courts may be somewhat constrained by a desire not to collapse this distinction completely. Space precludes a full discussion of this thorny issue here, but my own view would be that extending the employee concept to cover 'regular casuals' like the waiters in *O'Kelly* would not fall foul of this problem, since it would broaden but not abolish mutuality.[83] And although there is some authority to the contrary,[84] mutuality is best viewed as a distinctive requirement of employee status, not as a requirement of worker status too.[85]

In practice, we may never see a case in which these issues are explored in precisely these circumstances, because a casual worker who had been discriminated against on trade union grounds would nowadays have an avenue of recourse that does not depend on proving employee status. Section 146 TULRCA (as amended in 2004[86]) protects a 'worker' against detrimental treatment (which includes not being offered any more work) on trade union grounds, such as asking a trade union representative to approach the employer on their behalf.[87] Although the waiters in *O'Kelly* were found to have been self-employed, the worker option was not before the tribunal at the time, and the suggestion that they were in business on their own account is one of the least plausible elements of the case. Indeed, the waiters had less autonomy than the drivers in *Uber* in the sense that there were penalties for not accepting work as well as substantial control over their activities during engagements. The protection afforded by section 146 is not as good as that afforded to employees – there is no possibility of re-employment, nor is there any opportunity to seek interim relief – but these elements of the employee right are rarely used in practice.[88]

[81] ibid [91]–[101].

[82] Where a fundamental human right is at stake, as it was in *O'Kelly*, it is arguable that any limitation of protection to employees could be challenged using the Human Rights Act 1998, though the courts' track-record on Article 11 is mixed at best. Space precludes a full discussion of this issue here.

[83] It might, however, have a more radical effect when combined with a re-think of status during the wage-work bargain, as discussed in the next section.

[84] Eg, *Byrne Bros (Formwork) Ltd v Baird* [2002] ICR 667 (EAT).

[85] See *Nursing and Midwifery Council v Somerville* [2022] EWCA Civ 229 [52].

[86] Employment Relations Act 2004, s 30(2).

[87] Trade Union and Labour Relations (Consolidation) Act 1992, s 146(2A)–(2B).

[88] Respectively ERA 1996, ss 113–117; TULRCA 1992, s 161.

IV. 'LANDMARK' ELEMENT 2: STATUS WHILE WORKING

A second element of *O'Kelly*, which continues to cast a long shadow over the current law, is its treatment of the claimants' status while working. The Employment Appeal Tribunal attempted to solve the mutuality problem by finding that the claimants were employees during the wage-work bargain, but the Court of Appeal rejected this approach and upheld what it claimed was the tribunal's original finding that they were self-employed even at this time. I consider here how this approach might have improved the lot of casual workers and its ongoing relevance today.

A. Strategic Importance

A finding that a casual worker is an employee during the wage-work bargain has two potential benefits.

First, it would open up access to those employment rights which apply during the working day and do not depend on any continuous period of employment. A simple example is the right to unpaid emergency leave to care for a dependent under section 57A of the Employment Rights Act 1996. However, the exact list of rights to which employee status during the wage-work bargain would give access remains somewhat unclear. The right at stake in *O'Kelly* itself, the right not to be dismissed on trade union grounds, is a 'day one' right not requiring any period of continuous employment.[89] But Ackner LJ's obiter view in the Court of Appeal was that the claimants would only have had an arguable case had they been sent home in the middle of a shift (when they had employee status), not if the relationship had been terminated between engagements (when they did not have that status).[90] While this is hard to challenge as a matter of logic, it would be highly problematic in practice because it would give the employer a very easy route to avoid its obligations. This issue was never resolved because the claimants were not found to be employees in any event.

Second, a casual worker who is an employee during the wage-work bargain may be able to use the statutory continuity provisions in section 212 of the Employment Rights Act 1996 to gain access to rights requiring a qualifying period of continuous employment, such as the right to a redundancy payment or the right not to be unfairly dismissed.[91] This approach is exemplified by the

[89] TULRCA 1992, s 154.

[90] *O'Kelly* (n 1) 118. A refusal to offer a worker future shifts on trade union grounds could now be challenged under TULRCA 1992, s 146.

[91] For early discussions of this possibility, see H Collins, 'Employment Rights of Casual Workers (2000) 29 *ILJ* 73, 77–78; S Anderman, 'The Interpretation of Protective Statutes and Contracts of Employment' (2000) 29 *ILJ* 223, 235–37, 239–40.

decision in *Cornwall CC v Prater*.[92] In that case, the claimant was a tutor for pupils not attending school and was found to have a contract of employment in respect of each pupil. These could be tied together using section 212 into a lengthy period of continuous employment with the council.

The 'employee while working' analysis does not solve every problem associated with mutuality of obligation, but it would have broadened the application of the employee concept and helped some working people in some situations. Indeed, it is arguable that there would have been much less need to develop and invoke a concept of worker had this aspect of *O'Kelly* been decided differently.

B. Subsequent Case Law

Once again, the particular approach to determining employment status – each case turning on its own facts and circumstances – means that there are different lines of case-law on status during the wage-work bargain.

The most radical approach is simply to ignore mutuality of obligation in the context of the wage-work bargain, treating it as relevant only to the presence or absence of a global contract. This approach is exemplified by *McMeechan*.[93] The claimant agency worker was seeking a payment from the Secretary of State in respect of unpaid wages when the agency became insolvent. The Court of Appeal held that although he had no mutuality of obligation between assignments and no global contract, this did not stop him from being an employee of the agency during the wage-work bargain.

An alternative approach is to hold that mutuality is relevant during the wage-work bargain, but to reinterpret it as a pair of promises relating to the duration of the *current* engagement, not the offer or acceptance of future engagements. This approach is most visible in *Prater*.[94] While there was no obligation on the local authority to find new pupils for the claimant to teach or on her to accept future assignments, it was held that there was mutuality once she had taken on a particular pupil. She was expected to see the assignment through and the authority was expected to provide her with future work and pay in connection with that pupil until such time as her services were no longer needed. Although some of the assignments in *Prater* were quite long, this analysis could work for any wage-work bargain, including a shorter one, in which there is no right for either the employer or the employee to end the shift before the agreed time.

However, a prominent line of cases has taken *O'Kelly* as authority for the proposition that absence of mutuality *between* wage-work bargains can be a

[92] *Cornwall CC v Prater* [2006] EWCA Civ 102, [2006] ICR 731. See further ACL Davies, 'Casual Workers and Continuity of Employment' (2006) 35 *ILJ* 196.

[93] *McMeechan v Secretary of State for Employment* [1997] ICR 549 (CA) 565 (Waite LJ).

[94] *Prater* (n 92) [33] (Mummery LJ).

sign that the working person is self-employed *during* the wage-work bargain. This view was neatly summarised by Elias LJ in *Quashie*:

> … whilst the fact that there is no umbrella contract does not preclude the worker being employed under a contract of employment when actually carrying out an engagement, the fact that a worker only works casually and intermittently for an employer may, depending on the facts, justify an inference that when he or she does work it is to provide services as an independent contractor rather than as an employee.[95]

This approach was adopted in the *Windle* case,[96] concerning court interpreters who sought to bring race discrimination claims under the Equality Act 2010.[97] Underhill LJ said:

> I accept of course that the ultimate question must be the nature of the relationship during the period that the work is being done. But it does not follow that the absence of mutuality of obligation outside that period may not influence, or shed light on, the character of the relationship within it. It seems to me a matter of common sense and common experience that the fact that a person supplying services is only doing so on an assignment-by-assignment basis may tend to indicate a degree of independence, or lack of subordination, in the relationship while at work which is incompatible with employee status even in the extended sense.[98]

This was approved by the Supreme Court in *Uber*.[99] It is important to acknowledge that Underhill LJ's statement is carefully worded: it preserves the possibility that someone might be an employee during the wage-work bargain without mutuality of obligation between assignments, and it does not treat the absence of mutuality as conclusive. However, it remains very unclear how cases like *McMeechan* and *Prater* are properly to be distinguished from *O'Kelly* and *Windle*.

To untangle the conflicting lines of case law, it may be helpful to focus on the courts' purpose in drawing this distinction. This is rarely stated with any clarity, but a clue may be found in the judgment of Sir John Donaldson MR in *O'Kelly*.[100] He suggested that the Employment Appeal Tribunal's approach in that case would have had the effect of making everyone an employee during an exchange of work for pay. Although he did not articulate this concern very fully, one possible worry is that a person hiring a genuinely self-employed person to perform a specific task might find themselves unexpectedly subject to employer obligations during the wage-work bargain.

[95] *Quashie v Stringfellow Restaurants Ltd* [2012] EWCA Civ 1735, [2013] IRLR 99 [12] (Elias LJ).
[96] *Windle v Secretary of State for Justice* [2016] EWCA Civ 459, [2016] ICR 721.
[97] Equality Act 2010, s 83(2)(a). Arguably, this definition is broad enough on its face to cover genuinely self-employed people who perform work personally, but it was significantly narrowed in *Jivraj v Hashwani* [2011] UKSC 40, [2011] ICR 1004.
[98] *Windle* (n 96) [23].
[99] *Uber* (n 4) [91] (Lord Leggatt JSC).
[100] *O'Kelly* (n 1).

One obvious response to this concern is to argue that it does not matter if the law is over-inclusive in its treatment of the wage-work bargain. Genuinely self-employed people might technically acquire some employee rights but they would be unlikely to invoke them, and over-inclusivity might be preferable to the alternative, which is to exclude vulnerable working people from protection. More profoundly, these boundaries are now blurred to a considerable extent by the worker definition, which can operate to afford some employment rights even to the genuinely self-employed, as the *Westwood* case so clearly illustrates.[101]

My own view is that even if the courts' concern to remove the genuinely self-employed from employee protection is legitimate as a matter of principle, it has been undermined by their spectacular failure to decide cases in a way that achieves this objective. This is exemplified by *O'Kelly* itself. There was no suggestion whatsoever that the waiters were in business on their own account or (to use modern language) that the hotel was their client or customer. They did not, for example, fix a price for their services, and the only way they could earn more money was by working more hours. During the wage-work bargain, there were many indicators of employee status: the waiters worked under the direction of the hotel's managers, wore a uniform and were fully integrated into the hotel's operations. The Court of Appeal's decision to uphold the tribunal on this point is particularly disappointing because, on any fair reading of the tribunal's decision, it had not squarely addressed the matter of status during the wage-work bargain as a separate question.

In conclusion, while *O'Kelly* is often thought of primarily in connection with mutuality of obligation, it has also had a significant, and malign, influence on the way we think about the wage-work bargain. This seems particularly unfortunate since the idea of focusing on status during the wage-work bargain stemmed from a well-meaning attempt on the part of the Employment Appeal Tribunal to find an alternative route to protecting Mr O'Kelly and his colleagues. Conceptually, it seems correct to suggest that where the parties' wider relationship is one of self-employed person and customer or client, the exchange of work for pay should not normally be treated as a contract of employment. However, care must be taken to ensure that this approach is only applied in clear-cut cases of genuine self-employment.

V. CONCLUSION

O'Kelly is undoubtedly a landmark case, but it is not a particularly attractive landmark. It stands out for the procedurally-driven, formalistic and unsympathetic nature of its reasoning, showing limited concern for working people

[101] *Hospital Medical Group v Westwood* [2012] EWCA Civ 1005, [2013] ICR 415.

facing discrimination on trade union grounds, and little understanding of the realities of precarious working relationships.

Much has been written about the law on employment status, including powerful critiques of the very requirement to show mutuality of obligation in order to be classified as an employee.[102] There is much force in these critiques. However, mutuality of obligation would have been less problematic had the courts been more willing to find it in cases where work was intermittent but regular, and had the courts made greater use of employee status during the wage-work bargain as an alternative route to protection. The *O'Kelly* decision is partly responsible for both of these difficulties. First, a more sympathetic tribunal could have held that the promises between the parties were sufficient for mutuality of obligation: the employer clearly promised to offer available work to regular casuals in preference to others, and there were sanctions in operation for turning down shifts. This would have pushed a greater proportion of casual workers – typically those with relatively regular and reliable work for one employer – across the boundary into the employee category. Second, the option of finding employee status during the wage-work bargain could have been remitted to the tribunal at the very least. Greater use of this approach would have created the potential, depending on the drafting of statutory employment rights, to afford some protection to all working people except the genuinely self-employed, including those working on a very short-term basis. Frustratingly, the tribunal clearly understood that part of its task was to work out whether the claimants were in business on their own account, but it failed to apply that test in any meaningful way on the facts of the case.

Nowadays, greater use of the term 'worker' as the key to unlocking statutory employment rights, coupled with the Supreme Court's decision in *Uber* that statutory rights should be afforded to those Parliament intended to protect, has overcome many of the practical difficulties generated by *O'Kelly* and related cases. Significant (and growing[103]) protections can be secured without the need to show employee status, and the courts are much less likely to be swayed by employer efforts to create false impressions of self-employment. However, this has come at a price. A 'three-tier' approach to employment rights has become firmly entrenched in the law, with workers missing out on some important

[102] See, eg, Z Adams, 'Labour Law and the Labour Market: Employment Status Reconsidered' (2019) 135 *LQR* 611; S Fredman, 'Women at Work: the Broken Promise of Flexicurity' (2004) 33 *ILJ* 299; M Freedland, *The Personal Employment Contract* (Oxford, Oxford University Press, 2003); P Leighton and M Wynn, 'Classifying Employment Relationships – More Sliding Doors or a Better Regulatory Framework?' (2011) 40 *ILJ* 5.

[103] See, eg, Personal Protective Equipment at Work (Amendment) Regulations 2022 (SI 2022/8) enacted in response to the decision in *R (Independent Workers' Union of Great Britain) v Secretary of State for Work and Pensions* [2020] EWHC 3050 (Admin), [2021] ICR 372.

rights such as the right not to be unfairly dismissed. The pressure to expand the employee definition has diminished because, understandably, strategic litigation has tended to focus on worker claims, and the purposive approach set out in *Uber* may not extend as far as disrupting the logic of the statutory scheme. A different decision in *O'Kelly* (coupled with a sympathetic legislature) might have been able to achieve appropriate protections for working people through creative application of the employee concept alone.

9

A Half-Forgotten Landmark: Enderby v Frenchay *and the Continuing Challenges of Equal Pay Laws*

SANDRA FREDMAN

I. INTRODUCTION

THERE ARE MANY ways in which *Enderby v Frenchay Health Authority*[1] deserves the acclaim of a landmark case. Yet, nearly 30 years after it was decided, the issues are depressingly familiar. Indeed, the case note I wrote for the *Industrial Law Journal* in 1994 could just as easily have been written today.[2] In that note, I argued that the decision was to be welcomed on several counts. In the last resort, however, it did not go far enough. So, what have three decades taught us, and what have we failed to learn?

Enderby exposed the dilemma at the heart of equal pay legislation. If a group of predominantly female workers is paid significantly less than a group of predominantly male workers doing work of equal value, to what extent can the pay disparity be attributed to the differences in gender rather than being a product of other factors, such as bargaining systems or market forces? Courts, concerned to prevent widespread challenges of pay inequities per se, have quickly reverted to a fault-based understanding of discrimination, looking to finding clear prejudicial conduct or exclusionary processes on the part of employers. However, this risks neglecting the social forces which operate most effectively to perpetuate women's disadvantage in the workforce. The stubborn persistence of pay discrepancies between men and women makes it imperative for equal pay legislation to penetrate apparently neutral pay structures to address these underlying structural factors. The judgment of the European Court in *Enderby* went some distance towards this goal, recognising that the

[1] Case C-127/92 *Enderby v Frenchay Health Authority* [1994] ICR 112 (ECJ).
[2] S Fredman, 'Equal Pay and Justification' (1994) 23 *Industrial Law Journal* 37.

mere fact of a pay discrepancy was sufficient to shift the burden to the employer to justify the difference on grounds unrelated to gender. However, the Court's continued endorsement of 'market forces' as a potential justification for pay differentials, albeit in a more limited manner than that of the referring court in the UK, has considerably detracted from this recognition. This chapter begins with the perspectives from 1994, when *Enderby* was decided. It then assesses *Enderby's* legacy, first from the standpoint of the litigants and the other women whose pay was at issue; and then in relation to the overall development of the law. I conclude that, while *Enderby* has dented the pervasive resistance to equal pay for women workers, like many cases which have come later, it merely triggered a regrouping of forces in a different part of the equal pay structure. Both the legislation and the courts' interpretation of the law need far more radical revision to genuinely fulfil the promise of equal pay for work of equal value in EU and UK law.

II. *ENDERBY*: THE PERSPECTIVE FROM 1994

Behind the question referred to the ECJ lies one of the key challenges of equal pay legislation. Was it merely a coincidence that senior speech therapists were paid on a rate that was 60 per cent lower than that of senior psychologists and pharmacists doing work of equal value? The answer to this depends on whether courts are able to surmount their instincts to look for fault and recognise structural inequalities. In the EAT, Wood J had no doubt of the answer. 'The purpose of the Act was to prevent discrimination – not to provide equal pay.'[3] The pay disparity alone did not raise a prima facie case of discrimination: it was necessary to prove that the process of decision-making tended to exclude women. Since pay was set by separate collective bargaining structures, which were not internally discriminatory, there was no discrimination.

The ECJ was able to rely on a more incisive notion of discrimination. Instead of searching for an exclusionary process, it focussed on the fact of the pay discrepancy. A disparity in pay between two highly segregated jobs of equal value, it held, was sufficient to raise a prima facie case of sex discrimination, putting the onus on the employer to justify the difference on the basis of objective reasons. Importantly, it held, '[w]orkers would be unable to enforce the principle of equal pay before the national courts if evidence of a prima facie case of discrimination did not shift to the employer the onus of showing that the pay differential is not in fact discriminatory.'[4]

This decision was important in its recognition that job segregation itself raises a strong suspicion of discrimination. The fact that speech therapists

[3] *Enderby v Frenchay Health Authority* [1991] ICR 382 (EAT) [75] (Wood J).
[4] *Enderby* (n 1) para 18.

were a low paid profession relative to the comparators was closely related to its status as a female dominated profession. As evidence before the EAT revealed, the profession had at least two central hallmarks of 'women's work'. First, the nature of the work made it possible to practise part-time. In 1980, over a third of all speech therapists worked part-time. Second, the pay was too low to attract men. An inquiry in 1972 established that the pay and career structure were glaringly out of proportion to the responsibilities of the job, acting as a disincentive to recruitment, particularly of men.

Having shifted the burden to the employer to justify the discrepancy, the next crucial question was to determine what sort of justifications were permissible. The respondents mounted two defences: one based on collective bargaining and the second on market forces. In relation to the collective bargaining defence, the respondents argued that speech therapists' pay had always been negotiated in a different committee from that of clinical psychologists. On the evidence, there was no prejudice against women within each bargaining committee. Wood J in the EAT regarded this as an unassailable defence. The legislation, he held, could not have been intended to 'disrupt[ed] the well-tried and established negotiating machinery which is totally untainted by gender'.[5] He was clearly impressed by the good faith of the union and employer representatives in the collective bargaining process. However, focussing on the fault or absence of fault of individual actors obscures the extent to which entrenched social institutions perpetuate inequalities regardless of individual actions. The collective bargaining structure then in existence, based on Whitley Committees which had been unchanged since the NHS was founded in 1947, clearly simply replicated the gender inequalities found in the workforce. Speech therapists had always been in a weak bargaining position, and no amount of good faith by representatives could remedy this. Here too, the ECJ's decision was of crucial importance. Focussing on the results, rather than on individual actors, it held that where the results show that two groups with the same employer and the same trade union are treated differently, the mere fact that rates of pay were decided by separate collective bargaining processes did not preclude a finding of prima facie discrimination. Otherwise, the principle of equal pay could easily be circumvented by using separate bargaining processes.

It is in relation to the market forces defence that the ECJ's stance is weaker, coming close to abandoning its insistence on a results-oriented view. Most worryingly, it held that the state of the employment market, which might lead an employer to increase the pay of a particular job to attract candidates, might constitute an objective justification for a pay discrepancy. The Court did seem to temper this approach by stating that, where a national court can determine precisely what proportion of the increase is attributable to market forces, it must accept that the pay differential is only objectively justifiable to the extent of that

[5] *Enderby* (n 3) [186].

proportion. This might seem to be an important innovation. However, there are at least three problems with this position. First, even if it is possible to demonstrate precisely what proportion of a pay discrepancy is due to market forces, there is no mechanism within equal pay legislation, either at EU or domestic level, to reflect that proportion within the pay structures. Article 119 of the EEC Treaty, and its successor Article 157 of the TFEU, only require equal pay for equal work, precluding the possibility of proportional pay. This is particularly difficult to implement as part of a defence to a claim for equal pay for work adjudged to be of equal value. This contrasts with Canada, where several jurisdictions specify pay equity as achieving proportional pay for work of proportional value.[6]

Even more problematic, the Court's approach assumes that market forces, such as supply and demand, work independently of policy choices. In *Enderby* itself, there had been a shortage of speech therapists, but this had not led to an increase in pay because a decision had been taken not to expand the number of training places available. Finally, and more fundamentally, allowing the state of the job market to act as an ostensibly objective justification for a difference in pay for work of equal value ignores the fact that market forces themselves create and perpetuate inequalities. For example, low pay for work with part-time opportunities may be explained in market terms by the oversupply of women requiring part-time work. Yet the underlying reason for the over-supply is that women remain primarily responsible for child-care. Permitting market forces to constitute a sufficient justification simply entrenches stereotypes and biases which equal pay legislation, especially the right to equal pay for work of equal value, is designed to pierce.

III. ENDERBY'S LEGACY

Given both the strengths and flaws of the *Enderby* decision, as I saw them as a contemporaneous observer, what has its enduring legacy been, and how can we judge it with the benefit of hindsight? This question can be addressed on three levels. The first is to ask what its effect was on Pamela Enderby, her 1,500 co-applicants, and other speech therapists. Second, what was its influence on equal pay laws in the EU and the UK? Third, to what extent has its broader recognition of the structural and institutional nature of unequal pay for women been realised?

So far as its effect on the plaintiffs themselves and the wider group of speech therapists goes, there is some good news. The case was eventually settled, with a reported £30 million paid out by the government in back-pay. Concurrently, a large number of equal pay claims, estimated at 10,000, were lodged. In 2005, Unison and the North Cumbria Acute Hospitals NHS Trust reached an

[6] See further S Fredman, *Discrimination Law*, 3rd edn (Oxford, Oxford University Press, 2022) ch six.

agreement to settle the claims of 1,500 female staff working in posts ranging from nurses to catering assistants and clerical officers. They claimed equal pay for work of equal value with craft operatives, labourers and maintenance assistance and received compensation ranging from £35,000 to £200,000 each.[7]

Enderby is also attributed with leading the Labour Government to a review of pay in the NHS, known as *Agenda for Change*.[8] This overhauled the Whitley Council-based pay system, which was based on national bargaining units, each involving numerous unions covering different groups.[9] Instead, the aim was to set up simplified national pay 'spines' for the various staff groups, removing at least in principle the separate bargaining unit defence. More important for our purposes was that the Labour Government in power at the time took seriously the requirement of equal pay for jobs of equal value[10] and instituted a huge job evaluation programme, leading to the revaluation of jobs in the NHS across the board. This job evaluation scheme was based on 16 factors, including 'analytical and judgement skills', 'emotional effort', and 'working conditions'.[11] It was therefore capable of piercing the many stereotypes attached to women's work and of leading to real and lasting increases in pay. Particularly salient is the fact that it led to an increase in the basic salary for a qualified nurse of about 15 per cent in the first three years of its operation, between 2004 and 2007.

However, this was not an unadulterated positive outcome for protagonists in the case and the wider group of NHS women workers. This was because, although early estimates suggested more than 90 per cent of staff would receive an immediate pay increase as a result of the implementation, *Agenda for Change* also included some prospective downgrading of pay. To prevent this, the pay of 7.5 per cent of staff was protected or 'red-circled'.[12] The likelihood is that these jobs were overwhelmingly male, further delaying women's right to equal pay for work of equal value. A similar pattern of red-circling in local government led to its own set of equal pay claims, with courts eventually holding that it was discriminatory to exclude women from pay protection.[13]

Enderby also exposed the slow and lumbering nature of the statutory machinery for achieving the right to equal pay for work of equal value. It involved 26 court appearances, 1,500 applicants and 16 test cases.[14] It took ten

[7] J Buchan and D Evans, *Realising the Benefits? Assessing the Implementation of Agenda for Change* (London, King's Fund, 2007) 15

[8] TUC, 'Speaking out for Change: Winning Equal Pay for NHS Speech and Language Therapists' (2007) www.tuc.org.uk/publications/speaking-out-change-winning-equal-pay-nhs-speech-and-language-therapists-1985 (accessed 15 February 2022).

[9] Department of Health, *Agenda for Change Final Agreement* (2004) webarchive.nationalarchives.gov.uk/ukgwa/20130103005856/http://www.dh.gov.uk/en/Publicationsandstatistics/Publications/PublicationsPolicyAndGuidance/DH_4095943 (accessed 15 February 2022).

[10] ibid para 13.4, Annex M1.

[11] Buchan and Evans (n 7) 4

[12] ibid 8.

[13] *Redcar and Cleveland BC v Bainbridge* [2008] EWCA Civ 885, [2009] ICR 133.

[14] 'Equal Pay' www.tolpuddlemartyrs.org.uk/story/tuc-150/post-war-and-heady-days-unions/equal-pay (accessed 15 February 2022).

years to achieve a settlement. When the case began in 1986, Margaret Thatcher and her Conservative Government were implacably opposed, sensing the potential for wide ripple effects on NHS pay structures. It was only when the Labour Government came to power that it was brought to its conclusion, and new pay structures put into place.[15] Even then, the long delays in negotiating and implementing the new pay structure meant that by the time it was in place, the financial situation was much tighter than at the start. Matters got even worse after 2010, after Labour lost power to a Conservative-Liberal Democrat coalition Government determined to impose deep cuts in public spending. For seven years, from 2010, pay rises in the NHS were limited to zero or one per cent. Three year pay deals agreed in 2018 did not make up for the real cuts in pay since 2010. So much so that in 2021, nurses argued that only a 12.4 per cent pay rise will bring them back to their 2010 position.[16] Yet they were offered a derisory three per cent.[17]

Notably, Pam Enderby was backed by her union, MSF, now part of UNITE, a fact which was key to her ability to sustain the long and difficult journey through the court process. Trade union support for equal pay claims is crucial. But the absence of proper funding has made it inevitable that equal pay claims for women will be represented as a cost to male workers, leading to acute dilemmas for trade unions representing both constituencies.[18] Two major sources of dispute concerned bonuses paid to predominantly male occupations and the protection of pay for men who stood to lose in the process of implementing new job evaluation schemes ('red-circling'). Trade unions, such as the GMB, opted to favour their male members, not only by negotiating schemes protecting male workers' pay, but also by agreeing a low settlement for women's past pay inequalities to release more money for future pay protection.[19] There was also evidence that unions were negotiating to protect male workers on a longer term basis through job enrichment schemes, so that workers in male-dominated manual grades had been put at the top of their new grades.[20] This meant that women would continue to earn less than men for years ahead, and they also were required to forego backpay. The unedifying result was a Court of Appeal finding of indirect discrimination against the GMB.[21] As the employment tribunal put it: 'It is striking how much care, effort and discussion went into pay protection

[15] TUC (n 8).

[16] Royal College of Nursing, 'NHS Pay: RCN Submits Official Case for 12.5% Rise' (2021) www.rcn.org.uk/news-and-events/news/uk-nhs-pay-rcn-submits-official-case-for-12-5-rise-250121 (accessed 15 February 2022).

[17] 'NHS Staff to Receive 3% Pay Rise' (2021) www.gov.uk/government/news/nhs-staff-to-receive-3-pay-rise (accessed 15 February 2022).

[18] S Fredman, 'Reforming Equal Pay Laws' (2008) 37 *Industrial Law Journal* 193, 209.

[19] *GMB v Allen* [2008] EWCA Civ 810, [2008] ICR 1407.

[20] S Deakin and others, 'Are Litigation and Collective Bargaining Complements or Substitutes for Achieving Gender Equality? A Study of the British Equal Pay Act' (2015) 39 *Cambridge Journal of Economics* 381.

[21] *GMB* (n 19) [12].

and how little into back pay. We believe the union officials in Middlesbrough knew that they were neglecting the interests of the back pay claimants.'[22] The union, it was held, deliberately omitted to 'us[e] its influence to press the employer to comply with its obligation under the Equal Pay Act, those obligations not only being to achieve equal pay going forward but to compensate for past inequality'.[23] Even more disturbing, '[i]n order to justify persuading a group which was overwhelmingly women to be altruistic we believe that the union must be able to demonstrate their members were persuaded by truth to be so as opposed to duped or frightened into being so.'[24] Upholding these findings, the Court of Appeal held that, although the union's aims were legitimate, the means used to achieve these aims were disproportionate.

There is some evidence, although not uncontested, that this acted as a catalyst in encouraging unions to pursue back pay claims on behalf of women members.[25] Deakin and his colleagues conclude that collective bargaining and litigation strategies in Britain have been intertwined at every stage of the history of equal pay legislation.[26] However, it is also clear that the cumbersome nature of litigation has impeded real progress towards equal pay. It is unfortunate that the opportunity was not taken in the Equality Act 2010 to introduce effective enforcement mechanisms.

The second question concerns the impact of *Enderby* on subsequent EU and UK law. Surprisingly, *Enderby* itself is only infrequently cited either in EU or domestic law. Nevertheless, its central insight, namely that a prima facie case of pay discrimination arises simply from the fact of a pay disparity between men and women doing the same work or work of equal value, is now familiar in both legal systems. *Enderby* clarified and strengthened the finding of the earlier case of *Danfoss*.[27] In *Danfoss*, the ECJ held that where an undertaking applies a system of pay which is totally lacking in transparency, and the average pay for women over a relatively large number of employees is less than that for men, the burden shifts to the employer to show that their practice is not discriminatory. In *Danfoss*, the pay disparity arose as a result of the award of individual pay supplements to workers, on the basis of criteria which were not divulged to each worker. *Enderby* took this further and applied it even though there was no lack of transparency, and no evidence of discrimination within the regular collective bargaining processes themselves. The Court's recognition in *Enderby* of the crucial function of a shift in the burden of proof 'where necessary to avoid depriving workers … of any effective means of enforcing the principle of

[22] ibid [12].
[23] ibid.
[24] ibid.
[25] Deakin and others (n 20) 401.
[26] ibid 400–01.
[27] C-109/88 *Handels-og Kontorfunktionaerernes Forbund I Danmark (Union of Clerical and Commercial Employees) v Dansk Arbejdsgiverforening (Danish Employers' Association)* [1991] 1 CMLR 8 (ECJ).

equal pay'[28] received legislative endorsement in the Burden of Proof Directive in 1997.[29] It is now transcribed in the Recast Directive[30] as well as the Race[31] and Employment Directives.[32] These Directives provide that the burden should shift when the complainant establishes facts from which it may be presumed that there has been direct or indirect discrimination. They leave it open as to what facts would give rise to this presumption. This is where *Enderby* still holds sway, standing for the further insight that a disparity in pay can itself lead to such a presumption. This can be seen in the ECJ case of *Kenny v Minister of Justice* in 2013, in which the Court reiterated the *Enderby* principle that if the pay of a predominantly or exclusively female group of workers is significantly lower than a predominantly male group of workers doing work of equal value, there is a prima facie case of discrimination.[33]

More complex in evaluating the *Enderby* legacy is the decision to allow a market forces defence with the caveat that, where a national court can determine precisely what proportion of the increase is attributable to market forces, it must accept that the pay differential is only objectively justifiable to the extent of that proportion. The fears that permitting a market forces defence would erode the right to equal pay have been somewhat allayed by subsequent case law. In *Schönheit* in 2006, the ECJ held that a state cannot rely on the aim of restricting public expenditure to justify a difference in treatment on grounds of sex. To hold otherwise might mean that 'the application and scope of a rule of Community law as fundamental as that of equal treatment between men and women might vary in time and place according to the state of the public finances of Member States'.[34] Properly applied, this standard can be exacting. In *Schönheit* itself, it was held that while it is acceptable to pay part-timers a pro rata pension, a measure which reduces the pension by a proportion greater than warranted by their part-time work is disproportionate and cannot be objectively justified.[35] This chimes with its consistent view in part-time workers cases, that an employer cannot justify indirect discrimination solely on the ground that avoidance of such discrimination would involve increased costs.[36] More concerning is the

[28] *Enderby* (n 1) para 14.

[29] Council Directive 97/80/EC of 15 December 1997 on the burden of proof in cases of discrimination based on sex [1998] OJ L014.

[30] Directive 2006/54/EC of the European Parliament and of the Council of 5 July 2006 on the implementation of the principle of equal opportunities and equal treatment of men and women in matters of employment and occupation (recast) [2006] OJ L204, Art 19.

[31] Council Directive 2000/43/EC of 29 June 2000 implementing the principle of equal treatment between persons irrespective of racial or ethnic origin [2000] OJ L180, Art 8.

[32] Council Directive 2000/78/EC of 27 November 2000 establishing a general framework for equal treatment in employment and occupation [2000] OJ L303, Art 10.

[33] Case C-427/11 *Kenny v Minister for Justice* [2013] 2 CMLR 50 (CJEU).

[34] Joined Cases C-4 and 5/02 *Schönheit v Stadt Frankfurt am Main* [2006] 1 CMLR 5 (ECJ), paras 84–85.

[35] ibid.

[36] Case C-243/95 *Hill v Revenue Commissioners* [1999] ICR 48 (ECJ) para 40.

decision in *Kenny v Minister of Justice*[37] that the interests of good industrial relations may be one factor in the determination of whether differences in pay between two groups of workers are due to objective factors unrelated to discrimination on grounds of gender and are proportional.[38] This could weaken the *Enderby* finding that separate bargaining units are not themselves sufficient to constitute a justification.

The third question relating to the *Enderby* legacy concerns whether its broader recognition of the structural and institutional nature of unequal pay for women has been realised. It is striking that the important points of principle made in the judgment have not oiled the wheels of equal pay litigation. Employers, faced with the potential of large payments to compensate women from whom they have benefited by underpaying for decades, have searched for other parts of the legislation to contest. *Enderby* stood powerfully for the principle that the onus should quickly pass to the employer to justify patent discrepancies. Employers responded by contesting claims at the preliminary stages, aiming to avoid the merits stage altogether, or at least protract the time and expense involved in bringing an equal pay claim. One fertile cause of litigation has been the 'same establishment' requirement. A woman can only claim equal pay if she is paid less than a man doing equal work and employed contemporaneously for the same employer at the same or 'equivalent' establishment.[39] Not only must the comparator be employed by the same employer: he must also be at the same establishment. The requirement that the comparators be employed at the same establishment inevitably obstructs the potential to achieve equal pay for work of equal value, given that one of the chief causes of low pay among women is the fact that so many women work in segregated workplaces or in the lower grades of mixed professions. A woman working in a segregated workplace is unlikely to find a male comparator doing equal work for higher pay at the same establishment. As presaged in *Enderby*, where the ECJ warned that allowing different bargaining units to function as a justification would incentivise employers to resort to such bargaining, the 'same establishment' requirement might easily tempt employers to reorganise their establishments to avoid equal pay claims.

This risk is heightened by the opaque definitions in the Equality Act 2010, where the same establishment requirement is somewhat widened to allow A to compare herself with B if B is employed by the same employer at a different establishment in situations in which 'common terms apply at the establishments (either generally or as between A and B)'.[40] Employers have consistently used this formulation to raise preliminary points as part of an attempt to have the claim struck out. Indeed, there have been four cases in the Supreme Court and

[37] *Kenny* (n 33).
[38] ibid para 50.
[39] Equality Act 2010, s 79.
[40] ibid.

one in the ECJ determining the meaning of this formulation in preliminary proceedings.[41] This is despite the fact that in each of these cases, the apex courts, following in the footsteps of the ECJ in *Enderby*, have opted for a more flexible application of the test in favour of the claimants. There have also been clear dicta in several of these cases, underlying the importance of proceeding to the substance of the claim.

To achieve this, several principles have been crafted.[42] The first is that establishments can be compared where the woman and the male comparator are covered by the same collective agreement.[43] This principle is helpful for segregated workplaces in those parts of the labour force where there are still collective agreements which span more than one workplace. However, these conditions are increasingly difficult to meet, due to the steep decline in collective bargaining, particularly in the private sector, and the technical approach of courts to the interpretation of the statutory provisions. Moreover, where several collective agreements cover different parts of the workforce, a woman's right to equal pay might depend on historical patterns of collective bargaining.[44] This was the case in *British Coal Corp v Smith*,[45] where women canteen workers and cleaners, a paradigmatically female and undervalued occupation, sought to compare themselves to surface mineworkers, an overwhelmingly male and better paid group of workers. Although they were employed by the same employer, many worked at different establishments and their terms and conditions were covered by a variety of collective agreements. In a dictum resonant of the ECJ in *Enderby*, Lord Slynn stated that it was obvious why a woman was not limited to comparing herself with men employed in the same workplace: 'Otherwise an employer could arrange things to ensure that only women worked at a particular establishment or that no man who could reasonably be considered as a possible comparator could work there.'[46] The Court therefore sought to provide an alternative pathway for cross-establishment comparisons even in the absence of a collective agreement covering both workplaces. If there are no male comparators at the claimant's place of work, it held, a cross-establishment comparison can be drawn where like terms and conditions would apply if men were employed at her establishment in the particular jobs concerned.[47]

[41] *Leverton v Clwyd County Council* [1984] IRLR 28 (HL); *British Coal Corp v Smith* [1996] ICR 515 (HL); *North v Dumfries and Galloway Council* [2013] UKSC 45, [2013] ICR 993; *Asda Stores Ltd v Brierley* [2021] UKSC 10, [2021] ICR 786; Case C-624/19 *K v Tesco Stores Ltd* [2021] 3 CMLR 33 (ECJ).

[42] This section draws on Fredman, *Discrimination Law* (n 6) ch six; S Fredman, 'Inching Forward: Preliminary Victory for Equal Value at Tesco and Asda' (2022) 51 *Industrial Law Journal* 166

[43] *Leverton* (n 41).

[44] *South Tyneside Metropolitan BC v Anderson* [2007] ICR 1581 (CA).

[45] *British Coal Corp* (n 41).

[46] ibid 525H.

[47] ibid 526.

However, this formulation was equally opaque, inviting further contestation from employers at the preliminary stages. In *North v Dumfries Council*,[48] the Supreme Court refined the test to create what it called the *North* hypothetical. The question was whether, if the comparators were transferred to do their present jobs in a different location, however unlikely, they would remain employed on the same or broadly similar terms and conditions to those applicable in their current place of work. Lady Hale reiterated that

> [i]t is well known that those jobs which require physical strength have traditionally been better rewarded than those jobs which require dexterity. It is one of the objects of the equality legislation to iron out those traditional inequalities of reward where the work involved is of genuinely equal value.[49]

Importantly, too, she stressed that the same employment test should not be used as a way of avoiding all the remaining steps in the claim.

> The 'same employment' test should not be used as a proxy for those tests or as a way of avoiding the often difficult and complex issues which they raise (tempting though this may be for large employers faced with multiple claims such as these).[50]

This must surely be the right approach. If it is believed that there might be good reasons why a woman is paid less than a man doing work of equal value at a different establishment of the same employer, this should be raised as part of a justification defence.[51] Allowing complex skirmishes on the threshold question of cross-establishment comparison has simply protracted proceedings and allowed employers to delay implementation of the right to equal pay by many years. The *North* case, for example, began in 2006. It was not until 2013 that the Supreme Court held that the first hurdle had been surmounted. Job evaluation, justification and other key steps still needed to be taken.

Nevertheless, large employers continue to contest this point in an attempt to protract potentially very costly equal pay claims. Two large supermarkets, Tesco and Asda, took this approach when faced with multiple claims by low paid women workers. The *Asda* case, which reached the Supreme Court in 2021, was brought by 7,000 workers, overwhelmingly women, employed in Asda supermarkets.[52] They claimed that their work was of equal value to that of the male workforce at Asda's distribution depots, who were paid substantially more and worked at locations separate from the retail stores. As in *Enderby*, the employers protracted the procedure by taking preliminary points all the way to the Supreme Court. Rejecting their claim, Lady Arden held that there was a short and direct answer to the case, provided by the *North* case. Echoing the

[48] *North* (n 41).
[49] ibid [34]
[50] ibid [35]
[51] Equality Act 2010, s 69.
[52] *Asda Stores Ltd* (n 41).

concerns in *Enderby* that there might be incentives for employers to rearrange their business or collective bargaining to avoid equal pay claims, Lady Arden warned that 'if the threshold test is elevated into a major hurdle mirroring other elements of an equal pay claim, the purpose of equal pay legislation will be thwarted, and the pay disparities will not be investigated'.[53]

The attempt of Tesco to thwart equal pay claims at the threshold stage was similarly imaginative, and similarly rejected. It argued before the ECJ that, even though the right to equal pay for like work was directly effective under Article 157 of the Treaty on the Functioning of the European Union (TFEU), the right to equal pay for equal value was not directly effective under Article 157. This was quickly rejected by the ECJ.[54] In the alternative, Tesco argued that the workers were not covered, because they did not work at the same establishment. Importantly, the Court held that Article 157 of the TFEU could be relied on in relation to a comparator with the same employer but in different establishments, provided the employer of both the claimant and the comparator can be regarded as a 'single source' in that it was responsible for the inequality and could restore equal treatment. In this case, the Court held, Tesco Stores could constitute such a single source to which the pay and conditions of shop workers and distribution centres may be attributed, and which could be responsible for any discrimination.

The EU concept of a 'single source' is a much simpler formula than the one developed by the UK Supreme Court. By permitting cross establishment comparisons in most cases where the employer has control over setting terms and conditions, it sidesteps the complex requirements of the 'common terms and conditions' formula and the technicalities of the 'North hypothetical'. However, its applicability in the UK after Brexit is still unclear. No further guidance was available from *Asda*, where the Supreme Court held that, since the case could be resolved on the basis of the *North* hypothetical, it was unnecessary to decide whether the claimants could succeed on the basis of a 'single source' where the common terms requirement is not met.[55] In the meanwhile the optimism of the victory in both these cases is tempered by the sobering reality that the cases have simply overcome the preliminary stages and now need to return to the tribunals to continue the process. Predictably, given the sums involved, employers will continue to find further snares along the way.

Since it is unusual, as we have seen for cases to get to the justification stage, it is not possible to assess the *Enderby* legacy from the position of actual cases. What is important to explore, however, is the germ of the idea that pay should be proportional to value.[56] As mentioned above, this has never been

[53] ibid [71].
[54] *K v Tesco Stores Ltd* (n 41).
[55] *Asda Stores Ltd* (n 41) [6].
[56] See further Fredman (n 6) ch six.

possible under equal pay legislation. However, the inclusion of pay relativities has begun to surface through the separate mechanism of gender pay gap reporting. Introduced in 2017, these provisions require large private sector employers (employing 250 or more workers) to report annually on the gender pay gaps in their institutions.[57] The same threshold applies to public sector employers in England, but it is much lower at 20 in Scotland. Notably, 'gender pay gap' is defined more widely than equal pay for work of equal value to encompass the spread of pay across the whole establishment. This casts light on occupational segregation and disproportionate pay, as well as unequal pay for work of equal value. Importantly, employers must publish information not only about pay differences but also about differences in bonuses, which are well known to contribute significantly but also invisibly to gender pay gaps. For example, in an inquiry into the gender pay gap in the financial services sector in 2009, the Equality and Human Rights Commission found that annual bonuses had a striking impact on earnings. Indeed, female full-time employees on average received only a fifth of the annual bonuses of men working full-time in the sector.[58] Transparency is also increased by requiring separate information about the proportions of male and female relevant employees who were paid bonus pay. Finally, since much of the pay gap is due to segregation of women in lower paying grades, the regulations require employers to also include the proportions of male and female relevant employees in the lower, lower middle, upper middle and upper quartile pay band. The information should be published on the government portal and the organisation's website. Failure to comply with the reporting requirement can lead to hefty fines. However, due to the Covid-19 pandemic, the government decided to suspend the reporting requirement in 2020, with a further extension of six months granted in 2021.

The reporting obligation depends for its efficacy entirely on the expected reputational risk to organisations with high gender pay gaps. There is no duty on private sector employers to take action to reduce the gap or indeed to even produce a plan to do so. Instead, government encourages employers to publish a narrative explaining why the pay gap exists, and to voluntarily produce and publish an action plan for closing it. In fact, about half published a plan in 2018–19.[59] Only in Wales is there a requirement on public sector employers to publish an action plan where the report reveals gender pay differences, while there is no such requirement for England or Scotland.

Initially, the 'name and shame' tactic appeared successful. The first two years of reporting attracted much negative publicity for companies and organisations

[57] The Equality Act 2010 (Gender Pay Gap Information) Regulations 2017.

[58] Equality and Human Rights Commission, *Financial Services Inquiry* (2009) 6 www.equalityhumanrights.com/en/publication-download/financial-services-inquiry-sex-discrimination-and-gender-pay-gap-report (accessed 15 February 2022).

[59] Fawcett Society, Global Institute for Women's Leadership and Thomson Reuters Foundation, *Gender Pay Gap Reporting: A Comparative Analysis* (2020) 24.

whose published reports demonstrated striking inequalities. There was also initially a high level of compliance with the duty, with 100 per cent of eligible employers fulfilling the obligation in 2019.[60] However, a more comprehensive study of the first three years of reporting revealed a much gloomier picture. Analysis by the Equality Trust showed that despite increasing transparency, the same names have continued to appear every year in the list of those with the worst records. Even more worrying is the fact that, while there has been a tiny narrowing of the gap in hourly pay (the average gender pay gap for reporting companies decreased by a mere 0.5 per cent since 2018–19), the bonus gap has soared, increasing as much as 178.7 per cent between 2017–18 and 2019–20 reporting years.[61] Indeed, in 2019–20, as many as 82 companies reported a gender bonus gap of 100 per cent, many of them in the public sector.[62] As the Equality Trust report puts it, this suggests that 'companies are paying men increasingly higher bonuses while placating women with minute pay rises'.[63] There are other weaknesses in the provisions. The 250 threshold is comparatively high, with many countries in Europe having a lower threshold, clustering around 50.[64] Similarly, the data requirements are relatively undemanding, with the lack of detail making it difficult to diagnose the cause of the problem. For example, Australian private sector employers are required to report not just on wage levels, but also on the number of promotions and resignations, and on the gender composition of governing bodies.[65]

In the meanwhile, the European Commission has proposed a similar measure, in the form of the Draft Pay Transparency Directive.[66] Like the UK provision, it requires employers with at least 250 employees to publish information on the pay gap between female and male workers in their organisations. The concept of pay is a wide one, to include additional benefits, such as bonuses, overtime compensation, travel facilities (including cars provided by the employer), housing allowances, compensations for attending training, occupational pensions and other complementary or variable components. Importantly too, the draft Directive requires an overall picture of gender differences in pay in the organisation, such as the distribution of workers by gender in the quartile pay bands, which can demonstrate the proportion of women in the highest and the lowest

[60] ibid 17.

[61] The Equality Trust, *UK Gender Pay Gap Reporting 2017–2020: Patterns and Progress* (2020) equalitytrust.org.uk/resource/uk-gender-pay-gap-reporting-2017–2020-patterns-and-progress (accessed 15 February 2022).

[62] ibid.

[63] ibid 11.

[64] Fawcett Society, Global Institute for Women's Leadership and Thomson Reuters Foundation (n 60) 17.

[65] ibid 18.

[66] Commission, 'Proposal for a Directive of the European Parliament and of the Council to strengthen the application of the principle of equal pay for equal work or work of equal value between men and women through pay transparency and enforcement mechanisms' COM (2021) 93 final.

paid positions. But it goes beyond the UK in proposing that, where there is a pay gap of at least five per cent, employers will be required to carry out a pay assessment in co-operation with workers' representatives. The aim of the joint pay assessment is to trigger mandatory action by employers to address potential gender bias in pay. Where differences in average pay levels between male and female workers doing work of equal value cannot be objectively justified, the employer is required to take remedial measures. This is further backed up by remedies such as injunctions which can be issued by courts or other competent bodies. Particularly important is the proposal that courts should have the power to require the defendant to take structural or organisational measures to comply with its obligations. What is not clear, however, is whether these remedies are confined to achieving equal pay for work of equal value within the organisation, or whether the measures encompass a broader notion of pay equity, which can address proportionate pay too.

Much more promising are the Canadian provisions on pay equity, which centrally embrace proportionality and are able to address job segregation. Proportional value schemes look at the relationship between the value of the work performed and the compensation received by male job classes. The same ratio should then be applied to the relationship between value and compensation for female job classes. For example, the Ontario Pay Equity Act specifies that pay equity is achieved when the relationship between value of the work performed and the compensation received is the same for both female and male job classes.[67]

IV. CONCLUSION

At one level, *Enderby* certainly ranks as a landmark case. This is especially true of its move away from a fault-based understanding of pay discrimination to one based on the simple fact of pay disparities patterned along gender lines. In this way, the judgment made some progress towards using equal pay law to address the structural forces fuelling gender pay gaps. Also, a lasting contribution of the *Enderby* judgment was its recognition that, without shifting the burden rapidly to the employer, applicants would have little chance of success. *Enderby* is therefore the precursor of several subsequent cases, including *Leverton*,[68] *British Coal*,[69] *North*,[70] *Asda*[71] and *Tesco*,[72] where the highest courts aim to remove some of the obstacles to equal pay claims. However, the acquiescence of the ECJ

[67] Pay Equity Act 1990 (Ontario), s 21.3(1).
[68] *Leverton* (n 41).
[69] ibid.
[70] ibid.
[71] ibid.
[72] ibid.

in *Enderby* to a market forces defence, limited only by a relatively unworkable proportionality requirement, is a significant limitation. More than anything, the legacy of *Enderby* is a symbol of the mighty wall of resistance by employers in both the public and private sectors to truly valuing women's work. While from the employers' side the cost of equal pay might appear to be large, it only reflects decades of exploitation of women at work. Instead, the cost to women, and to society as a whole, should be brought into focus.

10

Wilson and Palmer: *A Biographical Portrait of a Landmark Case*

ALAN BOGG*

I. INTRODUCTION

As Lord Reed once observed in *UNISON*, '[e]very day in the courts and tribunals of this country, the names of people who brought cases in the past live on as shorthand for the legal rules and principles which their cases established.'[1] This is certainly true of *Wilson and Palmer*. Yet as far as we can tell, David Wilson and Terry Palmer never actually met. David Wilson was a London-based journalist, and Terry Palmer worked at the port in Southampton. Their legal cases started out in different disputes and in different tribunals. Yet they are now forever immortalised as a pair in a legal biography that began in 1989 and is still being written today.

This chapter draws upon archival material and interviews with key people in the *Wilson and Palmer* litigation. In so doing, it charts the biography of a landmark case. The dramatis personae extend far beyond the claimants themselves. The story that follows includes trade union leaders, managers, lawyers, judges, academics, and legislators. Landmark cases are fashioned by the hands of many people. Nor was there a single 'eureka' moment. The development of the law was a story of victories, defeats, and (sometimes) unintended consequences, and it has spanned decades. Indeed, it is still being written today.

The second section examines the domestic litigation in the case, culminating in the workers' defeat in the House of Lords. The third section then follows the parties to Strasbourg, and the remarkable transformation of Article 11 of the European Convention on Human Rights (ECHR). The next stop in section IV

* I would like to record my gratitude to Jenny Eady, Sir Patrick Elias, Keith Ewing, John Foster, Lord Hendy QC, and Paul Statham, who generously gave their time and shared their thoughts, recollections, and personal papers, arising out of the litigation. I am grateful to ACL Davies, Keith Ewing, and Lord Hendy for comments on an earlier draft of the chapter.

[1] *R (UNISON) v Lord Chancellor* [2017] UKSC 51, [2020] AC 869.

is Parliament, and the indispensable role of legislation in the specification of fundamental human rights.[2] The leading history of *Wilson and Palmer* to date is Keith Ewing's 'Dancing with the Daffodils?'.[3] It has often been overlooked that this was a literary reference to Wordsworth's paean to daffodils in 'I Wandered Lonely as a Cloud' which was inspired by Wordsworth's time in Ullswater. As we shall see, Viscount Ullswater introduced a hasty legislative amendment in the House of Lords to reverse the protective effects of the Court of Appeal judgment. This should remind us that landmark cases can have a life in Parliament too. Furthermore, statutory interpretation has been central to *Wilson and Palmer* from the first Industrial Tribunal decision through to the present day.

The biography of this landmark case is therefore testament to the fact that strategic litigation is usually an amalgam of legal and political action, and the interactions between courts and legislators are central to this. The presentation of legal mobilisation and political mobilisation as alternative rather than complementary approaches is often unhelpful. It certainly distorts the legal story of *Wilson and Palmer*. The final substantive section considers the recent United Kingdom Supreme Court judgment in *Kostal v Dunkley*, which is the latest chapter in *Wilson and Palmer's* legal biography.[4] The conclusion reflects back on what this biographical portrait reveals about 'landmark' cases in the law.

II. *WILSON* AND *PALMER* IN THE DOMESTIC COURTS

A. *Wilson* and *Palmer* in the Industrial Tribunals: A Purposive Approach

The story of *David William Wilson v Associated Newspapers* (*Wilson*) *plc* really begins on 16 February 1989 when the editors of the *Evening Standard* and *Mail on Sunday* attended a meeting under the chairmanship of Sir David English, the then Editor-in-chief of the *Daily Mail*.[5] During that meeting, it was agreed that the employer would no longer engage in collective bargaining with the National Union of Journalists (NUJ). To this end, recognition of local NUJ 'chapels' would be withdrawn by 31st March 1990. During the 1980s, industrial relations in the newspaper and print industry was undergoing significant upheaval as a result of rapid technological changes. This was occurring against the backdrop of a fundamental realignment in public policy between 1979 and 1997 in trade union law, described in gentle terms by Davies and Freedland as 'reducing the

[2] G Webber and others, *Legislated Rights: Securing Human Rights through Legislation* (Cambridge, Cambridge University Press, 2018).

[3] KD Ewing, 'Dancing with the Daffodils?' (2000) 50 *Federation News* 1.

[4] *Kostal UK Ltd v Dunkley* [2021] UKSC 47, [2022] ICR 434.

[5] *Wilson v Associated Newspapers plc* (Industrial Tribunal, 22 October 1990) [7].

power of trade unions'.[6] Statutory recognition machinery and other auxiliary props to collective bargaining had been repealed in the Employment Act 1980. This marked the beginning of 'step by step' legislative reforms in collective labour law across the 1980s. This legislative programme was aimed at restricting solidaristic practices, especially through reform of strike laws, to facilitate a restructured 'labour market' based upon individual bargaining. The 'Wapping Dispute' between News International and the print unions between 1985–1986 exemplified these political and economic tensions in the print industry.[7] Rupert Murdoch dismissed his entire workforce and relocated production from Fleet Street to Wapping, utilising technological developments and deskilling to reassert managerial control over its new production site. The transition from collective bargaining to 'personal contracts' was often central to this general process of restructuring.[8] The derecognition of the NUJ at Associated Newspapers was a less dramatic instalment in the de-collectivisation of the print industry that had been fought out in open industrial warfare at 'Fortress Wapping'. In due course, however, its legacy in the law would be far more enduring.

The linkage between union derecognition and the issuing of new 'personal contracts' was designed to mark a definitive exclusion of trade unions from future pay determination. It was especially prominent in certain industries like shipping, printing, and publishing.[9] It was perhaps no accident then that *Wilson* should be the first case to test the legality of the practice. David Wilson was 'father of chapel' at the *Daily Mail* when the case was argued in the London (South) Industrial Tribunal during September and October 1990. At this point he was 37 years old and had an impeccable record of service with his employer. He had worked for Associated Newspapers since 1977. As he would later recount, 'I am no politically motivated union firebrand.'[10] Yet he did have a keen sense of justice and fairness. So did his union.

When David Wilson learned of what was afoot at Associated Newspapers, he met with the national organiser of the NUJ at that time, Mr John Foster. Foster recalls that they met in a pub in Hampstead on a Sunday evening. The NUJ was facing severe challenges across different employers, with withdrawals of recognition even where the union had 100 per cent membership in bargaining units. Bert Hardy had joined Associated Newspapers in 1989 as managing director,

[6] PL Davies and MR Freedland, *Labour Legislation and Public Policy* (Oxford, Oxford University Press, 1993) ch 9.

[7] KD Ewing and BW Napier, 'The Wapping Dispute and Labour Law' (1986) 45 *Cambridge Law Journal* 285.

[8] In the Wapping Dispute, News International entered into a 'sweetheart' recognition deal with the Electrical, Electronic, Telecommunications and Plumbing Union (EEPTU). The EEPTU was expelled from the TUC in 1986.

[9] KD Ewing, 'Trade Union Derecognition and Personal Contracts: a Note on Recent Developments' (1993) 23 *ILJ* 297. See also P Smith and G Morton, 'Union Exclusion and the Decollectivization of Industrial Relations in Contemporary Britain' (1993) 31 *British Journal of Industrial Relations* 97.

[10] 'Saint, Sinner or Scapegoat?' *UK Print Gazette*, 3 July 1995, 14.

and this no doubt reflected the shift in managerial approach at Associated Newspapers. Hardy had previously worked for Murdoch during the 1970s. Growing up in poverty in Mill Hill, Hardy had a reputation as a tough and uncompromising negotiator for employers.[11] For Foster, the issue was essentially a collective one, namely the complete legal freedom of employers to derecognise in circumstances where the union was a legitimate representative and enjoyed strong worker support. That night, he resolved that 'they would go all the way to Europe to challenge the anti-union laws' in the European Court of Human Rights (ECtHR). While the NUJ legal team could see the mileage in a complaint to the International Labour Organisation, they were more sceptical about the ECtHR. He also warned David Wilson that this undertaking might come at a great personal cost to him. Foster would have had little sense of how prophetic all this would be.

Wilson's case was argued by John Hendy QC, already a seasoned class warrior in the English courts and who had acted for the NUJ on previous occasions. A certain rising star of the Employment Bar, Nicholas Underhill, acted for Associated Newspapers. In her opening remarks to the Industrial Tribunal decision, the chair Mrs Stella Hollis acknowledged that the case involved what Mr Hendy had described as a 'clash of philosophies'.[12] In this respect, he was invoking what would become one of Lord Wedderburn's most celebrated academic articles, the recently published 'Freedom of Association and Philosophies of Labour Law', charting the clash between Hayekian neoliberalism and worker-protective collective laissez-faire during the 1980s.[13]

Mr Wilson's claim was based on section 23(1)(a) of the Employment Protection (Consolidation) Act 1978, which prohibited employers from taking 'action short of dismissal' against an employee where the employer's 'purpose' was to 'deter' or 'prevent' or 'penalise' trade union membership. Following the termination of recognition, the employer issued new 'personal contracts' with the inducement of a 4.5 per cent pay rise. This pay rise was withheld from those employees who insisted on their existing contracts which was subject to the House Agreement with the NUJ. There was a ballot in favour of strike action in December 1989.[14] However, the workers were unwilling to strike and by April 1990 all but 15 of the 173 affected employees had signed the new personal contracts providing for individualised pay assessments. The signatories benefited from the pay rise whereas the remaining 15 employees did not. The employer indicated it was prepared to 'recognise' the union for discussions on health and safety matters,

[11] R Greenslade, 'Bert Hardy: The Veteran Newspaper Executive's Wapping 'Folly' Proved the Undoing of the Fleet Street Unions' *The Guardian*, 10 March 2009 www.theguardian.com/media/2009/mar/10/bert-hardy-obituary-fleet-street (accessed 29 March 2022).

[12] *Wilson* (n 5) [5].

[13] Lord Wedderburn, 'Freedom of Association and Philosophies of Labour Law' (1989) 18 *ILJ* 1.

[14] *Wilson* (n 5) [31].

and it would permit union representation in individual disciplinary and grievance procedures. During a meeting with the chapel representatives, Sir David English had expressed the view that he would prove to them that 'in two years … the Trade Union was not necessary and the Chapel would "wither away"'.[15]

The Tribunal's legal findings take up a small proportion of the overall judgment which is mostly focused on explaining the factual context of the dispute. The derecognition of the union did not fall within the scope of 'action short of dismissal' because it was not action taken against the applicant 'as an individual'.[16] It was action taken against the union itself. By contrast, the modifications to the individual contracts and the withholding of the 4.5 per cent pay increase did constitute 'action' within the scope of the statutory provision. Given what was to come later in the appeals, it is particularly striking that there was no discussion at all of the act/omission distinction. Perhaps this was because in *Ridgway* a majority of the Court of Appeal held that 'action short of dismissal' encompassed omissions. This was clear authority and it was binding on the tribunal. At this stage, it had occurred to neither party to raise this issue, and both Hendy and Underhill had appeared in *Ridgway*. Even so, the tribunal appears to treat the employer's conduct as straightforward instances of acts; there is no mention of omission in its reasoning.

The liability discussion then turned to the factual enquiry into the employer's subjective 'purpose', and whether it was directed at deterring, preventing or penalising 'trade union membership'. The tribunal concluded that it was because 'the respondents purpose was so to reduce the power of the union as to negate it totally … they were effectively rendering the union powerless and thus membership pointless'.[17] This obviously had strong evidential support in the reported statements of Sir David English, who had confidently predicted the disappearance of the union within two years of the new contractual arrangements. As with the 'action' enquiry, this was treated as an uncontroversial application of settled law to the facts in the case. In *Discount Tobacco & Confectionary Ltd v Armitage*, the Employment Appeal Tribunal upheld an Industrial Tribunal decision that an employee had been dismissed for trade union membership where this related to the use of an essential union service.[18] On the facts of this case, the dismissal was triggered by the employee seeking union assistance in an individual grievance in elucidating and negotiating her terms of employment with the employer. The Employment Appeal Tribunal judgment was handed down on 17 October 1989 and reported in the 1990 Industrial Relations Law Reports. It is not mentioned in the *Wilson* judgment although the parties would not have been aware of that judgment at the time of the hearing. In any event, it

[15] ibid [32].
[16] This was a well settled distinction in the case law. See *NCB v Ridgway* [1987] ICR 641 (CA).
[17] *Wilson* (n 5) [60]–[61].
[18] *Discount Tobacco & Confectionary Ltd v Armitage* [1990] IRLR 15 (EAT).

supported the robust and purposive approach to union membership adopted in the Industrial Tribunal judgment in *Wilson*.

At this stage, there is little to suggest a landmark case in the making. The political context to the litigation was no doubt interesting as an example of Wedderburn's 'clash of philosophies'. Yet the Industrial Tribunal judgment reads like a run of the mill case where the law is uncontroversial and settled by authorities, and the factual evidence relatively clear. There is nothing *legally* momentous afoot. A couple of years later, in the Southampton Industrial Tribunal on 20 January 1992, Terence Palmer, Brian Stedman and Arthur Wyeth succeeded in their section 23(1)(a) claims against Associated British Ports (*Palmer*). While recognition continued with the union in this case, employees who signed new personal contracts without collective bargaining received a higher pay rise than those employees who continued under the collective bargaining framework. This was again treated as 'action short of dismissal' for the unlawful purpose of deterring union membership.

B. *Wilson* and *Palmer* in the Employment Appeal Tribunal: Asserting Control

The Employment Appeal Tribunal heard appeals in both *Wilson* and *Palmer* in 1992. In fact, in *Palmer* it was merely a matter of months between the original Industrial Tribunal decision in January 1992 and the hearing in the Employment Appeal Tribunal later that year in July. This haste may have reflected the wider political importance of the litigation. In labour law, legally mundane points can be highly politically charged when they touch upon matters of high controversy. The appeals were each considered by tripartite panels chaired by the President of the Employment Appeal Tribunal, Sir John Wood. Although not an employment lawyer by training, Wood J had specialised in family law. He was approached to take on the Presidency by Lord Lane, who had charmingly described it as a 'stinking job'.[19] Sir John had a reputation for fierce independence and he had famously clashed with the Lord Chancellor, Lord Mackay, in insisting on a fair consideration of whether litigants in person had an arguable point of law to take an appeal. Interestingly, Sir John's obituary describes his preparedness to be guided by the industrial common sense of lay members in the Employment Appeal Tribunal. Yet in both cases here, the employer appeals were allowed by a majority, in the face of strong dissents by the 'worker' member of the Panel. It may be that Sir John had some of the qualities of that other judicial resident of Hampshire, Lord Denning, in his fierce attachment to justice for the individual, access to justice, and the independence of the judiciary. It was sometimes challenging for judges to translate these values of individual fairness into collective disputes.

[19] 'Obituary: Sir John Wood' *The Times*, 13 February 2017 www.thetimes.co.uk/article/sir-john-wood-6h62ctvgk (accessed 29 March 2022).

The dissents by the 'worker' members were also testament to the dubious legitimacy of the claim that these cases simply involved a neutral application of settled law to agreed facts. Instead, Hendy's 'clash of philosophies' perspective was prescient. The splits in the Employment Appeal Tribunal exposed the deep conflict between management and labour on the appropriate role of law in collective labour relations. In both *Wilson* and *Palmer*, Wood J adopted strained legal arguments to allow the employers' appeals. Any challenge to the 'action short of dismissal' aspect was effectively closed off because the court was bound by *Ridgway*: 'action' encompassed omissions. The focus would necessarily be on the factual findings of 'purpose', a matter that was squarely within the fact-finding remit of the Industrial Tribunal.

In *Wilson*, John Hendy QC was joined by Jennifer Eady, and Nicholas Underhill continued to act for Associated Newspapers. In upholding the employer's appeal, the reasoning of Wood J is somewhat opaque. However, the principal objection appeared to be based in a narrow conceptualisation of what 'trade union membership' entailed. The only 'action' that the Employment Appeal Tribunal regarded as relevant to the statutory right was the withholding of the pay rise. The employees who signed the new contracts were entitled to remain as trade union members, and 138 employees did in fact retain their NUJ membership while accepting the personal contracts and the 4.5 per cent pay rise. According to Wood J, 'experience tells us that there may well have been other fields in which the benefit of membership could still have been felt. Legal and financial advice could no doubt be obtained. Thus, we could find no evidence that membership of the NUJ would be pointless.'[20] For this reason, there was no evidence to support the tribunal's finding that the employer had acted with an unlawful purpose. The tribunal's approach was based upon an elision between 'union membership', which was protected, and the incidents of membership, including collective bargaining, which were not.

The Employment Appeal Tribunal's intervention in these terms, based on an assertion of no evidence, was certainly out of step with the prevailing approach of appellate courts in their oversight of tribunals. In a series of important judgments, the appeal courts had emphasised the paramount importance of self-restraint on their part, reflected in a high threshold for interference in questions of fact.[21] There is no sense of that restraint in the Employment Appeal Tribunal in *Wilson*. Furthermore, Knox J's reasoning on the purposive construction of 'membership' in *Armitage* provided strong support to the Industrial Tribunal's general approach. This must also be considered in light of critical evidence before the Industrial Tribunal where Sir David English confidently anticipated the disappearance of the trade union within two years

[20] *Associated Newspapers Ltd v Wilson* [1992] ICR 681 (EAT) 694.

[21] See, eg, *Piggott Brothers v Jackson* [1991] IRLR 309 (CA). On employment status and the limited role of appellate courts, see *O'Kelly v Trusthouse Forte* [1983] ICR 728 (CA).

of the new pay arrangements. While *Armitage* was cited in argument to the Employment Appeal Tribunal, there is no reference to it in Wood J's judgment. There is however a crucial aside that may give a truer picture of what was really at stake in the case. In commenting on the submissions of Mr Hendy QC, Wood J remarked that 'the collective agreement could never have been terminated without an employer incurring some form of liability. The legislature envisaged that de-recognition was an option open to an employer.'[22] This reveals a concern that statutory liability needed to be circumscribed with legal certainty. Otherwise the resulting risks of legal liability, particularly where that was based upon controversial findings about mental states, would always hover above the employer's legally sanctioned freedom to derecognise the union. These concerns with entrepreneurial freedom, legal certainty, and anxieties about 'union vetoes' of managerial decisions, would recur throughout *Wilson*'s biography as a landmark case. It would be central many years later in the *Kostal* appeal.

The facts in *Palmer* were somewhat different to those in *Wilson*, in that the employer had continued to recognise the National Union of Rail, Maritime and Transport Workers (RMT) for collective bargaining. It offered enhanced pay rises to those who relinquished union representation and signed new 'personal contracts'. The legal teams in *Palmer* were similarly impressive. Peter Clark acted for the claimants, with Patrick Elias QC and Alan Wilkie QC acting for Associated British Ports. The employer's arguments in the appeal again attacked the findings of the Industrial Tribunal on 'purpose'.[23] The Industrial Tribunal had drawn a distinction between 'purpose' and 'objective'. This supported its factual finding that while the employer's admitted 'objective' might have been to achieve greater flexibility in its contractual and pay arrangements, this was to be achieved through an unlawful purpose: using financial inducements to persuade employees to give up their union representation. There was no strong coordination between the NUJ and the RMT. They were both facing similar industrial relations problems, but the *Palmer* case had arisen independently of *Wilson* (though it is highly likely that the RMT was aware of the outcome in *Wilson*).

Wood J accepted counsel's argument that 'objective' and 'purpose' were synonyms. On this specific point he was on relatively safe ground. He then reintroduced his own sophistry by drawing a distinction between the 'purpose' of an action and the 'means' by which that purpose was to be achieved.[24] In *Palmer*, the purpose ('flexibility') was to be achieved through the means (the use of pay rises to induce 'personal contracts').[25] Unlike his judgment in *Wilson*, Wood J

[22] *Wilson* (n 20) 695.

[23] *Associated British Ports v Palmer* [1993] ICR 101 (EAT).

[24] ibid 111.

[25] This takes us into unfamiliar territory on the philosophy of intentional action. Wood J's distinction between 'ends' and 'means' is misleading: there is no reason at all why there cannot be purpose in relation to both ends *and* means. The analysis of intentional action in law is at its most highly

did give explicit consideration to the authority of *Armitage*. With great respect, Sir John's treatment of *Armitage* was confused and confusing: 'We cannot accept that Knox J was intending to indicate that an employee had a statutory right as against his employer, not only to recognition of his trade union, but to have his terms and conditions of service negotiated by that employer only through that trade union.'[26] Yet this was no part of Mr Clark's arguments on behalf of the claimants.[27] There was no possible basis for deriving a positive right to union representation from section 23(1)(a), with correlative duties on an employer. The argument based on *Armitage* was far narrower: that it was open to the tribunal to find discrimination on the ground of 'union membership' where the employer was reacting to the essential incidents of union membership. We will never know Wood J's answer to Mr Clark's powerful point because it was never addressed in the judgment.

As in *Wilson*, the most revealing parts of the judgment are the asides rather than the legal reasoning itself. In reflecting on the potential consequences of a broader view of statutory liability, Wood J articulated the following concern:

> even where an individual employee for his own benefit was anxious and willing to enter into a fresh and individual contract of service, which gave greater benefits to an employer – eg, by flexibility or increased productivity – for which the employer was prepared to increase pay, that employer could not negotiate such a fresh contract with that employee if he was a member of a trade union without incurring liability under section 23(1)(a) to the other members of his staff who are members of that trade union.[28]

This is the same 'union veto' worry that was articulated in *Wilson*, corresponding to the need to preserve individual freedom of contract.[29] Wood J was also more forthright about the inadequacies of the existing legal framework. While he was bound by *Ridgway*, he opined that 'as this branch of the law is of such importance throughout the economic activity in this country, it would be of enormous help if consideration could be given to it by a higher court'.[30] Having invited the higher courts to tighten up the law on 'action', he gave the parties leave to appeal.

developed in the criminal law. For the leading discussion of 'purpose' and means and ends in the law on 'direct' intent, see AP Simester and others, *Simester and Sullivan's Criminal Law: Theory and Doctrine*, 7th edn (Oxford, Hart, 2019) ch 5. There was greater merit in the dissenting member's view, Ms Brenda Dean, that the tribunal was entitled to take an overall view of the employer's plan as a purposive exercise.

[26] *Palmer* (n 23) 112.

[27] ibid 109.

[28] ibid 113.

[29] *Wilson* (n 20) 695.

[30] *Palmer* (n 23) 110.

C. *Wilson* and *Palmer* in the Court of Appeal: Orthodoxy Restored

The appeals in *Wilson* and *Palmer* were considered together by the Court of Appeal, although the outcome may not have been what Wood J expected. A single judgment was given by Dillon LJ, with whom Butler-Sloss LJ and Farquharson LJ agreed.[31] In both cases, the original decisions of the tribunals were restored. When we look back at the litigation in *Wilson* and *Palmer*, it is sometimes tempting to view the Court of Appeal judgment as a brave rearguard action in support of a collectivist judicial approach. In fact, a careful reading of Dillon LJ's judgment reveals a strong restatement of orthodox legal principles. The reasoning is attentive to the precise statutory language and it applies the existing authorities with scrupulous care. The legal claims against the employers succeeded, but this did not depend upon the stretching of doctrinal categories to fit the facts. On the contrary, the legal outcomes in both cases are treated as unexceptionable. Indeed, it would seem to require a contorted legal argument to reach the opposite conclusion of no liability for 'action short of dismissal'. This is reflected in Dillon LJ's critical engagement with some of the reasoning of Wood J in the Employment Appeal Tribunal.

The fundamental basis of Dillon LJ's approach was to emphasise the limited remit of the appellate courts in disturbing findings of fact by the tribunal. At this point, the appeals had all been focused on the determination of the employer's 'purpose'. Mental states are issues of fact. In the Employment Appeal Tribunal, Wood J had adopted a highly interventionist approach in holding that it was not open to the tribunal in either case to find an unlawful purpose to 'deter' union membership. This interventionism was heterodox. In the Court of Appeal, Dillon LJ restored an orthodox circumscribed approach to the appellate court's role:

> it is common ground that on an appeal of this nature the question is whether the industrial tribunal was right, not whether the appeal tribunal was right. This is set out in the judgment of Mustill LJ in *Campion v Hamworthy Engineering Ltd*.[32] He quoted a statement from a judgment of Sir John Donaldson MR in *Hennessy v Craigmyle & Co Ltd*.[33] Mustill LJ went on to point out that whether the decision of the industrial tribunal was 'right' must be understood as meaning 'not so demonstrably wrong as to be beyond reason.[34] The appeal from the industrial tribunal as the tribunal of fact only lies on grounds of law.[35]

The factual findings on 'purpose' were pre-eminently for the tribunal, and the appeal courts ought only to intervene where those findings were perverse. That

[31] *Associated Newspapers Ltd v Wilson* [1994] ICR 97 (CA).
[32] *Campion v Hamworthy Engineering Ltd* [1987] ICR 966 (CA) 972.
[33] *Hennessy v Craigmyle & Co Ltd* [1986] ICR 461 (CA) 470.
[34] (n 32) 972e.
[35] *Wilson* (n 31) 111.

was very far from being the case in both *Wilson* and *Palmer*, where the evidence provided ample support for the tribunals' conclusions. In this emphasis on appellate deference, Dillon LJ's judgment is aligned with the orthodox approach in cases such as *O'Kelly v Trusthouse Forte*.[36] These procedural considerations are more concerned with the efficient administration of justice than aligning with a pro- or contra- worker-protective approach to substantive rights.

To support this 'deference' approach to the tribunal's factual findings on 'purpose', the Court of Appeal also considered and approved the Employment Appeal Tribunal judgment in *Armitage*. According to Dillon LJ, it was 'unreal' to divorce union membership from the essential incidents of that membership.[37] The reasoning in *Armitage* provided a critical legal underpinning to the tribunals' factual findings on purpose. For such an important case, it is therefore surprising that the Employment Appeal Tribunal had either simply ignored *Armitage* (as in *Wilson*) or badly misconstrued it (as in *Palmer*). Since *Armitage* provided a sound interpretation of 'membership' as encapsulating the essential incidents of trade union membership, it was open to a tribunal in an appropriate case to address the issue of union membership 'robustly'.[38] This was so in both *Wilson* and *Palmer.* In *Wilson*, the evidence of Sir David English indicated that the disappearance of the union within two years had been anticipated as the natural (and welcome) result of the new contracts.[39] That supported the tribunal's finding on 'purpose' based on the fact that employer's purpose was to negate the union's power totally. In *Palmer*, Dillon LJ emphasised the similarities between the facts in *Palmer* and *Armitage*. He agreed with the dissent of Ms Brenda Dean in the Employment Appeal Tribunal in *Palmer*, that the purpose of the personal contracts was that the union would eventually 'wither on the vine'.[40] Ms Brenda Dean had of course been the General Secretary of the print union, the Society of Graphical and Allied Trades (SOGAT), before and during the Wapping Dispute, and so was intimately familiar with the broader economic context.

Dillon LJ also took the opportunity to clear up some analytical confusions about the nature of 'purpose' introduced by the Employment Appeal Tribunal. In the *Palmer* case, Wood J had proposed a distinction between the purpose and the intermediate means by which that purpose was to be achieved. This provided the justification for interfering with the tribunal because it had elided purpose with the means used to achieve it. Dillon LJ rejected this distinction as unhelpful. It was logically possible for an agent to act with a number of different purposes, and those purposes may relate to the means as well as the ends: 'a person invited to stay with a friend in the Highlands who therefore takes the

[36] *O'Kelly v Trusthouse Forte* (n 21).
[37] *Wilson* (n 31) 104.
[38] ibid 102.
[39] ibid 110.
[40] ibid 103.

night train from Kings Cross to Edinburgh may say that his purpose in catching the train was to get to Edinburgh, or that his purpose was to join his friend in the Highlands and shoot grouse'.[41] In *Wilson*, the relevant 'action' to be considered in the statutory enquiry was the withholding of the 4.5 per cent pay rise. While there were multiple purposes in the employer's plan – to achieve derecognition, to end collective bargaining, to ensure that the new terms and conditions were accepted by employees – it was open to the tribunal to take a view of the employer's overall purpose in implementing that plan. As with the Court of Appeal's emphasis on deference and appellate self-restraint, these interventions by Dillon LJ should be understood as an attempt to realign the law on 'purpose' to restore an orthodox legal view of its meaning. As we shall see, the Court of Appeal judgment was reversed with great urgency by legislative intervention through the 'Ullswater' amendment. As it turned out, the judgment in the House of Lords rendered this legislative reversal superfluous.

D. *Wilson* and *Palmer* in the House of Lords: The Appeal Takes a Surprising Turn

In the House of Lords events took a surprising turn.[42] The panel had a mix of conservative and more liberal Law Lords. On the liberal side, Lords Browne-Wilkinson and Slynn had both served with distinction as Presidents of the Employment Appeal Tribunal between 1978 and 1983, and (in contrast to the conservatives, Lords Bridge and Keith) bringing a deeper empathy to the collective dimensions of the case. The lower courts had been bound by *Ridgway* so that the 'omission', in the form of withholding pay rises, was included within the statutory formulation of 'action short of dismissal'. Everything had been focused on 'purpose'. Given the factual nature of this enquiry, any appellate supervision of the tribunals was liable to be unstable and unpredictable. A new point of law on the omission issue was taken on appeal to the House of Lords. The point was suggested by Nigel Giffin, and he had some difficulty persuading his leader (Elias QC) that it was worth taking. Lord Bridge, with whom Lord Keith and Lord Browne-Wilkinson agreed, decided that 'omission' was not included within the statutory phrase 'the right not to have action … taken against him'. On this basis, the employers' appeals were allowed. According to Lord Bridge, the grammatical difficulties involved in the inclusion of 'omission' within the scope of 'action short of dismissal' necessitated consideration of the legislative history. The original provisions in the Industrial Relations Act 1971 had dealt with the conferral of benefits in a specific provision, section 5(4), but that language was not carried over into the Employment Protection Act 1975.

[41] ibid 103.
[42] [1995] 2 AC 454 (HL).

Lord Slynn and Lord Lloyd were content to treat omissions as included within 'action short of dismissal', and both were evidently moved by the lacuna that would otherwise be left in the statutory protections. In response to the argument that the exclusion of omissions would undercut the collectivist and protective purpose of the 'social contract' legislation, Lord Bridge articulated a 'traditional' approach to statutory interpretation. In so doing, the ordinary meaning of the words carefully chosen by Parliament were usually determinative of legislative intent:

> A purposive construction to resolve ambiguities of statutory language is often appropriate and necessary. But this is the first time I have heard it suggested that the policy of an enactment to be presumed from the political complexion of the government which introduced it may prevail over the language of the statute. The courts' traditional approach to construction, giving primacy to the ordinary, grammatical meaning of statutory language, is reflected in the parliamentary draftsman's technique of using language with the utmost precision to express the legislative intent of his political masters and it remains the golden rule of construction that a statute means exactly what it says and does not mean what it does not say.[43]

All of their Lordships, with the exception of Lord Browne-Wilkinson, cast doubt on the broad concept of union membership that had been applied in the tribunals and the Court of Appeal. While *Armitage* was not overruled, it was confined to its own particular facts which were said to be remote from those in *Wilson* and *Palmer*. In *Armitage*, the employee had been dismissed for seeking assistance from the union in an individual grievance. In *Wilson* and *Palmer*, by contrast, the employer was at liberty to discontinue recognition of trade unions following the repeal of statutory recognition machinery in 1980. The exposure of the employer to the risk of liability for 'action short of dismissal', in circumstances where Parliament had repealed compulsory union recognition, was an unwarranted extension of the statutory provision. It was encroaching upon a freedom that had been permitted to employers under the statutory framework. For Lord Slynn, the employer's purpose was to achieve flexibility, and this was not an unlawful purpose.[44] Lord Lloyd also took the view that the evidential basis for a finding of unlawful purpose was slender to non-existent.[45] Lord Slynn's judgment also displayed analytical sensitivity to the legal difficulties at the intersection between (collective) union derecognition and (individual) trade union discrimination. In both cases, the employees were permitted to retain their trade union membership; the real issue was the derecognition. Underlying these reservations is the concern that section 23(1)(a) was being strained beyond its natural remit and used as an auxiliary prop to collective bargaining. This was illegitimate because section 23(1)(a) was really concerned with individual

[43] ibid 475.
[44] ibid 482–83.
[45] ibid 487.

discrimination wrongs against employees. Of course, their Lordships were on shakier legal ground on the 'union membership' issue. The original findings on the employers' mental states were squarely within the fact-finding remit of the tribunals. The act/omission distinction spared their Lordships blushes; they were all good enough lawyers to see the cogency of the Court of Appeal's more orthodox approach on this point. Having allowed the employers' appeals, the House of Lords also made an order for full indemnity costs against the respondents which was backdated to the date of the Court of Appeal judgment. This was regarded at the time as gratuitously punitive.

By March 1995, there was nowhere left for David Wilson to go in the domestic courts. The unions had suffered a heavy blow in the House of Lords. From time to time, an issue comes before the English courts that touches a neuralgic point in the English judicial psyche. When this happens, there is a psychic revolt reflected in 'a volley of bullets aimed at a number of possible grounds or bases'.[46] We see something of this kind in *Addis v Gramophone Co Ltd*[47] and *Edwards v Chesterfield Royal Hospital NHS Foundation Trust*.[48] A battery of arguments, often scattered across different judgments, is arrayed at an outcome regarded by the judges as intolerable to the basic values of the English common law. In my view, the House of Lords judgment in *Wilson* and *Palmer* is just such a case. In *Addis* and *Edwards*, it was that most totemic of employer powers in the managerial prerogative, dismissal. In *Wilson and Palmer*, it was the intolerable uncertainty created by a statutory liability, the effect of which was to overshadow and fetter the individual freedom of contract between employers and employees.

We should also note the play of chance in the formulation of the original legal arguments. The complaint in *Wilson* was not about the original decision terminating the collective bargaining arrangements, made on 10 November 1989, but the fact that from 31 January 1990 employees who did not sign up were denied a pay rise paid to others. This was easily characterised as an omission. If the originating complaint had encompassed that positive decision in November 1989, as a positive act in a further sequence of omissions, might this case have been successfully argued as a positive act?[49] That may well have been unlikely to succeed because it was an act against the union itself which was not protected under the statutory provision. One suspects anyway that the 'volley of bullets' in the judgments in *Wilson and Palmer* meant that the eventual success of the employer appeals was a forgone conclusion in the politics of that time.

[46] A Bogg and MR Freedland, 'The Wrongful Termination of the Contract of Employment' in MR Freedland and others (eds), *The Contract of Employment* (Oxford, Oxford University Press, 2016) 537, 541.

[47] *Addis v Gramophone Co Ltd* [1909] AC 488 (HL).

[48] *Edwards v Chesterfield Royal Hospital NHS Foundation Trust* [2011] UKSC 58, [2012] 2 AC 22.

[49] I am grateful to Professor Michael Ford QC, who raised this issue in his skeleton argument submitted to the Court of Appeal in *London Borough of Southwark v Whillier* [2001] EWCA Civ 808, [2001] ICR 1016.

In assessing the landmark status of *Wilson* and *Palmer* in 1995, one would conclude that it was a landmark for the wrong reasons. John Foster recalls a sense of despair and devastation when they learned of the result, which came as a great shock to them. The House of Lords judgment represented a narrow and formalistic interpretation of the relevant statutory provisions which, by some of their Lordships' own admissions, opened up regrettable lacunae in the law on freedom of association. The effect of this was to remove an important legal obstacle to the de-collectivisation of the workplace. The direct aftermath of *Wilson* and *Palmer* is also worth recounting. By 1996, counsel for Palmer, Mr Peter Clark, had become Judge Peter Clark in the Employment Appeal Tribunal. In *Speciality Care v Pachela* the question arose whether Knox J's reflections in *Armitage* on the conceptual limits of union membership remained good law after the House of Lords judgment in *Wilson* and *Palmer*.[50] According to Clark J, the judgments in the House of Lords on this point were strictly obiter, and in any event, it was difficult to distil a clear principle from the various speeches. Since *Armitage* was undoubtedly correct on its own facts, it remained open to tribunals to address the question of union membership 'robustly'. In *Pachela*, the alleged dismissal of employees because they had sought union assistance in a disciplinary procedure was remitted to the tribunal for consideration under the union membership provision. This was something of a poke in the eye for the House of Lords with Clark J achieving what Mr Clark could not. For David Wilson, sadly, the outcome was less satisfactory. Two months and ten days after the House of Lords judgment, he was sacked by Associated Newspapers. The dismissal letter from the *Daily Mail* Editor Paul Dacre criticised his 'provocative attitude' as a shop steward.[51] He was just 41 and looking for a new job. In retrospect, the original findings of the tribunals on 'purpose' may not have been so wide of the mark.

III. *WILSON* AND *PALMER* IN THE EUROPEAN COURT OF HUMAN RIGHTS

The first major academic critique of *Wilson* and *Palmer* was undertaken by Bob Simpson in a widely admired and wide ranging consideration of the law on the 'right to organize'.[52] It invoked many of the values of the collective laissez-faire tradition as developed in the hands of Kahn-Freund and Wedderburn. In particular, Simpson criticised the conservative role of the judiciary in interpreting the individual statutory rights introduced in the Employment Protection Act 1975.

[50] *Speciality Care v Pachela* [1996] IRLR 248 (EAT).

[51] Dismissal letter from Paul Dacre to David Wilson, (on file with author from the *Journalist*, June/July 1995).

[52] B Simpson, 'Freedom of Association and the Right to Organize: The Failure of an Individual Rights Strategy' (1995) 24 *ILJ* 235. See further, A Bogg, 'Individualism and Collectivism in Collective Labour Law' (2017) 46 *ILJ* 72.

Judicial interpretation was often narrow and formalistic and accentuated the individualistic features of the right to organise. This was especially pertinent to his close critique of *Wilson* and *Palmer* in the House of Lords. An agenda for law reform would need to be based in extensive statutory reforms focused on the values of collectivism and joint regulation through autonomous collective bargaining. This would necessitate a scheme of freestanding collective rights for trade unions themselves to support their collective regulatory role in the workplace. It would need to be buttressed by strong remedies such as penal financial awards for breach of collective rights. What is absent from Simpson's critique is an engagement with fundamental human rights, including the right to freedom of association under Article 11. This is not surprising. At this time, there was a high degree of scepticism about the role of fundamental human rights in collective labour law.[53] The ECtHR had been scrupulous in protecting the negative right to disassociate while giving only limited recognition to positive trade union rights. Article 11 was regarded as superfluous at best and potentially disruptive through its protection of negative freedom of association.

This 'traditional' view of *Wilson* and *Palmer*, where human rights are marginal to the early domestic story, is incomplete. During the 1980s, unions and their lawyers were increasingly turning to human rights arguments. International human rights law provided a powerful language of universal social justice. The characterisation of an entitlement as fundamental to one's human dignity provided a strong normative response to regulatory arguments based on economic efficiency and deregulation. Human rights arguments were also a practical imperative where the legislature and statutory law was so hostile to trade unions across a long period of time. In these circumstances, unions began to use human rights arguments in domestic courts. Unions also made more extensive use of complaints mechanisms under the International Labour Organisation and the European Social Charter. In terms of landmark status, one of the most significant aspects of *Wilson* and *Palmer* was that it marked a decisive turning point in Article 11 as a foundation for trade union rights.

An early example of the use of human rights' arguments can be seen in *Express Newspapers v Keys*.[54] This involved proceedings for interlocutory injunctions following the TUC's call for a national 'Day of Action', adjudged to be a political strike. The arguments based on the freedoms of assembly and association were dealt with briskly by Griffiths J. These fundamental freedoms were to be exercised within the existing constraints of the general civil law, and so were of no assistance where the proposed action was independently unlawful.[55] Later in

[53] KW Wedderburn, 'Freedom of Association or Right to Organise? The Common Law and International Sources' in KW Wedderburn, *Employment Rights in Britain and Europe* (London, Lawrence & Wishart, 1991) 138, originally published in (1987) 18 *IRJ* 244.

[54] *Express Newspapers v Keys* [1980] IRLR 247 (QB). John Hendy was junior counsel in *Keys*, led by J Melville Williams QC.

[55] ibid [13]–[15].

the famous *GCHQ* case, a case with its own claim to landmark status, the Prime Minister imposed a peremptory ban on trade union membership at GCHQ Cheltenham on the grounds of national security. The decision was challenged through judicial review in the domestic courts, an application under Article 11 ECHR, and complaints to the ILO. The domestic judicial review failed on the grounds of national security. The Court of Appeal considered legal arguments based on the relevant ILO Conventions on freedom of association, and it reached a different conclusion to the ILO Committee on Freedom of Association in finding that the Prime Minister was entitled to take the view that the prohibition did not violate ILO standards.[56] The Article 11 complaint was declared inadmissible because the workers fell within the Article 11(2) exception for workers engaged in the administration of the state. By contrast with the Court of Appeal, various ILO committees upheld the GCHQ complaints based on ILO Conventions.[57] Finally, in *Cheall v APEX* the House of Lords considered whether the right to be a trade union member under Article 11 supported public policy restriction of the 'Bridlington Rules' (TUC rules regulating inter-union competition).[58] Lord Diplock rejected this argument on the basis that freedom of association could only be mutual: there was no right to associate with another who did not wish to associate with him. Overall, the impact of Article 11 in the domestic courts was muted; the unions enjoyed much greater success through the ILO supervisory mechanisms.[59]

In its way, *Wilson* and *Palmer* in the domestic courts can also be viewed as a human rights case too. On first appearances, that may seem like a surprising claim. After all, the judgments in the House of Lords treat the legal crux as a technical issue of statutory construction. In the official reports, however, the record of the oral arguments reveals that international human rights law was an important part of Hendy's and Eady's submissions to their Lordships:

> International conventions (e.g. article 8 of the International Covenant on Economic, Social and Cultural Rights and International Covenant on Civil and Political Rights (1977) (Cmnd. 6702); article 11(1) of the Convention for the Protection of Human Rights and Fundamental Freedoms (1953) (Cmd. 8969); International Labour Organisation Convention (No. 87), Freedom of Association and the Protection of the Right to Organise (1948); International Labour Organisation Convention (No. 98),

[56] *R v Secretary of State for Foreign and Commonwealth Affairs, ex p Council of Civil Service Unions* [1984] IRLR 353 (CA) [44]–[51].

[57] See KD Ewing, *Britain and the ILO*, 2nd edn (London, Institute of Employment Rights, 1994) ch 5.

[58] *Cheall v APEX* [1983] 2 AC 180 (HL).

[59] An important complaint was brought to the ILO by the TUC and NUM alleging multiple violations of ILO standards in 1988. Lord Hendy was integral to the preparation of this complaint. For discussion and detail of the complaint, see Ewing, *Britain and the ILO*, 1st edn (London, Institute of Employment Rights, 1989) ch 4.

> Right to Organise and Bargain Collectively (1949)) recognise that the right to union membership extends to protection of the individual members' interests. That right does not protect collective bargaining as such but it protects more than merely holding a union card. Derecognition or refusal of recognition led to breach of the requirement of consultation under European Directives: see Commission of the European Communities v United Kingdom (Case C-382/92-C-383/92) [1994] I.C.R. 664.[60]

Two features warrant particular emphasis. The first is the identification of a range of instruments that are convergent and thereby identify a particularly important principle of social law. This may be regarded as an early example of 'integrated' human rights argumentation, whereby common standards are constructed by reference to relevant UN Conventions, ILO standards, European law, and Article 11 ECHR.[61] The second is the content of this principle. It is described in the following terms: 'the right to union membership extends to protection of the individual members' interests'. In retrospect, it is now possible to understand this argument as anticipating the Article 11 challenge to UK law. At this point, the ECtHR had rejected the proposition that the fundamental right to collective bargaining was intrinsic to Article 11 freedom of association. A much stronger argument was that the 'right that the trade union should be heard' was given strong and explicit judicial protection under Article 11, and UK law failed to implement this. It is also notable that there was no engagement with the human rights argument in any of the speeches in *Wilson* and *Palmer*, not even to dismiss it. The argument was set out in both the written submissions and oral arguments and relied upon heavily by Hendy. It was simply ignored by the Court.

Undeterred, Mr Wilson and the NUJ lodged an application with the European Commission on Human Rights on 7 September 1995. This had been on Foster's mind right at the outset when he met David Wilson in the pub back in 1990. Subsequent applications followed from the RMT and employees at Southampton and Cardiff ports later that year. It was clear that the potential for a human rights challenge had been identified early in the litigation. This reflected a strategic assessment that the facts in both cases were strong for an innovative Article 11 challenge given that they encompassed discrimination against individual trade unionists. The paradigm of an individual discriminatory wrong was more propitious for a strong Article 11 challenge than a 'pure' collective dispute.

[60] *Wilson* (n 42) 461. In his oral reflections to this author, Lord Hendy recalls that the author of the official report had initially omitted this material because it had been ignored by the House of Lords. Lord Hendy insisted on its inclusion to ensure that this important aspect of the legal arguments was recorded.

[61] V Mantouvalou, 'Labour Rights in the European Convention on Human Rights: An Intellectual Justification for an Integrated Approach to Interpretation' (2013) 13 *HRLR* 529. Interestingly, there is no reference to the European Social Charter in the reported oral submission in the official reports.

This 'individual right to union representation' as a corollary of union membership was crystallised in two academic papers authored or co-authored by Hendy in 1997 and 1998.[62] However, Foster recalls that the fundamental linkage between the individual right to be a trade union member and the individual right to be represented by that trade union emerged in public meetings of the 'Press for Union Rights', a pressure group set up by Foster to agitate for law reform. This was an important pressure group centred on the print unions, that coordinated with other pressure groups and think tanks such as the Institute of Employment Rights. He recalls that a Catholic Bishop, 'Bishop John', whose Personal Assistant was a retired miner, emphasised how this fundamental idea was rooted in Catholic social thought. In the dreadful jargon beloved of research bureaucrats, this was an early instance of 'co-production of knowledge'. The activities of these grassroots organisations were pivotal in the formulation of the overall legal strategy.

The first academic piece in 1997 was co-authored with Michael Walton, a leading Australian advocate acting exclusively for the trade union movement who would later become a justice of the Supreme Court of New South Wales.[63] It examined industrial relations and judicial developments in the UK and Australia, and then analysed international human rights instruments addressing trade union representation. According to them, the right to trade union membership was a fundamental human right in international law. This individual human right to union representation was an essential corollary of this fundamental right to union membership. In placing this individual right in focal position, the theoretical shift was important. It might be more attractive to a human rights court focused on the human rights of individual claimants. It was also more likely to get traction in a political environment dominated by neoliberal governments committed to liberal individualistic tenets in Australia and the UK. Bob Simpson's work was an exemplar of the mainstream hostility to this individual rights strategy in collective laissez-faire. Methodologically, this was rooted in an 'industrial relations' framing of the relevant issues. For Hendy and Walton, by contrast, the analysis was formulated in the domain of fundamental human rights. The simple vesting of this fundamental right in individuals circumvented the difficult and complex regulatory schemes needed to implement a legal duty to bargain. The individual right could be exercised collectively, and its aggregative realisation would be akin to members-only bargaining. It would also be amenable to enforcement by the trade union itself, which would have standing to vindicate the individual right. Moreover, this also had the important

[62] I recall discussing these papers as a student in Oxford BCL seminars in the late 1990s with Professors Davies and Freedland, as we reflected on the tantalising prospect of a potential Article 11 challenge along these lines.

[63] J Hendy QC and M Walton, 'An Individual Right to Union Representation in International Law' (1997) 26 *ILJ* 205.

virtue that it was *already recognised* in Article 11 by the ECtHR, in its notion of a right that the trade union should be heard 'for the protection of his interests'.[64] In 1998, these arguments were developed more comprehensively by Hendy in a long booklet for the Institute of Employment Rights, *Every Worker shall have the Right to be Represented by a Trade Union*.[65] Yet we can already see these arguments beginning to take shape in the oral submissions to the House of Lords back in 1995.

This tension between an 'industrial relations' and a 'human rights' formulation of the right to freedom of association was a critical fault line in the academic literature.[66] Hendy took the view that the choice between them ought to reflect strategic judgements of which was most likely to advance the union's case in a particular time and place. This fault line was reflected in the preparation of a joint submission of the TUC-Liberty to the ECtHR. On 20 April 2000 the General Secretaries of the NUJ and the RMT wrote to Mr John Monks, the General Secretary of the TUC, requesting that Professor Keith Ewing be commissioned to prepare a submission to the ECtHR on behalf of the TUC.[67] On 12 October 2000 Dianne Luping, the Legal Officer at Liberty (the National Council for Civil Liberties), wrote to the Registrar of the ECtHR asking for permission to submit a joint submission with the TUC. The joint submission was coordinated by Sarah Veale at the TUC, who would later become its Head of Equality and Employment Rights. The first part of the joint submission, 'Collective Trade Union Rights', was prepared by Professor Keith Ewing on behalf of the TUC. The second part of the joint submission, 'Comparison of Individual Rights', was prepared by Brian Langstaff QC and Paul Epstein on behalf of Liberty. In a letter from Ewing to Veale on 3 February 2001, Ewing noted this key philosophical difference between the 'human rights' and 'comparative industrial relations' framings in the first and the second parts of the joint submission.[68]

The first part was addressed to the distinctive position of 'trade union action' in the ECHR: these arguments were internal to Article 11. Article 11 envisaged something more than the protection of general associational activities. The explicit recognition of special 'trade union' freedom of association in Article 11 meant that '[c]ontracting States must permit and make possible some form of action which relates to *the core activity of trade unions which is regulating relations between employers and workers*'.[69] In *Wilson* and *Palmer*, domestic law

[64] *Swedish Engine Drivers' Union v Sweden* (1979–80) 1 EHRR 617 [40].

[65] J Hendy QC, *Every Worker shall have the Right to be Represented by a Trade Union* (London, Institute of Employment Rights, 1998).

[66] See, eg, Wedderburn, 'Freedom of Association or Right to Organise?' (n 53).

[67] Letter on file with author.

[68] Letter on file with author.

[69] Joint Submission by Liberty and the Trades Union Congress to the European Court of Human Rights, (5 January 2001) [5] (*emphasis added*).

severed 'union membership' from 'union services'. This failure to protect use of union services did not meet the Article 11 standard as reflected in the textual formula 'for the protection of his interests'. According to the submission,

> the right to be a trade union member for the protection of one's interests does not only impose a duty on the part of the State to enable the union to be heard (albeit by indeterminate means): it must also impose a duty on the part of the State to ensure that the worker is not penalised because he or she is a trade union member or his or her interests are being protected by trade union membership.[70]

Interestingly, this argument was based upon the individual right to union representation intrinsic to the individual right to be a trade union member 'for the protection of his interests'. In this way, it was grounded in the existing jurisprudence of the ECtHR.

The argument was also formulated as a *positive duty* on the state to prevent employers from penalising workers for exercising this fundamental right. This was critically important as the legal arguments shifted from employer responsibilities (in the domestic courts) to the state's responsibilities (in international law). The second part provided a detailed comparative examination of law and practice in Australia, Canada, New Zealand, the US, and Italy. In each case, union membership extended to the 'protection of the worker's employment interests vis-à-vis his employer'.[71] The identification of a universalist consensus on fundamental features of the human right was likely to provide indirect support to the key 'internal' arguments in the first part. However, these examples of English-speaking common law systems were unlikely to be directly persuasive to the ECtHR which was more likely to focus on European national legal practices.

The decision in *Wilson v UK* was handed down on 2 July 2002.[72] In the oral submissions to the ECtHR, John Hendy QC and Jenny Eady had been joined by Lord Wedderburn QC. Along with the joint written submission of TUC-Liberty, this was a formidable team of lawyers. Foster recalls that the advocates were unsure of how to address the judges in the ECtHR as they were unused to the forum. The ice was broken when it emerged that Lord Wedderburn had taught comparative labour law to some of the judges at the LSE. Hendy also attaches importance to the fact that Lord Phillips of Worth Matravers was sitting in the case, and his questions to the advocates revealed a helpful familiarity with the distinctive contours of the UK system. In the definitive academic article on the case, Ewing described it as 'probably the most important labour law decision for at least a generation'.[73] Here again we are in 'landmark' territory in terms of the reception of the case, albeit for very different reasons to the House of

[70] ibid [7].
[71] ibid [34].
[72] *Wilson v UK* [2002] 35 EHRR 20.
[73] KD Ewing, 'The Implications of *Wilson and Palmer*' (2003) 32 *ILJ* 1, 20.

Lords' judgment in *Wilson and Palmer*. The most surprising part, of course, was that the workers and trade unions won a famous Article 11 victory establishing important trade union rights in the ECtHR.[74] The unions' submission was building upon a body of academic work that had been developing the 'individual right to union representation' within the existing doctrinal parameters of Article 11 and its protection of union membership. For its own part, the ECtHR recognised that the case did not involve a direct state interference with Article 11 rights. Instead, it engaged the state's positive duty to protect the Article 11 rights of both workers *and* the trade union itself from interference by employers.[75] The Court went on to observe,

> it is of the essence of the right to join a trade union for the protection of their interests that employees should be free to instruct or permit the union to make representations to their employer or to take action in support of their interests on their behalf. If workers are prevented from so doing, their freedom to belong to a trade union, for the protection of their interests, becomes illusory. It is the role of the State to ensure that trade union members are not prevented or restrained from using their union to represent them in attempts to regulate their relations with their employers.[76]

UK law at the time of the complaints was such that it 'permitted employers to treat less favourably employees who were not prepared to renounce a freedom that was an essential feature of union membership. Such conduct constituted a disincentive or restraint on the use by employees of union membership to protect their interests.'[77] It provided a strong reaffirmation of the right to be represented by a trade union as protected under Article 11. It also identified 'inducements' as liable to 'prevent' or 'restrain' essential trade union freedoms, on a par with more overt and coercive employer actions such as dismissal or demotion at work. Accordingly, the Court found a violation of Article 11. The Court did not go on to examine whether the interference under Article 11(1) was justified under Article 11(2).

Apart from the outcome itself, were there other features that justified its landmark status? In certain respects, the Court was keen to emphasise the doctrinal limits of its reasoning. So, there was no fundamental right to bargain collectively under Article 11 since this was not 'indispensable' to trade union freedoms; the state enjoyed 'a wide margin of appreciation' in how these freedoms were to be secured in view of 'the sensitive character of the social and political issues involved in achieving a proper balance between the competing interests and the wide degree of divergence between the domestic systems in this field'.[78] The explicit recognition of an individual right to union representation,

[74] There were also signs of such a shift in *UNISON v UK* [2002] IRLR 497 which also gave early and cautious recognition to a right to strike under Article 11.
[75] *Wilson* (n 72) [41].
[76] ibid [46] (*emphasis added*).
[77] ibid [47].
[78] ibid [44].

as a corollary of the fundamental right to be a trade union member, nevertheless provided a strong normative foundation for subsequent Article 11 developments. Furthermore, the judgment exemplified an 'integrated' approach to legal reasoning in referencing ILO and ESC provisions, and decisions of the ESC's Committee of Independent Experts and the ILO's Committee on Freedom of Association that had been critical of the relevant UK law. While it was not the first time that these legal regimes had been used by the ECtHR to interpret Article 11,[79] it was significant that they were being used in *Wilson* to *extend* trade union protections. This can surely be traced back to the 'integrated' submissions in the House of Lords in *Wilson and Palmer*.

Wilson was also a landmark in terms of its significant normative effects on subsequent Article 11 development. It enlivened the dynamic potential of the ECHR for trade unions and workers engaged in litigation, leading to an expansion in its strategic use. In *Demir and Baykara v Turkey*, the Grand Chamber finally recognised the fundamental right to bargain collectively as protected under Article 11.[80] This development was supported by the 'integrated' method that had been honed in *Wilson*. There can be little doubt that *Wilson* provided the critical bridge between the cautious 1970s case law (Article 11 did not secure any particular treatment of trade unions) and the judgment in *Demir* (Article 11 protected the fundamental right to bargain collectively). It is significant that the Court in *Demir* observed that the Court considers that

> its case-law to the effect that the right to bargain collectively and to enter into collective agreements does not constitute an inherent element of article 11 (see *Swedish Engine Drivers' Union*, cited above, § 39, and *Schmidt and Dahlström*, cited above, § 34) should be reconsidered, so as to take account of the perceptible evolution in such matters, in both international law and domestic legal systems.[81]

Wilson itself is not mentioned because it is treated as in broad alignment with *Demir* and therefore part of the *new* era of Article 11. The recognition of the right to strike as 'protected' under Article 11 then followed on quickly from *Demir*.[82] In this way, one of the most remarkable landmark legacies of *Wilson* is as a juridical gateway between the 'old' and the 'new' Article 11 jurisprudence.

Yet it would be a mistake to view *Wilson* as a historical relic that has been superseded by an ever-expanding horizon for the right to bargain collectively under Article 11. In *UNITE v UK*, an Article 11 challenge to the abolition of the Agricultural Wages Board (AWB) was declared inadmissible because it was

[79] *Sigurdur Sigurjónsson v Iceland* (1993) 16 EHRR 462. This case involved the recognition of 'negative' freedom to disassociate under Article 11. I am grateful to Kalina Arabadjieva for a very helpful discussion of this point, based on her excellent DPhil work on Article 11.

[80] *Demir and Baykara v Turkey* (2009) 48 EHRR 54.

[81] ibid [153].

[82] See *Enerji Yapi-Yol Sen v Turkey* App No 68959/01 (ECtHR, 21 April 2009); *National Union of Rail, Maritime and Transport Workers v UK (RMT)* (2015) 60 EHRR 10.

'manifestly ill-founded'.[83] There are two limiting factors in the reasoning in *UNITE*, both of which were also present in the earlier 'right to strike' case in *RMT*.[84] First, the Court emphasised the extremity of the facts in *Demir* which involved the judicial annulment of the collective agreement. *Demir* involved direct state interference with freedom of association which was 'a very far-reaching interference with freedom of association'.[85] In *Unite*, by contrast, the state had withdrawn a specific legal model of collective bargaining while leaving no other legal mechanisms practically available to agricultural workers.[86] This re-interpretation of *Demir*, which elides the specific facts of that case with the general legal principles it establishes, is designed to entrench a wide margin of appreciation in state positive obligation cases under Article 11. The Court in *Unite* also exaggerated the specific factual context in *Demir* by describing it as involving a formal dissolution of the trade union. Second, the Court emphasised the democratic process whereby the legislature had consulted widely and given explicit consideration to the human rights dimension before repealing the AWB. Again, and following the earlier judgment in *RMT*, the democratic quality of legislative restriction was taken to support a wide margin of appreciation for the state. In *Wilson*, the Court found a violation of Article 11 in respect of the state's failure of its positive obligation to protect workers and their trade unions. The fact that this violation was underpinned and facilitated by democratically enacted legislation did not figure in the Court's analysis. Some 20 years on, *Wilson* may still represent a high watermark in terms of a practical and effective enforcement of Article 11 rights.[87] It also reflects the basic distinction between 'individual' and 'collective' Article 11 cases, with instances of individual victimisation attracting a far narrower margin of appreciation than purely collective cases.[88]

The *Wilson* era was also marked by the emergence of a new genre of legal scholarship. During the 1980s, scholarship on freedom of association as a human right was often strongly critical in its orientation. This was aligned with a more general attitude of scepticism towards law as an instrument of progressive social change. As with Article 11 itself, *Wilson* represented something of a transition point here too. Labour lawyers increasingly turned to international instruments as a *standard of critique* of deregulatory national laws and practices. This led

[83] *Unite the Union v UK* App No 65397/13 (ECtHR, 3 May 2016).

[84] K Arabadjieva, 'Another Disappointment in Strasbourg: *Unite the Union v United Kingdom*' (2017) 46 *ILJ* 289.

[85] *Unite the Union* (n 83) [60].

[86] As Arabadjieva points out, these alternative methods of collective bargaining are theoretical rather than practical and effective given the specific labour market disadvantages of agricultural workers in the UK: Arabadijeva (n 84).

[87] The formula of 'practical' and 'effective' guarantee of Convention rights is specified in *Artico v Italy* (1981) 3 EHRR 1 [33].

[88] See, eg, *Ognevenko v Russia* (2019) 69 EHRR 9.

to a developing body of scholarship teasing out the regulatory implications of those international norms for statutory reform and judicial interpretation of domestic law.[89] Ewing was at the forefront of this methodological turn with his signature 'The Implications of [INSERT] v United Kingdom …' articles. It was also reflected in his sustained engagement with *Wilson* itself. He drafted the first part of the TUC-Liberty joint submission. Following *Wilson* and then *Demir*, he developed a 'reconstructive' critique of domestic law, identifying its deficiencies against the measure of Article 11 and proposing regulatory solutions for reform. While recent scholarship has been more despondent, reflecting frustration with the apparent timidity of the ECtHR in its relationship with the UK,[90] this genre of 'reconstructive' labour law scholarship is likely to be enduring. Immanent critique is focused on the inner resources of the law to repair itself in light of its own aspirational standards.

IV. *WILSON* AND *PALMER* AND STATUTE LAW

Fundamental labour rights depend upon statutes for their specification and full realisation.[91] Freedom of association in labour law is pre-eminently a 'legislated right'. The central role of legislation and legislatures to freedom of association is reflected in *Wilson*'s biography as a landmark case. In the domestic courts, the legal arguments were concerned exclusively with statutory interpretation. The choice to pursue the case to the ECtHR reflected a strategic judgement that this was the most effective way of securing broader changes to the legislative framework. After *Wilson v UK*, attention then shifted to how legislation could be reformed to bring domestic law into compliance with the directive guidance of Article 11. This would lead to a specific statutory provision introduced in the Employment Relations Act (ERA) 2004, inserted into TULRCA 1992 as section 145B, which would become known colloquially as the '*Wilson and Palmer*' provision.

Through much of this period, unions were engaged concurrently with the courts *and* the legislature. Strategic litigation was instrumental to a wider objective of legislative reform. In this way, legal and political modes of action were complementary. This case study also reveals the complexity of the interaction

[89] For notable early examples, see KD Ewing, 'Freedom of Association and the Employment Relations Act 1999' (1998) 28 *ILJ* 283; T Novitz, 'International Promises and Domestic Pragmatism: To What Extent Will the Employment Relations Act 1999 Implement International Standards Relating to Freedom of Association?' (2000) 63 *MLR* 379; KD Ewing, 'The Implications of the *ASLEF* Case' (2007) 36 *ILJ* 425; KD Ewing and J Hendy QC, 'The Dramatic Implications of *Demir and Baykara*' (2010) 39 *ILJ* 2.

[90] KD Ewing and J Hendy QC, 'The Trade Union Act 2016 and the Failure of Human Rights' (2016) 45 *ILJ* 391.

[91] Webber and others (n 2).

between courts and legislatures in securing fundamental rights through legislation. There are three main periods in the statutory history of *Wilson*: (i) the enactment of the 'Ullswater' amendment following the Court of Appeal judgment; (ii) the Employment Relations Act 1999; (iii) the ERA 2004 reforms in response to *Wilson v UK*. In the first two periods, unions were unable to secure significant concessions through statutory reform. It was only during the third period, following *Wilson v UK*, that statutory reforms were focused specifically on the best way to specify and realise the right to freedom of association. Yet *Wilson v UK* did not pre-empt a creative legislative specification. It triggered a democratic and deliberative engagement with the precise requirements of freedom of association and how best to implement those through statute.

A. The 'Ullswater' Amendment

Viscount Ullswater has already made a cameo appearance in this story, and it is now time to reveal his role more fully. Following the Court of Appeal judgment in *Wilson*, the government reversed the effect of the decision with great urgency. The legislative history of the amendment has been explained fully by Ewing in 'Dancing with the Daffodils?'[92] The Court of Appeal decision was handed down on 30 April 1993 and the intention to reverse it was announced a week later on 6 May 1993. The amendment was tabled at the Third Reading of the Trade Union Reform and Employment Rights Bill in the House of Lords by Viscount Ullswater. As Ewing observed, this was described with some justification by some members of the Lords as an abuse of parliamentary process.[93] It curtailed the scope for a democratic assessment of an amendment with far-reaching substantive effects on fundamental rights. The amendment was passed and introduced in section 13 of the Trade Union Reform and Employment Rights Act 1993, inserting it as section 148(3)–(5) TULRCA 1992. The provision operated through modifying the evidential rules on 'purpose'. Where there was: (a) evidence 'that the employer's purpose was to further a change in his relationship with all or any class of his employees'; and (b) evidence of an unlawful purpose, the tribunal was directed to disregard the unlawful purpose. The lawful purpose was determinative 'unless it considers that the action was such as no reasonable employer would take'. This would cover most scenarios involving offers of 'personal contracts' as part of a plan to restructure contractual relations on a more individualised basis. It was aimed at preserving maximal scope for individual freedom of contract. Up until this point, the law permitted the derecognition of trade unions. The 'Ullswater' amendment was a kind of legislative 'prop' that provided positive statutory support to derecognition.

[92] Ewing (n 3) 5–7.
[93] ibid 6.

The 'Ullswater' amendment was subjected to strong criticism by the ILO Committee on Freedom of Association and the Committee of Experts, both in terms of the democratic flaws in the process of enactment and its substantive content.[94] The truncated process meant that any democratic consultation with the social partners was flawed. This had resulted in a statutory provision that effectively legitimised anti-union discrimination. It was also subjected to criticism in the 13 and 14 cycles of supervision by the Committee of Independent Experts of the European Social Charter.[95] In due course, the 'Ullswater' amendment was relevant to the conclusion of the ECtHR that UK law violated Article 11.

Whatever else might be said of the 'Ullswater' amendment, it was not an example of the 'central case' of legislating in favour of rights and the common good.[96] While a conscious deliberative orientation to fundamental rights might not be *essential* to conscientious legislating, it would at least encourage an explicit deliberative assessment of the requirements of the common good. Indeed, in *Unite the Union* the ECtHR identified the legislature's explicit human rights consideration of a legislative measure as a factor favouring a broader margin of appreciation.[97] There was no evidence of this in the 'Ullswater' episode. Instead, it was a hasty intervention to restore a legal position that was the subject of universal criticism by bodies with expertise in administering international human rights instruments.

B. The Employment Relations Act 1999

The election of 'New Labour' in 1997 signalled an important political shift for collective labour rights. The White Paper, *Fairness at Work*, formulated its critique of the law in *Wilson and Palmer* in individualistic terms.[98] The law permitted discrimination that was 'contrary to its commitment to ensuring individuals are free to choose whether or not to join a trade union'.[99] To address this, it proposed to extend 'action short of dismissal' to cover discrimination by omission. Interestingly, this proposal was contained in the same paragraph dealing with measures to prohibit blacklisting of trade unionists. This would suggest that *Wilson and Palmer* was now being conceptualised as an individual freedom of association issue by the government. Despite this, there was an ominous silence on the 'Ullswater' amendment that had been subject to such

[94] ibid 12–13.
[95] ibid 13–16.
[96] For discussion of this legislative responsibility, see Webber and others (n 2).
[97] *Unite the Union* (n 83).
[98] Department of Trade and Industry, *Fairness at Work* (Cm 3968, 1998).
[99] ibid 4.24–4.25.

strong criticism as a violation of freedom of association. This may have reflected the wider philosophical context to the White Paper, which was that collective representation should 'facilitate negotiation on terms and conditions without preventing the recognition of good individual performance'.[100] This exposed a fault line that had been present throughout the biography of *Wilson and Palmer* but became more prominent in the 1999 settlement: the tension between (individual) freedom of contract and the right to bargain collectively.

As the details of the Employment Relations Bill were being formulated, the general secretaries of the NUJ and the RMT had been in correspondence with Ian McCartney MP, Minister of State at the Department of Trade and Industry.[101] The unions were focused on the repeal of the 'Ullswater' amendment, and this was linked explicitly with the unions' pending Article 11 case. The ongoing litigation in the courts was not being treated as a substitute for political engagement. On the contrary, it was being harnessed by the unions to shape and influence legislative activity. In a longer letter to David Winnick MP, who had been relaying the unions' concerns to the Secretary of State Peter Mandelson, McCartney provided a fuller explanation of government policy and the retention of 'Ullswater'.[102] According to McCartney, it was 'our intention to retain the existing freedoms of employers and employees to reach individual contracts which differ from the terms of any collective agreement'.[103] He went on to emphasise the cogency of the distinction between 'union membership' and 'collective bargaining', thereby endorsing the obiter statements in the House of Lords in *Wilson and Palmer*. Furthermore, the retention of 'Ullswater' 'serves a useful purpose and ought to be retained' in circumstances where an employer sought 'legitimately' to pursue voluntary or statutory derecognition.[104] This reflected a conception of freedom of association that encompassed the negative freedom to disassociate from collective arrangements, especially where this negative freedom promoted individualised pay flexibility.

The ERA modified 'action short of dismissal' to include protection for omissions in a new 'detriment' provision in section 146 TULRCA 1992.[105] The narrow judicial interpretation of 'union membership' was unaffected. Predictably, the 'Ullswater' amendment was not repealed. Section 17 ERA gave the Secretary of State a power to make Regulations where a worker was dismissed or subjected to a detriment on the grounds that 'he refuses to enter into a contract which includes terms which differ from the terms of a collective agreement which applies to him'.[106] According to section 17(4), there would be no 'detriment' where the

[100] ibid 4.3.
[101] Letter from Ian McCartney MP to John Foster, 10 February 1999 (on file with author).
[102] Letter from Ian McCartney MP to David Winnick MP, 19 January 1999 (on file with author).
[103] ibid.
[104] ibid.
[105] ERA 1999, Sch 2.
[106] ERA 1999, s 17(1)(b).

contract contained no inhibition on union membership and 'payments of higher wages or rates of pay or overtime or bonuses or the provision of other benefits are in accordance with the terms of a contract of employment and reasonably relate to services provided by the worker under that contract'. Regulations were never introduced, but the solicitude for individual freedom of contract and pay flexibility was striking.

C. The Employment Relations Act 2004

In February 2003 the Department of Trade and Industry (DTI) launched the 'Review of the Employment Relations Act 1999' to assess the operation of the legislation.[107] While the bulk of the review was focused on the statutory recognition procedure, the DTI used it as an opportunity to consider the legal implications of *Wilson v UK*.[108] Overall, the DTI adopted a narrow view of the legal changes needed. It proposed the repeal of the 'Ullswater' amendment, a necessary step given that this statutory provision was considered specifically by the ECtHR in *Wilson*. It also proposed the introduction of a 'clear positive right' to use the services of an independent trade union.[109] At this stage, it was not clear whether this would simply involve a new additional ground of unlawfulness in the detriment/dismissal provisions, or a freestanding right correlative to positive duties on an employer to consider the union's representations. In response to the specific facts in *Wilson* itself, the Review was anxious to preserve the scope for individual contractual flexibility and rewarding individual performance. The proposal was strongly in favour of a wide scope for individual negotiation, limited only by the exclusion of overt 'quid pro quo' anti-union inducements: 'the entering of individualised contracts would not constitute unlawful union discrimination against those union members not offered them, as long as there was no inducement to relinquish union representation and no pre-condition in the contracts to relinquish it'.[110] The power in section 17 of the ERA 1999 would also be repealed.

The consultation on the Review attracted a significant number of responses from employer and trade union organisations. It also attracted submissions from the main protagonists in *Wilson and Palmer* (including one by David Wilson himself). These were considered in the 'Review of the Employment Relations Act 1999: Government Response to the Public Consultation'.[111] There was

[107] Department of Trade and Industry (DTI), *Review of the Employment Relations Act 1999* (DTI, February 2003).

[108] ibid 3.5.

[109] ibid 3.11.

[110] ibid 3.13.

[111] DTI, *Review of the Employment Relations Act 1999: Government Response to the Public Consultation* (December 2003).

unanimous agreement from all consultees that the 'Ullswater' amendment and section 17 of the ERA 1999 should be repealed. The DTI rejected the extension of freestanding rights to trade unions in *Wilson and Palmer* situations; these Article 11 protections were rights principally for individuals.[112] The use of union services provided to individual members would be included alongside union membership and trade union activities in the existing detriment and dismissal protections. There would be a separate provision to regulate *Wilson and Palmer* situations. Where it was the 'main purpose' of the employer to induce workers to have terms of employment determined outside the collective agreement, this would be unlawful.[113] Liability would not arise where the employer's 'main purpose' was a legitimate business reason, so that 'the law should give room for employers and individuals to enter individualised contracts designed to reward or retain key workers'.[114] Finally, the Review proposed extending core freedom of association rights to 'workers' from the narrower category of employee.[115] While this point did not arise specifically in *Wilson v UK*, it was justified by reference to Article 11.

The human rights scrutiny of the Employment Relations Bill was undoubtedly enhanced by the involvement of the Joint Committee on Human Rights (JCHR). This select committee was first proposed in 1998 but it had its first meeting on 31 January 2001. The initial view of the JCHR was that the relevant provision in the Bill, which reflected the basic shape set out in the DTI Review, was compatible with Article 11. There then followed an intensive dialogue between Lord Wedderburn QC and John Hendy QC, both of whom had appeared before the ECtHR in Strasbourg. They identified three main issues: (i) the absence of a trade union right; (ii) the stringency of the 'sole or main' purpose threshold which had the potential to permit discriminatory inducements that violated Article 11; and (iii) the absence of a remedy for derecognised or non-recognised unions. The JCHR was persuaded by these criticisms in its 10th Report of 2003–04. In the final version of the Bill that received Royal Assent, an amendment to protect unions that were 'seeking recognition' was introduced. This was a valuable change brought about through a process of deliberative dialogue and reflection. However, the 'sole or main purpose' test was retained because of concerns that a wider 'purpose' test might impede individualised merit payments. The government did not agree that compliance with *Wilson* necessitated specific provision for a trade union right. Nevertheless, the discussion that occurred around the JCHR reports prompted a good faith dialogue about the specification of the fundamental right in legislation. In this respect, it can be contrasted with earlier legislative engagements which were less structured around questions of human rights implementation.

[112] ibid 3.09.
[113] ibid 3.12.
[114] ibid.
[115] ibid 3.13.

The ERA 2004 introduced significant changes that went beyond the specific facts in *Wilson v UK*. The 'Ullswater' amendment and section 17 of the ERA 1999 were repealed. The 'detriment' protections in section 146 were extended to 'workers'. The 'use of union services' was inserted as a new ground of unlawfulness in both the section 146 detriment and section 152 dismissal provisions. The ERA 2004 also introduced two new additional rights. Under section 145A, a worker had a right not to have an offer made to him if the 'sole or main purpose' was to induce the worker not to be a union member, to participate in the activities of an independent trade union, or to use union services. Under section 145B, a worker who was a member of an independent trade union that was recognised or seeking recognition had a right not to have an offer made to him in certain 'collective bargaining' contexts. Those offers must, if accepted, lead to the 'prohibited result'. This was that the workers' term or terms of employment would not (or no longer) be determined by collective agreement. If this counterfactual condition was satisfied, the liability enquiry shifted to the employer's 'sole or main purpose'. The assessment of the employer's 'sole or main purpose' was guided by section 145D which provided (amongst other things) 'that the offers were made only to particular workers, and were made with the sole or main purpose of rewarding those particular workers for their high level of performance or of retaining them because of their special value to the employer'. While 'Ullswater' was gone, the scope for individual contractual flexibility, particularly on issues of pay and reward, was a persistent concern for courts and legislators throughout the *Wilson and Palmer* story.

V. *KOSTAL V DUNKLEY*: THE LATEST CHAPTER OF *WILSON*

In *Kostal v Dunkley*, the United Kingdom Supreme Court considered section 145B for the first time.[116] The facts were different to *Wilson and Palmer* in that they did not involve derecognition. Following a recent recognition agreement, which set out a detailed bargaining procedure, Kostal and Unite the Union commenced collective negotiations. Before the exhaustion of the agreed procedure, the employer issued direct offers to the workforce which contained the proposals that had been rejected by the union. The facts of the case exemplify an important evolution in the legal character of the relevant statutory provision. *Kostal* is much more like a 'collective' dispute than *Wilson and Palmer*, and section 145B sits as easily in the family of 'collective' statutory provisions supporting collective bargaining as in the 'individual' anti-discrimination provisions protecting freedom of association. The issue of a duty to bargain in good faith is latent in *Kostal* even if it is not explicit. In the Supreme Court, both the majority and

[116] *Kostal UK Ltd v Dunkley* [2021] UKSC 47, [2022] ICR 434.

minority agreed that the facts gave rise of a breach of section 145B. The majority and minority disagreed on the correct interpretation of section 145B. It is interesting to consider this disagreement against the backdrop of the *Wilson and Palmer* story, and to contrast the styles of reasoning with the House of Lords back in 1995. What, if anything, has changed?

The majority judgment was given by Lord Leggatt (with whom Lord Briggs and Lord Kitchin agreed). According to the majority, the precise wording of section 145B indicated that statutory liability required the 'offers' to have potential causal salience: would acceptance of those offers contribute to the 'prohibited result' in that the term or terms might otherwise have been collectively agreed?[117] The practical effect of this was that 'quid pro quo' offers or offers issued during the collective bargaining process would satisfy the objective causal test, but not otherwise. The 'sole or main purpose' test was subsidiary to this objective enquiry. The minority judgment was given by Lady Arden and Lord Burrows. They treated the objective element of section 145B as merely a de minimis threshold. Whenever multiple offers were issued to workers, their hypothetical acceptance would always mean that those terms were not being determined by collective agreement: they were by definition being determined by individual agreement. Liability would then depend principally on the 'sole or main purpose' enquiry. Where the employer could identify a credible legitimate business purpose for the offers, it was likely to avoid section 145 liability. Where it could not, a tribunal might infer that it had made the offers with an unlawful 'sole or main purpose'.

Starting with the majority, it is worth recalling Lord Bridge's reflections on statutory interpretation in *Wilson and Palmer*: 'giving primacy to the ordinary, grammatical meaning of statutory language, is reflected in the parliamentary draftsman's technique of using language with the utmost precision to express the legislative intent of his political masters'.[118] For Lord Leggatt,

> as with any question of statutory interpretation, the task of the court is to determine the meaning and legal effect of the words used by Parliament. The modern case law – including, in the field of employment law, the recent decision of this court in *Uber BV v Aslam* [2021] UKSC 5; [2021] ICR 657, para 70 – has emphasised the central importance of identifying the purpose of the legislation and interpreting the relevant language in the light of that purpose. Sometimes the context and background, or the statute viewed as a whole, provides clear pointers to the objectives which the relevant provisions were seeking to achieve. In other cases, however, *the purpose needs to be identified at a level of particularity which requires it to be elicited mainly from the wording of the relevant provisions themselves.* The present case is one in which, although the legal context and aim of seeking to secure article 11 rights is important,

[117] ibid [65]–[66].
[118] *Wilson* (n 42) 475.

> the somewhat complicated and elaborate wording of section 145B (and section 145D) calls, in my view, for *a careful linguistic analysis on the assumption that the words used have been chosen with precision.*[119]

Lord Leggatt's judgment is attentive to the requirements of Article 11 and the reasoning in *Wilson v UK*. This provided the 'context and background' to the enactment of section 145B. However, the statutory interpretation in *Kostal* is not treated as a special genre of 'human rights' interpretation based upon section 3 of the Human Rights Act 1998. It is 'ordinary' statutory interpretation, and it reflects a view that the words in section 145B had been chosen with 'precision' (and compare Lord Bridge, where the words had been chosen with 'the utmost precision'). Furthermore, the background concern for the majority is the spectre of uncertain statutory liability for employers. The importance of 'legal certainty' demanded a bright line (albeit a relatively arbitrary) specification of the limits of liability, and this was provided by the parties' own agreed bargaining procedure.[120] If one listens carefully, it is possible to detect the echoes of Wood J in the Employment Appeal Tribunal in *Wilson* and *Palmer*, who had expressed his own anxieties about the ambiguities of 'purpose' deterring employers and workers from negotiating advantageous individual bargains. Likewise, the anxieties in *Kostal* about a 'union veto' flowing from a wide interpretive approach to section 145B is a different way of making the same basic point that had been expressed by Sir John in the early 1990s.

By contrast, the minority judgment focuses on 'sole or main purpose', with liability turning on whether the employer had a legitimate business reason for the offers. As with the majority, the exercise is treated as one of 'ordinary' statutory interpretation. The critical difference is that the minority emphasise statutory purpose and context over the precise statutory language as it relates to the objective effects of acceptance of offers. The precise statutory wording in section 145B supported the majority's view that there was a requirement of causal nexus between the acceptance of the offers and the 'prohibited result': that the term or terms of employment will not or no longer be determined by collective agreement. For the minority, this insistence upon causation would subvert the effectiveness of the statutory provision and its protective purpose. Accordingly, the focus should be on the employer's 'sole or main purpose', and whether it had a legitimate business purpose for making the offers. This would enable tribunals to scrutinise different bargaining situations, which often involve subtle distinctions of fact and degree, to determine liability. The rule of law cost in terms of a loss of maximum legal certainty is counterbalanced by the rule of law gain of an effectively enforced statutory provision. It is strongly rooted in a 'labour law' mode of thinking, developing legal doctrine with an eye on practicability and enforcement in first instance tribunals. It is the kind of approach that

[119] *Kostal* (n 116) [30] (*emphasis added*).
[120] ibid [60].

would lend itself well to the intensive focus on facts and 'industrial morality' in the employment tribunals. Indeed, it is very much in the protective spirit of Mrs Stella Hollis' landmark Industrial Tribunal judgment back in 1991. It is difficult to imagine that the minority judgment in *Kostal* could have been handed down by the House of Lords circa 1995. In this sense, *Kostal* does represent progress.

VI. *WILSON AND PALMER*: THE MAKING OF A LANDMARK CASE

There can be no question that *Wilson and Palmer* is a 'landmark' case. This conclusion is fully vindicated by this biographical portrait. This story also illuminates some interesting features of the very idea of a 'landmark'. The first is that landmark cases often have a diachronic dimension. The landmark significance of *Wilson and Palmer* changed over time. The reasons why the House of Lords judgment is a landmark case are quite different to the reasons why the ECtHR judgment is a landmark. Furthermore, we could only really see how much of a landmark the ECtHR judgment was by tracing the jurisprudential shifts in the decade that followed it. This retrospective examination also highlights the phenomenon of the 'slow burn' legal argument/strategy. Lord Hendy's use of an 'integrated' human rights argument in the House of Lords, judged at the time in 1995, was a spectacular failure. In due course, it would become embedded in the standard reasoning pattern of the ECtHR in its interpretive approach to Article 11. Arguments that fail today may end up succeeding many years later. Moreover, the story of *Wilson and Palmer* is continuing to be written some 30 years after the original Industrial Tribunal judgment, reflected in the recent *Kostal* judgment (described by two errant commentators as a '*Wilson and Palmer* for the twenty-first century'[121]). It will no doubt continue to be made and remade by judges, lawyers, and academics, and its meaning will remain contingent and negotiable in this process of reinterpretation and narrative reconstruction.

The second feature is how the making of a landmark case is a collaborative enterprise. Different unions have taken the lead at different times over the last 30 years: NUJ, RMT, TUC, Unite the Union. They have been supported by legal teams, academic lawyers, and the workers themselves prepared to make great personal sacrifices to see these cases through. While the making of *Wilson and Palmer* involved only relatively loose coordination between the NUJ and the RMT, there is no doubt that these landmark cases reflect the aggregated efforts of many remarkable individuals.

The third feature is the role of serendipity. What if Patrick Elias QC and Nigel Giffin had not decided to pursue the relatively obscure and technical act/

[121] A Bogg and KD Ewing, 'Collective Bargaining and Individual Contracts in *Kostal UK Ltd v Dunkley: A Wilson and Palmer* for the 21st century?' (2020) 49 *ILJ* 430.

omission point in the House of Lords? Perhaps the unions might have won the domestic case. Had they done so, we have no idea how Article 11 might then have developed if there had been no *Wilson v UK* in the ECtHR. Landmark cases are made or unmade through planning, resources, and hard work. They are also made or unmade through the accidental play of fate and the legal flutter of a butterfly's wings.

The fourth feature is the collaborative interaction between courts and legislatures in constituting fundamental human rights. *Wilson and Palmer* has been made through an ongoing dialogue between different courts (both national and transnational) and legislatures engaged in statutory reform. For the NUJ and RMT, litigation was always an element in a broader approach of strategic law-making. Justice for the individuals in the specific litigation was a means of seeking structural legal changes to benefit every worker. This story demonstrates that courts play a vital supporting role in the democratic specification of 'legislated rights' in legal orders.

Above all, landmark cases are human stories about landmark people. It is fitting, therefore, to close this chapter with the people that made *Wilson and Palmer*. John Foster became General Secretary of the NUJ from 1992 until 2001, and was an active supporter of the Institute of Employment Rights. Lord Hendy QC was given a life peerage in 2019 and currently sits in the House of Lords as a Labour peer. Professor Keith Ewing continues to this day as a Professor at King's College, London, and one of the leading labour law and public law academics of his generation. At different stages of the litigation, no less than four future Presidents of the Employment Appeal Tribunal were involved in the case: Patrick Elias, Nicholas Underhill, Brian Langstaff, and Jennifer Eady. Peter Clark served as a widely admired judge on the Employment Appeal Tribunal. Patrick Elias and Nicholas Underhill both went on to serve with great distinction in the Court of Appeal, and in their different ways have shaped modern employment law through their own landmark judgments. And what of David Wilson himself? Following a period as a freelance journalist, where his professionalism was widely respected across the industry, he was employed by the architect of Fortress Wapping, Rupert Murdoch. Wilson worked at *The Times* and then *The Sunday Times* as deputy news editor (nights). The final detail may be apocryphal but here it is. At his retirement event, the speech was given by none other than Rebekah Brooks, that controversial member of Rupert Murdoch's tight inner circle. In landmark cases as in life, the truth is often far stranger than fiction.

11

Malik v BCCI: *The Impact of Good Faith*

DOUGLAS BRODIE

I. THE EMERGENCE AND ACCEPTANCE OF MUTUAL TRUST AND CONFIDENCE

A. Introduction

THE DECISION OF the House of Lords in *Malik v BCCI* (*Malik*) confirmed that the employment contract contained an implied term in law of mutual trust and confidence.[1] *Malik* was the end point of a journey that had begun some 20 years before when a version of the term first emerged at tribunal level. The catalyst had been the enactment of the statutory law of unfair dismissal which meant that, in constructive dismissal cases, employees were required to demonstrate that they were justified in resigning given the conduct of the employer. For a period of time in the 1970's the basis upon which the employer's behaviour was to be assessed was unclear. Matters were resolved by the decision of the Court of Appeal in *Western Excavating v Sharp* (*Sharp*) which held that a contractual test should be deployed and not one of reasonableness.[2] As a result, a repudiatory breach of contract must have occurred before an industrial tribunal would have jurisdiction.[3] Thereafter, the law of implied terms took on added significance as many instances of objectionable behaviour will not amount to a breach of an express term of the contract. Against this backdrop, the emergence and subsequent affirmation of mutual trust and confidence was a matter of considerable consequence for the law of the employment contract. I will though conclude this chapter by suggesting that the element of affirmation is not what makes *Malik* a landmark case.

[1] *Malik v BCCI* [1998] AC 20 (HL). As an implied term in law it was an incident of all employment contracts.

[2] *Western Excavating v Sharp* [1978] 1 QB 761 (CA).

[3] Prior to 1 August 1998 employment tribunals were known as industrial tribunals.

An illuminating explanation of the origins of the term is provided by Hepple. In 2005 in the course of delivering the Hamlyn lectures he revisited a decision of an industrial tribunal which he had chaired in 1977 and which had promulgated the first iteration of the obligation of trust and confidence.[4] The case concerned was *Wood v Freeloader (Freeloader)* where a live-in nanny had been seduced by her employer into conducting a sexual relationship.[5] She had resigned and claimed to have been constructively dismissed. The lay members regarded the employer's conduct as utterly unacceptable but the key question was whether there had been a breach of contract and they looked to Hepple for guidance. It would almost certainly have been possible to have looked to the old master and servant cases and, through a modicum of modernisation, found a solution. Several years later in the Court of Appeal Lord Denning MR appeared to be drawn to such an approach when he invoked the language of yesteryear and said that an employer 'must be good and considerate to his servants'.[6] The employer in *Freeloader* could hardly be said to have been 'good and considerate' but Hepple chose to disregard the language and formulations of the past. Instead, the general principles of the law of contract and, in particular, the implied duty of co-operation offered a way forward. The tribunal went on to hold that that duty was part of the law of the employment contract and, in addition, it gave rise to a more specific duty in the employment context; viz. a duty implied by law that an employer will not do anything which would undermine the continuation of the confidential relationship between employer and employee.[7] The soundness of such a term was accepted with alacrity in subsequent cases.[8]

The term as articulated in *Freeloader* was not yet expressed in its current form but the arrival of the contemporary formulation was not to be delayed for long. The subsequent case of *Robinson v Crompton Parkinson* expressed the term in a more recognisable manner and also stressed that the obligation was reciprocal.[9] In the EAT in December 1978, in *Courtaulds Northern Textiles v Andrew*, the formulation put forward by the claimant's solicitor was accepted: 'the employers would not, without reasonable and proper cause, conduct themselves in a manner calculated or likely to destroy or seriously damage the relationship of confidence and trust between the parties'.[10] The process of composition of the term was now complete. This definition was again followed by the EAT in

[4] B Hepple, *Rights at Work: Global, European and British Perspectives* (London, Sweet and Maxwell, 2005) 51–52.

[5] *Wood v Freeloader* [1977] IRLR 455 (Industrial Tribunal).

[6] *Woods v WM Car Services* [1982] ICR 693 (CA) 698.

[7] *Freeloader* (n 5) [12] (the Tribunal). It is worthy of note that the phrase 'trust and confidence' does not appear at this stage.

[8] *Woods v WM Car Services* [1981] ICR 666 (EAT).

[9] *Robinson v Crompton Parkinson* [1978] ICR 401 (EAT).

[10] *Courtaulds Northern Textiles v Andrew* [1979] IRLR 84 (EAT) [10] (Arnold J). On the role of the claimant's solicitor see F Reynold, 'Bad Behaviour and the Implied Term of Mutual Trust and Confidence: Is There a Problem?' (2015) 44 *ILJ* 262, 264.

Woods v WM Car Services who were also of the view that the term (its seeming youth notwithstanding) was 'clearly established'.[11] Highly significantly, the term was said to be one of general application where the employment contract was concerned and was therefore one in law. This was consistent with Hepple's approach in *Freeloader* where the term devised was categorised as an aspect of the general duty of co-operation. *Freeloader* also displayed an awareness that tribunals and lay members in particular were likely to be untroubled by the precise crafting of the implied term and be more concerned with a common sense assessment of the employer's conduct: 'the tribunal's function is to look at the employer's conduct as a whole and determine whether it is such that its effect, judged reasonably and sensibly, is such that the employee cannot be expected to put up with it'.[12]

The emergence and rapid acceptance of the term owed a great deal to the decision of the Court of Appeal in *Sharp* where, as we have seen, a contractual test rather than one of reasonableness had been favoured where constructive dismissal was concerned.[13] As a corollary, the law of implied terms began to be looked to by aggrieved employees far more. In an extremely perceptive article, published in 1978, Elias highlighted that implied terms could bridge the gap between a contractual test and one based on reasonableness.[14] Subsequent developments were to show just how prescient this observation was.

B. The Term Appraised

It is undoubtedly the case that had someone other than Hepple chaired the tribunal in *Freeloader* the claimant would still have been likely to have won. The circumstances were such that it would have reflected badly upon the laws of employment protection had the employer avoided liability given the abuse of power which had taken place. It may be noted that Lawton LJ, without reference to *Freeloader*, had suggested in *Sharp* that a breach of contract would arise should there be '[p]ersistent and unwanted amorous advances by an employer to a female member of his staff …'.[15] This speaks to the emergence of a judicial consensus that inappropriate conduct of this sort should be excluded from the workplace. Had the case been decided by a different tribunal chair I would suggest though that the reasoning would have been likely to have been very different. Most chairs would have painted on a much smaller canvas and any

[11] *Woods* (n 8). The EAT also held that they were not entitled to interfere with the decision of the tribunal below, which had found against the employee, because there had been no error of law. Their view on jurisdiction was confirmed by the Court of Appeal: *Woods* (n 6).

[12] *Woods* (n 8) 670 (Browne-Wilkinson J).

[13] *Sharp* (n 2).

[14] P Elias, 'Unravelling the Concept of Dismissal – II' (1978) 7 *ILJ* 100.

[15] *Sharp* (n 2) 772 (Lawton LJ).

term implied to govern the situation would, in all probability, have been closely confined to the factual circumstances in issue. I would also hazard that it would have been one in fact rather than law. Had the case been decided in such a way its influence would have been far less and would have been confined to cases of a closely analogous nature.

The design of the term, initiated by Hepple and crystallised in *Andrew*, merits careful attention. A less carefully constructed obligation might have been problematic and far less likely to have had a wider and lasting impact. The 1978 decision in *British Aircraft Corp v Austin*, for example, put forward an implied duty that appears wide and loose.[16] It was said that 'it must ordinarily be an implied term of the contract of employment that employers do not behave in a way which is intolerable or in a way which employees cannot be expected to put up with any longer'.[17] A term expressed along those lines would have been unlikely to have found favour with the higher courts. It is too vague and would not have lent itself to consistency of outcome. Most significantly of all, it might well have been viewed as an illegitimate attempt to circumvent *Sharp*.

Nevertheless, it must be acknowledged that mutual trust and confidence was itself formulated in a broad and open-textured manner. This has rendered it equipped to cover a wide range of workplace situations and its utility continues to be evident:

> the stark reality is that on countless occasions practitioners have resorted to the implied term as the only effective way of characterising bad and/or unreasonable behaviour on the part of an employer where otherwise such behaviour would not (even remotely) have attracted any sanction under any other terms of the contract.[18]

However, the sophisticated construction of the term also provided reassurance that it was a measured development of the law of implied terms in the employment context. It contains an element of balance in that the employer's behaviour can be justified should reasonable cause exist. It is also reciprocal though decisions addressing breach on the part of the employee are uncommon. Such features help explain the ease of judicial endorsement.

I would further suggest that the very language of trust and confidence has also played a part in the ready acceptance of the term and its durability. The notion that both sides to an employment relationship should be able to trust one another resonates widely. A parallel might be drawn with the great negligence case of *Donoghue v Stevenson* where the language of neighbour may well have contributed to the ongoing influence of the Atkin dictum.[19] Where mutual trust was concerned, Hepple's original articulation of the term evolved at great pace to emerge in its current form.

[16] *British Aircraft Corp v Austin* [1978] IRLR 332 (EAT).
[17] ibid [13] (Phillips J).
[18] Reynold (n 10) 262.
[19] *Donoghue v Stevenson* [1932] AC 562 (HL).

C. Wider Acceptance: The Judiciary and the Academy

The term has always tended to be viewed positively by the academy. There has been little by way of criticism and academic validation was not slow in arriving. The evident utility of the term was helpful in this regard; writing in 1986 Carty noted that '[c]ontract theory has had to cede to employment reality'.[20] Hepple had also ensured that a sound juridical basis existed through his explanation that the term should be seen as an instance, in the employment context, of the general duty of co-operation. Writing extra-judicially in 1981 he explained that the early mutual trust cases could be 'rationalised as examples of the application of the duty of co-operation, although it must be recognised that in reality these are practical decisions on their own facts by tribunals'.[21] The gap-filling function anticipated by Elias also played its part in fostering a favourable reception. Academic endorsement continues to remain in place. Mark Freedland in his seminal work *The Personal Employment Contract* declared that the term was 'undoubtedly the most powerful engine of movement in the modern law of the employment contract'.[22] There are of course those who would wish for something more radical.[23]

As we have seen, judicial acceptance in the EAT had been swift and unequivocal. Two major Court of Appeal decisions in the mid-1980s confirmed that the term was an established part of the legal landscape. The Court in *Bliss v South East Thames RHA* was able to note the 'ample authority' for the existence of the term.[24] *Lewis v Motorworld Garages* not only endorsed the term's existence but also confirmed that a breach could arise through a course of conduct.[25] It was said that 'it is now established that the repudiatory conduct may consist of a series of acts or incidents, some of them perhaps quite trivial, which cumulatively amount to a repudiatory breach of the implied term …'.[26] *Lewis* is a great example of the wide-ranging utility of the term given that such behaviour is all too common in the workplace.

D. Malik: The Courts Below

The nub of the litigation in *Malik* was very different to a typical employment dispute. It is possible to portray the case as being about redundancy but the crux

[20] H Carty, 'Contract Theory and Employment Reality' (1986) 49 *MLR* 240, 240.
[21] BA Hepple, *Employment Law*, 4th edn (London, Sweet & Maxwell, 1981) 134.
[22] MR Freedland, *The Personal Employment Contract* (Oxford, Oxford University Press, 2003) 166.
[23] S Anderman, 'Termination of Employment: Whose Property Rights?' in C Barnard et al (eds), *The Future of Labour Law* (Oxford, Hart, 2004) 108–111.
[24] *Bliss v South East Thames RHA* [1987] ICR 700 (CA).
[25] *Lewis v Motorworld Garages* [1986] ICR 157 (CA).
[26] ibid 167 (Neill LJ).

of the matter was the heads of damages that were sought given the alleged severity and distinctive nature of the impact of the redundancies on the claimants. The latter had been made redundant when their employer (BCCI) went into liquidation. After a winding-up order was made, liquidators were appointed and they subsequently advertised for proofs of debt. Mr Malik and Mr Mahmud submitted proofs, including claims for 'stigma damages'. Mr Malik claimed £50,000 under this head and Mr Mahmud £99,753.35, on the basis that their mere association with BCCI at the moment of its liquidation and its widely known fraudulent practices stigmatised them and put them at a disadvantage in the employment market. Those proofs were rejected by the liquidators which led to the High Court considering the following preliminary issue: 'whether the evidence of the two applicants was sufficient to disclose a cause of action that they have suffered what have been referred to in these proceedings as stigma damages capable of being proved in the liquidation'.[27]

Before the High Court the case proceeded on the basis of an assumed set of facts:

> The facts and matters upon which the applicants rely are as follows: (a) the applicants were employees of BCCI; (b) BCCI operated in a corrupt and/or dishonest manner; (c) the applicants were innocent of any involvement in BCCI's corruption and/or dishonesty; (d) following the collapse of BCCI its corruption and/or dishonesty has become widely known; (e) in consequence the applicants are now at a handicap on the labour market because they are stigmatised by reason of their previous employment by BCCI; (f) the applicants have suffered loss in consequence of (e) above.

Much of the judgment is devoted to a discussion of the permissible heads of claim in an action for breach of an employment contract. After a thorough review of the authorities Evans-Lombe J concluded that it was not open to him to allow a claim for reputation damages.

Before the Court of Appeal the existence of the implied term of mutual trust and confidence was not in dispute.[28] The liquidators sought instead to impose limitations on its scope and, in particular, argued that conduct rendered impermissible was restricted to that which involves the direct treatment of the employee in question. In addition, it was said to be a pre-requisite of a claim that the employee be aware of such conduct whilst he is an employee. Not surprisingly, the liquidators also maintained that Evans-Lombe J had been correct to deny recovery for reputation damages. The Court of Appeal took the view that the former limitation could be said to be inherent in the definition of the term. Nevertheless, mutual trust was capable of extension to forms of behaviour whose impact on the employee was indirect. The second basis of limitation was though held to exist

[27] *Re BCCI SA* [1994] IRLR 282 (Ch) [1] (Evans-Lombe J).
[28] *Malik v BCCI* [1996] ICR 406 (CA).

> ... it is inherent in conduct of the kind which we are required to assume in this case that, if it is to be successful, it is secret and hidden from most of the employees as well as the rest of the world. So long as it remains secret it can have no effect on the trust and confidence of the employee from whom it is concealed. Moreover, not only could there be no breach without knowledge, there could be no stigma damage either until the fraud was revealed. Once the employee has left his employment the subsequent revelation of the fraud can have no effect on the trust and confidence for, by definition, it has ceased anyway.[29]

This conclusion was obviously pivotal in *Malik* itself. In any event, the Court of Appeal were at one with Evans-Lombe J where reputation damages were concerned. The case therefore proceeded to the House of Lords with the implied term untarnished save for the imposition of the limitation based on knowledge.

E. *Malik*: The House of Lords

Malik gave the House of Lords the opportunity to review the implied term of trust and confidence which had emerged in the tribunal decisions discussed above. The existence of the term was not in dispute and it was explained by counsel for the defendants that '[t]he wider term is a manifestation of the principle in *MacKay v Dick* (1881) 6 App.Cas. 251, that one is not to frustrate the objective of the contract and make it in practice impossible to perform.'[30] This reflected a key element of Hepple's intellectual endeavour in depicting the term as the progeny of an older more general obligation; viz. the implied duty of co-operation. The language of impossibility was though left behind as the term was crafted and applied in a way that made sense within the four walls of employment relations. The term was already established to such a degree that counsel for the claimants saw no reason to downplay its significance and its width was portrayed as a virtue: 'It is a term which is flexible in its nature and which is intended to cover the multitude of circumstances in which the employer's right to manage has to be balanced with the employee's right not to be unfairly exploited by his employer.'[31] Argument continued to rage over recoverable heads of claim and *Addis v Gramophone Co* (*Addis*) loomed large.[32] This dimension of the dispute was said by Lord Nicholls to be 'at the heart of this case'.[33] As in the Court of Appeal the scope of the term also remained in dispute; the employer argued that the employee must be directly affected by the behaviour in question and be aware of it whilst in employment.

[29] ibid 412 (Morritt LJ).
[30] *Malik* (n 1) 29 (counsel's arguments).
[31] ibid 24 (counsel's arguments).
[32] *Addis v Gramophone Co* [1909] AC 488 (HL).
[33] *Malik* (n 1) 34.

The House of Lords found for the claimants. Two speeches were handed down: one by Lord Nicholls and one by Lord Steyn. It was held that the defendants, by conducting a dishonest or corrupt business, had breached the implied obligation. BCCI's behaviour did not comply with 'the portmanteau general obligation not to engage in conduct likely to undermine the trust and confidence required if the employment relationship is to continue in the manner the employment contract implicitly envisages'.[34] The restriction sought on the basis of knowledge was rejected.[35] In some ways the decision of the Law Lords was unremarkable. It was abundantly clear that there was already a consensus over the existence of the term of trust and confidence; both sides accepted that the law was now settled and indeed it had been for some time. It is probably the case that, in terms of authoritative judicial acceptance, the 1980s Court of Appeal decisions in *Bliss* and *Lewis* were more significant. *Malik*, by allowing for reputation damages, moved the law forward where the law of secondary obligations was concerned. It is interesting to note, in stark contrast to the subsequent case of *Johnson v Unisys* (*Johnson*),[36] that the position under statute was seen as a stimulus in this regard rather than a constraint: 'I am reinforced in this view by the consideration that such losses are in principle recoverable in respect of unfair dismissal: see section 123(1) of the Employment Rights Act 1996 and *Norton Tool Co Ltd v Tewson* [1973] 1 WLR 45, 50–51.'[37] *Addis* was not simply distinguished but depicted as representing the values and approach of a bygone age and the prospect of a more extensive attack in later litigation was thereby opened up. Lord Steyn observed that '*Addis* was decided in 1909 before the development of modern employment law, and long before the evolution of the implied mutual obligation of trust and confidence.'[38]

The true significance of *Malik* lies, in my view, in its contribution to a change in 'legal culture'.[39] The decision articulated, at the highest judicial level, the contemporary judicial understanding of (and approach to) the employment contract. The nature of the relationship was expressed in the following terms: 'An employment contract creates a close personal relationship, where there is often a disparity of power between the parties. Frequently the employee is vulnerable.'[40] This recognition of the key attributes of the contract pointed towards the law evolving in a very different way from its historical path. The

[34] ibid 35.
[35] ibid.
[36] *Johnson v Unisys* [2003] 1 AC 518 (HL).
[37] *Malik* (n 1) 52 (Lord Steyn).
[38] ibid 50 (Lord Steyn).
[39] ibid 46 (Lord Steyn).
[40] ibid 37 (Lord Nicholls). For some it did not go far enough. See, eg, F Carrigan, 'The Implications of Implied Terms in the Common Law Contract of Employment' (2009) 9 *Oxford University Commonwealth Law Journal* 73.

realities of a relationship underpinned by an imbalance of power were taken on board and the implied term struck at 'harsh and oppressive behaviour' and 'any other form of conduct which is unacceptable today'.[41]

Malik, by confirming the existence and importance of the trust and confidence term, installed an obligation of the good faith type at the heart of the employment relationship. To borrow from the language of the Canadian Supreme Court in *Bhasin v Hyrnew* the term can be viewed as the 'organising norm' of the employment contract.[42] The open-textured construction of the obligation allows it to continue to expand and embrace a wider range of workplace issues. The sophistication of the formulation guards against ossification; it is readily applicable to new or untested forms of behaviour that could damage employment relations. Writing in 2010 Bogg drew attention to 'a whole range of misdeeds that have breached the implied term'.[43] The range becomes ever wider. *Rawlinson v Brightside* provides a recent example of how the term can, through incremental steps, expand its coverage so that the workplace is run in line with contemporary expectations of good behaviour. In *Rawlinson*, the employer misled the employee about the reason for termination of his employment which was, in truth, about performance.[44] To 'soften the blow' for the employee, who the employer wanted to work through his notice period to ensure a smooth handover of work, the employer did not tell him the real reason for its decision but told him instead that there was to be a re-organisation of his work, which would be carried out by an external service provider. Such behaviour was seen as disrespectful and a breach of the implied obligation:

> In all but the most unusual of cases, the implied term must import an obligation not to deliberately mislead – after all, how can there be trust and confidence between employer and employee if one party has positively determined to mislead the other? That does not mean an employer is necessarily placed under some broader obligation to volunteer information, but where a choice has been made to do so, the implied term must require that it is done in good faith. And, even if I allow that there may be particular cases in which the operation of the implied term would permit some element of deceit (the white lie that serves some more benign purpose), I cannot see how that was so in this instance.[45]

[41] *Malik* (n 1) 38 (Lord Nicholls).
[42] *Bhasin v Hyrnew* [2014] 3 SCR 494 (SCC).
[43] A Bogg, 'Good Faith in the Contract of Employment: A Case of the English Reserve' (2011) 32 *Comparative Labor Law and Policy Journal* 729, 756.
[44] *Rawlinson v Brightside* [2018] IRLR 180 (EAT). *Johnson* (n 36) was distinguished: 'this was a case where the complaint was in respect of financial loss suffered as a result of the Respondent's breach of the implied term that preceded and stood apart from the dismissal; indeed, it arose at a time when the employment relationship was intended to continue'.
[45] *Rawlinson* (n 44) [38] (Eady J).

This conclusion mandates respect for the employee but also requires greater transparency in decision making.

The term has been rendered more secure by its impact on the law of contract more widely. Somewhat unusually for a term which is specific to the employment context it has served as the catalyst for developments in the general principles of contract law. It would, at least in modern times, be difficult to think of another example of this dynamic. The developing law on control of discretionary clauses in commercial contracts illustrates the point.[46] The fact that the general stance has changed makes it much more likely that the position under the employment contract will remain sacrosanct. No special pleading on the worker's behalf is required; the term has become an instance of and not an exception to the general law.

II. MUTUAL TRUST AFTER *MALIK*

In the years since the decision of the House of Lords the term has assumed the status of absolute orthodoxy; there has never been any suggestion that it was in any way unsound or required to be reconsidered. Somewhat ironically, given the catalyst provided by the statutory law of unfair dismissal, statute has operated to provide a constraint on the expansion of the scope of the term. *Johnson* decided that the employer's right to terminate at common law was not subject to the operation of trust and confidence. *Johnson* though remains the only major encroachment on the term's evolution and, as will be shown in the next part of this chapter, statute has not led to the impact of the term being diminished further. At the same time, it may be claimed that *Malik* has done less than might have been anticipated to inspire further common law developments. It might have been expected that the law of damages would have evolved further. Again, one might have thought that other implied terms in law would have been subject to modernisation. I would suggest that the continued failure of the law of the employment contract to protect the employee's economic interests is highly relevant at this juncture.

Malik has given rise to a significant body of case law which can be regarded as largely settled. There are though several questions that one would have expected to have been answered by the courts by now. One relates to the relationship between the implied term and the traditional usage of 'trust and confidence'; another to the test to be applied when the appropriateness of an exercise of discretion is in issue. The most significant outstanding issue remains the position on derogation. It is somewhat surprising that it is still not clear whether contracting-out is permissible.

[46] M Arden, 'Coming to Terms with Good Faith' (2013) 30 *Journal of Contract Law* 199.

A. The Impact of Statute

Since *Malik* mutual trust and confidence has shown great vitality.[47] The decision in *Johnson*, by taking account of the statutory context, restricted the evolution of the term but reference to statute has not otherwise constrained its growth and operation. The courts have shown themselves sensitive to the danger of restricting the common law more than the rationale of *Johnson* required. Two examples might be given which evidence a reluctance to allow arguments based on statute to have a greater influence. The first lies in the area of the procedural safeguards afforded to employees at common law. The modern employment contract, particularly through the medium of mutual trust and confidence, places much greater weight on procedural fairness than was the case traditionally. Strong affinities with natural justice are now apparent.[48] There have been attempts to restrict this development by importing the band of reasonable responses test from the statutory law of unfair dismissal. The decision of the Court of Appeal in the constructive dismissal case of *Buckland v Bournemouth University* repelled this attack and denied statute a role.[49] *Buckland* endorsed 'the unvarnished *Mahmud* test' and indicated that to do otherwise would be to contrary to the stance taken in *Sharp* which had made clear that the test was contractual should constructive dismissal be in issue.[50] Matters are never entirely straightforward and the subsequent decision of the Court of Appeal in *Yapp v FCO* would though seem to be inconsistent with *Buckland* by appearing to favour the band of reasonable responses test.[51]

The second example is provided by the treatment of situations where entitlement to an element of the remuneration package (such as an income protection clause) is contingent on the beneficiary retaining the status of employee. Given the decision in *Johnson* there was a concern that, in a termination situation, an employer might be able to deprive an employee of not just his employment but also the benefit of a contractually provided scheme. The courts though have responded consistently and effectively and have been at pains to ensure that the employee does not forfeit more than his employment. Admittedly, as a result of *Johnson*, there can be no implied restraint on the notice clause as such. However, there has been found to be room for implied constraints where the post-employment implementation of the remuneration package is in issue

[47] But see D Cabrelli, 'Receding Confidence in Trust and Confidence?' (2019) 23 *Edinburgh Law Review* 411.

[48] In *Burn v Alder Hey* [2021] EWCA Civ 1791 [35] Underhill LJ observed that '[t]here may not on the orthodox view be a general implied duty on an employer to act fairly in all contexts; but such a term is very readily implied in the context of disciplinary processes …'. It is not apparent to me what such a term would achieve that is not already brought about through mutual trust and confidence.

[49] *Buckland v Bournemouth University* [2010] EWCA Civ 121, [2011] 1 QB 323.

[50] On the issue of coherence with statute see A Bogg, '*Bournemouth University HEC v Buckland*: Re-Establishing Orthodoxy at the Expense of Coherence?' (2010) 39 *Industrial Law Journal* 408.

[51] *Yapp v FCO* [2014] EWCA Civ 1512, [2015] IRLR 112.

to ensure that the employee gains the full benefit of the work-wage bargain. The courts have permitted challenges by employees which are directed against breach of the employer's obligations under the clause bestowing a benefit rather than the notice clause.

In the last few years, the Privy Council has confirmed the appropriateness of this approach in *Ali v Petroleum Co* (*Ali*).[52] There the employee received a loan from the employer for study abroad. The loan agreement provided that repayment was to be waived if he worked for five years after return. *Ali* required that the Privy Council consider what the impact on the right of waiver would be if the contract was terminated by the employer before the expiry of the five-year period. In particular, the Board considered whether a term should be implied into the contract of loan restricting the capacity of the employer to terminate the employment. It was noted that the claimant could only benefit from the clause if he was allowed to remain in employment for five more years. The Privy Council accepted that the duty of co-operation dictated that an appropriate term be implied to protect the employee's interests.[53] The Board went on to hold that it was implicit in the agreement that 'if Mr Ali completed five further years of service that the company would do nothing of its own initiative to prevent him from providing such service, justified dismissal for repudiatory breach and compulsion excepted …'.[54] A more expansive interpretation of *Johnson* might have led to a very different outcome by viewing such an implied term as an inappropriate restriction on the employer's capacity to terminate at common law. It must be said though that mutual trust and confidence has been conducive to the emergence of a presumption against expropriation.

B. Limitations in Impact: (1) Economic Interests

Mutual trust and confidence has, of itself, made a very considerable contribution to the modernisation of the law of the employment contract that has occurred over the last 40 years. It might though have been expected to have prompted further reforms in the law of implied terms. I would suggest, in particular, that the position where the employee's economic interests are concerned is very much a case in point. The implied obligation of reasonable care is pivotal here given the utterly inequitable way it has always operated and continues to do so where economic losses are concerned. Careless performance by the employee will lead to an obligation to compensate the employer yet the latter has, in general, no obligation to protect the former's economic interests. In the years preceding *Malik* the law appeared to be beginning to move in

[52] *Ali v Petroleum Co* [2017] UKPC 2, [2017] ICR 531.

[53] The Board referred to the judgment of Cockburn CJ in the old case of *Stirling v Maitland and Boyd* (1864) 5 B&S 840; 122 ER 1043.

[54] *Ali* (n 52) [11] (Lord Hughes).

favour of employees. The House of Lords had held for the claimant(s) in both *Spring v Guardian Assurance* (*Spring*) and *Scally v Southern Health Board* (*Scally*).[55] *Spring* offered greater protection to the employee by providing, where references were concerned, that a claimant could look to the law of negligence and not just the law of defamation. *Scally* provided the employee with a right of information (admittedly in tightly defined circumstances) for the better protection of his economic interests. *Malik*, by confirming that an obligation of the good faith type lay at the centre of employment relations, might have been expected to prompt further such reforms. However, the position has changed very little since *Malik* and the recent decision of the Supreme Court in *James-Bowen v Commissioner of Police* confirms that the courts are not yet minded to engage in reform at common law.[56] As Morgan points out, mutual trust 'has never been generalised into an overarching duty to protect employees' economic well-being'.[57] It, therefore, remains the case that the current position on risk allocation sits uneasily with a contractual relationship with a good faith obligation at its core. It does not seem consonant with fair dealing to impose such a disproportionate burden on the weaker party to the relationship.

The current position is strongly engrained. The recent case of *Greenway v Johnson Matthey* offered the Court of Appeal an excellent opportunity to carve out an exception where 'advance mitigation' was in issue.[58] The claimant in that case incurred financial losses when he moved to a lower paid position to avoid risks to his physical safety. The Court showed no interest in developing the law and the Supreme Court was not, on appeal, required to consider the point.[59] The judicial view is that

> it would be an illegitimate extension of the law to make the leap from the standard employer's duty to safeguard its employees against personal injury, to a broad duty to safeguard them against pure economic loss incurred as a result of the claimant's need to cease working to avoid a threat to his physical safety.[60]

The harshness of the position is reinforced by the fact that it is the employer's careless creation of the risk of physical harm that leads to financial loss arising.

It does not seem likely that the position will change in the immediate future though the possibility of common law reform cannot be altogether discounted. Enterprise liability has had a major impact on risk allocation within the law of tort and could still prove to be of influence where the employment contract is concerned.[61]

[55] *Spring v Guardian Assurance* [1995] 2 AC 296 (HL); *Scally v Southern Health Board* [1992] 1 AC 1 (HL).

[56] *James-Bowen v Commissioner of Police* [2018] UKSC 40, [2018] WLR 4021.

[57] J Morgan, 'Novelty in Negligence: Policy Reasoning Survives' (2019) 78 *CLJ* 15, 16.

[58] *Greenway v Johnson Matthey* [2016] EWCA Civ 408, [2016] IRLR 526.

[59] In *Dryden v Johnson Matthey* [2018] UKSC 18, [2019] AC 403 the claimants succeeded on other grounds.

[60] *Rihan v E & Y* [2020] EWHC 901 (QB) [476] (Kerr J).

[61] D Brodie, *The Future of the Employment Contract* (Cheltenham, Edward Elgar, 2021) ch 5.

C. Limitations in Impact: (2) Damages

A further area where one might have expected *Malik* to have had a greater impact is where the law of remedies is concerned. *Malik* itself was a relatively rare instance of a modern decision resulting in an expansion of the availability of damages at common law. Achieving this had required that *Addis* be distinguished but, in the process, hope emerged that further marginalisation of that decision might occur. The statutory framework, providing for compensation should an unfair dismissal arise, served as a catalyst for change in the law of damages for injury to reputation. Might the statutory position on compensation more widely provide the inspiration for further change? The question is an important one as the strength of the protection afforded to the employee turns not only on the content of primary obligations but also on the secondary obligations which arise in the event of breach. The lack of movement on the latter front has been disappointing and statutory provision has, in this context, not proved to be a stimulus. The failure to depart from the traditional denial of recovery for injury to feelings offers a particularly cogent example of an area where statutory protection has improved but the common law has been left behind. One thinks of Sedley LJ's hypothetical employee in *Dunnachie v Kingston upon Hull CC* 'who had been appallingly treated and finally driven out of his job with his self-confidence in tatters'.[62] The options open to such an employee are decidedly limited and the position is particularly constrained where the employer's breach has not caused pecuniary loss. It is conceivable that this could arise in a significant number of cases where the obligation breached is mutual trust and confidence. In the absence of pecuniary loss, the only remedy open to the employee is to resign and claim constructive dismissal; the choice has to be made between vindicating one's right to dignity in the workplace and preserving job security.

Why have these limitations not been addressed? After *Malik* a claim for reputation damages became possible but it was anticipated by the House of Lords that the number of awards would be low. Common law reform to allow for injury to feelings would be a far more significant change. There may be a judicial belief that the magnitude of any such decision points to it being left to the legislature. The restrictive policy with regard to compensation for psychiatric harm may offer some insights. The Court of Appeal in *Hatton v Sutherland* laid down a number of barriers should an employee bring forward a claim.[63] The underlying notion was that the risk should normally lie where it fell and the Court thought that ascription of fault was inappropriate. Somewhat disappointingly, the Court of Appeal in *Yapp v FCO* has extended the policy of restriction to include situations where the employer is actually at fault by,

[62] *Dunnachie v Kingston upon Hull CC* [2004] EWCA Civ 84, [2004] ICR 481 [43] (Sedley LJ).
[63] *Hatton v Sutherland* [2002] EWCA Civ 76, [2002] 2 All ER 1.

for example, conducting a disciplinary process in breach of natural justice.[64] The law of remoteness is also applied in a way that renders the prospects of recovery unlikely even though the standard tests in contract and tort were still said to apply. The claim in *Yapp* itself failed because it was held not to be foreseeable in the absence of any sign of special vulnerability, that the claimant might develop a psychiatric illness. There was, however, a reticence to let fundamental principles apply in the courts below in future litigation without direction: '[I]t will in my view be exceptional that an apparently robust employee, with no history of any psychiatric ill-health, will develop a depressive illness as a result even of a very serious setback at work.'[65] Upset to feelings may be seen in a similar light. The view may be taken that such an impact is inevitable in employment relations and that therefore recovery should not arise. This of course is to ignore the fact that a damages claim could only arise should the employer's behaviour constitute a breach of contract through, for example, failure to follow due process.

D. Unresolved Questions: (1) Conflicting Meaning

The language of 'trust and confidence' continues to be used in two senses by the law of the employment contract. Its traditional usage was a factual one and was relevant where the employee was at risk of termination and sought the protection of an equitable order. The absence of trust and confidence in that latter sense went against the granting of such an order. Many years ago Elias pointed out the power that this gave to employers.[66] This was demonstrated yet again by the decision of the High Court in *Ashworth v Royal National Theatre* where an order for specific performance was sought.[67] The employer's view was that 'there has been a loss of confidence in the sense that the producers and directors of War Horse do not believe that the musicians can contribute positively to the play and that the play is better off without them'.[68] This led to a denial of the remedy sought:

> That to my mind is precisely the type of situation where on the authorities it would be inappropriate for the court to enforce a contract by specific performance or analogous injunction. There is clearly an absence of personal confidence on the part of the National Theatre.[69]

On such a traditional analysis (and one still prevailing where equitable orders are concerned) subjective loss of confidence is the 'primary block' to this type

[64] *Yapp* (n 51).
[65] ibid [125] (Underhill LJ).
[66] P Elias, 'The Structure of the Employment Contract' (1982) 35 *CLP* 95.
[67] *Ashworth v Royal National Theatre* [2014] EWHC 1176 (QB), [2014] IRLR 526.
[68] ibid [24] (Cranston J).
[69] ibid [25] (Cranston J).

of relief.[70] It has been argued that 'the very recognition of the legal obligation of mutual trust and confidence as the core common law duty dictating how employees should be treated during the employment relationship greatly advances the quest to be awarded specific implement'.[71] Given that the modern usage goes to legal obligation the foregoing argument would appear to be a good one. Unfortunately we continue to await the 'great advance'.

The issue is not simply an academic one but, as the preceding paragraph demonstrates, highly relevant in terms of the availability of remedies. It would be wrong to fail to acknowledge that judicial thinking has changed to some extent. There is, for example, an increased acceptance that damages may not be an adequate remedy and this increases the likelihood of an order, such as an interlocutory injunction, being granted.[72] There is though little to indicate that the obligation of mutual trust will prompt a review of traditional usage of the 'trust and confidence' factor. Similar issues also arise in the law of unfair dismissal and the recent decision of the Court of Appeal in *Kelly v PGA* may represent a step forward.[73] It concerned the proper approach to the making of orders for the re-engagement of employees who have been unfairly dismissed. The decision focussed in particular on the question of whether it is practicable to order re-engagement in cases where an employer asserts that the conduct of an employee led to a breakdown in trust and confidence between the employer and employee. It was held that the question for the Court was whether the employer had a genuine, and rational belief that the employee had engaged in conduct which had broken the relationship of trust and confidence between the employer and the employee.[74] This would seem to me to be an encouraging development. The reference to rationality would appear to exclude decisions made on the mere whim of the employer.

E. Unresolved Questions: (2) Regulating Discretion

A further area where there is a degree of uncertainty is where the regulation of discretion is concerned. This is in some ways surprising as key formative cases such as *United Bank v Akhtar* (*Akhtar*) dealt with the issue in a clear and straightforward way.[75] The position though has become unduly complicated. There is now said to be a 'distinction between cases where the employer is exercising an express or implied discretionary power, and cases where the concern

[70] ibid [23] (Cranston J).
[71] 'Specific Implement: How Far Have We Come? How Far To Go?' (2014) 123 *Employment Law Bulletin* 6, 8.
[72] *Avsar v Wilson* [2020] EWHC 3412 (QB), [2021] IRLR 300.
[73] *Kelly v PGA* [2021] EWCA Civ 559, [2021] ICR 1124.
[74] ibid [44]. And see *Jones v Gwent CC* [1992] IRLR 521 (Ch).
[75] *United Bank v Akhtar* [1989] IRLR 507 (EAT).

is simply with the conduct of the employer'.[76] The test for a breach of mutual trust is said to be rationality in the former situation whereas, in the latter, one simply asks whether there has been a breach of the term. It would seem to me that such differentiation is not called for and the latter approach should prevail across the board. In *Akhtar* the employer had sought to exercise his discretion under a mobility clause to require the employee to move to a different place of employment. The EAT had no difficulty in holding that the decision constituted a breach of mutual trust and the employee's resignation therefore constituted a constructive dismissal. As the case law has developed there are of course contexts where a less intensive degree of scrutiny is appropriate. Decisions concerning the remuneration package provide an excellent example. It may then be helpful, in determining whether a breach has occurred, to ask a supplementary question. *Clark v Nomura International* concerned entitlement to a discretionary bonus and Burton J stated that 'the right test is one of irrationality or perversity (of which caprice or capriciousness would be a good example) ie that no reasonable employer would have exercised his discretion in this way'.[77] This may well be an appropriate approach in a case of that sort but the fundamental question should always be whether a breach of mutual trust has occurred.

F. Unresolved Questions: (3) Entrenchment

The nature of the obligation of trust and confidence means that the question of derogation cannot be ignored. Lord Steyn in *Johnson* explained that it was an 'overarching obligation implied by law as an incident of the contract of employment'.[78] The logic of this analysis is that the term can be overridden and, in consequence, contracting-out can then occur. What is perhaps surprising is the fact that the case law has yet to explore the issue in detail. The judiciary have though appeared discouraging of such a possibility. Writing extra-judicially in 2002, with reference to mutual trust, Lord Bingham had indicated that attempts may 'be made to relax the obligations by express terms set out in a contract of employment, but I would not expect such terms to be sympathetically interpreted'.[79]

The insertion of an express term explicitly denying the existence of mutual trust has never seemed a particularly likely approach to drafting but it is important to appreciate that a variety of mechanisms can be used to achieve contracting-out of an implied term. Of late, for example, it has become apparent

[76] *Smo v Hywel DDA University Health Board* [2020] EWHC 727, [2021] IRLR 273 [205] (Linden J) with reference to *IBM UK Holdings Ltd v Dalgleish* [2017] EWCA Civ 1212, [2018] ICR 1681.

[77] *Clark v Nomura International* [2000] IRLR 766 (QB) [44].

[78] *Johnson* (n 36) [24].

[79] T Bingham, 'From Servant to Employee: A Study of the Common Law in Action' (2002) 13 *Singapore Academy of Law Journal* 253, 266.

that, in commercial cases, a narrower view will be taken of what constitutes a discretionary decision than has been the case in employment law. The courts have gone as far as holding that the exercise of a term which is expressed as an absolute right does not involve a discretionary decision at all. As a corollary, implied constraints to ensure fair dealing are not applicable: 'When a contract gives one of the parties an absolute right, a court will not usually imply any restrictions on it, even restrictions preventing the right from being exercised in an arbitrary, capricious or irrational manner.'[80] As yet, there are no indications that employment law will follow suit but the possibility cannot be altogether excluded. *IBM v Dalgleish* suggests though that a more protective approach will continue to be taken in the employment context.[81]

The most likely route to contracting-out may well be the one illustrated by *Burn v Alder Hey* where the express terms of the contract dealt with matters which, if nothing had been said, would have been addressed by the implied term.[82] The question then is whether the dissatisfied employee can look beyond the express obligation. It is not surprising that the issue has resulted in litigation as the modern employment contract is often extensive and, on occasion, unduly complicated. There may appear to be no space within which implication can operate. Such an approach worked in the employer's favour in *Burn* where the claimant was subject to an internal investigation and the parties were in dispute over the extent of her right to see documentation held by the employer. Under the express terms of the contract it was said that 'the practitioner must be given the opportunity to see any correspondence relating to the case'.[83] It was held that the 'natural and ordinary meaning of "correspondence" is an exchange of written communications, as for example by way of letter, email or similar'.[84] As a result of this interpretation the employer was held to have complied with the requirements of the express term. This meant that, for instance, documents relating to an earlier investigation did not have to be provided. The claimant, in addition, argued that the failure to provide the documents sought also amounted to a breach of the implied term of mutual trust and confidence. This argument was rejected. A traditional analysis of the relationship between express and implied terms was adopted and, as a result, it was not permissible to extend the employee's rights by way of implication: 'To permit the Claimant to see the documents, nonetheless, would be to allow her to use the implied term of trust and confidence to modify the express terms of the contract.'[85] Occupation of the same space allowed the employer to derogate.

[80] *Greenclose v National Westminster* [2014] EWHC 1156 [145] (Andrews J).
[81] *IBM* (n 76).
[82] *Burn v Alder Hey* [2021] EWHC 1674 (QB).
[83] ibid [94] (Thornton J).
[84] ibid [97] (Thornton J).
[85] ibid.

The extent to which the approach in *Burn* will determine the outcome of future cases is though debateable. A very different approach was taken in *Stevens v University of Birmingham* (*Stevens*).[86] In *Stevens* the employer was held to be in breach of mutual trust where they refused to allow the employee to be accompanied to an investigatory meeting by a member of his professional association. It should be said that the contract provided for a more limited right of representation. *Stevens* declines to allow the express terms of the contract to offer less by way of procedural protection than would be dictated by mutual trust and confidence. The position taken has been described by one commentator as 'remarkable'.[87] In the Court of Appeal decision in *North West Anglia v Gregg* it was argued that *Stevens* 'was open to the criticism that it allowed the implied term to modify the express terms of the contract, and may have confused the implied term of trust and confidence with a general duty to act fairly'.[88] The Court though did not need to determine the matter; nor did they express a view. It should be noted that *Stevens* was referred to, with apparent approval, by the Supreme Court in *James-Bowen*.[89]

In the face of diverging approaches is it possible to suggest a way forward? The obligation of trust and confidence allows the judiciary to play their part in determining acceptable standards of behaviour in the modern workplace; contracting-out would, prima facie, therefore seem objectionable. At the same time the function of the term is not to enable the re-writing of contractual provisions which seek to provide detailed guidance for the benefit of both employer and employee. The outcome in a case like *Burn* may be perfectly reasonable. In my opinion, however, more significant attempts at exclusion of the procedural protection afforded by mutual trust should merit very different treatment. What of a situation such as that which arose in *Gogay v Hertfordshire*?[90] There suspension took place though reasonable cause for the decision had not been established and the Court of Appeal held that a breach of mutual trust had arisen as a result. Suspension is a very significant and potentially hugely damaging act and I would argue that it would be grossly unsatisfactory if the protection afforded by mutual trust were to be diluted. What if the express terms of the contract in *Gogay* had allowed the employer to suspend at their absolute discretion? The imposition of such a limitation on the protection offered by process should be guarded against.

It is important that both employers and employees know what should happen where procedural matters are concerned. There is much to be said for the creation of detailed policies and procedures. The rights and obligations conferred will vary a great deal from employer to employer and that in itself is

[86] *Stevens v University of Birmingham* [2015] EWHC 2300 (QB), [2017] ICR 96.
[87] A Sanders, 'Fairness in the Employment Contract' (2017) 46 *ILJ* 508, 521.
[88] *North West Anglia v Gregg* [2019] EWCA Civ 387, [2019] ICR 1279 [99] (Coulson LJ).
[89] *James-Bowen* (n 56).
[90] *Gogay v Hertfordshire* [2000] IRLR 703 (CA).

not problematic. It is though essential that any policy does not serve to diminish the impact of mutual trust and confidence where fundamental aspects of procedural justice are in issue. The judgment of Cranston J in *Yapp v FCO* in the High Court may be seen as helpful in so far at it identifies some fundamental points of process.[91] He took the view that

> a golden thread through the case law on fair treatment is that those liable to be affected by a decision must be given prior notice of it so that they can make representations. A corollary is that any representations must be taken into account by the decision-maker. The greater detriment a decision is likely to cause the more demanding these duties.[92]

It would seem to me that derogation from such key aspects of procedural justice should be impermissible.

Given the fundamental nature of the term it would be regrettable if limitations were not placed on the employer's ability to contract-out. Further juridical development is required to reach a position whereby derogation is forbidden or at least restricted by the common law. It is of course the case that a term may be rendered mandatory on the basis of public policy.[93] It is to be hoped that such an approach will be taken where the employment contract is concerned and where key rights conferred by mutual trust are at stake.

III. THE PROPER LIMITS OF MUTUAL TRUST

The controversial decision in *Johnson* resulted in a limitation in scope of mutual trust where termination of the contract was in issue. Whatever the merits of that decision, I would suggest that a further self-imposed limitation makes good sense. The common law has long set its face (procedural impropriety aside) against assessing the substantive fairness of the bargain and the employment contract does not differ in this respect.[94] The decision in *Bateman v Asda* offers an instance of the sort of clause that employees find utterly unfair and objectionable but which is valid in judicial eyes.[95] *Bateman* held that the employer was entitled to unilaterally vary the terms of the bargain given the existence of the following term: Asda 'reserved the right to review, revise, amend or replace the contents of this handbook, and introduce new policies from time to time reflecting the changing needs of the business …'. Notwithstanding its utterly one-sided nature the common law will not intervene to prevent the insertion of a clause of this sort. The exercise of such a clause might be very much to the employee's

[91] *Yapp v FCO* [2013] EWHC 1098 (QB), [2013] IRLR 616.
[92] ibid [82].
[93] *Lee v Showmen's Guild* [1952] 2 QB 329 (CA).
[94] See Brodie (n 61) ch 10.
[95] *Bateman v Asda* (EAT, 11 February 2010).

detriment but, on the face of it, there are no restrictions on its use. However, that is not to say that the law of implied terms will not ameliorate the impact of the substantive terms. It was not argued before the ET in *Bateman* that the exercise of the clause was subject to mutual trust though, in my opinion, such an argument would have been perfectly feasible. The imposition of inferior new terms would have been unlikely to have given rise to a breach of the term. The absence of assessment of the fairness of the bargain at the outset would be mirrored at the point of variation. However, the application of mutual trust might have led to some implied constraints arising should the clause be invoked. Reasonable notice, for example, of the variation might have been required depending upon the nature of the change.

The longevity of such a non-interventionist stance notwithstanding, should contract law ever become underpinned by a norm of good faith the position may change. This has occurred in Canada where good faith has become an 'organising norm'. This development led to the Supreme Court subsequently upholding a challenge to the substantive terms found in an employment contract.[96] A dispute resolution clause was found to be unconscionable and void. The initial reaction in the UK may be one of envy but it is highly debateable whether such a tendentious task should be undertaken by the judges. I would suggest that such issues are best left to the legislature.

IV. CONCLUSION

It is fitting that *Malik* is accorded the status of a landmark case but not simply because it endorsed the now core obligation of mutual trust and confidence. The decision's greater significance lies in the part it played in the establishment of a new 'legal culture' where the contract of employment is concerned. It may be claimed that the impact of the term has been less extensive than might have been anticipated.[97] In so far as that is true, I would suggest that the position in contract law as a whole is relevant. English law has not adopted a general principle of good faith and, as a consequence, the stimulus of developments in the general law of contract has inevitably been less significant than would otherwise have been the case. The position does not seem likely to change in the foreseeable future. Lord Hodge, in the recent economic duress case *Pakistan International Airline* v *Times Travel*, maintained that the establishment of a general principle of good faith would 'be a radical move forward for the English law of contract and the uncertainty caused by it seems unlikely to be a price worth paying'.[98] The absence of an 'organising norm' denies the common law

[96] *Heller v Uber Technologies* [2020] SCC 16, 447 DLR (4th) 179.

[97] For an early attempt at predicting how the term might evolve after *Malik* see D Brodie, 'Beyond Exchange: The New Contract of Employment' (1998) 27 *International Law Journal* 97.

[98] *Pakistan International Airline* v *Times Travel* [2021] UKSC 40, [2021] 3 WLR 727 [95] (Lord Burrows).

of the employment contract the assistance of an important catalyst for radical reform. The law on disclosure of information for example might have moved on much more otherwise. It is instructive that the law has not changed a great deal since *Scally*.

Other developments in the law of obligations have also had, at best, a very limited impact on the law of the employment contract. Notions of enterprise liability have had a significant influence on the law of tort and, in particular, vicarious liability. The allocation of risk between employer and third party has been adjusted in favour of the latter. The underpinning reasoning is relevant to the two party relationship of employer and employee. However, instances in the case law are historical and are not the product of recent developments in the law of tort.[99] It is also the case that the recognition that the employment contract is relational in nature does not (perhaps contrary to initial expectations) appear to have stimulated much in the way of change. Initial excitement may have given way to a recognition that the term relational contract is little more than a 'convenient phrase' to capture the nature of the modern contract.

[99] See Brodie (n 61) ch 5.

12

Johnson v Unisys Ltd *(2001)*: *A Compelling Constitutional Vision of Common Law and Statute?*

JOE ATKINSON

I. INTRODUCTION

IN *JOHNSON V Unisys*[1] the House of Lords confirmed the longstanding orthodoxy that the common law places no restraints on the manner employers may exercise their power of dismissal. The decision is undoubtedly deserving of landmark status. Both because it sharply limited the ongoing development of implied terms as a means of constraining managerial power, and due to the reasoning adopted by the House of Lords, namely that the presence of the statutory unfair dismissal framework prevented them from developing the common law.

Unlike many of the cases discussed in this volume, *Johnson* has starkly divided opinion among labour lawyers. The initial wave of academic commentary subjected the decision to trenchant criticism on the basis that it left the common law in a confused and unsatisfactory state.[2] More recently, however, a second wave of literature has emerged which mounts a cautious defence of the decision on constitutional grounds.[3] These arguments undoubtedly have considerable force and are yet to be adequately addressed by scholars who are critical of the decision in *Johnson*. This chapter contributes to the ongoing debate by pushing back against the view that the uncertainty, inconsistency, and incoherence in

[1] *Johnson v Unysis Ltd* [2001] UKHL 13, [2003] 1 AC 518.

[2] As listed by Lord Steyn in *Eastwood & Williams v Magnox and McCabe v Cornwall County Council* [2004] UKHL 35, [2005] 1 AC 503 [43].

[3] C Barnard and L Merrett, 'Winners and Losers: Edwards and the Unfair Law of Dismissal' (2013) 72 *Cambridge Law Journal* 313; A Bogg, 'Common Law and Statute in the Law of Employment' (2016) 69 *Current Legal Problems* 67; ACL Davies, 'The Relationship between Contract of Employment and Statute' in M Freedland and others (eds), *The Contract of Employment* (Oxford, Oxford University Press, 2016).

the common law resulting from *Johnson* is required out of respect for constitutional principle.

The first part sets out the legal position regarding mutual trust and confidence and implied terms in the contract of employment prior to *Johnson*. The second focuses on the case itself and the reasoning of the House of Lords. The following parts then examine the problematic legacy of the decision before considering whether the pre-emption of the common law was nevertheless justified. The chapter concludes by identifying and highlighting an important exception to *Johnson's* exclusion of the common law, the scope and extent of which appears to have been so far overlooked.

II. IMPLIED TERMS AND THE CONTRACT OF EMPLOYMENT

To understand the significance of *Johnson* it is necessary to first detail two prior legal developments relating to implied terms in the contract of employment, which set the scene and provide important context for the litigation.

A. The Emergence of Trust and Confidence

The default position at common law is, and remains, that an employer may dismiss an employee 'at any time and for any reason or none' provided adequate notice is given,[4] and that no remedy is available for the manner of dismissal or reputational harm flowing from it (known as stigma damages).[5] Where an employer is in repudiatory breach of the contract, most often but not exclusively the contractual notice period, an employee may accept this breach and bring a common law action for wrongful dismissal.[6] However, damages will generally be limited to the contractual benefits that would have accrued during the notice period,[7] as it is assumed that the employer would perform the contract in the way most favourable to themselves, and so limit their liability by immediately dismissing the employee with notice. Changing societal understandings of employment and the breakdown of collective industrial relations as an effective

[4] *Ridge v Baldwin* [1963] 2 All ER 66 (HL).

[5] *Addis v Gramophone Co Ltd* [1909] AC 488 (HL).

[6] Wrongful dismissal is taken here as 'effectively synonymous' with wrongful termination of the employment contract as per A Bogg and M Freedland, 'The Wrongful Termination of the Contract of Employment' in M Freedland and others (eds), *The Contract of Employment* (Oxford, Oxford University Press, 2016) 537.

[7] With the possible extension to include benefits accruing during the period it would have taken to complete a contractually required disciplinary process, *Gunton v Richmond Upon Thames* [1980] ICR 755 (CA). Damages will also be reduced to account for the duty to mitigate losses and any amounts received through social security payments or other employment.

means of regulating job security led to dissatisfaction with this position.[8] The perceived inadequacy of the common law coupled with the need to maintain industrial peace led to the introduction of protections against unfair dismissal in the Industrial Relations Act 1971,[9] following the recommendation of the Donovan review in 1968.[10]

Somewhat ironically, it was the legislative framework of unfair dismissal that provided the catalyst for the development of the implied term of mutual trust and confidence, which was then itself rejected as a source of common law protection against dismissal in *Johnson*.[11] In 1974 the Union and Labour Relations Act introduced protection against constructive dismissal, where an employee resigns 'in circumstances in which [the employee] is entitled to terminate without notice by reason of the employer's conduct'.[12] In *Western Excavating v Sharp* the Court of Appeal interpreted constructive dismissals as involving the employee resigning in response to a repudiatory breach of contract by the employer, rather than other unreasonable treatment that did not amount to breach of contract.[13] This contractual approach to constructive dismissal in turn led to the emergence of the implied term of term of trust and confidence as a means of avoiding unduly narrowing the scope of constructive unfair dismissal.

In its canonical formulation, the term requires that both parties must not 'without reasonable and proper cause, conduct themselves in a manner calculated and likely to destroy or seriously damage the relationship of trust and confidence between employer and employee'.[14] It provides 'a general behavioural standard for judging whether the conduct of one of the parties had left an employment relationship in a condition of viable continuance or placed it in a state of breakdown'.[15] The threshold for breach of the duty of trust and confidence is not simply one of unreasonable behaviour, but the stricter one of whether the necessary conditions for a functioning employment relationship have been undermined without good reason. Initially implied 'in fact' into contracts on an individual basis,[16] the term became regarded as being implied 'in law' as a default rule in all employment contracts,[17] and was confirmed at the highest level in *Malik v Bank of Credit and Commerce International SA (in liq)* ('*Malik*').[18]

[8] M Freedland, 'Constructing Fairness in Employment Contracts' (2007) 36 *Industrial Law Journal* 136, 136.

[9] See P Davies and M Freedland, *Labour Legislation and Public Policy* (Oxford, Clarendon Press, 1993) 195–204.

[10] Royal Commission on Trade Unions and Employers Associations 1965–1968, *Report* (Cmnd 3623, 1968).

[11] For further discussion of this process, see ch 11 in this volume.

[12] Now contained in the Employment Rights Act 1996, s 95(1)(c).

[13] *Western Excavating Ltd v Sharp* [1978] QB 761 (CA).

[14] *Woods v WM Car Services* [1981] ICR 666 (EAT) 670.

[15] M Freedland, *The Personal Employment Contract* (Oxford, Oxford University Press, 2003) 156.

[16] *Courtaulds Northern Textiles Ltd v Andrew* 8 [1979] IRLR 84 (EAT).

[17] On this distinction, see *Scally v Southern Health and Social Services Board* [1991] IRLR 522 (HL).

[18] *Malik v Bank of Credit and Commerce International SA (in liq)* [1998] AC 20 (HL).

The scope and content of the implied term of trust and confidence are notoriously hard to pin down, as it applies in 'the great diversity of situations in which a balance has to be struck between an employer's interest in managing his business as he sees fit and the employee's interest in not being unfairly and improperly exploited'.[19] In short, employers must not exercise their contractual 'rights and powers' in a way that is likely to undermine the employment relationship, unless they have good and proper reason for their actions.[20] An employers' conduct will breach the term where 'its effect, judged reasonably and sensibly, is such that the employee cannot be expected to put up with it'.[21] As well as active mistreatment or mismanagement, trust and confidence may be breached by an employers' failure to act, for example in not investigating grievances or providing important information to an employee.[22] Subject to the establishment of the 'exclusion zone' discussed below, the term applies to constrain the exercise of employers' express contractual powers,[23] as well as their more general prerogative to manage workers and production processes conferred by the employment contract.[24]

B. Implied Terms and Managerial Power

The emergence of trust and confidence radically transformed the common law duties of employers,[25] with Freedland famously describing it as 'the most powerful engine of movement in the modern law of employment contracts'.[26] However, the application of trust and confidence to limit employers' contractual powers is an instance of a broader category of cases where implied terms have been used as a means of regulating managerial power.[27] In these cases implied terms function as a form of judicial review of managerial decision-making,[28] and provide

[19] ibid 46 (Lord Steyn).

[20] *Imperial Group Pension Trust Ltd v Imperial Tobacco Ltd* [1991] ICR 524 (Ch) 533.

[21] *Woods* (n 14). For an overview of the operation of trust and confidence, see S Deakin, G Morris and A Adams, *Labour Law* (Cambridge, Cambridge University Press, 2021), 3.76–3.78.

[22] *Visa International v Paul* [2004] IRLR 42 (EAT).

[23] As in *Gogay v Hertfordshire County Council* [2001] FLR 280 (CA); *United Bank Ltd v Akhtar* [1989] IRLR 507 (EAT).

[24] As in *Transco Plc v O'Brien* [2002] EWCA Civ 379, [2002] ICR 721; *French v Barclays Bank plc* [1998] IRLR 646 (CA). *cf* the limits of the term in respect of employees reputation and economic wellbeing in the context of litigation *James-Bowen v Commission of Police of the Metropolis* [2018] UKSC 40, [2018] 1 WLR 4021.

[25] Although the term applies to both parties the range of other implied terms that employees are subject to has meant the impact of the term has largely been on the duties owed by employers.

[26] Freedland (n 15) 166.

[27] It has been suggested that trust and confidence might operate as an umbrella term under which these more concrete terms might operate, but the better approach is to view them as distinct obligations, D Cabrelli, 'The Implied Duty of Mutual Trust and Confidence: An Emerging Overarching Principle?' (2005) 34 *Industrial Law Journal* 284.

[28] See J Morgan, 'Against Judicial Review of Discretionary Contractual Powers' [2008] *Lloyd's Maritime and Commercial Law Quarterly* 230; T Daintith 'Contractual Discretion and Administrative Discretion: A Unified Analysis' (2005) 68 *MLR* 554.

a 'prism … through which to evaluate whether there has been respect for the implicit behavioural commitments made by entry into, and continuance in, working relationships'.[29]

The primary example of this aside from trust and confidence is employers' implied duty of care, which also operates as a default term in all employment contracts.[30] For example, in *Johnstone v Bloomsbury Health Authority* the employers' contractual discretion to require employees to work up to 48 hours of overtime was found to be subject to their implied duty of care.[31] The application of the implied duty of care to constrain employers' express managerial powers is also supported by the Unfair Contract Terms Act 1977, which prevents liability for personal injury in negligence from being excluded by express terms that appear to provide employers with absolute discretion.[32] The term also conditions the general authority conferred on employers by the contract of employment to govern the workplace and production processes as they see fit. Employers have a duty to not act in an objectively unreasonable manner when exercising their managerial prerogative over matters such as hiring and supervising the workforce,[33] or the organisation of the workplace and performance of work.[34] Notwithstanding the limits to implied terms as a mechanism for governing managerial power imposed in *Johnson* they continue to develop and play an important role in regulating employer discretion.[35]

Implied terms have even been used to constrain employers' power of dismissal in some circumstances. These cases generally involve courts implying terms limiting employers' freedom to terminate where the effect of this would be to deny an employees' entitlement to health insurance payments or some other contractual benefit.[36] *Aspden v Webbs Poultry & Meat Group (Holdings) Ltd* is an example of this, where a term was implied preventing the employer from dismissing other than for good reason, as this was necessary to prevent contractual entitlement to incapacity benefits under a permanent health insurance scheme.[37] While these cases seem to involve terms being implied 'in fact'

[29] L Barmes, 'Common Law Implied Terms and Behavioural Standards at Work' (2007) 36 *Industrial Law Journal* 35, 41.

[30] *Lister v Romford Ice and Cold Storage Co Ltd* [1957] AC 555 (HL). Another example, which overlaps to at least some extent with trust and confidence, is the implied term requiring that employers not act in an arbitrary manner when awarding discretionary benefits, D Cabrelli, *Employment Law in Context* (Oxford, Oxford University Press, 2020) 202–07.

[31] *Johnstone v Bloomsbury Health Authority* [1992] QB 333 (CA).

[32] Unfair Contract Terms Act 1977, s 2. See, also, L Barmes, 'The Continuing Conceptual Crisis in the Common Law of the Contract of Employment' (2004) 67 *MLR* 435, 442–43.

[33] *Hudson v Ridge Manufacturing Co* [1957] 2 All ER 229 (Assizes).

[34] *Wilsons & Clyde Coal Co Ltd v English* [1938] AC 57 (HL); *Speed v Thomas Swift & Co Ltd* [1943] KB 557 (CA); *Sutherland v Hatton* [2002] EWCA Civ 76, [2002] 2 All ER 1.

[35] *Braganza v BP Shipping Ltd* [2015] UKSC 17, [2015] 1 WLR 1661. See, also, A Sanders, 'Fairness in the Contract of Employment' (2017) 46 *Industrial Law Journal* 508.

[36] See, also, *Hill v General Accident Fire and Life Assurance Co plc* [1998] IRLR 641 (CSOH).

[37] *Aspden v Webbs Poultry & Meat Group (Holdings) Ltd* [1996] IRLR 521 (QB). For a recent example, see *Union of Shop, Distributive and Allied Workers v Tesco Stores Ltd* [2022] EWHC 201 (QB).

on the basis that they are necessary and obvious in the specific circumstances, they can also be formulated as instances of a more general principle that an 'anti avoidance' term will be implied constraining employers' freedom to terminate without good reason where doing so would deprive the worker of some benefit they have contracted for.[38]

These developments in the common law frame the central question addressed in *Johnson*, of whether the implied term of trust and confidence applies to constrain an employers' freedom to dismiss. Given the discussion above, this might appear a natural and incremental way for the law to proceed. Writing shortly before *Johnson* Ford argued 'there is every reason why [trust and confidence] should apply to the exercise of an express right to terminate a contract' given the central importance of the term to the employment relationship.[39] This seems to make sense as a matter of principle, because it is artificial to distinguish between implied terms as a valid constraint on some express contractual powers but not on an employers' decision to exercise a notice clause or otherwise terminate the contract. As articulated by Leggatt J in the commercial context, the exercise of termination and non-termination powers both involve circumstances where 'one party to the contract has a decision to make on a matter which affects the interests of the other party to the contract whose interests are not the same'.[40]

However, the implications of finding that mutual trust and confidence applies to the termination of employment contracts should not be underplayed. Taking this step would create a common law action for damages where a dismissal is carried out in a manner incompatible with the duty of trust and confidence. It would still be relatively easy for employers to dismiss without breaching the term by having a good and proper reason for their actions, albeit that more detailed guidance would need to be provided by the courts on what amounts to these reasons. But the longstanding position that there is no common law remedy for the manner of dismissal would be reversed. Moreover, recovery for wrongful dismissal would be extended significantly beyond the current standard of the employees' notice period, irrespective of whether the claim involved a breach of trust and confidence or another term such as an express notice clause. Damages for lost earnings would have to be calculated based on the estimated length of time the contract would have continued before the employer would have been able to terminate without breaching trust and confidence. An employee dismissed in breach of contract who would otherwise have continued to work for the employer for several years would therefore be entitled to lost

[38] Cabrelli, *Employment Law in Context* (n 30) 207.

[39] M Ford, 'Rethinking the Notice Rule' (1998) 27 *Industrial Law Journal* 220, 228.

[40] *MSC Mediterranean Shipping Co SA v Cottonex Anstalt* [2015] EWHC 283, [2015] All ER (Comm) 614 [97]. Despite the persuasiveness of this reasoning, the courts have been unwilling to regard termination as an exercise of contractual discretion that is subject to implied duties, see *Monde Petroleum SA v Westernzagros Ltd* [2016] EWHC 1472 (Comm), [2017] All ER (Comm) 1009 [261].

wages for that period. Awards could be even more extensive where a dismissal in breach of contract prevented the employee from working again due to psychiatric injury. Recovery would of course be limited by the normal rules of causation and remoteness, as well as the employees' duty to mitigate losses, but there would nevertheless be the prospect of substantial common law damages following dismissal.

III. THE CASE

A. Facts

Mr Johnson began working for Unisys Ltd in 1971 at the age of 23 and remained there for 16 years before being made redundant. During this period, he had time off for work-related stress issues, was prescribed anti-depressants, and offered counselling by his employer. After three years away from the company Mr Johnson was re-employed in 1990 and became a company director in 1992 until the dismissal in 1994 which forms the basis of the litigation in question.

In January 1994 Mr Johnson was informed that there had been complaints made against him relating to his conduct. He was called to a disciplinary meeting at which he was not told the substance or specifics of the allegations and was summarily dismissed later the same day with four weeks wages in lieu of his notice. An internal appeal was rejected, and his dismissal confirmed on 3 March 1994. The circumstances of his dismissal caused Mr Johnson to suffer a major psychiatric illness, which included hospitalisation from March to August 1994. Following his dismissal and resulting psychiatric injury Mr Johnson brought a successful claim for unfair dismissal. The industrial tribunal found the dismissal process had been procedurally unfair, and in July 1995 awarded him the statutory maximum allowed compensation at the time of £11,691.[41]

After claiming for unfair dismissal, however, Mr Johnson continued to suffer from serious psychiatric issues which required ongoing psychotherapy and treatment via antidepressants and twice led to his re-admittance to hospital. Three years after his dismissal, and now in his late forties, he found himself still unable to find employment. It was at this point, in August 1997, that he brought a claim alleging his treatment during the dismissal amounted to a breach by Unisys of the implied terms in their contract, including mutual trust and confidence and their duty of care. These were alleged to have been breached by the failure to follow internal disciplinary processes, and not informing him of the allegations against him or providing an opportunity to defend himself. Mr Johnson further

[41] The cap was increased to £50,000 and linked to inflation by the Employment Relations Act 1999, s 34. As of April 2021, the maximum compensation for unfair dismissal is the lesser amount of £89,493 or 52 weeks' pay.

claimed these breaches caused his psychiatric breakdown and subsequent inability to find work, which was said to be foreseeable given his personal history of stress-related absence from work, and sought special damages of £400,000 to compensate for lost earnings.

This claim was struck out in both the County Court and Court of Appeal. The Court of Appeal decided the case based on the rule in *Addis*, that no compensation is available for losses due to an inability to find employment caused by the manner of dismissal.[42] Lord Woolf distinguished the case of *Malik v BCCI*,[43] where the House of Lords had found that employees can in principle claim for financial losses due to an inability to find future employment caused by a breach of trust and confidence,[44] on the grounds that *Malik* related to anterior breaches of contract rather than being about the manner of dismissal as in *Johnson*.

B. Johnson in the House of Lords

The claim was also rejected in the House of Lords. The majority decision declining to extend the term of trust and confidence to dismissal was given by Lord Hoffmann, with Lords Bingham and Millet agreeing and Lord Nicholls deciding the case on analogous grounds. Lord Steyn dissented on the reasoning, finding that the term of trust and confidence should apply to constrain dismissal, but concluded that the claim in *Johnson* failed on remoteness grounds.

Lord Hoffmann identified two problems with extending the implied term of trust and confidence to fetter dismissal. The first was based in general contract law reasoning and the need for implied terms to be consistent with the parties' express agreement, while the second was grounded in constitutional principle and parliamentary intent.[45] Beginning with the common law reasoning, Lord Hoffmann believed the express term permitting Unisys to terminate with notice presented a significant barrier to Mr Johnson's claim.[46] He reasoned this was difficult to reconcile with an implied term restricting how this power was exercised, as the notice clause was likely to displace any implied term. In contrast, Lord Steyn in his judgment emphasised that trust and confidence was 'an overarching obligation implied by law as an incident of the contract of employment', and believed express and implied terms regarding dismissal could 'live together'.[47] Lord Hoffmann also doubted whether the implied term of trust and confidence could apply to the act of dismissal because it is concerned with continuing employment relationships, and trust

[42] *Johnson v Unisys Ltd* [1999] 1 All ER 854 (CA).
[43] *Malik v BCCI* (n 18).
[44] See ch 11 in this volume.
[45] *Johnson* (n 1) [37].
[46] ibid [42].
[47] ibid [24].

and confidence would necessarily be lost in the circumstances surrounding dismissal.[48] For this reason, he thought a distinct term would have to be implied in order for the claim to succeed, such one requiring good faith in dismissal, rather than being based in trust and confidence. Lord Steyn again dissented on this point. In his view, the 'obligation aims to ensure fair dealing between employer and employee, and that is as important in respect of disciplinary proceedings, suspension of an employee and dismissal as at any other stage of the employment relationship'.[49]

Notwithstanding these issues, Lord Hoffmann thought that it would be 'jurisprudentially possible' as a matter of contract law to imply a term restricting the exercise of dismissal power and giving a remedy in this case.[50] But he questioned whether 'it would necessarily be wise to do so', due to the risks of 'disproportionate' and open-ended liability for employers, as well as difficulties of causation and identifying the relevant damage,[51] which meant it would be a substantial rather than incremental development of the law which might therefore be best left to Parliament. As a result, the question of whether to imply a term was 'finely balanced'.[52]

Given these statements it is unclear whether, if approached purely as a matter of contract law reasoning, Lord Hoffmann would have been willing to develop an implied term constraining employers' power of dismissal. He was spared from adopting a conclusive position on this question, however, as he regarded the presence of the statutory unfair dismissal framework as determinative in barring the free development of the common law in this area. It would 'go contrary to the evident intention of Parliament' for implied terms to fetter dismissal, as this would 'develop the common law to give a parallel remedy' to unfair dismissal that was not subject to the limits on liability contained in the legislation.[53] The unfair dismissal framework was said to represent 'an attempt to balance fairness to employees against the general economic interests of the community' by Parliament.[54] The imperative for the common law to 'be consistent with legislative policy' and 'proceed in harmony with Parliament' therefore made it impermissible to imply any terms circumventing the statutory limits on unfair dismissal liability.[55]

Two further aspects of Lord Hoffmann's judgment are worth highlighting. First, parliamentary intent and the legislative context was found to equally exclude claims for breaches of duty of care in the context of dismissal.[56]

[48] ibid [46]. See, also, Lord Millet at [78].
[49] ibid [26].
[50] ibid [47].
[51] ibid [47]–[49].
[52] ibid [50].
[53] ibid [56]–[58].
[54] ibid [54].
[55] ibid [37].
[56] ibid [59].

Second, he also commented obiter that express contractual disciplinary procedures would be unlikely to give rise to damages at common law. It was 'impossible' to think that Parliament had intended that the inclusion of disciplinary rules in the statements of particulars required under the Employment Rights Act 1996 would 'give rise to a common law action in damages ... circumventing the restrictions and limits' placed on unfair dismissal claims.[57] The statutory background also meant the parties themselves would be unlikely to intend any express disciplinary procedures to 'create contractual duties which are independently actionable'.[58]

The other majority judgments closely echoed the reasoning adopted by Lord Hoffmann. In his concurring judgment Lord Millet noted that had unfair dismissal framework not existed the courts might have developed a similar common law remedy to reflect 'changing perceptions of the community',[59] but that 'the creation of the statutory right has made any such development of the common law both unnecessary and undesirable'.[60] It would be unnecessary to imply a term that merely replicated claims for unfair dismissal, and 'inconsistent with the declared policy of Parliament' to imply a term that extended beyond the statutory scheme.[61] In addition, the co-existence of two systems with different rules and routes to enforcement would be 'a recipe for chaos'.[62] Lord Nicholls similarly believed that developing the common law would 'defeat the intention of Parliament' that claims for the manner of dismissal should be subject to prescribed limits and decided by specialist tribunals.[63] The unfair dismissal framework therefore presented an 'insurmountable obstacle' to developing the common law as an implied term limiting the power of dismissal 'cannot satisfactorily co-exist with the statutory right not to be unfairly dismissed'.[64]

Lord Steyn was unpersuaded by both the common law and constitutional reasoning of the majority. He began by questioning whether on close analysis the ratio of *Addis* did in fact rule out pecuniary damages for loss of employment prospects following breach.[65] But even if this were true, he would have been willing to depart from this approach.[66] In addition to finding Lord Hoffmann's reasoning on express terms and the limited scope of trust and confidence unconvincing, Lord Steyn rejected the finding that the common law had been pre-empted by statute. In his view it was 'unrealistic' to think Parliament would

[57] ibid [66].
[58] ibid [66].
[59] ibid [77].
[60] ibid [80].
[61] ibid.
[62] ibid.
[63] ibid.
[64] ibid [2].
[65] ibid [15]–[16].
[66] ibid [17]–[20].

have assumed (much less intended) that the common law be set in stone when introducing legislation on unfair dismissal.[67] Ultimately, however, he concluded that the claim must fail on the facts, as there was no prospect of success due to the remoteness of the alleged damages and level of foresight that could be expected of the employer.

IV. THE LEGACY OF *JOHNSON*

This section explores the troubling legacy of *Johnson*, and sets out the uncertainty, inconsistency, and incoherence created by the decision. The analysis focusses on the pre-emption finding as this was determinative in the House of Lords, but the contract law reasoning has also been subject to thorough and persuasive critiques.[68]

A. Parliamentary Intent

The reliance on parliamentary intention as a key basis of the pre-emption finding in *Johnson* is, with respect, somewhat unsatisfactory. We should be wary about deploying parliamentary intent in this way given its existence, meaning, and role in questions of legal interpretation are all contested.[69] Even allowing that it is conceptually possible for an institution constituted by a multitude of individuals to have a single intention,[70] it is difficult to identify in practice.[71] Barmes rightly points out that these difficulties are especially acute for employment legislation given the constantly evolving and 'internally contradictory' nature of the policy environment.[72]

It can also be questioned whether parliamentary intent should bar otherwise legitimate common law developments given the intention 'of the majority of the members of the legislature … does not have legal significance' under

[67] ibid [23].

[68] See, eg, Barmes, (n 32); A Bogg and H Collins, 'Lord Hoffmann and the Law of Employment: The Notorious Episode of *Johnson v Unisys Ltd*' in P Davies and J Pila (eds), *The Jurisprudence of Lord Hoffmann* (Oxford, Hart Publishing, 2015).

[69] For a sample of these debates see J Waldron, *Law and Disagreement* (Oxford, Oxford University Press, 1999) 119–46; R Ekins, *The Nature of Legislative Intent* (Oxford, Oxford University Press, 2012); J Goldsworthy, 'Legislative Intention Vindicated?' (2013) 33 *OJLS* 821; R Dworkin, *Law's Empire* (Cambridge Massachusetts, Harvard University Press, 1986) ch 9; P Craig, *UK, EU and Global Administrative Law: Foundations and Challenges* (Cambridge, Cambridge University Press, 2015) 125–27; J Raz, *Between Authority and Interpretation: On the Theory of Law and Practical Reason* (Oxford, Oxford University Press, 2009) ch 11; A Burrows, *Thinking about Statutes: Interpretation, Interaction, Improvement* (Cambridge, Cambridge University Press, 2018) 13–21.

[70] R Ekins, 'The Intention of Parliament' [2010] *Public Law* 709.

[71] Dworkin (n 69) 313–37; J Steyn, '*Pepper v Hart*: A Re-Examination' (2001) 21 *OJLS* 59.

[72] Barmes (n 32) 451.

the UK's constitutional settlement.[73] What matters instead is the statutory text, and while this is usually interpreted 'in line with the intention reasonably to be attributed to Parliament in using the language'[74] the hypothetical nature of this intent means legislation need not necessarily be construed in line with the actual intentions of those who enacted it.

These general concerns about parliamentary intent are evident in *Johnson* itself, where it is far from clear what Parliament's intention was in respect of the unfair dismissal legislation, or how this intent should be identified. Hepple's analysis of the Donovan Commission demonstrates the intent when introducing unfair dismissal was to preserve the common law, and that there is 'no reason to believe' the Commissioners 'thought that the common law they were preserving would stand still'.[75] Indeed, shortly after the introduction of unfair dismissal the Court in *Norton Tool v Tewson* regarded unfair dismissal as a distinct framework for redress, stating that damages for wrongful dismissal were 'quite unaffected by the [1971] Act which created an entirely new cause of action'.[76] The malleable nature of parliamentary intent is also apparent in *Johnson*, where it could just as well be argued that the silence of the legislation in respect of the common law indicates that 'Parliament was content to let the courts develop it in the usual way'.[77]

In truth, it is likely that Parliament simply did not have any specific intent regarding the future development of the common law when legislating for unfair dismissal. References to parliamentary intent in *Johnson* must therefore be to intentions attributed to Parliament rather than any actual existing intent. Not only does this make reliance on the concept 'more than slightly artificial',[78] but if parliamentary intention merely refers to an intent attributed to the legislature by the court for some other independent reasons the concept is doing little of the normative work in justifying pre-emption of the common law. In which case it would be preferable for the courts to have addressed these free-standing reasons supporting pre-emption directly.[79]

Given these critiques, defences of *Johnson* have understandably taken references to parliamentary intent as a placeholder for other considerations. Alan Bogg, for example, believes parliamentary intent can 'charitably' be read as 'shorthand' for more persuasive arguments.[80] This possibility is considered below. But even if the pre-emption in *Johnson* could ultimately be justified on

[73] Steyn (n 71) 61.

[74] *Ghaidan v Godin-Mendoza* [2004] UKHL 30, [2004] 2 AC 557 [30] (Lord Nicholls).

[75] B Hepple, *Rights at Work: Global, European and British Perspectives* (London, Sweet & Maxwell, 2005) 47–49.

[76] *Norton Tool v Tewson* [1972] ICR 501 (NIRC) [14].

[77] B Hepple and G Morris, 'The Employment Act 2002 and the Crisis of Individual Employment Rights' (2002) 31 *Industrial Law Journal* 245, 253.

[78] Freedland (n 15) 304.

[79] TRS Allan, *The Sovereignty of Law: Freedom, Constitution and Common Law* (Oxford, Oxford University Press, 2013) 192.

[80] Bogg (n 3) 77.

other grounds it is problematic from a rule of law perspective for these reasons to have been obscured by the notion of parliamentary intent.

B. The Exclusion Zone

There is considerable uncertainty and arbitrariness regarding the extent and operation of the 'exclusion zone' established by *Johnson*. In the immediate aftermath of the decision, it was feared that trust and confidence would also be barred from governing the termination of employment contracts in circumstances involving constructive dismissal,[81] and thus significantly reduce the protection available against unfair dismissal. Alternately, if the common law applied to employer conduct away from direct dismissals, it was unclear where the boundaries of the exclusion zone lay and when claims in contract would be available for breaches of trust and confidence by employers. If the implied term continued to apply outside the context of dismissal the decision in *Johnson* also appeared to give rise to what Barmes called 'the liability problem'.[82] Namely, that an employees' claim in contract following a breach of trust and confidence would rest on their response to the employers' repudiatory breach; with those accepting the breach by resigning seeming to bring their claim within the exclusion zone.

The scope of the exclusion zone was clarified to some extent by the House of Lords in the joined cases of *Eastwood v Magnox Electric plc* and *McCabe v Cornwall County Council*.[83] Both involved claims for psychiatric injury allegedly caused by breaches of the implied terms of trust and confidence and duty of care. In *Eastwood* the employees had been subjected to a persecutory campaign at work involving allegedly false accusations of sexual harassment and an unfair disciplinary process that ultimately led to their dismissal. *McCabe* involved a claim on the basis that the employer had breached trust and confidence in suspending him and failing to investigate allegations of misconduct prior to dismissal. Giving the majority judgment, Lord Nicholls asserted:

> [T]he boundary of the '*Johnson* exclusion area' … is comparatively straightforward. The statutory code provides remedies for infringement of the statutory right not to be dismissed unfairly. An employee's remedy for unfair dismissal, whether actual or constructive, is the remedy provided by statute. If before his dismissal, whether actual or constructive, an employee has acquired a cause of action at law, for breach of contract or otherwise, that cause of action remains unimpaired by his subsequent unfair dismissal and the statutory rights flowing therefrom.[84]

[81] M Freedland, 'Claim for Unfair Dismissal' (2001) 30 *Industrial Law Journal* 309; Barmes (n 32) 452–53.
[82] Barmes (n 32).
[83] *Eastwood* (n 2).
[84] ibid [27].

Following this, it was found that all three employees' claims could proceed to trial, as on the alleged facts their claims had arisen before dismissal.

The 'liability problem' identified by Barmes was therefore avoided in *Eastwood*, as the availability of an employees' claim for breach of contract that exists independently of dismissal does not depend on whether they choose to accept the repudiatory breach. However, Lord Nicholls also made clear that where a common law claim exists prior to dismissal, whether for breach of trust and confidence or otherwise, recovery cannot include any losses flowing from the dismissal itself.[85] As this includes losses resulting from constructive dismissals, any loss flowing from an employees' acceptance of the repudiatory breach by resigning will fall within the exclusion zone.[86]

Defining the exclusion zone in this way considerably weakens the practical significance of common law claims for breach of trust and confidence, as it means employees who resign following a breach of an implied term cannot claim for lost earnings during their notice period. Breaches of trust and confidence unrelated to dismissal will therefore not give rise to claims for damages in most cases. Substantial recovery will only be available in exceptional circumstances where pre-dismissal breaches cause psychiatric injury,[87] or demonstrable economic loss through damage to reputation.[88] The effect of this is to significantly curtail the protection (and deterrence) provided by the common law of wrongful dismissal against abuses of managerial power and unfair treatment within the employment relationship.

Despite the assurances of Lord Nicholls in *Eastwood*, the scope and effect of the exclusion zone remain deeply uncertain. First, where a breach of trust and confidence is independent from dismissal it will frequently be difficult to determine what can be recovered at common law. Indeed, it may be impossible to demarcate with any degree of accuracy the harms and losses caused by a prior breach of duty rather than resulting from the employees' acceptance by resignation. Second, and more fundamentally, it will often be unclear whether an employers' conduct is sufficiently independent from dismissal to fall outside the exclusion zone, and for common law duties in contract and tort to therefore apply. It is challenging to draw any bright lines in this area, as the implied term of trust and confidence can apply to disciplinary processes and suspension decisions leading up to a dismissal as well as to redundancy selection processes.[89] Disciplinary processes may therefore 'have to be chopped artificially into separate pieces',[90] with a somewhat arbitrary line being drawn where the

[85] ibid [28].
[86] ibid [31].
[87] See *Gogay* (n 23).
[88] *Malik* (n 18).
[89] *Gogay* (n 23); *Stevens v University of Birmingham* [2015] EWHC 2300 (QB), [2015] IRLR 899; *Yapp v Foreign and Commonwealth Office* [2014] EWCA Civ 1512, [2015] IRLR 112; *Gebremariam v Ethiopian Airlines Enterprise* [2014] IRLR 354 (EAT).
[90] *Eastwood* (n 2) [31] (Lord Nicholls).

court considers the employers' actions can no longer be regarded as sufficiently independent from the dismissal.

The boundaries of the exclusion zone are to be determined by tribunals as a question of fact, and it is difficult to predict where the line will be drawn. A striking example of trust and confidence being found to apply in circumstances that intuitively seem inextricably linked to dismissal is *Rawlinson v Brightside Group*, where the employer was held to have breached the implied term by giving the employee a false reason for their dismissal.[91] The uncertainty regarding this boundary is also demonstrated by *Monk v Cann Hall*, where an employee who was working out her notice after being made redundant was publicly escorted out of the workplace, and subsequently claimed this treatment had breached the duty of trust and confidence and caused psychiatric injury.[92] The Court of Appeal thought that if escorting the employee out of the workplace constituted a dismissal the claim would be covered by the exclusion zone, but as the dismissal did not in fact take place until a later date the treatment fell outside the exclusion zone. It is troubling for the availability of common law claims in contract and tort to turn on margins such as these.

The confusion surrounding the exclusion zone was further compounded by the Supreme Court in the linked cases of *Edwards v Chesterfield* and *Botham v Ministry of Defence*.[93] With the seven-member judicial panel giving five separate judgments adopting an array of different reasoning, the true ratio of the case is hard to identify, if one exists at all.[94] *Edwards* confirmed the exclusion zone applies to implied terms as set out in *Eastwood*.[95] However, it appears a majority also concluded the *Johnson* exclusion zone should be extended to some express terms, with Lords Dyson, Mance, and Walker finding the legislation on unfair dismissal meant that breaches of disciplinary processes incorporated into employment contracts would not ordinarily give rise to common law claims for damages.[96] Drawing on Lord Hoffmann's comments in *Johnson*, the legislative context of unfair dismissal was said to mean that contractual disciplinary procedures cannot be regarded as 'ordinary contractual terms agreed by parties to a contract in the usual way'.[97] So while potentially enforceable through injunctions, they will not give rise to damages claims unless expressly stated in the contract.[98]

[91] *Rawlinson v Brightside Group Ltd* [2018] IRLR 180 (EAT).

[92] *Monk v Cann Hall* [2013] EWCA Civ 826, [2013] IRLR 732.

[93] *Edwards v Chesterfield* and *Botham v Ministry of Defence* [2011] UKSC 58, [2012] 2 AC 22.

[94] Doubted in L Barmes, 'Judicial Influence and *Edwards v Chesterfield Royal Hospital NHS Foundation Trust & Botham v Ministry of Defence*' (2013) 42 *Industrial Law Journal* 192.

[95] *Eastwood* (n 2).

[96] While the judgment of Lord Phillips was principally based in *Addis's* case rather than this reasoning he also stated that it would undermine the decisions in *Johnson* and *Eastwood* to allow common law claims for breach of contractual disciplinary procedures, see *Edwards* (n 93) [87].

[97] ibid [38] (Lord Dyson).

[98] ibid [44].

While a full analysis of *Edwards* lies beyond the scope of this chapter it is notable that, in contrast to *Johnson*, labour lawyers have been united in opposition to the decision. Key criticisms include that the Supreme Court erred in thinking that the constitutional concerns present in *Johnson* should apply equally to exclude express terms;[99] wrongly treated employment legislation as a ceiling rather than floor of rights on which the parties can agree to go beyond;[100] adopted an unprincipled and anomalous approach to remedies for breach of contract;[101] created further uncertainty over the class of express terms which fall within the exclusion zone;[102] and overlooked earlier cases that awarded damages for breach of express disciplinary procedures.[103]

It is therefore understandable that supporters of *Johnson* have sought to argue that *Edwards* represents an unprincipled extension of the pre-emption finding and 'should not be regarded as the legitimate progeny of *Johnson*'.[104] It is certainly true that a distinction could and should have been made in *Edwards* between the pre-emption of implied terms and express terms. But although it might not inexorably follow from the decision, *Edwards* is undoubtedly part of *Johnson*'s legacy given it was clearly inspired by the judgment and reasoning of Lord Hoffmann. That the result in *Edwards* represents 'a perfectly possible sequel'[105] to *Johnson* is sufficiently damning of the earlier decision.

C. Apparent Inconsistency

Another feature of *Johnson's* legacy are the apparent inconsistencies it creates in the relationship between common law and statute in the employment sphere. One element of this being that it is hard to reconcile the decision in *Johnson* with instances where the common law does regulate the manner of dismissal. First, it seems that the common law continues to restrict employers' right to dismiss through the law of implied terms in cases involving attempts to deny employees health insurance or other contractual entitlements.[106] In *Briscoe v Lubrizol*, for example, the Court of Appeal found that where dismissal would

[99] Barnard and Merrett (n 3) 327–29; Bogg and Collins (n 68) 209–11; Davies (n 3) 92.

[100] Bogg and Collins (n 68) 211–12.

[101] A Bogg, 'Express Disciplinary Procedures in the Contract of Employment: Parliamentary Intention and the Supreme Court (2015) 131 *LQR* 15; Davies (n 3) 94.

[102] Barmes (n 94); D Cabrelli, 'Liability and Remedies for Breach of the Contract of Employment at Common Law: Some Recent Developments' (2016) 45 *Industrial Law Journal* 207, 217.

[103] *Barber v Manchester Regional Hospital Board* [1958] 1 WLR 181 (QB), as discussed in K Costello, '*Edwards v Chesterfield Royal Hospital* – Parliamentary Intention and Damages Caused by Maladministration of a Contractual Dismissal Procedure' (2013) 76 *MLR* 134. See, also, *Deadman v Bristol CC* [2007] EWCA Civ 822, [2008] PIQR P2.

[104] Bogg and Collins (n 68) 211.

[105] Bogg and Freedland (n 6) 557.

[106] Barmes (n 32) 461–62. See, also, *Jenvey v Australian Broadcasting Co* [2002] EWHC 927 (QB), [2003] ICR 79.

deny an entitlement to PHI benefits there was an implied term that the employer would not terminate other than for good cause.[107] The recent Privy Council case of *Ali v Petroleum Company of Trinidad and Tobago* similarly found an implied term preventing the employer from dismissing without good reason where this would deny the employee from being entitled to have a loan written off.[108]

Second, the common law also protects against the manner of dismissal through the judicial review of decisions to remove individuals from positions or offices created by statute.[109] This discrepancy might be explained by the established nature and limited distributional consequences of judicial review,[110] as well as the courts' greater willingness to scrutinise administrative decision-making than that of employers.[111] But it is hard to justify as a matter of principle given that there is often now little practical difference between office holders and employees,[112] and that the courts have recently included office holders within the protective scope of some employment law statutes.[113]

Another area of inconsistency is that the common law may provide remedies that extend beyond those available for unfair dismissal, contrary to the underlying logic of the *Johnson* exclusion zone. One example of this is that injunctions are sometimes available to prevent employers from breaching expressly incorporated disciplinary processes,[114] or breaching the implied term of trust and confidence in a disciplinary process.[115] In these circumstances the common law provides a pre-emptive remedy against attempted unfair dismissals and therefore offers better protection to employees than that available under statute, where claims must be brought on a retrospective basis and there is usually little prospect of reinstatement.

A further example is that employees who have claims for constructive unfair dismissal may sometimes recover significantly more in compensation for wrongful dismissal. Where a highly paid employee has a long notice period or large bonus entitlement and their employer is in repudiatory breach of an express term of the contract the employee can accept this breach and recover lost wages and benefits for their notice period that vastly exceed the statutory cap for unfair dismissal.[116] The same is true for breaches of express terms in high-value, fixed-term employment contracts that do not contain a break clause. The ex-Newcastle United manager Kevin Keegan, for example, was

[107] *Briscoe v Lubrizol* [2002] EWCA Civ 508, [2002] IRLR 607 [107].
[108] *Ali v Petroleum Company of Trinidad and Tobago* [2017] UKPC 2, [2017] ICR 531 [11].
[109] *R (Shoesmith) v OFSTED* [2011] EWCA Civ 642, [2011] IRLR 679.
[110] Bogg (n 3) 84.
[111] ACL Davies, 'Judicial Self Restraint in Labour Law' 38 *Industrial Law Journal* 278.
[112] Ford (n 39) 233.
[113] *Gilham v Ministry of Justice* [2019] UKSC 44, [2019] WLR 5905.
[114] *McMillan v Airedale NHS Foundation Trust* [2014] EWCA Civ 1031, [2015] ICR 747; *Mezey v South West London & St. George's Mental Health NHS Trust* [2010] EWCA Civ 293, [2010] IRLR 512. For discussion see Cabrelli (n 102) 214–17.
[115] *Chhabra v West London Mental Health NHS Trust* [2013] UKSC 80, [2014] 1 All ER 943.
[116] Eg, *Horkulak v Cantor FitzGerald International* [2004] EWCA Civ 1287, [2005] ICR 402.

awarded £2 million in lost earnings under his fixed-term contract for constructive wrongful dismissal, after he resigned in response to a repudiatory breach of an express term providing that he had final say over transfer decisions.[117] Cases such as these conflict with the underlying reasoning in *Johnson*, that the common law should not circumvent the remedies Parliament has provided for situations of unfair dismissal.

A final element of inconsistency created by *Johnson* is that the decision appears to adopt a markedly different approach towards the relationship between common law and statute than is in operation elsewhere in employment law. Notably, the implied term of reasonable notice for dismissal continues to be inserted into indefinite employment contracts that do not contain express notice clauses despite the existence of statutory minimum notice periods.[118] This discrepancy is no doubt due to the more established nature of the implied notice term, which is based on a general common law principle that such a term will be implied into contracts of indefinite duration.[119] However, it is nevertheless striking that legislation regulating one aspect of the manner of dismissal (fairness) displaces the common law while another statute also regulating the manner of dismissal (notice) does not.

Furthermore, and in contrast to the result in *Johnson*, the implied term of trust and confidence continues to run in parallel with a range of employment legislation away from the dismissal context. This includes statutes protecting trade union rights and against discrimination among others. In *Stevens v University of Birmingham*, for example, the term provided a right to be accompanied in an investigatory meeting, which extended beyond the rights provided by the Trade Unions Relations (Consolidation) Act 1992 (TULRCA).[120] Similarly, an employer who offers employees inducements not to join a union is likely to breach both the implied term and section 145A of TULRCA.[121] There is also a significant degree of overlap between common law implied terms and the Equality Act 2010, as employer conduct amounting to direct discrimination or harassment under the Act is likely to also breach trust and confidence and the employers' duty of care.[122]

Indeed, it is interesting to contrast the fate of trust and confidence in the context of discrimination with that of dismissal given the similarities between

[117] *Keegan v Newcastle United Football Co Ltd* [2010] IRLR 94 (Premier League Manager's Arbitration Tribunal).

[118] *McCelland v Northern Ireland General Health Service Board* [1957] 1 WLR 594 (HL); *Clark v Clark Construction Initiatives Ltd* [2008] IRLR 364 (EAT). For recent discussion of this issue in the Australian context, see *McAlister v Yara Australia Pty Ltd* [2021] FCCA 1409.

[119] See *Martin-Baker Aircraft Co v Canadian Flight Equipment* [1955] 2 QB 556 (QB).

[120] *Stevens v University of Birmingham* [2015] EWHC 2300, [2016] All ER 258.

[121] D Brodie, 'Mutual Trust and Confidence: Catalysts, Constraints and Commonality' (2008) 37 *Industrial Law Journal* 329, 334–35.

[122] *Weathersfield Ltd v Sargent* [1999] IRLR 94 (CA); *Waters v Commissioner of Police of the Metropolis* [2000] 1 WLR 1607 (HL). This was left open in *Sheriff v Klyne Tugs (Lowestoft) Ltd* [1999] ICR 1170 (CA).

them. In both contexts the implied term often overlaps with the protection provided by statute but remains a distinct behavioural standard.[123] In addition, as with unfair dismissal the implied term may sometimes provide more extensive protection against discrimination than the legislation. For instance, unlike statutory claims for discrimination or harassment, the term of trust and confidence may protect against arbitrary or discriminatory treatment by employers without needing to be linked to a protected characteristic,[124] and common law claims can be brought outside the time limits imposed by the Equality Act.

There are no doubt other examples of common law and statute happily co-existing that contrast with the finding of pre-emption in *Johnson*.[125] The diverse circumstances where common law and employment legislation operate in parallel mean they cannot easily be dismissed as 'red herrings' or 'remote statutory analogies'.[126] Rather, they are in genuine tension with the vision of the relationship between common law and statute endorsed in *Johnson*. Why must the implied term of trust and confidence be pre-empted by the unfair dismissal legislation but allowed to co-exist with statutory protections against discrimination and trade union rights among others? It might be possible to justify these apparent inconsistencies by reference to legislative context,[127] but at the very least they show the need for a more fully developed and nuanced approach to pre-emption than is evident in *Johnson*.

D. Legal Incoherence

The *Johnson* exclusion zone has created incoherence and anomalies in the common law remedies available for breach of the employment contract, and absurd legal consequences for the statutory unfair dismissal framework.

In respect of common law remedial rules, the position can be summed up as follows. An employee may accept an employer's repudiatory breach of an express term and claim damages for lost earnings during their notice period in an action for wrongful dismissal. But damages will not normally be available if the breach is of an express term incorporating disciplinary procedures, and possibly other express terms relating to dismissal. In such cases damages will only be available if expressly provided for in the contract, and injunctions must instead be used to enforce these terms; a position that is 'surely unique' in the common law of

[123] *Amnesty International v Ahmed* [2009] IRLR 884 (EAT).

[124] See *Manchester Passenger Transport Executive v Sands* EAT (11 January 2001); *Johnson v The Governing Body of Coopers Lane Primary School* (EAT, 1 December 2009).

[125] Such as the overlap between employers' duty of care and the Health and Safety at Work Act 1974, or the Workman's Compensation Act 1897, see Bogg and Collins (n 68) 193.

[126] Bogg (n 3) 77.

[127] As Bogg seeks to do in respect of workmen's compensation legislation, ibid 78.

contract.[128] In addition, an employers' breach of the implied term of reasonable notice may be accepted by an employee and give rise to damages for lost earnings during the notice period, whereas breaches of other implied terms such as trust and confidence or duty of care that are similarly accepted by an employee will not ground a claim for lost earnings during the notice period.

These varying results can be observed despite the basic legal position being the same in all situations: namely that there has been a repudiatory breach of contract, accepted by an employee who is claiming for breach of contract. The absurdity of the current position is illustrated by the fact that an employer who is in repudiatory breach of an express term will necessarily also breach the implied term of trust and confidence,[129] meaning that the same actions of an employer may ground a claim for breach of contract including lost earnings during the notice period if the action is brought as a breach of the express term, but no such recovery will be available if the claim is brought for breach of the implied term.

There is also little justification as a matter of common law principle for distinguishing between the implied term of trust and confidence as valid constraint on the exercise of employers' express and implied managerial powers other than their ability to terminate the contract. As Collins argues, it makes no sense doctrinally for the availability of a claim in contract to turn on whether an employers' breach of trust and confidence takes place the day before a dismissal or the same day.[130] This distinction also leads to the counterintuitive result that Parliament's decision to establish protections against unfair dismissal has ultimately resulted in *less* protection being offered by the common law in this context than other areas of managerial decision-making.

Another paradoxical outcome of *Johnson* is that in some circumstances the exclusion zone provides an incentive for employers to dismiss employees without full and fair procedures. The implied term of trust and confidence applies leading up to dismissal, so unfair disciplinary processes could potentially lead to employees recovering for psychiatric injury or economic losses caused by breaches of the term without being subject to the cap on compensation for unfair dismissal. Employers might therefore be better off, and avoid any such uncapped liability, by pre-emptively dismissing the employee rather than suspending them or undertaking thorough disciplinary processes. However unlikely this is to regularly occur in practice, it is perverse for the introduction of unfair dismissal to have the result of incentivising dismissal without due process in a manner which is diametrically opposed to the legislation's underlying goals.

[128] Bogg and Collins (n 68) 196.
[129] *Smith v Trafford Housing Trust* [2012] EWHC 3221 (Ch), [2013] IRLR 86; *Mostyn v S&P Casuals Ltd* (EAT, 22 February 2018).
[130] Bogg and Collins (n 68) 197.

V. A COMPELLING CONSTITUTIONAL VISION?

The preceding analysis demonstrates the 'awkward and unfortunate consequences' of *Johnson*,[131] and it is difficult to maintain that the courts have managed to avoid the 'recipe for chaos' that Lord Millet believed would result from developing the common law in the area of dismissal.[132] In spite of the problems created by *Johnson*, it might nevertheless be possible to justify the conclusion of the House of Lords that the normal application and development of the common law must be precluded by the statutory framework of unfair dismissal.

At the time of *Eastwood* Lord Steyn was able to refer to an impressive array of labour law scholarship and conclude that 'there is apparently no support for the analysis adopted in *Johnson*'.[133] This is no longer the case. More recently, a second wave of literature has emerged, with several leading labour lawyers mounting a cautious defence of the decision on grounds of constitutional principle.[134] These scholars largely acknowledge the problems with *Johnson* outlined above but view them as the necessary price for maintaining constitutional propriety. There are undoubtedly legitimate and weighty concerns about developing the common law in an area regulated by statute that were not fully accounted for in the original critiques of *Johnson*. However, this section seeks to push back against the view that *Johnson* represents a 'compelling constitutional vision of the interaction between common law and legislation' in the employment sphere.[135] While there are certainly plausible arguments in favour of pre-emption, and the question is finely balanced, it is argued that constitutional considerations did not necessitate the pre-emption of the common law in *Johnson*.

A. Coherence of Common Law and Statute

One argument made by Anne Davies in support of pre-emption in *Johnson* is that it promotes 'the overall coherence of the law'.[136] There are two key elements of this claim. First, that courts should seek to 'develop a coherent body of employment law in which statute and common law work together effectively',[137] including by developing the common law by 'considering its fit with statute'.[138] Second, that despite the doctrinal incoherence created by *Johnson*, pre-emption

[131] *Eastwood* (n 2) [31] (Lord Nicholls).
[132] *Johnson* (n 1) [80].
[133] *Eastwood* (n 2) [43].
[134] Barnard and Merrett (n 3); Davies (n 3); Bogg (n 3).
[135] Bogg (n 3) 68.
[136] Davies (n 3) 86.
[137] ibid 75.
[138] ibid 89.

was necessary to achieve coherence at the more macro level between common law and statute. But while the first of these seems entirely correct, it is less clear that the pursuit of coherence necessitated pre-emption in *Johnson*.

It is certainly welcome that the House of Lords in *Johnson* departed from the traditional 'oil and water' view of the relationship between common law and statute, which characterises them as distinct sources of law that flow beside each other through the legal system but do not comingle.[139] This approach tends to coincide with a belief that legislation represents an unprincipled intervention into the common law as the primary source of law,[140] epitomised by the statement that 'Parliament generally changes law for the worst … the business of the judges is to keep the mischief of its interference within the narrowest bounds'.[141]

The oil and water view of common law and statute is not tenable in the context of labour law. Employment legislation can no longer be seen as isolated interventions within the common law and is now an equally (or more) important source of regulation. Moreover, it is wrong to characterise common law and statute as separate bodies of law given that the common law is used to give meaning to legislation,[142] and legislation frequently triggers developments in the common law. As a result, a 'kind of legal partnership' exists between common law and statute.[143] This is certainly true for employment law. Not only does Parliament often choose to 'graft statutory protections on to the stem of the common law contract'[144] but, as Freedland states, the common law 'has evolved, in an intricate symbiosis with employment legislation and various adjacent kinds of legislation … so that it should be regarded as ultimately if not immediately inseparable from that large body of legislation'.[145]

Rather than treating them as oil and water, therefore, courts should aim for the 'emulsification' of common law and statute in employment cases. Emulsification occurs where two initially separate and immiscible liquids are combined to create a new substance. The process generally requires the use of a third substance, known as an emulsifier, in order for the two liquids to form a stable compound. Under this approach, rather than flowing through the legal system side-by-side, common law and statute should undergo a process of emulsification whereby these two distinct sources of law are rendered into a single stable compound by the courts, with the Rule of Law and other constitutional principles acting as the emulsifying agent.

[139] J Beatson, 'Has the Common Law a Future?' (1997) 56 *CLJ* 291, 308.
[140] ibid 299.
[141] F Pollock, *Essays in Jurisprudence and Ethics* (London, Macmillan, 1882) 85.
[142] Burrows (n 69) 58.
[143] P Atiyah, 'Common Law and Statute Law' (1985) 48 *MLR* 1, 6.
[144] *Buckland v Bournemouth University Higher Education Co* [2010] EWCA Civ 121, [2011] QB 323 [19] (Sedley LJ).
[145] M Freedland, 'The Legal Structure of the Contract of Employment' in M Freedland and others (eds), *The Contract of Employment* (Oxford, Oxford University Press, 2016) 34.

Given this, it is welcome that the House of Lords in *Johnson* were sensitive to the legislative context and did not view common law and statute as oil and water. It is not clear, however, that pre-emption was required in pursuit of coherence between common law and statute. The emulsification of common law and statute can be achieved in various ways, and pre-emption of the common law will not be necessary in every instance where Parliament has legislated.[146] For example, the process of emulsification might sometimes instead be best achieved by interpreting legislation in line with common law principles,[147] developing the common law by analogy to legislation,[148] or in a manner which best achieves the purposes of the legislation.[149] In any given context the courts must therefore decide which mode of interaction between common law and statute is most appropriate.

In *Johnson* itself the emulsification of common law and statute could arguably have been better achieved by developing the common law in a way that furthers the underlying goals of unfair dismissal, of providing justice and security for subordinate and dependent workers.[150] This would represent a deeper integration of the two, with the legislation being used as a source of principle for developing the common law.[151] Moreover, the finding of pre-emption damages the coherence of common law and statute, because it has the paradoxical result of legislation introduced to protect workers against unfair dismissal causing the common law to offer less protection in this context than other abuses of managerial power.

B. Legislative Finality

The most powerful arguments for pre-emption in *Johnson* are rooted in concerns that developing the common law would be contrary to democratic principle because it would undermine the finality of the unfair dismissal legislation enacted by a democratically legitimate Parliament.[152] The core idea is that Parliament has considered and answered the question of what remedy employees should

[146] On the various modes of interaction between common law and statute, see R Pound, 'Common Law and Legislation' (1907) 21 *Harvard Law Review* 383; Atiyah (n 143); Beatson (n 139); J Beatson, 'The Role of Statute in the Development of Common Law Doctrine' (2001) 117 *LQR* 247; A Burrows, 'The Relationship between Common Law and Statute in the Law of Obligations' (2012) 128 *LQR* 232; Davies (n 3); Bogg (n 3); Burrows (n 69).

[147] For examples of this in employment law, see Davies (n 3) 75–80.

[148] As in *Barber v RJB Mining (UK) Ltd* [1999] ICR 679 [QB].

[149] Eg, the departure from the standard postal rule in *Gisda Cyf v Barratt* [2010] UKSC 41, [2010] 4 All ER 851.

[150] On the goals of unfair dismissal and employment legislation, see H Collins, *Justice in Dismissal: The Law of Termination of Employment* (Oxford, Oxford University Press, 1992) ch 1; G Davidov, *A Purposive Approach to Labour Law* (Oxford, Oxford University Press, 2016) 98–112.

[151] For discussion of this see Pound (n 146).

[152] Bogg (n 3) 79–80.

have for unfair dismissal, and the courts should not undermine this framework by developing a common law remedy that extends beyond it.

Alan Bogg suggests the finding of pre-emption is also justified due to the polycentric nature of the issue in *Johnson* and the significant resource allocation implications of developing the common law.[153] These are certainly reasons for cautious incrementalism when developing the common law, and may heighten democratic concerns about the co-existence of common law and statute. But they are not, in themselves, sufficient to demand pre-emption of the common law. Polycentric questions involving the distribution of resources are pervasive in private law and so should not be equated with non-justiciability,[154] with employment law being no exception to this. For example, the application of the implied term of trust and confidence to balance the interests of employers and employees raises similar issues of polycentricity and resource allocation outside of dismissal, and it is only the additional concern of legislative finality that potentially justifies pre-emption in that context. Similarly, judicial determinations about which rights and interests can be vindicated in court necessarily have distributive impacts.[155] This includes the orthodox common law rule giving employers' freedom to dismiss, which places the allocative impacts of termination firmly on employees.[156] To regard these factors as sufficient to pre-empt the common law would represent a regressive level of judicial restraint, and signal a limited role for the common law in regulating employment that is out of step with the existing 'discrete body of worker-protective common law norms, which constitute a distinctive common law of the personal employment contract'.[157]

Considerations of democratic principle and legislative finality are therefore central to the constitutional propriety of developing the common law in an area regulated by statute. The key question is when will the legislative sovereignty and democratic legitimacy of Parliament make it inappropriate for the common law to apply and develop in its usual manner. This is most obviously the case where the statute *expressly* replaces or excludes the common law. But there will also be circumstances where legislation must be taken as *impliedly* pre-empting the common law in the absence of any explicit statement to this effect. This should not happen too readily, as the common law's authority is independent of Parliament and the courts provide an important forum for representation and participation.[158]

[153] ibid 80–83.

[154] J King, 'The Pervasiveness of Polycentricity' [2008] *Public Law* 101; J King, 'The Justiciability of Resource Allocation' (2007) 70 *MLR* 197.

[155] J Gardner, 'What Is Tort Law for? Part 2. The Place of Distributive Justice' in J Oberdiek (ed), *Philosophical Foundations of the Law of Torts* (Oxford, Oxford University Press, 2013).

[156] As well as the state to some extent, via the social security system.

[157] A Bogg and M Freedland, 'Pensions Law, *IBM v Dalgleish* and the Public/Private Divide' in S Agnew, P Davies, and C Mitchell (eds), *Pensions: Law, Policy and Practice* (Oxford, Hart, 2020) 230.

[158] R Alexy, 'Balancing, Constitutional Review, and Representation' (2005) 3 *International Journal of Constitutional Law* 572; P Pettit, 'Representation, Responsive and Indicative' (2010) 17 *Constellations* 426; J Waldron, *Political Political Theory* (Cambridge, MA, Harvard University Press 2016) 158–62.

But if the doctrine of implied repeal can operate to displace legislation enacted by a sovereign Parliament it must also be possible for statutes to impliedly displace or freeze the common law. While it there is not space here to explore this issue fully, or attempt to develop a theory of when legislation should impliedly pre-empt the common law, at least three such instances can be identified.

The first is where Parliament has introduced a comprehensive code of regulation in a particular area, and thereby 'occupied the field'.[159] This was the justification given for the *Johnson* exclusion zone by Lord Nicholls in *Eastwood*,[160] which has also been endorsed by academic commentators.[161] However, the statutory unfair dismissal scheme is not an exhaustive source of rules or remedies for dismissal. Not only are claims for wrongful dismissal still available (with remedies that overlap and may extend beyond unfair dismissal), but the courts use injunctions and implied terms to prevent unfair dismissals in some circumstances. The legislation is therefore not a complete code of remedies in the context of dismissal. It also seems unnecessary to regard the legislation as occupying the 'field' of employers' duties in contract and tort given that these are conceptually distinct from the statutory protections provided against unfair dismissal. No comprehensive scheme has been introduced to regulate trust and confidence or employers' duty of care within the employment relationship, and unfair dismissal no more occupies the field in respect of these duties than other legislation that happily co-exists with them, such as the Equality Act 2010. Finally, we should not be too quick to assume legislation occupies the field, because if Parliament has indicated the common law is unsatisfactory it may be appropriate for courts to be receptive to further readjustments.[162]

Second, implied pre-emption will be necessary where the common law would leave the legislation dead letter. This would effectively amount to the courts repealing the law, contrary to the core tenet of parliamentary sovereignty that only Parliament can set aside legislation.[163] It is not the case, however, that applying common law implied terms to constrain employers' power of dismissal would leave the law of unfair dismissal dead letter. The statutory framework would continue to exist and operate as before, and the availability of any common law claim would not prevent employees from relying on their statutory right not to be unfairly dismissed. Many employees would no doubt continue to bring claims for unfair dismissal even if a common law claim were also available, given the relatively user-friendly nature of tribunals compared to the procedural

[159] M Lee, 'Occupying the Field: Tort and the Pre-Emptive Statute' in TT Arvind and J Steele (eds), *Tort law and the Legislature: Common Law, Statute and the Dynamics of Legal Change* (Oxford, Hart, 2012); *R (Child Poverty Action Group) v Secretary of State for Work and Pensions* [2010] UKSC 54, [2011] 2 AC 15.

[160] *Eastwood* (n 2) [14].

[161] Davies (n 3) 89; Bogg (n 3) 79.

[162] Atiyah (n 143); Beatson (n 139) 311.

[163] AV Dicey, *Lectures Introductory to the Study of the Law of the Constitution* (London, Macmillan, 1885) 36.

formalities of ordinary courts, the (theoretical at least) possibility of reinstatement, and that tribunals will not generally award costs against unsuccessful employees. In addition, there are benefits to having one's case determined by a specialist tribunal with lay members and judges who have a good understanding of the industrial relations context,[164] albeit these may now be more limited given the infrequent use of lay members and increased juridification of tribunals.[165]

Unfair dismissal would also remain an important source of redress and not be left dead letter because employees may well be able to bring successful claims in circumstances where the employer is not in breach of the implied term of trust and confidence. The inquiry into fairness, and particularly procedural unfairness, is likely to be more searching under the statutory framework than under the implied term, where the employer merely needs to demonstrate they have good and proper reason for their actions to avoid being in breach.[166]

The final category of cases where implied pre-emption might be necessary is where applying the common law does not threaten parliamentary sovereignty or leave the legislation dead letter but nevertheless undermines or frustrates the goals of legislation to a constitutionally inappropriate degree. This is the basis on which pre-emption in *Johnson* can most plausibly be justified. It is also an important point of distinction between the case and *Rookes v Barnard*, where developing the common law undoubtedly had the effect of undermining the protective purposes of the legislation.[167] Although developing the common law in *Johnson* would arguably further the underlying principles and normative goals of unfair dismissal protection, allowing employees to claim for breaches of trust and confidence in the context of dismissal does appear to circumvent many of the limits Parliament has chosen to impose on recovery for unfair dismissal. This includes the statutory cap on compensation, the qualification period to be entitled to claim, and the three-month time limit for claims to be brought. It is for this reason that Barnard and Merrett conclude that developing the common law would 'undermine the statutory regime'.[168]

Rather than replicating the statutory framework, however, it can be argued that applying trust and confidence to employers' power of dismissal provides an entirely different action; namely one for breach of contract rather than the unfairness of dismissal. This seems convincing in relation to the implied duty of care, as recovery for personal injury seems quite different in nature and content than protection against unfair dismissal.[169] But the position is more

[164] KW Wedderburn, 'Change, Struggle and Ideology in British Labour Law' in KW Wedderburn (ed), *Labour Law and Freedom: Further Essays in Labour Law* (London, Lawrence and Wishart, 1995) 30–31.

[165] See S Corby, 'British Employment Tribunals: From the Side-Lines to Centre Stage' (2015) 56 *Labor History* 161.

[166] Ford (n 39) 231.

[167] *Rookes v Barnard* [1964] AC 1129 (HL).

[168] Barnard and Merrett (n 3) 324.

[169] Obiter comments along these lines were made by Underhill LJ in *Monk v Cann Hall* (n 92) [32].

difficult in relation to trust and confidence. The significant overlap and frequent co-existence of claims for breach of trust and confidence and unfair would not be overly problematic if there were a clear conceptual division between claims for breach of contract and the statutory framework. The two could then be regarded as concurrent but distinct actions. This line is blurred, however, because terms implied in law are often regarded as based on policy and efficiency considerations.[170] But if the term of trust and confidence is grounded in the same policy considerations as those underpinning the unfair dismissal legislation it seems inappropriate for the courts to provide a remedy for unfair treatment in dismissal that extends beyond the scheme that Parliament introduced in response to those same policy considerations.

One way this conclusion can be avoided and a sufficient conceptual distinction maintained between the common law and statutory claims is if implied terms in law, including the term of trust and confidence, are conceived as reflecting obligations of interpersonal justice between the parties,[171] which courts identify as intrinsically associated with the roles they are entering into when contracting. This proposed understanding of implied terms views them as legal embodiments of obligations of role morality, meaning those duties inherently linked to certain social roles such as being a parent, landlord or employer, which the parties undertake when entering into these relationships.[172] This interpretation also fits with the courts treatment of implied terms in law as 'necessary incidents' of particular categories of contract,[173] and with the view of trust and confidence as representing a general behavioural standard that reflects moral and societal expectations of acceptable conduct within an employment relationship.[174] Seen in this revised light, common law actions in contract for breaches of trust and confidence are sufficiently conceptually distinct from the statutory action for unfair dismissal to co-exist satisfactorily. Given this, and considering the problems for the rule of law flowing from the uncertainty and arbitrariness created by the decision, developing the common law in *Johnson* would not have undermined the legislation to such an extent that pre-emption was necessary.

Whether one accepts this conclusion ultimately turns on deeper normative commitments regarding the autonomy and role of the common law, the legitimacy of judicial law-making, and the appropriate relationship between courts and Parliament. Given Lord Steyn's comments on parliamentary sovereignty in *R (Jackson) v Attorney General*[175] it is perhaps unsurprising that he was more

[170] H Collins, 'Implied Terms: The Foundation in Good Faith and Fair Dealing' (2014) 67 *Current Legal Problems* 297.

[171] On contract law and relational justice see H Dagan and A Dorfman, 'Justice in Contracts' (2022) 67 The American Journal of Jurisprudence 1.

[172] M Hardimon, 'Role Obligations' (1994) 91 *The Journal of Philosophy* 333; J Andre, 'Role Morality as a Complex Instance of Ordinary Morality' (1991) 28 *American Philosophical Quarterly* 73.

[173] *Scally v Southern Health and Social Services Board* [1992] 1 AC 294 (HL).

[174] Barmes (n 29).

[175] *R (Jackson) v Attorney General* [2005] UKHL 56, [2006] 1 AC 262.

willing to support a robust role for the common law than the more conservative approach to the judicial role adopted by Lord Hoffmann and others. The relevance of these deeper commitments might also go some way to explaining the divide created among labour lawyers by *Johnson*, with scholars whose work emphasises the public law dimensions of the field perhaps being more receptive to the pre-emption finding than those who adopt an approach more grounded in private law.

VI. THE HUMAN RIGHTS EXCEPTION

A final important issue in *Johnson* that is often overlooked is the 'human rights exception' that must be carved out of the exclusion zone. The principle of legality and the Human Rights Act 1998 respectively mean that courts should not interpret the legislation on unfair dismissal as pre-empting the common law where it protects either fundamental common law rights or those contained in the European Convention. Although the existence of this exception was acknowledged in *Johnson* itself, its extent and significance are yet to be fully recognised.

The first dimension of the human rights exception flows from the principle of legality, which requires that legislation not be interpreted as removing the protection of fundamental common law rights unless expressly stated or strictly necessary.[176] In *R (Unison) v Lord Chancellor*, for example, the principle of legality meant that legislation providing for the introduction of employment tribunal fees was interpreted as not authorising the introduction of fees that would be contrary to the common law constitutional right of access to justice.[177] Although generally regarded as preventing the *removal* of existing protections of fundamental common law rights,[178] the principle of legality must logically also prevent legislation being interpreted as preventing the common law *developing* to protect these rights. Following this, because pre-emption in *Johnson* was not required by the express statutory text or necessary implication the principle of legality requires that the unfair dismissal framework not be interpreted as barring the protection of fundamental common law rights.

It is unclear, however, where if ever this aspect of the human rights exception to the *Johnson* exclusion zone will apply, as it seems fundamental common law rights will rarely be at stake in the context of dismissal. Certainly, the implied term of trust and confidence is not itself a fundamental common law right. One possibility is that freedom of contract might be regarded as a fundamental

[176] *R v Lord Chancellor, ex p Witham* [1998] QB 575 (QB); *R v Home Secretary, ex p Simms* [2000] 2 AC 115 (HL).

[177] *R (Unison) v Lord Chancellor* [2017] UKSC 51, [2020] AC 869.

[178] As in *R (Morgan Grenfell & Co Ltd) v Special Commissioner of Income Tax* [2002] UKHL 21, [2003] 1 AC 563. See Burrows (n 69) 68–73.

common law right that engages the principle of legality.[179] In which case, and contrary to the reasoning in *Edwards*, the unfair dismissal legislation should not be interpreted as pre-empting common law liability for breach of express contract terms that contain procedural or substantive restrictions on dismissal. Another possibility is that the exception to the exclusion zone demanded by the legality principle may become more significant as the courts come to recognise a wider range of common law constitutional rights, such as freedom of expression or association.[180] The exclusion zone would then not apply to dismissals where the common law of implied terms functions to protect these rights. The role of common law constitutional rights in the employment sphere may also become more important if the Human Rights Act 1998 is repealed and replaced with legislation that makes it harder for arguments grounded in the ECHR to gain traction.

The second dimension of the human rights exception results from the Human Rights Act 1998 (HRA) and European Convention of Human Rights (ECHR). Section 3 of the HRA requires the legislation on unfair dismissal be interpreted in line with Convention rights so far as possible,[181] and the positive obligations imposed by the ECHR mean that this legislation must not be interpreted as barring the protection of Convention rights through the application of the implied term of trust and confidence.[182]

Under the ECHR, Member States have positive obligations to protect Convention rights, including to secure employees' rights against disproportionate interferences by employers.[183] As part of this, *Redfearn v UK* makes clear that legal protections are required against dismissals that interfere with Convention rights.[184] In *Redfearn* the UK was found to breach its positive obligations where an employee was dismissed for his association with a political party and could not bring a claim for unfair dismissal due to the qualifying period. The case involved Article 11 but the reasoning is equally applicable to other Convention rights.[185] Following this, if a dismissal interferes with a Convention right but falls

[179] Although the right to restitution was not regarded as fundamental in *R (Child Poverty Action Group) v Secretary of State for Work and Pensions* (n 160).

[180] See generally M Elliott and K Hughes (eds), *Common Law Constitutional Rights* (Oxford, Hart, 2020).

[181] *X v Y* [2004] EWCA Civ 662, [2004] ICR 1634.

[182] For discussion of the circumstances where the implied term protects Convention rights see J Atkinson, 'Implied Terms and Human Rights in the Contract of Employment' (2019) 48 *Industrial Law Journal* 515.

[183] L Lavrysen, *Human Rights in a Positive State: Rethinking the Relationship Between Positive and Negative Obligations Under the European Convention on Human Rights* (Cambridge, Intersentia, 2016); V Mantouvalou, 'The Human Rights Act and Labour Law at 20' in A Bogg, A Young, and J Rowbottom (eds), *The Constitution of Social Democracy: Essays in Honour of Keith Ewing* (Oxford, Hart, 2020) 20.

[184] *Redfearn v UK* (2013) 57 EHRR 2.

[185] H Collins and V Mantouvalou, '*Redfearn v UK*: Political Association and Dismissal' (2013) 76 *MLR* 909.

outside the unfair dismissal framework it appears that there will be a breach of the state's positive obligations. In these circumstances, however, section 3 of the HRA requires that the unfair dismissal framework be interpreted consistently with the state's duty to secure Convention rights. The legislation must therefore not be interpreted as preventing the common law from protecting employees' Convention rights. As a result, the HRA requires that the *Johnson* exclusion zone must not be applied where Convention rights are not protected by unfair dismissal and the common law would function to fulfil the state's protective duties.[186]

The fact that the exclusion zone applies 'subject to observance of fundamental rights' was acknowledged by Lord Hoffmann in *Johnson* itself.[187] Despite this, the extent and implications of the human rights exception have so far largely gone unrecognised.[188] The HRA means that mutual trust and confidence should not be excluded where a dismissal interferes with a Convention right and a claim for unfair dismissal is not available. This exception to the exclusion zone encompasses a wide range of circumstances. Although *Redfearn* led to the removal of the qualifying period for unfair dismissal claims involving political association there continue to be many instances where dismissals interfere with Convention rights but nevertheless fall outside the unfair dismissal framework. This includes employees dismissed before the qualifying period because of how they have exercised their rights to freedom of expression, religion, and private life among others.[189] But the human rights exception created by the HRA extends beyond cases where the reason the employee is dismissed is how they have exercised their Convention rights, and also encompasses dismissals which interfere with the Article 8 right to private life because of the severe impact they have on an employees' ability to form relationships or work in their chosen sector or profession.[190]

The potential scope of the human rights exception based in the HRA is therefore substantial and deserves greater recognition. In future the courts should refrain from applying the *Johnson* exclusion zone in cases where dismissals engage Convention rights but fall outside the protective scope of

[186] HRA 1998, s 6 also supports the application of trust and confidence in these circumstances, as it requires that courts apply and develop the common law in a manner compatible with the positive obligation to protect Convention rights. For discussion of this indirect horizontal effect see G Phillipson and A Williams, 'Horizontal Effect and the Constitutional Constraint' (2011) 74 *MLR* 878; A Young, 'Mapping Horizontal Effect' in D Hoffman (ed), *The Impact of the UK Human Rights Act on Private Law* (Cambridge, Cambridge University Press, 2011).

[187] *Johnson* (n 1) [37].

[188] Bogg and Collins (n 68) 208.

[189] As in, eg, *Barbulescu v Romania* [2017] IRLR 1032 (ECtHR); *Vogt v Germany* (1996) 21 EHRR 20; *Smith and Grady v UK* (1999) 29 EHRR 493; *Eweida v UK* (2013) 57 EHRR 8.

[190] *Denisov v Ukraine* App No 76639/11 (ECtHR, 25 September 2018). For discussion of when a dismissal may engage Convention rights see H Collins, 'An Emerging Human Right to Protection against Unjustified Dismissal' (2021) 50 *Industrial Law Journal* 36.

unfair dismissal.[191] The exception to pre-emption created by the principle of legality is more limited, but may become significant over time if the jurisprudence on common law constitutional rights develops or the rights protections contained in the HRA are removed.

VII. CONCLUSION

Writing at the turn of the century, Roger Rideout argued that labour lawyers should abandon their historical scepticism of the common law and recognise it was now capable of adequately regulating the employment relationship and defending workers' interests.[192] This might appear premature given what was to follow shortly in *Johnson*, where the common law was excluded from the vitally important area of dismissal and the House of Lords implicitly endorsed a subsidiary role for the common law in governing employment relations. However, the argument made in this chapter, that the pre-emption of the common law in *Johnson* was not required on constitutional grounds, supports the view that the common law can, and should, play a central role alongside legislation in protecting workers and securing fundamental rights.

The decision in *Johnson* will no doubt continue to divide opinion, with this divergence reflecting fundamental differences of opinion regarding the authority and legitimacy of the common law, the appropriate limits of the judicial role, and faith in the ability of Parliament to regulate employment relations. The uncertainty and apparent inconsistencies surrounding the case also illustrate a pressing need to develop a deeper and more nuanced understanding of when the common law will be pre-empted by legislation. We must do our best to live with the troubling legacy of *Johnson*, as there is little prospect of the decision being revisited or of statutory intervention. In addition to further work clarifying the boundaries of the exclusion zone and advancing our understanding of pre-emption, one promising way forward would be for the human rights exception to gain wider recognition and be applied by the courts.

[191] Although not explored here, the exclusion zone should also not be applied if the unfair dismissal framework falls short of fulfilling the UK's positive obligations under the ECHR by failing to strike a fair balance between the competing rights and interests at stake.

[192] R Rideout, 'The Lack of Principles in Labour Law' (2000) 53 *Current Legal Problems* 409.

13

Autoclenz v Belcher *(2011)*: *Divining 'The True Agreement Between the Parties'*

JEREMIAS ADAMS-PRASSL*

I. INTRODUCTION

'THE MANUFACTURE OF a five-pronged implement for manual digging results in a fork even if the manufacturer, unfamiliar with the English language, insists that he intended to make and has made a spade', Lord Templeman famously stated in *Street v Mountford*:[1] mere labels could not detract from the contractual terms agreed between parties.

But what about the owner of an algorithmically controlled service sector job app, who, quite familiar with the intricacies of modern employment legislation, insists that she intended to create and has created exciting (micro-) entrepreneurship opportunities, rather than old-fashioned employment, thus conveniently side-stepping a raft of worker-protective norms?

Avoidance attempts are as old as employment law itself. For a long time, however, UK employment law was barely equipped to deal with employers' stratagems to designate workers as self-employed contractors beyond the protective scope of the contract of employment, and subsequently the workers' contract. An exceedingly high threshold rarely, if ever, allowed courts to look beyond contractual terms, even if carefully crafted to that very end.

The turning point came in the Supreme Court's 2011 decision in *Autoclenz*.[2] Even though it was relatively quickly overtaken by subsequent litigation, this

* Magdalen College, Oxford. I am grateful to my co-editors as well as participants at a workshop in Oxford for feedback and discussion, and to the Leverhulme Trust and the European Research Council (Grant agreement No 947806) for funding support. The usual disclaimers apply.

[1] Street *v Mountford* [1985] AC 809 (HL). The situation is somewhat more complex in reality: see S Bright, H Glover, and J Prassl, 'Tenancy Agreements' in E Simpson and M Stewart (eds), *Sham Transactions* (Oxford, Oxford University Press, 2013).

[2] *Autoclenz Ltd v Belcher* [2011] UKSC 41, [2011] 4 All ER 745.

chapter argues that *Autoclenz* deserves recognition as a landmark case in employment law: by breaking with the strict *Snook* approach to contractual shams, it brought employment law back in line with other areas of domestic statutory regulation, as well as international labour standards and a surprisingly consistent approach in jurisdictions across the world. It opened a path for courts to recognise the socio-economic realities of workplace inequalities, and played an important role in the development of the law of the contract of employment as distinct from commercial practice. Finally, and perhaps most importantly, *Autoclenz* laid the foundations for what might come to be seen as a decisive step towards breaking with contractual analyses at the heart of the legal regulation of employment relationships altogether.

II. BEFORE *AUTOCLENZ*

At first glance, attempts at 'contracting out' from the protective scope of employment law are explicitly forbidden in statute. Section 203 of the Employment Rights Act 1996 provides that:

> (1) Any provision in an agreement (whether a contract of employment or not) is void in so far as it purports—
>
> (a) to exclude or limit the operation of any provision of this Act, …

Despite this provision, however, a number of employers have long sought to (mis-)classify their workforce as independent contractors. Strategies vary in complexity – from mere labels and Orwellian doublespeak to legal tools, whether in contract or corporate law, and increasingly even the deployment of sophisticated technology enabling the diffuse exercise of tight control.[3]

The rise of the gig or platform economy and its enthusiastic embrace of the language of 'gigs', 'tasks', 'rides', 'lifts', 'hustles', 'hits' and 'favo(u)rs' to replace the traditional vocabulary of the workplace has brought debates about employment status back to the forefront. There is little that is fundamentally new or distinct – but the 'gig economy … has taken such abuse to an entirely new and dubious level: … language has become a weapon to be used in direct defiance of employment regulation'.[4] In the spring of 2017, for example, it emerged that Deliveroo, a London-based food-delivery platform, had drawn up an extensive list of 'vocabulary guidelines' for staff interactions with its couriers, including a long number of 'dos and don'ts', complete with sample phrases. Workers were not to be hired and issued with a uniform – they were onboarded and sold an equipment pack. The couriers were not paid a wage for their work: rider service

[3] This 'control/accountability paradox' is beyond the scope of the present discussion. See J Adams-Prassl, 'What if your Boss was an Algorithm?' (2020) 41 *Comparative Labor Law and Policy Journal* 123.

[4] 'Employers Rely on Euphemisms to Hide Gig Economy Realities' *Financial Times* www.ft.com/content/a5709f84-1ab3-11e7-bcac-6d03d067f81f (accessed 13 April 2022).

invoices had to be submitted instead. And when things went wrong, no one was to be fired: 'We are terminating your Supplier Agreement due to your failure to meet Service Delivery Standards' instead.[5]

Whilst these labels might be new, there is plenty of historic precedent for more sophisticated legal attempts at avoiding the ascription of employer responsibilities In *O'Kelly*,[6] function waiters at the Grosvenor House Hotel employed under a rostering system were referred to as 'regular casuals', despite evidence that they had worked 'virtually every week [… for] up to as much as 57' hours.[7] In *Carmichael*, tour guides in a power station were referred to as 'casual as required' staff.[8]

In these and similar cases, contractual agreements had been drafted specifically to avoid employment status by inserting terms and conditions designed to deny key legal requirements, including notably personal service and mutuality of obligations. Examples from the case law include:

> For the avoidance of doubt, the Company shall be under no obligation to offer you work and you shall be under no obligation to accept such work from the Company.[9]
>
> In the event that the contractor is unable or unwilling to perform the services personally he shall arrange at his own expense entirely for another suitable person to perform the services.[10]

Another way in which employers have sought to avoid employment law liabilities is through the use of corporate structures, in particular personal service companies: individuals are asked to set up and operate their own limited company, which in turn provides their services to the client or end-user. The ensuing absence of a direct contractual relationship between the individual and the employer is designed to avoid employment law liability, at least insofar as the end-user undertaking is concerned.[11] Additional strategies include the use of limited liability partnerships,[12] or indeed a combination of multiple strategies.[13]

[5] S Butler, 'Deliveroo Accused of "Creating Vocabulary" to Avoid Calling Couriers Employees' *The Guardian* (London, 5 April 2017) www.theguardian.com/business/2017/apr/05/deliveroo-couriers-employees-managers (accessed 13 April 2022); 'Deliveroo Pedals the New Language of the Gig Economy' *Financial Times* www.ft.com/content/9ad4f936-1a26-11e7-bcac-6d03d067f81f (accessed 13 April 2022).

[6] *O'Kelly v Trusthouse Forte Plc* [1984] QB 90 (CA). See ch 8 in this volume; N Countouris, 'Uses and Misuses of "Mutuality of Obligations" and the Autonomy of Labour Law' in A Bogg, C Costello, A Davies and J Prassl (eds), *The Autonomy of Labour Law* (Oxford, Hart, 2014).

[7] *O'Kelly* (n 6) 101B, 124H.

[8] *Carmichael v National Power plc* [1999] UKHL 47, [1999] 1 WLR 2042.

[9] *Pimlico Plumbers Ltd v Smith* [2018] UKSC 29, [2018] 4 All ER 641 [18].

[10] *Express & Echo Publications Ltd v Tanton* [1999] ICR 693 (CA) 696.

[11] See, eg, the facts of *Halawi v WDFG UK Ltd* [2014] EWCA Civ 1387, [2015] 3 All ER 543 (albeit technically in the context of the Equality Act 2010). Excellent analysis of this approach is provided by M Ford, 'The Fissured Worker: Personal Service Companies and Employment Rights' (2020) 49 *Industrial Law Journal* 35.

[12] *Clyde & Co LLP & Anor v Bates van Winklehof* [2014] UKSC 32, [2014] ICR 730.

[13] See *Protectacoat Firthglow Ltd v Szilagyi* [2009] EWCA Civ 98, [2009] ICR 835 and the discussion of this case in the text to nn 45–52.

A. The Strict *Snook* Approach

Autoclenz is a landmark case in tackling at least some of the most egregious of these evasion attempts: but like many a tectonic shift, it was preceded by tremors resulting from excessively hardened positions.

A simple declaration or label was never enough to defeat the applicability of employment law.[14] What mattered were 'the rights conferred and the duties imposed by the contract … it [was] irrelevant that the parties declared [their relationship] to be something else'.[15] Other approaches, notably the reliance on personal service companies and carefully constructed contractual clauses, however, frequently succeeded in denying individuals protection as employees or workers.

The reason for this can be traced back to the 'sham' doctrine, developed in the context of commercial contracting. The classic principle was set out in *Snook v London East Riding*: the courts will only question aside a contractual agreement as a 'sham' if *both* parties were involved in nefarious dealings. As Diplock LJ put it,

> if sham has any meaning in law, it means acts done or documents executed by the parties to the 'sham' which are intended by them to give … the appearance of creating between the parties legal rights and obligations different from the actual legal rights and obligations (if any) which the parties intend to create. But one thing, I think, is clear in legal principle, morality and the authorities … that for acts or documents to be a 'sham', with whatever legal consequences follow from this, all the parties thereto must have a common intention that the acts or documents are not to create the legal rights and obligations which they give the appearance of creating.[16]

The stark implications of this approach when translated into the employment context can be illustrated with the judgment of Rimer LJ in *Consistent Group Ltd v Kalwak*.[17] Polish workers had been employed in Consistent Group's hospitality and food processing businesses, under contracts carefully drafted to deny both mutuality of obligations and personal service, even though this was not reflected in the reality of the parties' relationships.[18] The Employment Tribunal thus felt able to classify the contractual arrangements as shams, an approach which was approved by Elias P in the Employment Appeal Tribunal, instructing tribunals to look at 'the reality of the situation'.[19]

[14] *Ferguson v John Dawson & Partners Ltd* [1976] 1 WLR 1213 (CA).

[15] *Ready Mixed Concrete (South East) Ltd v Minister of Pensions and National Insurance* [1986] 2 QB 497 (QB) 512 (Mackenna J).

[16] *Snook v London and West Riding Investments Ltd* [1967] 2 QB 786 (CA) 802.

[17] *Consistent Group Ltd v Kalwak* [2008] EWCA Civ 430, [2008] IRLR 505.

[18] ibid [19]ff, setting out the Employment Tribunal Chairman's conclusions.

[19] *Consistent Group Ltd v Kalwak* [2007] IRLR 560 (EAT) [58]. For further details, see A Bogg, 'Sham Self-Employment in the Court of Appeal' (2010) 126 *LQR* 166, 167–68.

Giving the leading judgment in the Court of Appeal, Rimer LJ allowed the employer's appeal, explicitly endorsing the orthodox *Snook* approach: 'Was there any evidence on which [the Employment Tribunal] could have found that the [contractual arrangement] was a sham? The judgment does not identify any.'[20] Elias P's approach came in for strong criticism:

> It is not the function of the court or an employment tribunal to recast the parties' bargain. If a term solemnly agreed in writing is to be rejected in favour of a different one, that can only be done by a clear finding that the real agreement was to that different effect and that the term in the contract was included by them so as to present a misleadingly different impression.[21]

As a result of the Employment Tribunal and Employment Appeal Tribunal's departure from the orthodox *Snook* approach, the appeal was allowed, and the case remitted to the employment tribunal.[22]

B. UK (Employment) Law as an Outlier

In the run-up to *Autoclenz*, this strict approach in employment law had become quite anomalous – both when compared to other areas of English law, and also in contrast with other jurisdictions and international labour standards.

As seen in the opening paragraphs of this chapter, one of the first contexts in which the narrow strictures of the sham doctrine were abandoned several decades before *Autoclenz* is housing.[23] With the Rent Acts[24] imposing a series of obligations on leasehold contracts between landlords and tenants, the former frequently sought to characterise the legal arrangement as a mere contractual licence. The strategies are similar to those deployed in the employment context, from mere relabelling to the use of service company lets and contractual terms designed to disguise the true nature of the relationship, for example by stipulating shared use of the property even when impossible in practice.[25] As Lord Jauncey put it, such clauses should be seen as 'mere dressing up' to disguise the true nature of the contractual agreement, and could thus be disregarded.[26] Whilst the label of 'pretence' often deployed in the landlord and tenant cases has itself been subject to intense academic and judicial discussion, the overarching message is clear: the courts are ready to exclude 'non-genuine' terms where

[20] *Kalwak* (n 17) [28].
[21] ibid [40] (Rimer LJ).
[22] ibid [50], [52].
[23] S Bright, H Glover, and J Prassl, 'Tenancy Agreements' in E Simpson and M Stewart (eds), *Sham Transactions* (Oxford, Oxford University Press, 2013).
[24] The most recent of which is the Rent Act 1977, which is the latest iteration of a series of similar measures collectively known as the Rent Acts.
[25] See, eg, *AG Secruities v Vaughan* [1990] 1 AC 417 (HL).
[26] ibid 477.

necessary to give effect to the statutory provisions which motivated evasive attempts in the first place.[27]

Another context in which the law has long struggled to counteract sham transactions is taxation. An individual or corporation might try and enter into a series of transactions, designed to create artificial losses, which can then be offset against taxable income or capital gains. Whilst clearly designed to evade legal liability, such schemes do not always fit into the *Snook* sense of sham.[28] That, however, 'does not compel the court to look at a document or a transaction in blinkers, isolated from any context to which it properly belongs', as Lord Wilberforce explained in *Ramsay*: 'It is the task of the court to ascertain the legal nature of any transaction.'[29] The question, ultimately, was one of statutory construction. As more recent decisions emphasise.

The driving principle in the *Ramsay* line of cases continues to involve a general rule of statutory construction and an unblinkered approach to the analysis of the facts. The ultimate question is whether the relevant statutory provisions, construed purposively, were intended to apply to the transaction, viewed realistically.[30]

What these seemingly quite distinct areas of law have in common, Simpson argues, is that 'there is relevant legislation in play, and the purposes of that legislation may be influencing such developments at least as much as any analysis of what it is that the parties have done'[31] – an important point to consider in light of the development of *Autoclenz* in the Supreme Court's 2021 *Uber* decision, as explored further in section V, below.

The UK courts' strict approach to sham in employment law appears similarly anomalous when compared against other jurisdictions and international norms. Most employment jurisdictions recognise the principle of the primacy of facts.[32] The French Court de Cassation, for example, relied on the doctrine in reclassifying taxi drivers' rental contracts and franchised delivery services as employment contracts.[33] In *Île de la tentation*, the Social Chamber explicitly noted that neither 'the will expressed by the parties or … the name they have

[27] Bright, Glover and Prassl (n 23) 6.31ff.

[28] ibid 338. M Gammie, 'Tracing the Boundaries of Sham and *Ramsay*' in E Simpson and M Stewart (eds), *Sham Transactions* (Oxford, Oxford University Press, 2013) 12.14.

[29] *WT Ramsay Ltd v IRC* [1982] AC 300 (HL) 323–24.

[30] *Collector of Stamp Revenue v Arrowtown Assets Ltd* [2003] HKFCA 46, (2004) 6 ITLR 454 [35] (Ribeiro J); as endorsed by the House of Lords in *Barclays Mercantile Business Finance Ltd v Mawson* [2005] 1 AC 684 (HL) [35] and quoted in Gammie (n 28) 12.11.

[31] E Simpson, 'Sham and Purposive Construction' in E Simpson and M Stewart (eds), *Sham Transactions* (Oxford, Oxford University Press, 2013) 5.22. See also T Honoré, *The Quest for Security: Employees, Tenants, Wives* (London, Stevens, 1982).

[32] B Waas, 'Comparative Overview' in B Waas and GH van Voss (eds), *Restatement of Labour Law in Europe: Volume I The Concept of Employee* (London, Hart, 2017) li.

[33] Court de Cassation, Chambre Sociale, 19 December 2000, No 98-40572; Court de Cassation, Chambre Sociale, 4 December 2001, Nos 50105034, 35, and 36. For details, see F Kessler, 'The Concept of "Employee": The Position in France' in B Waas and GH van Voss (eds), *Restatement of Labour Law in Europe: Volume I The Concept of Employee* (London, Hart, 2017) 208–09.

given to their agreement', but only 'the conditions under which the activity of the workers is exercised' were relevant factors in determining the existence of an employment relationship.[34]

In Italy, the principle of primacy of fact is anchored in Article 4 of the Constitution, in which '[t]he Republic recognises the right of all citizens to work and promotes those conditions which render this right effective.'[35] In a high-profile decision in 1994, the Constitutional Court censured domestic labour courts for their excessive focus on the *nomen iuris* adopted by contracting parties: the 'concrete relationship and the modalities of work performance' were to trump 'the conditions agreed by the parties'.[36] German courts, too, seek to determine the 'true nature' of a purported employment contract, rather than looking to contractual terms alone.[37] The principle is closely linked to the rule of law. According to the Federal Labour Court,

> the basic idea of employment law as an instrument of protecting employees from the (regularly economically more powerful) employer would be impaired if the latter could set aside this protection by simply using contractual language that points in the direction of a 'free service contract.[38]

Many US states similarly recognise the principle. When the Court of Appeals for the Ninth Circuit in 2014 upheld FedEx drivers' claims that they were employees under Californian law, with Circuit Judge Trott adding the following observations:

> Abraham Lincoln reportedly asked, 'If you call a dog's tail a leg, how many legs does a dog have?' His answer was, 'Four. Calling a dog's tail a leg does not make it a leg.' Justice Cardozo made the same point … counselling us, when called upon to characterize a written enactment, to look to the 'underlying reality rather than the form or label.' … Bottom line? Labeling the drivers 'independent contractors' in FedEx's Operating Agreement does not conclusively make them so.[39]

[34] Court de Cassation, Chambre Sociale 3 June 2009, Nos 08-04982 et seq (translation by Kessler (n 33)).

[35] *Constitution of the Italian Republic* www.senato.it/documenti/repository/istituzione/costituzione_inglese.pdf (accessed 13 April 2022).

[36] Corte Costituzionale, Judgment of 31 March 1994. For details, see E Ales, 'The Concept of "Employee": The Position in Italy' in B Waas and GH van Voss (eds), *Restatement of Labour Law in Europe: Volume I The Concept of Employee* (London, Hart, 2017) 366–67.

[37] Bundesarbeitsgericht, Judgment of 19 November 1997 – 5 AZR 653/96. For details, see B Waas, 'The Concept of "Employee": The Position in Germany' in B Waas and GH van Voss (eds), *Restatement of Labour Law in Europe: Volume I The Concept of Employee* (London, Hart, 2017) 268–69.

[38] Waas (n 37), citing Federal Civil Court of 25 June 2002 – X ZR 83/00.

[39] *Alexander v FedEx Ground Package System* 764 F 3d 981 (9th Cir 2014). It is important to note that not all decisions in the FedEx litigation came to the same conclusion: given the wide range of tests used for employment classification across different US states and statutes, this is not necessarily surprising. See M Cherry, 'Beyond Misclassification: The Digital Transformation of Work' (2016) 37 *Comparative Labor Law and Policy Journal* 577.

Primacy of facts has also been firmly established as a principle of international law, notably in the International Labour Organisation's Employment Relationship Recommendation: worker classification 'should be guided primarily by the facts relating to the performance of work and the remuneration of the worker, notwithstanding how the relationship is characterized in any contrary arrangement, contractual or otherwise, that may have been agreed between the parties'.[40] A closely aligned approach is reflected in EU law, notably by the Court of Justice's decision in *FNV Kunsten*.[41] When faced with individuals who are potentially '"false self-employed", that is to say, service providers in a situation comparable to that of employees', the Court recalled, 'the classification of a "self-employed person" under national law does not prevent that person being classified as an employee within the meaning of EU law if his independence is merely notional, thereby disguising an employment relationship'.[42]

C. Towards a Recognition of Socio-Economic Realities

Whether compared with domestic law in other regulatory domains or with domestic law in Europe and the US, as well as international law at the European and International Labour Organisation level, it is clear that the narrow *Snook* approach was a far outlier in restricting employment tribunals' attention to the written terms of individuals' contracts.

Some fractures accordingly began to appear in the edifice. We have already encountered the attempt by Elias P in the Employment Appeal Tribunal in *Kalwak* to explore 'the reality of the situation', which could not be altered by unrealistic express contractual provisions.[43] This was driven not least by a concern at the prospect that 'armies of lawyers will simply place substitution clauses, or clauses denying any obligation to accept or provide work in employment contracts, as a matter of form, even where such terms do not begin to reflect the real relationship'[44] – and promptly rejected by Rimer LJ upon appeal.

Perhaps the clearest departure from *Snook*, and thus the Court of Appeal's decision in *Kalwak*, came in the judgment of Smith LJ in *Protectacoat v Szilagyi*.[45] The employer there had combined a number of stratagems in attempting to misclassify the claimant as an independent contractor, including a partnership

[40] International Labour Organisation, Recommendation 198 of 2006 [9]. For a detailed guide, see ILO, *Regulating the Employment Relationship in Europe: A Guide to Recommendation No 198* (Geneva, 2013) 33ff.

[41] Case C-413/13 *FNV Kunsten Informatie en Media v Staat der Nederlanden* [2015] 4 CMLR 1.

[42] ibid [31], [35].

[43] *Kalwak* (n 19) [58]. For further details, see Bogg (n 19) 167–68.

[44] *Kalwak* (n 19) [57] (Elias P).

[45] *Protectacoat v Szilagyi* (n 13). Though *cf* her Ladyship's comment (at [48]) that 'it seems … that Rimer LJ approved the test as enunciated by Elias J as being in compliance with Diplock LJ's definition of a sham'.

agreement and a services contract explicitly denying mutuality of obligations.[46] In upholding the Tribunal's finding that these arrangements amounted to a sham, her Ladyship surveyed the authorities including *Kalwak*, concluding that

> [w]ith great respect to Rimer LJ, it appears … that Elias J's way of putting the question may be of greater assistance to employment judges when deciding whether a services agreement is a sham … To speak of terms 'solemnly agreed in writing' is more redolent of a commercial agreement reached between two parties of equal bargaining power than the kind of 'take it or leave it' situation which can prevail in some agreements in the field of work.[47]

The test was 'always what the true legal relationship is between the parties. If there is a contractual document, that is ordinarily where the answer is to be found. But, if … the document does not represent or describe the true relationship, the court or tribunal has to decide what the true relationship is.'[48]

The socio-economic reality underpinning most employment relationships was central to this approach – 'in the field of work, it is sometimes on party and only one which dictates the terms of the "agreement"'.[49] In endorsing Smith LJ's approach, Sedley LJ went potentially even further in questioning the applicability of the sham doctrine, suggesting that tribunals

> ask in a case like this not whether the written agreement is a sham but simply what the true legal relationship is. Although there will be in many cases (as there was in this one) an intention to conceal or misrepresent the actual relationship, there is no logical reason why this should be a universal requirement.[50]

The 'refreshingly enlightened' decision in *Protectacoat* was warmly welcomed in the academic literature, not least for its recognition 'that employment usually involves unequal bargaining power', and a realignment of employment law with other areas such as land law.[51] It was 'nevertheless … too early to declare the death of contract', as Davies concluded: '*Protectacoat Firthglow* has demolished one big hurdle faced by claimants, but a number of others remain.'[52]

III. *AUTOCLENZ*

The claimants in *Autoclenz* were 20 valets, providing car-cleaning services to British Car Auctions in Measham, Derbyshire, through the eponymous company,

[46] ibid [11]–[12].
[47] ibid [51].
[48] ibid [55] (Smith LJ).
[49] ibid [52] (Smith LJ).
[50] ibid [74].
[51] ACL Davies, 'Sensible Thinking About Sham Transactions: *Protectacoat Firthglow Ltd v Szilagyi*' (2009) 38 *Industrial Law Journal* 318, 327.
[52] ibid 327–28.

a country-wide provider of business-to-business car cleaning and valet services. They brought a series of claims under the National Minimum Wage Act 1998, and the Working Time Regulations 1998,[53] which inter alia set out entitlements to be paid a minimum wage and receive paid holidays. In order to qualify, the valets had to show that they were employees or workers, defined in the relevant provisions as

> (3) … an individual who has entered into or works under (or, where the employment has ceased, worked under)—
>
> (a) a contract of employment, or
>
> (b) any other contract, whether express or implied and (if it is express) whether oral or in writing, whereby the individual undertakes to do or perform personally any work or services for another party to the contract whose status is not by virtue of the contract that of a client or customer of any profession or business undertaking carried on by the individual.[54]

The sample claimant, Paul Huntington, was described as a 'sub-contractor' in his original contract of June 1991. The original contractual terms included confirmation that he was 'a self-employed independent contractor', who 'agree[d] and acknowledge[d] that the Sub-contractor is not, and that it is the intention of the parties that the Sub-contractor should not become, an employee of Autoclenz'.[55] Following a 2004 review of Autoclenz's employment arrangement by the Inland Revenue which seemed to challenge the company's assertions, new and more extensive documentation was issued in 2007.

First, there was a document which required confirmation that the valets' relationship with Autoclenz was 'one of client and independent contractor and not one of employer/employee', as well as setting out a number of internal management rules, including a (limited) right to engage substitutes, and specifications for overalls and cleaning materials to be supplied, before concluding that

> YOU WILL NOT BE OBLIGED TO PROVIDE YOUR SERVICES ON ANY PARTICULAR OCCASION NOR, IN ENTERING INTO SUCH AGREEEMENT, DOES AUTOCLENZ UNDERTAKE ANY OBLIGATION TO ENGAGE YOUR SERVICES ON ANY PARTICULAR OCCASION.[56]

Mr Huntington and his fellow valets were asked to sign a second document, which reflected many of the original terms of his 1991 contract.[57] This was designed to provide watertight protection against employment claims to Autoclenz – with some apparent success: '[i]f the relevant contract was, as a matter of law, solely contained in those two documents,' Lord Clarke explained, 'it would be

[53] SI 1998/1833.

[54] Employment Rights Act 1996, s 230(3). Materially identical provisions can be found in s 54(3) of the National Minimum Wage Act 1998 and Regulation 2(1) of the Working Time Regulations 1998.

[55] *Autoclenz* (n 2) [4].

[56] ibid [8].

[57] ibid [9] and Annex to the Judgment.

impossible to bring the cases within limb (a) of the [statutory] definition and very difficult to bring it within limb (b).'[58]

Upon closer investigation of the contracting process, the Employment Tribunal found that whilst Autoclenz had not sought to hide its workers' legal status, all terms and conditions of employment were unilaterally imposed.[59] The weight of evidence that the valets were not independent contractors was overwhelming, given a lack of control over how and when the work was to be done, no economic interest in the long-term success of the enterprise, provision of materials, and clearly structured team work. Invoices were generated by the employer, who also set the levels of deductions for associated cost and determined wage increases and deductions unilaterally.[60]

The site manager's evidence before the tribunal furthermore confirmed that claimants were required to provide personal service, the contractual clauses to the contrary notwithstanding: valets had to notify the site manager in advance if unavailable for work on any given day, and in turn offered 'work provided that it was there for them to do'.[61]

A. Appellate History

Applying the approach set out in Elias P's judgment in *Consistent Group Ltd v Kalwak*, the Employment Tribunal set out to determine 'whether the written agreement between Autoclenz and the valeters described the true nature of the relationship between them. He was satisfied that it did not'.[62] On the basis of these facts, it was unsurprising that Employment Judge Foxwell concluded that the claimants had entered into contracts of employment, with all the hallmarks of personal service, mutuality of obligations, and tight employer control: 'the claimants entered into contracts under which they provided personal service, where there were mutual obligations ... and that the degree of control exercised by Autoclenz ... placed them in the category of contracts of employment'.[63]

On the employer's appeal, discussion before the Employment Appeal Tribunal focused on whether the employment judge had misdirected himself in law by adopting Elias P's test in *Kalwak*. HH Judge Clark did so find in the light of Rimer LJ's explicit disapproval and emphasis on the written terms of the agreement; as there had been no evidence of any mutual intention to mislead, the case

[58] ibid [10].

[59] ibid [11].

[60] *Autoclenz Ltd v Belcher* (Employment Tribunal, 1 March 2008) [35], as cited in *Autoclenz* (n 2) [37].

[61] *Autoclenz Ltd v Belcher* (Employment Tribunal, 1 March 2008) [37], as cited in *Autoclenz* (n 2) [37].

[62] *Autoclenz Ltd v Belcher* [2009] EWCA Civ 1046, [2010] IRLR 70 [30] (Smith LJ).

[63] *Autoclenz Ltd v Belcher* (Employment Tribunal, 1 March 2008) [38], as cited in *Autoclenz* (n 2) [37].

would not be remitted to the Employment Tribunal. At the same time, however, the Employment Appeal Tribunal upheld Foxwell J's alternative conclusion, *viz* that there had been an undertaking personally to perform the work, and the valets were accordingly reclassified as limb (b) workers.[64]

The Court of Appeal restored the Employment Tribunal's finding that the claimants were employees. Giving the leading judgment, Smith LJ reasserted her (with respect, difficult to accept) earlier position that there was little by way of difference in the approach taken by the authorities, and held that 'where there is a dispute as to the genuineness of a written term in a contract, the focus on the enquiry must be to discuss the actual legal obligations of the parties. To carry out that exercise, the tribunal will have to examine all the relevant evidence.'[65]

Aikens and Sedley LLJ agreed with reinstating the Employment Tribunal's findings; albeit on distinct grounds: 'whereas Aikens LJ's reasoning embodies a striking endorsement of the orthodox "contract law" approach to the task of characterising contractual arrangements, this can be contrasted with Sedley LJ's equally striking endorsement of a more purposive "labour law" approach'.[66] As Bogg explains, 'although Smith LJ's judgment is elusive on the point [as to which approach should be preferred], dispensing with the terminology of "sham" suggests a tentative alignment with Aikens LJ's contractual approach', thus giving rise to serious concerns: 'If this is the future of the doctrine, that will be the biggest swindle of all, as the radical promise of a purposive "labour law" sham doctrine disappears from view almost as rapidly as it appeared in the EAT in *Kalwak*.'[67]

B. In the Supreme Court

The stage was thus set for the Supreme Court's decision. Having set out the detailed facts and appellate history, Lord Clarke (with whom Lords Hope, Walker, Collins, and Wilson agreed) turned to the appropriate legal test in determining 'what were the terms of the agreement', endorsing Aikens LJ's approach in the Court of Appeal, particularly as regards the parol evidence rule in *L'Estrange v Graucob Ltd* [1934] 2 KB 394.[68] Whilst highlighting that '[n]othing in [the Supreme Court's] judgment [was] intended in any way to alter those principles, which apply to ordinary contracts and, in particular to commercial contracts', however, his Lordship also recognised 'a body of case law in the context of employment contracts in which a different approach has been taken', in particular, the decisions of the Employment Appeal Tribunal

[64] *Autoclenz* (n 62) [31]–[34].
[65] ibid [53].
[66] Bogg (n 19) 169.
[67] ibid 169, 171.
[68] *Autoclenz* (n 2) [20].

and Court of Appeal discussed in section II.C, above.[69] In any event, *Snook*-style shams were not the 'only circumstance in which the court may disregard a written term which is not part of the true agreement', as the landlord and tenant cases had shown.[70]

When faced with the competing approaches of Rimer LJ and Elias P in the earlier decisions, and in line with academic analyses by Alan Bogg and Anne Davies,[71] Lord Clarke 'unhesitatingly prefer[red] the approach of Elias J in *Kalwak* and of the Court of Appeal in *Szilagyi*' and *Autoclenz* itself: 'The question in every case is … what was the true agreement between the parties.'[72]

The context-specific approach to divining that 'true agreement' as developed in the lower courts was justified by the socio-economic realities of employment relationships, a 'critical difference between [employment law cases] and the ordinary commercial dispute':

> The relative bargaining power of the parties must be taken into account in deciding whether the terms of any written agreement in truth represent what was agreed and the true agreement will often have to be gleaned from all the circumstances of the case, of which the written agreement is only a part. This may be described as a purposive approach to the problem. If so, I am content with that description.[73]

On this basis, Lord Clarke entirely agreed with Sedley LJ's conclusion in the Court of Appeal the 'elaborate protestations in the contractual documents that the men were self-employed were odd in themselves and, when examined, bore no practical relation to the reality of the relationship'.[74] As a result, the claimant valets were limb (a) employees, and, whilst the question as to their limb (b) worker status did therefore not arise, 'like the Employment Tribunal, [his Lordship] would have held that they were in any event working under contracts within' the latter category.[75]

IV. *AUTOCLENZ:* IMMEDIATE IMPLICATIONS

Do the immediate repercussions of *Autoclenz* justify its status as a landmark case? The evidence is mixed: whilst it proved an important step in the right direction insofar as a strict application of the *Snook* test was for once at all rejected in the employment context, the Supreme Court's decision left unanswered a host of fundamental questions recognised in extensive academic commentary, whilst subsequent litigation quickly showed continued vulnerability to more sophisticated attempts by employers to avoid the application of employment law norms.

[69] ibid [21]–[22].
[70] ibid [23].
[71] Specifically, Bogg (n 19); Davies (n 51).
[72] *Autoclenz* (n 2) [29].
[73] ibid [34], [35] (Lord Clarke).
[74] ibid [36], citing the Court of Appeal decision in *Autoclenz* (n 62) [104].
[75] ibid [39] (Lord Clarke).

A. Academic Reaction

The general tenor in academic commentary was welcoming of a 'judicial decision of profound importance in the development of the common law of the personal employment contract', albeit with the potential to turn into a 'mixed blessing'.[76] Whilst arguing that 'the Supreme Court in *Autoclenz* ha[d] not strayed too far from the doctrines and techniques … in the Commercial Court's toolkit', for example, Bogg suggested that the decision had nonetheless opened up at least 'three more radical lines of development':[77] a much broader understanding of admissible evidence in interpreting the terms and conditions of personal employment; a shift from contractual interpretation to contractual characterisation; and, perhaps most importantly, a shift towards more explicit purposive interpretation. Indeed, a 'strong purposive approach' would suggest 'that any interpretative doubts will be resolved in the putative worker's favour, so as to further the protective reach of the specific statutory right being claimed'.[78] Ultimately, however, the continuing significance of contractual interpretation, even if set against the socioeconomic realities of employment relationships, meant that '[w]hether this acquisition of relative doctrinal autonomy is enough to render the device of contract something other than an instrument of subordination for working people must, for the time being at least, remain an open question.'[79]

Davies similarly notes that employment lawyers' welcome of the *Autoclenz* decision was 'hardly surprising, since the courts' traditional approach had been the subject of considerable criticism within the discipline',[80] reflecting at the same time on the uncertainty left behind as to the future of contractual and purposive interpretation. While 'a better explanation of the decision … [would be] to acknowledge the role being played by the statutory regime of protection for employees and workers', ultimately, the 'debate about whether employment relationships should be treated as a matter of status or of contract therefore remain[ed] unresolved'.[81]

Simpson, on the other hand, clearly characterised *Autoclenz* as one of two ways of tackling 'avoidance-motivated transactions' – 'escap[ing] the restrictive *Snook* formulation of the factual circumstances to which the sham doctrine is applicable' by extending it to include settings of unequal bargaining power. This he contrasts with 'some form of purposive, or extended, statutory construction. The modern understanding of the *Ramsay* technique, denying the desired effect

[76] A Bogg, 'Sham Self-Employment in the Supreme Court' (2012) 41 *Industrial Law Journal* 328, 344–45.
[77] ibid 336.
[78] ibid 343.
[79] ibid 344.
[80] ACL Davies, 'Employment Law' in E Simpson and M Stewart (eds), *Sham Transactions* (Oxford, Oxford University Press, 2013) 10.40.
[81] ibid 10.47.

to certain transactions in the face of relevant taxing statutes, is of this kind.'[82] However, he also recognised that 'it would equally be possible for both types of analysis to be available in certain circumstances'.[83]

B. Implications in Practice

The practical implications of *Autoclenz* were similarly mixed. On the one hand, the decision is clearly a milestone in English law's broader move away from treating contracts of employment with the tools of commercial law, as well as opening an avenue for arguments based on purposive interpretation; on the other, it has failed to provide a silver bullet to the plethora of evasion strategies which continue to be deployed by employers across the socio-economic spectrum.

The core themes of Lord Clarke's speech in *Autoclenz* continue to resonate in subsequent appellate decisions, even where the case is not explicitly referenced. In *Braganza v BP Shipping Ltd*, for example, the Supreme Court explicitly noted the 'significant imbalance of power between the contracting parties as there often will be in an employment contract' in deciding that employers' exercise of broad discretionary powers should come under increased scrutiny when compared to traditional arms-length commercial bargains.[84] The purposive approach has similarly been reflected in subsequent judgments on employment status, for example in Baroness Hale's emphasis on consistency 'with the underlying policy' of whistle-blower protection legislation in *Bates van Winkelhof*,[85] or Lord Wilson's explanation of Parliament's 'view that, while only employees under a contract of service should have full statutory protection against various forms of abuse by employers of their stronger economic position in the relationship, there were self-employed people whose services were so largely encompassed within the business of others that they should also have limited protection, in particular against discrimination but also against certain forms of exploitation on the part of those others' in *Pimlico Plumbers*.[86]

Autoclenz was also enthusiastically embraced by the Employment Tribunals, notably in grappling with a surge of claims for limb (b) status brought by gig economy workers. In *Dewhurst v Citysprint UK Ltd*, for example, a cycle courier brought a claim for unpaid holiday pay in the face of contractual documentation alleging that she was an independent contractor.[87] In determining the appropriate legal test, Employment Judge Wade turned to *Autoclenz* to determine

[82] E Simpson, 'Sham and Purposive Statutory Construction' in E Simpson and M Stewart (eds), *Sham Transactions* (Oxford, Oxford University Press, 2013) 5.04.

[83] ibid 5.05.

[84] *Braganza v BP Shipping Ltd* [2015] UKSC 17, [2015] 1 WLR 1661.

[85] *Clyde & Co LLP v Bates van Winkelhof* [2014] UKSC 32, [2014] 1 WLR 2047.

[86] *Pimlico Plumbers* (n 9) [9].

[87] *Dewhurst v Citysprint UK Ltd* (Employment Tribunal, 5 January 2017).

what primacy, if any, should be given to the contractual agreement between the parties, concluding that in 'the post-*Autoclenz* … era I understand the law to be that whilst the express terms of the contract are key pieces in the jigsaw, the bar is a low one before the true situation can be explored. … As Lord Clarke said, I have to look at all the circumstances.'[88] Given the 'inequality of bargaining power at work' in the courier's relationship with the delivery service,[89] it was clear on the facts that Ms Dewhurst was a worker.

There is, then, a pervasive sense of rupture following the Supreme Court's decision: 'I do not think that the old pre-*Autoclenz* cases of *Mingeley v Pennock* and *Smith v Hewitson* have enough weight to impact on these conclusions.'[90] At the same time, however, *Autoclenz* has proved unable to defeat all attempts at worker misclassification. When the Independent Workers' Union of Great Britain sought statutory recognition by RooFoods Ltd, operators of the Deliveroo gig economy platform, it was common ground between the parties that *Autoclenz* was the correct legal approach for the Central Arbitration Committee to take.[91] At the outset, the CAC noted an important limitation of the Supreme Court's approach: 'the question of whether Deliveroo's true purpose in constructing the contracts as they did was to avoid their Riders gaining worker status is not relevant[;] the proper question is what was actually achieved'.[92] As the company had been able to demonstrate that on (rare) occasion drivers had in fact made use of the substitution clause, the Riders could not qualify as limb (b) workers. As counsel for the Respondent argued,

> [e]ven if [that option existed solely] in order to defeat this claim and in order to prevent the Riders from being classified as workers, then that too was permissible: all that mattered was the terms of the agreement, analysed in the holistic and realistic way set out in *Autoclenz*.[93]

Autoclenz has similarly failed to address the personal service company evasion route. Whilst Ford has identified a 'patchwork of means by which domestic law might protect some employment rights of individuals engaged via PSCs in some circumstances', he also notes that '[i]n almost no case is there a simple, secure legal link between the substantive right and a legal claim by the individual.'[94] The *Autoclenz* approach is thus unlikely to extend to personal service companies, especially where they have played an actual role in the transaction (such as by receiving payment from the putative employer).[95]

[88] ibid [59], [63].
[89] ibid [49] (Wade J).
[90] ibid [77] (Wade J).
[91] *Independent Workers' Union of Great Britain v RooFoods Ltd* [2018] IRLR 84 (CAC) [93].
[92] ibid [94].
[93] ibid [99]. See now (post-Uber) also *Independent Workers' Union of Great Britain v CAC* [2021] EWCA Civ 952, [2022] ICR 84.
[94] Ford (n 11) 79.
[95] ibid 75–77.

V. BEYOND AUTOCLENZ: UBER

None of this is to doubt the fact that *Autoclenz* is a landmark case in labour law. In hindsight, however, its most important and lasting significance may well become seen as providing a crucial stepping stone on the way to the Supreme Court's decision in *Aslam* v *Uber*.

The employment status of Uber drivers was the first gig economy decision to reach the UK Supreme Court. The company's business model requires little explanation, and has become an archetype of the organisation of platform-mediated work.[96] This is true in particular as regards its carefully crafted complex contractual structures which underpin the transport provision, and combine many of the evasion strategies encountered thus far. The language of 'Partner Terms' and 'Services Agreement[s]' is not surprising in and of itself. What is more perplexing, on the other hand, is the fact that the contractual arrangements then refer to drivers as 'Customers' and passengers as 'Users'. Under this setup, Uber purports to provide electronic services […] to the driver, which include access to the Uber app and payment services, and the driver agrees to provide transportation services to passengers […]. The agreement states that the Customer acknowledges and agrees that Uber BV does not provide transportation services and that, where the Customer accepts a User's request for transportation services made through the Uber app, the Customer is responsible for providing those transportation services and, by doing so, 'creates a legal and direct business relationship between Customer and the User, to which neither Uber [BV] nor any of its Affiliates in the Territory is a party'.[97]

Further complex arrangements regulate the relationship between different corporate entities on Uber's side, including a Dutch parent company (Uber BV), operator of the Uber app, and UK subsidiaries (Uber London Ltd and Uber Britannia Ltd), which hold the relevant private hire licences in London and the rest of the country, respectively.[98]

A. Litigation History

The Uber litigation spanned a period of five years. In 2016, a group of Uber drivers led by Yaseen Aslam and James Farrar brought a number of claims, including for failure to pay the National Minimum Wage and grant paid annual leave, against the platform. In a first instance judgment handed down that autumn, Employment Judge Snelson at the London Central Employment Tribunal was

[96] J Prassl, *Humans as a Service: The Promise and Perils of Work in the Gig Economy* (Oxford, Oxford University Press, 2017) ch 1. See also *Uber BV v Aslam* [2021] UKSC 5, [2021] 4 All ER 209 [6]–[21].

[97] *Uber* (n 96) [24].

[98] ibid [3], [30]–[33].

unequivocal in finding that claimant drivers were workers, rather than independent contractors. The language in *Aslam, Farrar v Uber* was unusually pointed. The tribunal, the judge noted, were struck by the remarkable lengths to which Uber has gone in order to compel agreement with its (perhaps we should say its lawyers') description of itself and with its analysis of the legal relationships between the two companies, the drivers and the passengers. Any organisation (a) running an enterprise at the heart of which is the function of carrying people in motor cars … (c) requiring drivers and passengers to agree, as a matter of contract, that it does not provide transportation services … and (d) resorting in its documentation to fictions, twisted language and even brand new terminology, merits, we think, a degree of scepticism. Reflecting on [the platform's] general case, and on the grimly loyal evidence of [Uber Manager] Ms Bertram in particular, we cannot help being reminded of Queen Gertrude's most celebrated line:

> The lady doth protest too much, methinks.[99]

A detailed analysis of the facts before the tribunal led to the conclusion that Uber's extensive contractual documentation did not reflect the reality of its relationship with the drivers, and was therefore to be disregarded. 'This is, we think, an excellent illustration of the phenomenon of which Elias J warned in the *Kalwak* case of "armies of lawyers" contriving documents in their clients' interests which simply misrepresent the true rights and obligations on both sides.'[100] As a result, 'just as in *Autoclenz*, the employer is precluded from relying upon its carefully crafted documentation because, we find, it bears no relation to reality'.[101]

In November 2017, the Employment Tribunal's decision was fully vindicated in a carefully argued decision denying Uber's appeal. Her Honour Judge Eady QC, sitting in the London Employment Appeal Tribunal, upheld the first instance decision, confirming the drivers' worker status. Whilst more measured in terms of language, her substantive finding on the question of worker status was unequivocal. Uber's appeal had focused on the argument that in the absence of direct contractual relationships as set up in its terms and conditions, the business model could be explained in entirety as the result of regulatory requirements, including in particular Transport for London's Private Hire Licensing regime,[102] and that the purely commercial approach in *Secret Hotels2* was to inform the construction of the parties' contractual agreements.[103] In rejecting these arguments, HHJ Eady emphasised the importance of *Autoclenz*, 'that is an approach properly to be described as "purposive", taking into account the

[99] *Aslam v Uber BV* (London Employment Tribunal, 28 October 2016) [87] (citations omitted).
[100] ibid [96] (citations omitted).
[101] ibid [93].
[102] *Uber BV v Aslam* [2018] ICR 453 (EAT) [32]ff.
[103] *Secret Hotels2 Ltd v Revenue and Customs Commissioners* [2014] UKSC 16, [2014] 2 All ER 685.

relative bargaining power of the parties when deciding whether the terms of any written agreement represented their true intentions'.[104] She thus returned to the key question at stake:

> The issue at the heart of the appeal can be simply put: when the drivers are working, who are they working for? The ET's answer to this question was that there was a contract between ULL and the drivers whereby the drivers personally undertook work for ULL as part of its business of providing transportation services to passengers in the London area.[105]
>
> Following extensive scrutiny of Uber's challenges to the tribunal's judgment, the Employment Appeal Tribunal was 'satisfied [that] the ET did not err either in its approach or in its conclusions … [and was therefore] entitled to conclude there was a [worker] contract between [Uber] and the drivers'.[106]
>
> Just over a year later, in December 2018, the majority of the Court of Appeal arrived at a similar conclusion in rejecting Uber's further appeal. The Master of the Rolls, Sir Terence Etherton, and Bean LJ found that the Employment Tribunal had been 'not only entitled, but correct, to find that each of the Claimant drivers was working for [Uber] as a "limb (b) worker".'[107]

At this point in the litigation, the company's focus had firmly turned to the relationship between its written contractual arrangement (which it argued conclusively settled the question as to worker status) and the facts as determined by the Employment Tribunal. Adopting a nuanced position to determining the contractual position, and carefully highlighting relevant factors in support of both sides' arguments, the majority adopted a broad reading of the Supreme Court's '*Autoclenz*' sham contracting doctrine:

> We consider that the extended meaning of 'sham' endorsed in *Autoclenz* provides the common law with ample flexibility to address the convoluted, complex and artificial contractual arrangements, no doubt formulated by a battery of lawyers, unilaterally drawn up and dictated by Uber to tens of thousands of drivers and passengers, not one of whom is in a position to correct or otherwise resist the contractual language. As to the reality, not only do we see no reason to disagree with the factual conclusions of the ET as to the working relationship between Uber and the drivers, but we consider that the ET was plainly correct.[108]

Underhill LJ, on the other hand, disagreed with the approach adopted by his brethren, notably with regard to the extent that *Autoclenz* could assist the drivers case: the case could not

> be treated as a tool to re-write any disadvantageous contractual provision that results from the disparity of bargaining power between (putative) employer and (putative)

[104] *Uber* (n 102) [99].
[105] ibid [103].
[106] ibid [116] (Eady J).
[107] *Uber BV v Aslam* [2018] EWCA Civ 2748, [2019] 3 All ER 489 [71].
[108] ibid [105] (Sir Terence Etherton and Bean LJ).

> worker: in cases of the present kind the problem is not that the written terms misstate the true relationship but that the relationship created by them is one that the law does not protect.

On the basis of this reticence to depart from the contractual terms set out, above, his Lordship instead gave precedence to the intricate set of arrangements put in place by the company: 'standing back so as to be able to see the wood as well as the trees, it still seems to me that the relationship argued for by Uber is neither unrealistic nor artificial. On the contrary, it is in accordance with a well-recognised model for relationships in the private hire car business'.[109]

This split, Bogg and Ford argued, 'highlights the uncertain effect of *Autoclenz*' in scenarios where the difference between the factual matrix and the contractual term was less stark than what had happened in *Autoclenz*.[110] The way forward, they suggested was to recognise the 'two distinct streams' in previous decisions – contractual analysis, and '"statutory" *Autoclenz*' with an emphasis on purposive interpretation. The litigation thus offered a unique opportunity 'to clarify the distinctive ambits of "contractual" and "statutory" *Autoclenz*, and to give the purposive "statutory" dimension of *Autoclenz* a more prominent role'.[111]

B. The Supreme Court Ruling

In a decision handed down on 19 February 2021, seven Justices unanimously rejected Uber's final appeal, and fully vindicated the Employment Tribunal's findings both as to employment status and the applicability of the working time regime.

Following a detailed analysis of the relevant facts, statutory provisions, and litigation history, Lord Leggatt, with whom all Justices agreed, first turned to the core of submissions made on Uber's behalf, viz. whether drivers were 'performing services solely for and under contracts made with passengers through the agency of Uber London', rather than working for the platform.[112] Having rejected Uber's arguments as to the importance of the private hire licensing regime and its role as a booking agent on 'ordinary principles of the law of contract and agency',[113] his Lordship turned to the central question: in determining worker status, is the interpretation of the parties' written agreements an appropriate starting point?[114]

The answer to this question required a detailed examination of *Autoclenz*. Given that inequality of bargaining power can be a feature of contractual

[109] ibid [146].
[110] A Bogg and M Ford, 'Between Statute and Contract: Who is a Worker?' (2019) 135 *LQR* 347.
[111] ibid.
[112] *Uber* (n 96) [42].
[113] ibid [45].
[114] ibid [57].

relations in various contexts, Lord Leggatt set out to explore more fully the 'theoretical justification for [the *Autoclenz*] approach'. The critical distinction, his Lordship suggested, could be found in the fact that 'the rights asserted by the claimants were not contractual rights but were created by legislation. Thus, … the primary question was one of statutory interpretation, not contractual interpretation.'[115]

The appropriate approach was thus 'to have regard to the purpose of a particular provision and to interpret its language, so far as possible, in the way which best gives effect to that purpose'.[116] In the context of employment legislation, that meant the protection of vulnerable workers. Given their subordination to employer control, 'such relations cannot safely be left to contractual regulation'.[117] To do otherwise 'would reinstate the mischief which the legislation was enacted to prevent'. Indeed, the efficacy of [employment law] protection would be seriously undermined if the putative employer could by the way in which the relationship is characterised in the written contract determine, even prima facie, whether or not the other party is to be classified as a worker. Laws such as the National Minimum Wage Act were manifestly enacted to protect those whom Parliament considers to be in need of protection and not just those who are designated by their employer as qualifying for it.[118]

Taking the contractual documentation at face value, or even as the starting point in the classification exercise, in other words, 'would in effect … accord Uber power to determine for itself whether or not the legislation designed to protect workers will apply to its drivers'.[119] This had long been recognised by Parliament, not least in specifically voiding any clauses purporting to contract out of the Employment Rights Act 1996 and other employment legislation.[120]

How, then, should the worker test be applied? It is necessary for tribunals

> both to view the facts realistically and to keep in mind the purpose of the legislation. … The greater the extent of … control [exercised by the putative employer over the work or services performed by the individual concerned], the stronger the case for classifying the individual as a 'worker' who is employed under a 'worker's contract'.[121]

This approach, Lord Leggatt noted, was also in line with the jurisprudence of the European? Court of Justice.[122]

On the facts of the case, five elements of Uber's business model were highlighted as particularly salient for the question of worker status: the power to

[115] ibid [69].
[116] ibid [70] (Lord Leggatt).
[117] ibid [75] (Lord Leggatt).
[118] ibid [76] (Lord Leggatt).
[119] ibid [77] (Lord Leggatt).
[120] ibid [79].
[121] ibid [87] (Lord Leggatt).
[122] ibid [88], citing Case C-610/18 *AFMB Ltd v Raad van bestuur van de Sociale verzekeringsbank* [2021] 1 CMLR 17 paras 60–61.

set rates and determine the percentage of Uber's 'service fee'; full control over contractual terms and conditions; information asymmetries created by the app to exercise tight algorithmic control once a driver is logged on; a 'significant degree of control over the way in which drivers deliver their services'; and tight restrictions on communications between drivers and passengers.[123]

The tribunal was thus 'entitled to find that the claimant drivers were "workers" who worked for Uber London under "worker's contracts" within the meaning of the statutory definition. Indeed, that was, in [his Lordship's] opinion, the only conclusion which the tribunal could reasonably have reached'.[124]

VI. CONCLUSION

Even when read on its own terms, *Autoclenz* represents a fundamental development in UK employment law. By breaking with the narrow *Snook* sham approach, it decisively shifted judicial attention from primacy of contract to primacy of facts, and brought UK employment law in line both with other areas of domestic statutory regulation and the approach taken by national courts in other jurisdictions, as well as the Court of Justice. At the same time, however, its practical implications have been limited to a relative narrow factual matrix, whilst from a theoretical perspective, more questions were opened than answered.

Its long-lasting status as a landmark case is nonetheless assured, given the central role it played in subsequent litigation. The Supreme Court's decision in *Uber* has already been the subject of extensive academic commentary, both in terms of its implications for labour law,[125] and the political economy of labour market regulation more broadly.[126] The significance of how *Uber* developed the *Autoclenz* approach is central to many, if not all, of these debates, even though not all commentators agree with the notion that Lord Leggatt's judgment has sounded 'the death knell for the written contract [thus marking] a paradigm shift in the law on employment status'.[127] Atkinson and Dhorajiwala, for example, suggest that it would be a

> mistake … to view the contractual and statutory purposive approaches as mutually exclusive or in tension with each other such that there is a need to choose between

[123] ibid [94]–[101].

[124] ibid [119] (Lord Leggatt).

[125] See notably A Bogg and M Ford, 'The Death of Contract in Determining Employment Status' (2021) 137 *LQR* 392; D Brodie, 'Confronting the Gig Economy' (2021) 2 *Jur Rev* 102; J Atkinson and H Dhorajiwala, 'The Future of Employment: Purposive Interpretation and the Role of Contract after Uber' (2022) *MLR* (forthcoming); Z Adams, 'One Step Forwards For Employment Status, Still Some Way To Go: The Supreme Court's Decision in Uber v Aslam Under Scrutiny' (2021) 80 *CLJ* 221.

[126] A Adams-Prassl, J Adams-Prassl, and D Coyle, *Uber and Beyond: Policy implications for the UK* (Cambridge, The Bennett Institute for Public Policy, 2021) www.bennettinstitute.cam.ac.uk/publications/uber-and-beyond-policy-implications-uk/ (accessed 13 April 2022).

[127] Bogg and Ford (n 125) 399.

> them. Rather, they are *mutually supporting* elements of an overarching purposive approach to employment status which are relevant at different stages of the courts' deliberation.[128]

Brodie similarly suggests a sense of continuity,[129] and is 'far from convinced' by Lord Leggatt's emphasis on the fact that the rights asserted were statutory rather than contractual.[130]

Present space limitations prohibit a detailed engagement with these arguments, and broader questions, such as the applicability of *Uber* to limb (a) employee cases. Either way, however, it is clear that the decision in *Uber* could not have happened without the landmark decision in *Autoclenz* removing any lingering doubts about the role of *Snook* shams, and the rich judicial and academic debates about the role of contractual interpretation in employment law which ensued.

[128] Atkinson and Dhorajiwala (n 125) 4.
[129] Brodie (n 125) 103.
[130] ibid 105.

14

Headscarves, Tolerance and EU Law: Achbita, Bougnaoui *and* WABE

CATHERINE BARNARD*

I. INTRODUCTION

THERE IS ALWAYS something of a problem in defining what actually constitutes a landmark case. Under general European Union law, most would agree that *Van Gend en Loos*,[1] *Costa v ENEL*,[2] and *Cassis de Dijon*[3] stand out for having fundamentally changed the legal landscape.[4] But in the field of EU employment law it is hard to identify a case that is totally transformative. So I prefer to think about cases which are important, which have shaped future thinking on EU (employment) law, and which have paved the way for legal and, ultimately, social change. *Achbita*[5] and *Bougnaoui*,[6] and then *WABE*[7] are three such cases. They all concern the wearing of Islamic headscarves in the workplace.[8] They were the first cases where the Court of Justice was required to examine difficult issues of discrimination law in this sensitive area, against the backcloth of divergent Member State approaches to

* Thanks to the editors and to Sarah Fraser Butlin for helpful comments.

[1] Case 26/62 *Van Gend en Loos v Netherlands Inland Revenue Administration* [1963] ECR 1.

[2] Case 6/64 *Costa v ENEL* [1964] ECR 1141.

[3] Case 120/78 *Rewe-Zentral AG v Bundesmonopolverwaltug fur Branntwein ('Cassis de Dijon')* [1979] ECR 649.

[4] See, eg, M Maduro and L Azoulai (eds), *The Past and Future of EU Law: The Classics of EU Law Revisited on the 50th Anniversary of the Rome Treaty* (Oxford, Hart Publishing, 2010); A Albors-Llorens, C Barnard and B Leucht (eds), *Cassis de Dijon: Forty years On* (Oxford, Hart Publishing, 2021).

[5] Case C–157/15 *Achbita v G4S Secure Solutions NV* [2017] 3 CMLR 21.

[6] Case C–188/15 *Bougnaoui v Micropole SA* [2017] 3 CMLR 22.

[7] Joined Cases C–804/18 and C–341/19 *IX v WABE eV* [2022] 1 CMLR 11.

[8] Ie, not the niqab or the burka. As former AG Sharpston notes, while covering the woman's hair, headscarves leave her face completely visible, 'the least intrusive and thus the most proportionate way of complying with that particular [Muslim] obligation', see E Sharpston, 'Shadow Opinion: Headscarves at Work (Cases C–804/18 and C–341/19)' (2021) para 47 eulawanalysis.blogspot.com/2021/03/shadow-opinion-of-former-advocate.html (accessed 23 April 2022).

a multi-cultural, multi-faith Europe, where issues of integration, assimilation, diversity and tolerance are increasingly the subject of public debate.

By virtue of Article 2 of the Treaty on European Union (TEU), the EU is committed to the values of respect for human dignity, freedom, democracy, equality, the rule of law and respect for human rights, including the rights of persons belonging to minorities.[9] Article 2 TEU also notes that '[t]hese values are common to the Member States in a society in which pluralism, non-discrimination, tolerance, justice, solidarity and equality between women and men prevail.' It is easy to express – and indeed sign up to – these values in the abstract. But how do they play out in practice, specifically in the context of the workplace? To what extent can, and should, private considerations (religion and its manifestation) be taken into account in the public space of a working environment? For some, the answer is advocating tolerance and respect for diversity. This might be termed the human rights approach, an approach which prioritises the rights of the individual over those of the employer, subject to limitations laid down by the law. For others, it is about doubling down and reasserting values of neutrality of image at work and respect for employers' decisions as to how to manage staff at work. This might be termed the managerial prerogative approach. This places the Court of Justice in a difficult position. The managerial approach underpins the case law of other courts.[10] The human rights approach would be more compatible with the Court's embrace of the Charter of Fundamental Rights.[11] Should the Court of Justice lead or should it follow?

Achbita and *Bougnaoui* are a first attempt at tackling issues of diversity at work. The judgments read as a terse, technical exercise in interpreting Directive 2000/78;[12] the outcome largely supports the managerial prerogative approach. The decisions attracted considerable (mainly negative) academic

[9] See ibid, paras 38–39: 'I shall start by recalling the background of our shared, and not so distant, European history. The rise to power of the National Socialist Party in Germany during the 1930s led in very short order to overt and horrifying discrimination on grounds of race, religion and ethnic origin. That poison was allowed to spread unchecked. It resulted in the Second World War and the accompanying catalogue of genocide and crimes against humanity. The focussed and deliberate attempt to eradicate all Jews from territories under Nazi control – the Shoah – was accompanied by other, equally deliberate moves to exterminate other despised racial groups and unwanted minorities (Roma, homosexuals, Communists, Sinti …). Out of the devastation – the casual killing in the slave labour camps; the ashes of the industrial-style crematoria of the Konzentrationslager – came, thank heavens, the collective recognition that we Europeans had to ensure that such atrocities would never happen again. That is what gave birth to the "European project". The language of article 2 of the TEU … is there to entrench our collective memory of what went wrong and why we must do better than that in our shared European future. By the same token, article 22 of the Charter enjoins the European Union to "respect cultural, religious and linguistic diversity".'

[10] See, eg, *Ladele v United Kingdom* App Nos 52671/10 and 36516/10 (Statement of Facts) hudoc.echr.coe.int/fre# (accessed 23 April 2022).

[11] See, eg, Case C–336/19 *Centraal Israëlitisch Consistorie van België (CICB) v Vlaamse Regering* [2021] 2 CMLR 12.

[12] Council Directive 2000/78/EC of 27 November 2000 establishing a general framework for equal treatment in employment and occupation [2000] OJ L303/16 ('Framework Employment Directive').

comment, which we consider below. Some media commentary was also damning.[13] For example, *The New York Times* noted with concern[14] that '[r]ight-wing politicians were quick to hail the ruling[s]', including supporters of France's far-right National Front candidate for president, Marine Le Pen.[15] It noted too that the Conference of European Rabbis condemned the rulings, saying:[16] 'With the rise of racially motivated incidents and today's decision, Europe is sending a clear message: Its faith communities are no longer welcome.' *The New York Times* concluded: 'Instead of guarding against rising prejudice across the continent, the European Court of Justice shows that it is not immune to the same political pressures.'

Such criticisms must have hurt the Court of Justice, a Court which has prided itself on developing a human rights jurisprudence,[17] and on upholding the rule of law and other Article 2 TEU values.[18] Nevertheless, *Achbita* and *Bougnaoui* provided a platform on which other cases could build, contest, and develop the points that the Court had made.[19] A first reassessment can be seen in *WABE*, decided four years later. *WABE*, another Grand Chamber case, shows a greater understanding by the Court of the significance of wearing of headscarves for Muslim women, a more nuanced approach to discrimination law, a recognition of the need to balance competing human rights at stake, and a greater advocacy of the value of pluralism. While not quite a full human rights approach, it comes much closer to recognising the rights of the individual and not just those of employers.

A similar process of refinement can be seen following another major ruling of the Court of Justice in the social field more than 40 years before, the 1976

[13] Eg, 'Legalizing Discrimination in Europe' (*The New York Times*, 15 March 2017) www.nytimes.com/2017/03/15/opinion/legalizing-discrimination-in-europe.html (accessed 23 April 2022): 'The European Court of Justice handed right-wing nationalists a victory on Tuesday that allows employers to ban Muslim women and others who wear signs of their faith. With rising anti-Muslim sentiment in Europe, and elections coming in several nations where the populist right is expected to do well, this decision sends exactly the wrong message.'

[14] ibid.

[15] At the time this chapter was being prepared, Marine Le Pen, was a serious contender for the French presidency and made it to the run-off in the presidential election. One of her policies was to ban the wearing of headscarves: see, eg, 'Macron Clashes with Le Pen Over Islamic Head-Scarf Ban' (*France 24*, 15 April 2022) www.france24.com/en/live-news/20220415-macron-clashes-with-le-pen-over-islamic-headscarf-ban (accessed 23 April 2022).

[16] 'European Rabbis: EU Court's Ruling on Religious Garb Means Jews, Muslims Unwelcome' (*JTA*, 14 March 2017) www.jta.org/2017/03/14/global/european-rabbis-eu-ruling-on-religious-garb-means-jews-muslims-unwelcome (accessed 23 April 2022).

[17] For a history, see S Peers and others, *The EU Charter of Fundamental Rights: A Commentary*, 2nd edn (Oxford, Hart Publishing, 2021).

[18] See, eg, Case C–64/16 *Associação Sindical dos Juízes Portugueses v Tribunal de Contas* [2018] 3 CMLR 16.

[19] As Sharpston (n 8) para 77 noted, 'I do not believe that the Grand Chamber was wrong, in *G4S Secure Solutions*, to look at the directive more widely than through the sole prism of article 21 of the Charter. However, as the two orders for reference make clear, there is further work to be done in clarifying and explaining the ruling in that case.' This, she explains, is why the case was given to the Grand Chamber and has the benefit of an AG's Opinion (para 78).

decision of *Defrenne v SABENA*.[20] The Court recognised that Article 157 of the Treaty on the Functioning of the European Union (TFEU) on equal pay for men and women was directly effective and thus created a powerful tool for interest groups[21] and others to challenge conflicting domestic legislation. It also indicated that Article 157 TFEU was not purely an economic tool, but also had social objectives.[22] And from there, the Court was able to navigate the consequences of its decision. The developments have often been slow and by no means linear (one of the implications of *Defrenne* was resolved only in *Tesco*[23] 45 years later) but there is now a substantial body of case law on the meaning and effectiveness of Article 157 TFEU where the principles laid down, somewhat awkwardly in *Defrenne*, have become refined and polished. So judicial landmarks come in different shapes and sizes and it is only with hindsight that their significance may be revealed.

The chapter is structured as follows. First, it briefly sets out the facts of the three cases (section II) before focusing on those aspects of the judgments where, from a broadly liberal perspective, the Court got it right in *Achbita* and *Bougnaoui* (section III), and those where it did less well (section IV). It then looks at how *WABE* has made a difference. Section V considers what we learn about discrimination law from these cases. Section VI concludes.

II. THE CASES

A. *Achbita* and *Bougnaoui*

The facts of *Achbita* are well known. She was a Muslim woman who worked for G4S as a receptionist. There was an unwritten rule within G4S that workers could not wear visible signs that showed their political, philosophical or religious beliefs in the workplace. Ms Achbita had been working for G4S for three years, when she informed her line managers that she intended to wear an Islamic headscarf during working hours. She was told that this would not be tolerated, because of G4S's policy of neutrality. She went on a period of sick leave, and when she returned, she said she would be wearing her headscarf. Shortly afterwards, the G4S works council approved an amendment to the workplace regulations, according to which 'employees are prohibited in the workplace, from wearing any visible signs of their political, philosophical or religious beliefs, and, or

[20] Case 43/75 *Defrenne v SA Belge de Navigation Aérienne (SABENA)* [1976] ECR 455.

[21] C Barnard, 'A European Litigation Strategy: the Case of the Equal Opportunities Commission' in J Shaw and G Moore (eds), *Dynamics of European Integration* (Oxford, Clarendon, 1996) 253.

[22] C Barnard, 'The Economic Objectives of Article 119' in: T Hervey and D O'Keeffe (eds), *Sex Equality Law in the EU* (Chichester, Wiley, 1996).

[23] Case C–624/19 *K v Tesco Stores Ltd* [2021] 3 CMLR 33 (Article 157 of the TFEU has direct effect in 'proceedings between individuals in which failure to observe the principle of equal pay for male and female workers for "work of equal value", as referred to in that article, is pleaded'.)

from engaging in any observance of such beliefs'. The day before this new rule came into force Ms Achbita was dismissed due to her insistence on wearing a headscarf at work. The Belgian Court of Cassation asked the Court of Justice whether Article 2(2)(a) of Directive 2000/78 meant that the prohibition on wearing, as a female Muslim, a headscarf at the workplace, constituted *direct* discrimination. It did not ask whether the case concerned indirect discrimination, the more traditional legal route for analysing dress-code cases.

Bougnaoui concerned a Muslim woman employed as a design engineer by Micropole. Prior to being recruited, she was told that the wearing of an Islamic headscarf might pose a problem when she was in contact with customers of the company. When she started working as an intern for Micropole, she wore a simple bandana. At the end of her internship Micropole employed her and she wore a headscarf. She worked for the company for about a year when she was told that a customer had complained to Micropole that her wearing of a veil had 'upset a number of its employees' and that the customer had 'requested that there should be "no veil next time"'.[24] She refused to accept the 'professional requirements' not to wear the veil, and was dismissed, even though the employer 'regret[ted] this situation as your professional competence and your potential has led us to hope for a long working relationship'.[25] The French Cour de Cassation referred a question to the Court of Justice on the application of Article 4(1) of Directive 2000/78. It asked whether the wish of a customer no longer to have the services of Micropole, which provided an employee who wore a headscarf, was a genuine and determining occupational requirement (GOR) by reason of the nature of the particular occupational activities concerned or the context in which they are carried out. So, the question referred focused on the defences (GORs) not on the type of discrimination at issue.

Achbita and *Bougnaoui* were separate cases, each with their own Advocate Generals' Opinions (by AG Kokott and AG Sharpston respectively), but the (Grand Chamber) judgments were handed down on the same day and so were very much seen as linked.

B. *WABE*

Four years later came the decision in *WABE*. In fact, *WABE* involved two joined cases, Case C–804/18 *IX* v *WABE* and Case C–341/19 *MJ*.[26]

In *IX*, WABE ran a number of child day care centres in Germany, in which more than 600 employees worked, caring for 3,500 children. WABE was non-partisan and non-denominational and it followed the recommendations of the

[24] Case C–188/15 *Bougnaoui* (n 6) para 14.

[25] ibid.

[26] In the discussion that follows '*WABE*' will be used to refer to both cases; *IX* and *MJ* will be used when specific points are made about the particular rulings in their cases.

City of Hamburg that '[a]ll child day care facilities have the task of addressing and explaining fundamental ethical questions as well as religious and other beliefs as part of the living environment.' IX had worked for WABE for two years when, at the start of 2016, she decided to wear an Islamic headscarf. From October 2016 to May 2018, she was on parental leave. In March 2018, WABE adopted '[i]nstructions on observing the requirement of neutrality' which said that

> [i]n order to guarantee the children's individual and free development with regard to religion, belief and politics, … employees are required to observe strictly the requirement of neutrality that applies in respect of parents, children and third parties. WABE pursues a policy of political, philosophical and religious neutrality in respect thereof.

An information sheet made clear that no symbols could be worn: neither the Christian cross, Islamic headscarf nor Jewish kippah.

IX came to work wearing an Islamic headscarf; she was suspended. At about the same time WABE required a female employee to remove a cross that she wore around her neck. The Labour Court referred questions to the Court of Justice on whether the case raised issues of direct or indirect discrimination under Directive 2000/78 and, if the latter, whether the discrimination could be objectively justified.

In the second case, *MJ*, a Muslim woman had worked as a sales assistant for MH, a drug store, since 2002. In 2014, she started wearing an Islamic headscarf. Because she did not comply with MH's request to remove the headscarf, she was transferred to another post allowing her to wear the headscarf. In June 2016, MH again asked her to remove the headscarf. She refused and was sent home. In July 2016, MH adopted an internal directive prohibiting the use of conspicuous, large-sized political, philosophical or religious signs in the workplace. According to MH, the aim of that directive was to maintain neutrality within the undertaking and thus to prevent conflicts between employees. It said that such conflicts, arising from the different religions and cultures represented in the undertaking, had 'already occurred several times in the past'.[27] The German Federal Labour Court referred questions to the Court of Justice on objective justification, assuming that the employer's conduct was indirectly discriminatory.

WABE was clearly seen as important and so was allocated to the Grand Chamber. Eleanor Sharpston was due to be the Advocate General on the case and she had done much work in preparing a draft of her Opinion. However, in a twist on the fall-out from Brexit, even though she continued serving as AG after the UK had left the EU, she was eventually removed, a decision which she unsuccessfully challenged,[28] but before her Opinion was published. She therefore

[27] Joined Cases C–804/18 and C–341/19 *WABE* (n 7) para 36.

[28] For the background, see O Bowcott, 'British Lawyer Sues EU Over Her Removal From its Court Due to Brexit' (*The Guardian*, 1 May 2020) www.theguardian.com/law/2020/may/01/british-lawyer-sues-eu-over-her-removal-from-its-court-due-to-brexit (accessed 23 April 2022); J Rozenberg,

decided to publish her opinion independently, as a 'shadow' opinion.[29] She was replaced by AG Rantos who wrote his own opinion in the *WABE* case.

Having looked at the facts of the cases, we now turn to how the Court addressed the questions posed in these cases. I begin by examining those aspects of the *Achbita and Bougnaoui* rulings seen as positive, and how *WABE* improved on them (section III). Section IV looks at the less successful aspects of the Court's rulings and what *WABE* did to address them.

III. THE GOOD(ISH)

From a classical liberal perspective, based on recognising the freedom of the individual, equality and tolerance, the decisions in *Achbita* and *Bougnaoui* offer a number of positives, but each is qualified.

A. The Scope of 'Religion'

First, the Court in *Achbita* gave a broad reading to the term 'religion' to include not just the right to hold the belief but also its manifestation (the 'belief-action distinction').[30] It said:

> In so far as the ECHR and, subsequently, the Charter use the term 'religion' in a broad sense, in that they include in it the freedom of persons to manifest their religion, the EU legislature must be considered to have intended to take the same approach when adopting Directive 2000/78, and therefore the concept of 'religion' in Article 1 of that directive should be interpreted as covering both the *forum internum*, that is the *fact of having a belief*, and the *forum externum*, that is the *manifestation of religious faith* in public.[31]

And, in reaching this conclusion, the Court drew on the 'constitutional traditions common to the Member States, as general principles of EU law … which have been reaffirmed in the Charter of Fundamental Rights of the European Union'[32] ('the Charter'). The right to freedom of conscience and religion, enshrined in

'British Lawyer Kicked Off EU Court' (10 September 2020) rozenberg.substack.com/p/british-lawyer-kicked-off-eu-court?s=r (accessed 23 April 2022); D Vladimirovich Kochenov and G Butler, 'The Independence and Lawful Composition of the Court of Justice of the European Union: Replacement of Advocate General Sharpston and the Battle for the Integrity of the Institution' (Jean Monnet Center for International and Regional Economic Law and Justice, 2020) jeanmonnetprogram.org/paper/the-independence-and-lawful-composition-of-the-court-of-justice-of-the-european-union-replacement-of-advocate-general-sharpston-and-the-battle-for-the-integrity-of-the-institution/ (accessed 23 April 2022).

[29] Sharpston (n 8).

[30] See also Case C–188/15 *Bougnaoui* (n 6) para 30.

[31] Case C–157/15 *Achbita* (n 5) para 28 (emphasis added).

[32] ibid, para 27.

Article 10(1) of the Charter, 'includes freedom to change religion or belief and freedom, either alone or in community with others and in public or in private, to manifest religion or belief, in worship, teaching, practice and observance' and corresponds to the right guaranteed in Article 9 of the European Convention on Human Rights (ECHR).[33] This is a textbook example by the Court of ensuring that the general principles, the European Convention, and the Charter all work together in a mutually supportive fashion.

In *WABE* the Court went further and was clearer: 'The wearing of signs or clothing to manifest religion or belief is covered by the "freedom of thought, conscience and religion" protected by Article 10 of the Charter.'[34] But to protect itself from being dragged into future disputes as to what constitutes religion-required dress, it said: 'The specific content of religious precepts is based on an assessment which it is not for the Court to carry out.'[35]

In *WABE* the Court also made clear that the terms 'religion' and 'belief' had to be analysed as two facets of the same single ground of discrimination. Referring to Article 21 of the Charter, it said that 'the ground of discrimination based on religion or belief is to be distinguished from the ground based on "political or any other opinion" and therefore covers both religious beliefs and philosophical or spiritual beliefs'.[36] The Court is also more robust as to why freedom of conscience and religion need to be protected: they represent 'one of the foundations of a "democratic society" within the meaning of [the ECHR]' and constitute, 'in its religious dimension, … one of the most vital elements that go to make up the identity of believers and their conception of life' and 'a precious asset for atheists, agnostics, sceptics and the unconcerned', contributing to 'the pluralism indissociable from a democratic society, which has been dearly won over the centuries'.[37] This is an important statement of principle which had been lacking in *Achbita* and *Bougnaoui*. Freedom of religion is being protected not just as an individual right but also as a key pillar in a democratic society, including the Member States of the EU.

B. Customer Preference

Second, in *Bougnaoui* the Court firmly rejected the argument that 'my customers do not like veil wearers' as a justification for (direct?[38]) discrimination.[39] The Court said the GORs in Article 4(1) of Directive 2000/78 could not 'cover subjective considerations, such as the willingness of the employer to take account of

[33] ibid.
[34] Joined Cases C–804/18 and C–341/19 *WABE* (n 7) para 46.
[35] ibid.
[36] ibid, para 47.
[37] ibid, para 48 citing *Dahlab v Switzerland* App No 42393/98 (ECtHR, 15 February 2001).
[38] No question was referred on the type of discrimination at issue (see section II.A above).
[39] We return to the question of the type of discrimination at issue in section IV.A below.

the particular wishes of the customer'.[40] This is consistent with the robust stance taken by the Court in *Firma Feryn*.[41] That case concerned public statements by the director of Feryn that his business was looking to recruit fitters, but that it could not employ 'immigrants' because its customers were reluctant to give them access to their homes.[42] The Court said:

> The fact that an employer declares publicly that it will not recruit employees of a certain ethnic or racial origin, something which is clearly likely to strongly dissuade certain candidates from submitting their candidature and, accordingly, to hinder their access to the labour market, constitutes direct discrimination in respect of recruitment within the meaning of Directive 2000/43.

It added that the existence of such direct discrimination was not dependent on the identification of a complainant who claimed to have been the victim.[43]

The Court's approach in *Feryn* and now *Bougnaoui* is an important statement and one many would embrace enthusiastically. Had the Court found otherwise, it would have risked rolling back decades of progress in the field of equality law stopping employers running arguments that, for example, they would employ only (young) women as bar staff/air stewards/shop assistants because that is what the customers want.[44]

However, the ruling does pose a problem for particular employers. Consider the following. One of the little discussed aspects of dementia is that patients become less rational and at times deeply racist.[45] They will not let someone of a different skin colour come near them. What does a care home/care services supplier do in these circumstances about hiring and providing staff? Do they

[40] Case C–188/15 *Bougnaoui* (n 6) para 40.

[41] Case C–54/07 *Centrum voor Gelijkheid van Kansen en voor Racismebestrijding v Firma Feryn NV* [2008] ECR I–5187.

[42] ibid, para 16. The importance of the customer preference was emphasised in the question from the referring court: 'Is there direct discrimination within the meaning of Article 2(2)(a) of Council Directive 2000/43/EC of 29 June 2000 implementing the principle of equal treatment between persons irrespective of racial or ethnic origin where an employer, after putting up a conspicuous job vacancy notice, publicly states:

> "I must comply with my customers' requirements. If you say "I want that particular product or I want it like this and like that", and I say "I'm not doing it, I'll send those people", then you say "I don't need that door". Then I'm putting myself out of business. We must meet the customers' requirements. This isn't my problem. I didn't create this problem in Belgium. I want the firm to do well and I want us to achieve our turnover at the end of the year, and how do I do that? – I must do it the way the customer wants it done!"'.

[43] ibid, para 25.

[44] H Williamson, 'Model Workers: The Clothes Shops That Only Hire Beautiful People' (*New Statesman*, 18 July 2004) www.newstatesman.com/culture/2014/07/model-workers-clothes-shops-only-hire-beautiful-people (accessed 23 April 2022).

[45] 'Racism: A Ticking Time Bomb in Dementia Care?' www.tn-elderlaw.com/free-resources/blog/june-2020/racism-a-ticking-time-bomb-in-dementia-care (accessed 23 April 2022); 'Dementia and Racism' www.tn-elderlaw.com/free-resources/blog/august-2020/dementia-and-racism (accessed 23 April 2022).

advertise widely but then select, say, only white staff to look after white customers, or do they try relying on a GOR to justify direct discrimination and then be subject to public opprobrium (and possibly failing to meet the relevant standards for GORs (considered in section IV.C below))? This is where the binary divide between direct and indirect discrimination becomes problematic.

WABE offered a different way forward, albeit one based on objective justification (which is available only in the case of indirect, not direct, discrimination). The Court said that 'account may be taken, in the first place, of the rights and *legitimate* wishes of customers or users'.[46] On the facts of the case, it noted parents' right to ensure 'the education and teaching of their children in accordance with their religious, philosophical and teaching beliefs recognised in article 14 of the Charter or their wish to have their children supervised by persons who do not manifest their religion or belief when they are in contact with the children'.[47] These, the Court suggests, are legitimate customer interests, unlike the customer interests in *Bougnaoui* and *Feryn*.[48]

However, it could be argued, as AG Sharpston did in her shadow opinion, that permitting staff to wear a headscarf would allow children to ask questions about faith and its manifestation, and thus grow up as informed (and tolerant?) members of a democratic society, a view with which I have considerable sympathy. The Court did not go down this route. Rather it suggested there were legitimate customer preferences (the rights of parents to a neutrality policy by staff in an education setting),which could be upheld, and illegitimate customer preferences (not wanting to have those of other races/religions in their home/at their workplace), which could not.

This raises further difficulties. Where does the reach of discrimination law stop? I have argued elsewhere that, in the light of *Jivraj*,[49] it currently does (and probably should?) stop at an individual's front door.[50] In other words, in my own home I can choose who comes into my house to provide me with services and I can choose to discriminate on grounds of the providers' race/sex/sexual orientation/religion etc. Discrimination law has nothing to say about this: it does not apply to discriminatory purchasing decisions by private individuals. Freedom of contract and personal autonomy trump discrimination law. By contrast, the moment I open my house up to the public (for example to offer services via AirBnB and the like), *Bull v Hall*[51] tells us that discrimination law does apply. In the same way, in a workplace – a public forum – discrimination law does and should apply. So from that point of view, *Bougnaoui* is the right decision. The problem comes where the workplace spans the public and private sphere, as is

[46] Joined Cases C–804/18 and C–341/19 *WABE* (n 7) para 65 (emphasis added).
[47] ibid.
[48] ibid, para 66.
[49] *Jivraj v Hashwani* [2011] UKSC 40, [2011] 1 WLR 1872.
[50] C Barnard and A Blackham, 'Discrimination and the Self-Employed: The Scope of Protection in an Interconnected Age' in H Collins and others (eds), *European Contract Law and the Charter of Fundamental Rights* (Cambridge, Intersentia, 2017).
[51] [2013] UKSC 73, [2013] 1 WLR 3741.

the case with the provision of care in the home of a dementia sufferer, or in the less sympathetic case of a racist client as in *Firma Feryn*. What do employers do when clients refuse to welcome certain people into their homes? It maybe that now the Court has recognised that there are legitimate reasons to allow for discrimination, balancing the rights of the service recipient (parents under Article 14 of the Charter/patients under, for example, Article 25 of the Charter) this could be read across to the GORs, albeit in very narrowly defined circumstances of the Article 4(1) GORs.

C. Reasonable Accommodation

It is well known that the principle of reasonable accommodation applies only to disability discrimination[52] and not more generally. Attempts to read reasonable accommodation into the proportionality principle have also fallen largely on deaf ears.[53] Yet *Achbita* points towards allowing for some adjustment:

> ... it is for the referring court to ascertain whether, taking into account the inherent constraints to which the undertaking is subject, and without G4S being required to take on an additional burden, it would have been possible for G4S, faced with such a refusal, *to offer her a post not involving any visual contact with those customers, instead of dismissing her*. It is for the referring court, having regard to all the material in the file, to take into account the interests involved in the case and to limit the restrictions on the freedoms concerned to what is strictly necessary.[54]

In applying a strict proportionality principle the Court finds room for some reasonable accommodation (to offer her a post not involving any visual contact with those customers). In this there is some attempt to mirror the Canadian case of *Simpsons-Sears*[55] and the Court of Human Rights decision in *Thlimmenos*.[56] This effectively means that states should accommodate individuals who have different needs unless there is an 'objective and reasonable justification' not to do it. However, the duty of reasonable accommodation, if it does exist, is hemmed in with caveats ('taking into account the inherent constraints to which the [employer] is subject, and without G4S being required to take on an additional burden'). So the obligation in *Achbita* is not strong.

It is also not clear that the duty of reasonable adjustment – if it involves moving the employee from face to face contact with the public to a backroom role – can actually be considered a success when judged against the yardstick of tolerance and pluralism, which the Court itself recognised in *WABE*.[57] The

[52] Framework Employment Directive, Art 5.
[53] See, eg, *Ladele v United Kingdom* (n 10).
[54] Case C–157/15 *Achbita* (n 5) para 43 (emphasis added).
[55] *Ontario Human Rights Commission (O'Malley) v Simpsons-Sears Ltd* [1985] 2 SCR 536.
[56] *Thlimmenos v Greece* App No 34369/97 (ECtHR, 6 April 2000).
[57] Joined Cases C–804/18 and C–341/19 *WABE* (n 7) para 48.

effect of *Achbita* is that anyone who is different is removed from a frontline/customer facing role. This leads to segregation, something that is expressly prohibited in the UK legislation if done on the grounds of race.[58] The argument goes that if the individual who has been moved does not like the new job, he or she can resign. This approach hints at the 'specific situation' rule developed by the Court of Human Rights: that if individuals choose to put themselves in a position limiting their rights (eg, employment) their freedom is protected by leaving their job. Yet, this is not good for the individual, nor for the firm that has trained them, nor for society. This is particularly the case in respect of a group such as Muslim women who already suffer considerable economic disadvantage. The Court of Human Rights has started to move away from this approach in respect of other rights;[59] it is unfortunate to see it alluded to in *Achbita*.

IV. THE LESS GOOD

A. Direct v Indirect Discrimination

i. What Type of Discrimination?

Although in *Achbita* the question referred concerned direct discrimination, the Court addressed the issue through the more traditional lens: it considered controls on manifestation of religion to be indirectly discriminatory (the point was not considered in *Bougnaoui* since no question was referred on the point). The Court noted that the neutrality policy had to be 'regarded as treating all workers of the undertaking in the same way by requiring them, in a general and undifferentiated way, …, to dress neutrally, which precludes the wearing of such signs'.[60] The Court said that '[i]t was not evident that the internal rule was applied differently to Ms Achbita as compared to any other worker and so the rule was not directly discriminatory under article 2(2)(a) of Directive 2000/78'.[61]

Yet the facts suggest that G4S's focus was, in fact, only on Muslim women wearing headscarves, as the chronology shows (see section II.A). Although there had been an informal neutrality policy when Ms Achbita was employed, this was formalised only on 29 May 2006, less than two weeks after Ms Achbita returned to work after a period of sickness, wearing the headscarf. She was dismissed on 12 June and the formal policy came into operation the following day. When viewed against this background it could be argued that this case

[58] Equality Act 2010, s 13(5).
[59] *Vogt v Germany* (1996) 21 EHRR 205. This is happening more slowly in respect of religion, although *Eweida v United Kingdom* (2013) 57 EHRR 8 did suggest a turning point. See further L Vickers, '*Achbita* and *Bougnaoui*: One Step Forward and Two Steps Back for Religious Diversity in the Workplace' (2017) 8 *European Labour Law Journal* 232.
[60] Case C–157/15 *Achbita* (n 5) para 30.
[61] ibid, para 32.

actually concerned direct, not indirect, discrimination and that Muslim women were being targeted. This would have followed the earlier case of *CHEZ*.[62]

In *CHEZ* the Court had advocated a broad reading of the principle of direct discrimination. The case concerned the placing of electricity meters at a height of between six and seven metres in traditionally Roma districts (but at eye height in other areas) on the grounds of preventing of tampering with those meters and of unlawful connections. The Court took into account contextual factors, such as the fact that the electricity meters were placed up very high only in urban districts where the majority population were Bulgarian nationals of Roma origin (even though the claimant was not herself Roma). It also noted that CHEZ, the electricity company, had said that it was mainly Bulgarian nationals of Roma origin who interfered with the electricity meters. Such assertions, said the Court, could 'in fact suggest that the practice at issue is based on ethnic stereotypes or prejudices, the racial grounds thus combining with other grounds'.[63] The Court concluded that Article 2(2)(a) of Directive 2000/43 meant that the practice at issue constituted direct discrimination 'if that measure proves to have been introduced and/or maintained for reasons relating to the ethnic origin common to most of the inhabitants of the district concerned'.[64]

Advocate General Sharpston built on *CHEZ* in her shadow opinion in *WABE* when she proposed a revised formulation for direct discrimination:

> [W]here an employer imposes a criterion that he either knows or ought reasonably to have known will inevitably place a member of a particular group in a less favourable position on the basis of any of the grounds referred to in Article 1 of Directive 2000/78, that should be assimilated to treating that person less favourably than another in a comparable situation on the basis of a prohibited ground for the purposes of Article 2(2)(a) of that directive (direct discrimination).[65]

She recognised that the Court might not be prepared to go this far – yet.

Had the Court's approach in *CHEZ* (and AG Sharpston's proposal in *WABE*) been applied to the facts of *Achbita* the outcome could have been different: the neutrality measure was introduced and/or maintained for reasons relating to the religious beliefs common to many (female) Muslims, placing them in a less favourable position on the grounds of their religion. This would have amounted to direct discrimination. In *MJ* the Court showed some signs of moving in this direction. Although the reference from the German Court was premised on the existence of indirect discrimination, the Court of Justice said an internal rule of an undertaking which 'prohibits only the wearing of conspicuous, large-sized signs is liable to have a greater effect on people with religious, philosophical or

[62] Case C–83/14 *CHEZ Razpredelenie Bulgaria AD v Komisia za zashtita ot diskriminatsia* [2016] 1 CMLR 14.

[63] ibid, para 82.

[64] ibid, para 91.

[65] Sharpston (n 8) para 263.

non-denominational beliefs which require the wearing of a large-sized sign, such as a head covering'.[66] It continued:

> unequal treatment resulting from a rule or practice which is based on a criterion that is inextricably linked to a protected ground, in the present case religion or belief, must be regarded as being directly based on that ground. … [T]he prohibition imposed by an employer on its employees on wearing those signs on the basis of that criterion will mean that some workers will be treated less favourably than others on the basis of their religion or belief, and that direct discrimination, within the meaning of Article 2(2)(a) of Directive 2000/78, may therefore be established.[67]

ii. Intersectionality

If there is direct, or indirect, discrimination, the question is on the basis of what protected characteristic? The obvious answer is religion (see section III.A). However, *Achbita* and *WABE* raise a further issue: intersectionality. As noted above, there are hints in *Achbita* that the rule at issue did not just target one protected characteristic (religion: headscarves required by the Islamic faith) but two (religion and sex: headscarves required to be worn by *women* of the Islamic faith). The intersectionality argument was hinted at in *WABE*, too. The Court noted that that the neutrality rule 'concerns, statistically, almost exclusively female workers who wear a headscarf because of their Muslim faith'.[68] AG Sharpston in *WABE* went further: she said that female observant Muslims risk finding themselves subject to not just dual but *triple discrimination* in the employment market (on grounds of sex *and* race *and* religion).[69] She continued:

> To the extent that there may – unfortunately – be a degree of latent discrimination in our societies that perceives certain groups as identifiably 'other', it seems to me important to guard against the risk that, when an employer says that he 'merely' wishes to apply a policy of strict neutrality in his dealings with his clients and his customers, he may in reality be pandering to that latent discrimination.[70]

Addressing intersectionality proved too difficult for the Court and it avoided the issue.[71] Its focus was on the single protected characteristic, religion. At one level, this sharpened the focus on the key issue. The adherents to religions most affected by the neutrality policy are Muslims, Sikhs, and Jews. The adherents to the dominant Christian faith in western Europe, and those (the majority) who are secular, are not affected by this rule. Yes, Christians forced to remove a cross due to a neutrality policy may lament the instruction, but being asked to do so

[66] Joined Cases C–804/18 and C–341/19 *WABE* (n 7) para 72.
[67] ibid, para 73.
[68] ibid, para 59.
[69] Sharpston (n 8) para 41.
[70] ibid.
[71] See further R Xenidis, 'The Polysemy of Anti-discrimination Law: The Interpretation Architecture of the Framework Employment Directive at the Court of Justice' (2021) 58 *Common Market Law Review* 1649, 1695.

does not violate one of the fundamental tenets of their religion, since cross-wearing is a matter of personal choice.[72] This is different for many Muslims/Sikhs/Jews who believe that wearing a headscarf/turban/kippah is a mandatory requirement of their religion.[73] This points to the fact that a neutrality policy banning symbols is not in fact neutral but targeted and so should be considered directly discriminatory on the grounds of, at least, religion.

B. Objective Justification and Proportionality

i. Achbita

It matters, of course, whether the measure can be classified as directly or indirectly discriminatory because of the breadth of the defences. The former can be saved only by the narrow GORs (see below); the latter can be objectively justified, the route the Court went down in *Achbita*. It said that 'the desire to display, in relations with both public and private sector customers, a policy of political, philosophical or religious neutrality *must* be considered legitimate'.[74] It continued:

> An employer's wish to project an image of neutrality towards customers relates to the freedom to conduct a business that is recognised in Article 16 of the Charter and is, in principle, legitimate, notably where the employer involves in its pursuit of that aim only those workers who are required to come into contact with the employer's customers.[75]

Not only did the Court consider the neutrality policy to be objectively justified it also provided a strong hint that the policy was proportionate. On the first limb of the proportionality test, appropriateness, the Court assumed that the policy was suitable:

> it must be held that the fact that workers are prohibited from visibly wearing signs of political, philosophical or religious beliefs is *appropriate* for the purpose of ensuring

[72] Sharpston (n 8) para 115. She also says that 'there is a 'significant body of adherents to both the Muslim and Jewish faiths' who regard the wearing of, respectively, a hijab if one is female and a kippah if one is male as 'an essential aspect of a necessary religious rite' (para 119). For those reasons, in what follows I shall treat both the hijab and the kippah as being apparel *required of them by their religion* by those with a particular level of observance in their respective faiths. I shall refer to such items of apparel in shorthand as 'mandated religious apparel' (para 120).

[73] However, as Davies notes (G Davies, 'Achbita v G4S: Religious Equality Squeezed Between Profit and Prejudice' (*European Law Blog*, 6 April 2017) europeanlawblog.eu/2017/04/06/achbita-v-g4s-religious-equality-squeezed-between-profit-and-prejudice/ (accessed 23 April 2022), 'If the headscarf is presented as an empowering assertion of identity, and if this is put forward as a reason to defend women's choice to wear it, then that very vision undermines its legal protection. For the law protects religion, not culture or choice – it protects what we feel obliged to do, not what we are used to or what we want. The more the headscarf becomes personal, cultural, political, and assertive, the harder it is to claim that banning it violates religious beliefs, rather than simply violating personal preference.'

[74] Case C–157/15 *Achbita* (n 5) para 37 (emphasis added).

[75] ibid, para 38.

> that a policy of neutrality is properly applied, provided that that policy is genuinely pursued in a consistent and systematic manner.[76]

On the second limb, necessity, the Court provided a strong indication that the measure also satisfied this test:

> In the present case, what must be ascertained is whether the prohibition on the visible wearing of any sign or clothing capable of being associated with a religious faith or a political or philosophical belief covers only G4S workers who interact with customers. If that is the case, the prohibition *must be considered strictly necessary* for the purpose of achieving the aim pursued.[77]

There are four concerns about the Court's reasoning on objective justification and proportionality.

The first one is circularity: the provision, criterion or practice found to be indirectly discriminatory is the neutrality policy. The justification for the policy is – the employer's need to have a neutrality policy. There is no explanation why it actually needs to have such a policy. The Court also appears to conflate the employer's prerogative to have a dress code with the neutrality policy. As shown above, the neutrality policy is not, in fact, neutral. Adams and Adenitire go further: restricting the policy of ideological neutrality does 'not prevent a business activity from being carried out as such'.[78] In fact, the employer in *Achbita* would have been perfectly able to continue its activity of providing security and reception services without the policy. 'It was not argued that such a policy was central to its business operations.'

The second concerns the Court's reliance on Article 16 to help make out the justification. The Court considers Article 16 (on freedom to conduct a business) simpliciter – there is no attempt at balancing it with the interests of the worker,[79] nor is there any explanation as to why the neutrality policy is core to its business operations. No wonder, then, that the *New York Times* thought that '[t]he danger now is that companies will try to exclude Muslim and other religious minority workers who wear signs of their faith by imposing a seemingly neutral policy.'[80]

The third concerns proportionality. As Jolly puts it,[81] the proportionality exercise in *Achbita* was almost superficial. She notes that the Court did not consider whether appropriateness should be evidence-based, or related to the nature of the business the employer conducted, or the type of work which the

[76] ibid, para 40 (emphasis added).
[77] ibid, para 42.
[78] Z Adams and J Adenitire, 'Ideological Neutrality in the Workplace' (2018) 81 *MLR* 348.
[79] *cf* Joined Cases C–804/18 and C–341/19 *WABE* (n 7) paras 63–65 where a more nuanced approach was taken.
[80] 'Legalizing Discrimination in Europe' (n 13).
[81] S Jolly, 'Achbita & Bougnaoui: A Strange Kind of Equality' (2017) www.cloisters.com/achbita-bougnaoui-a-strange-kind-of-equality/ (accessed 23 April 2022).

employee was required to do. Yet this is a case which concerns fundamental rights where the proportionality review tends to be much stricter.

The arguments so far have been technical. There is a fourth and more fundamental concern: why does the employer need to have a neutrality policy at all? In *Achbita* the answer seemed to be – because the customers wanted it/did not want to be upset by the sight of someone wearing a religious symbol. Yet, as we saw above, the Court said clearly in *Firma Feryn* and *Bougnaoui* that customer preference is irrelevant and cannot justify discrimination. There is good reason for this: customer preference is based on stereotypes and prejudice. One of the justifications for equality law is to combat these prejudices, by regarding people as individuals rather than as members of a particular group (with the stereotypes which may be associated with that group). The neutrality policy risks being a cover for racism and prejudice. As Davies has suggested 'it would require a high degree of paranoia to worry about whether the engineer, nurse, waitress or postal worker will do her job properly because she is Muslim and the customer is not'.[82] He concludes: '[The neutrality policy] is not based on any genuine or objective threat to the interests of the customer, but simply on the fact that some customers may not like certain beliefs and if employees visibly have those beliefs the customers may shop elsewhere.' The Court was able to see this in *Firma Feryn* in the context of race discrimination but not in respect of religious discrimination.

This may suggest, at a minimum, a lack of consistency between the grounds or the development of some sort of hierarchy between the protected characteristics. Or it may be that the Court prioritises, in fact, protecting the religious belief itself over its manifestation. There are hints of this in AG Kokott's Opinion in *Achbita*:

> [T]he practice of religion is not so much an unalterable fact as an aspect of an individual's private life, and one, moreover, over which the employees concerned can choose to exert an influence … an employee may be expected to moderate the exercise of his religion in the workplace ….[83]

This, of course, oversimplifies the individuals' relationship with their faith. As Advocate General Kokott herself pointed out, Ms Achbita had a 'sincere belief' that she should wear the headscarf. In this respect her case differs very much from an individual wearing a 'Stop the War' t-shirt. All of this points to an increasing sense that religion – or at least its manifestation – is protected with less rigour than race (compare the strong judgment in *CHEZ*) and probably sex.

There is another way of looking at the Court's support for neutrality. As Hambler puts it, '"neutrality" … may be a synonym, in this context, for secularism; some versions of secularism are intrinsically hostile to, rather than

[82] Davies (n 73).

[83] Case C–157/15 *Achbita v G4S Secure Solutions NV* [2017] 3 CMLR 21, Opinion of AG Kokott, para 116.

symbiotic with, religion and so it is difficult to see it necessarily as a neutral creed'.[84] In other words, neutrality is also a policy choice, even if apparently a negative one. And this is favoured, even in the private sector, especially against the backcloth of French and Belgium state secularism/laïcité (considered by AG Kokott to extend to private employment).[85] In the UK many have difficulty understanding this attachment to laicité. AG Sharpston's view (let the carers wear headscarves in order to promote questions, understanding and, hopefully, tolerance) probably reflects the mainstream, broadly progressive British view.[86] However, as Kelly explains about French laïcité:

> What is at stake in these debates is not just the secular state, but also the wider framework of rights and responsibilities, and ultimately the very identity of the French Republic. So, from being the basis of a religious settlement, laïcité has increasingly become an expression of French identity. It now acts as a touchstone for le vivre-ensemble: how French people can live together.[87]

This might help to explain why it is easier for the Court of Justice ultimately to adopt a more secular approach and favour the employer's business interests over the individual's equality interests, the approach essentially endorsed by AG Kokott.

ii. WABE

In *IX* the Court was more nuanced on the question of objective justification than it had been in *Achbita*. It noted that 'an employer's desire to display, in relations with both public and private-sector customers, a policy of political, philosophical or religious neutrality *may* [not must as in *Achbita*] be regarded as legitimate'.[88] It continued: '[A]n employer's wish to project an image of neutrality towards customers relates to the freedom to conduct a business that is recognised in Article 16 of the Charter and is, in principle, legitimate'.[89] However, it added an additional requirement:

> *the mere desire* of an employer to pursue a policy of neutrality – while in itself a legitimate aim – *is not sufficient*, as such, to justify objectively a difference of treatment indirectly based on religion or belief, since such a justification can be regarded as being objective only where there is a *genuine need* on the part of that employer, which it is for that employer to demonstrate.[90]

[84] A Hambler, 'Neutrality and Workplace Restrictions on Headscarves and Religious Dress: Lessons from *Achbita* and *Bougnaoui*' (2018) 47 *ILJ* 149, 161.

[85] Case C–157/15 *Achbita v G4S Secure Solutions NV* [2017] 3 CMLR 21, Opinion of AG Kokott, para 125.

[86] *cf* E Bleich, 'Where Do Muslims Stand on Ethno-Racial Hierarchies in Britain and France? Evidence from Public Opinion Surveys, 1988–2008' (2009) 43 *Patterns of Prejudice* 379.

[87] M Kelly, 'France's Laïcité: Why the Rest of the World Struggles to Understand It' (*The Conversation*, 20 November 2020) theconversation.com/frances-la-cite-why-the-rest-of-the-world-struggles-to-understand-it-149943 (accessed 23 April 2022).

[88] Joined Cases C–804/18 and C–341/19 *WABE* (n 7) para 63.

[89] ibid.

[90] ibid, para 64 (emphasis added).

The genuine need might be found in the rights and legitimate interests of customers or users (such as parents – see above).[91] In *MJ* the Court noted that 'both the prevention of social conflicts and the presentation of a neutral image of the employer vis-à-vis customers may correspond to a real need on the part of the employer, which it is for the latter to demonstrate'.[92] However, there had to be a sufficiently specific 'risk of disturbances within the undertaking or the specific risk of a loss of income'.[93] The addition of the genuine need test helps to address some of the concerns around the blanket acceptance of the neutrality policy as justification in *Achbita*. However, the reference to a 'loss of income' raises concerns that employers could still say that without having a neutrality policy they risk losing customers, the very situation the Court appeared to outlaw in *Bougnaoui* and *Firma Feryn*.

The genuine need test now is a key part of the assessment of the legitimacy of the employer's actions defending the discrimination. The Court also indicates a more rigorous approach to the requirements of evidence in the proportionality review (see point (3) in the quote below). It spells this out in its conclusions in *IX*. It says the employer's neutrality policy may be justified provided that:

> (1) that policy meets a genuine need on the part of that employer, which it is for that employer to demonstrate, taking into consideration, inter alia, the legitimate wishes of those customers or users and the adverse consequences that that employer would suffer in the absence of that policy, given the nature of its activities and the context in which they are carried out;
> (2) that difference of treatment is appropriate for the purpose of ensuring that the employer's policy of neutrality is properly applied, which entails that that policy is pursued in a consistent and systematic manner; and,
> (3) the prohibition in question is limited to what is strictly necessary having regard to the actual scale and severity of the adverse consequences that the employer is seeking to avoid by adopting that prohibition.[94]

The Court also takes a much stricter line on the limb 'appropriateness' limb of the proportionality review: a policy of neutrality within an undertaking can be effectively pursued only if *no* visible manifestation of political, philosophical or religious beliefs is allowed when workers are in contact with customers or with other workers, since the wearing of any sign, even a small-sized one, undermines the ability of that measure to achieve the aim allegedly pursued and therefore calls into question the consistency of that policy of neutrality.[95]

[91] ibid, para 65.
[92] ibid, para 76.
[93] ibid, para 85.
[94] ibid, para 70. For a detailed and thorough suggestion as to how the Court could have tackled the substantive issues of objective justification in *IX*, see Sharpston (n 8) paras 201–260. Note in particular para 234.
[95] Joined Cases C-804/18 and C-341/19 *WABE* (n 7) para 77.

The Court also adopts a more rounded approach to balancing of competing rights as part of the 'strictly necessary' limb of the proportionality review.[96] In answer to questions in both *IX* and *MJ* it says:

> [W]hen several fundamental rights and principles enshrined in the Treaties are at issue, such as … the principle of non-discrimination enshrined in Article 21 of the Charter and the right to freedom of thought, conscience and religion guaranteed in Article 10 of the Charter, on the one hand, and the right of parents to ensure the education and teaching of their children in conformity with their religious, philosophical and pedagogical convictions recognised in Article 14(3) of the Charter and the freedom to conduct a business recognised in Article 16 of the Charter, on the other hand, the assessment of observance of the principle of proportionality must be carried out in accordance with the need to reconcile the requirements of the protection of those various rights and principles at issue, striking a fair balance between them.[97]

This is a very good example of the Court responding to the criticism of *Achbita* and adopting a more nuanced, refined approach to the question of balancing competing rights.

C. (G)ORs

In the UK sex and race discrimination legislation of the 1970s,[98] the Acts listed a number of Genuine Occupational Qualifications (GOQs) in which discrimination was lawful provided that the employer had taken reasonable steps to avoid imposing the GOQ. These included the cases of models, toilet attendants, hospital and prison staff, personal welfare counsellors, work in a private home involving close physical or social contact with a person living in the home, etc. The original Race Relations Act 1976 had a separate, also narrow, list of GOQs including the cases of actors, models, personal welfare counsellors, and work in a place where food and drink was provided 'in a special ambience' for which persons of a particular racial group are required for reasons of authenticity. This exhaustive list approach was replaced by an open-ended list of (Genuine) Occupational Requirements based on the delphic Article 4(1) of Directive 2000/78, the GOR defence. It provides:

> Notwithstanding Article 2(1) and (2), Member States may provide that a difference of treatment which is based on a characteristic related to any of the grounds referred to in Article 1 shall not constitute discrimination where, by reason of the nature of the particular occupational activities concerned or of the context in which they

[96] *cf* ibid, para 83 where it suggests that this balancing was already present in *Achbita*: 'Since the case which gave rise to that judgment concerned only the freedom to conduct a business, recognised in Article 16 of the Charter, it must be concluded that the other freedom to which the Court referred to in that judgment was the freedom of thought, conscience and religion, referred to in paragraph 39 of that judgment.'

[97] ibid, para 84.

[98] Sex Discrimination Act 1975, s 7; Race Relations Act 1976, s 5.

are carried out, such a characteristic constitutes a genuine and determining occupational requirement, provided that the objective is legitimate and the requirement is proportionate.

The following six criteria need to be met for Article 4(1) to be satisfied:

(1) difference of treatment;
(2) based on a *characteristic related* to any of the protected characteristics which is a genuine and determining occupational requirement;
(3) by reason of the nature of the particular occupational activities concerned or of the context in which they are carried out;
(4) such a characteristic constitutes a genuine and determining occupational requirement;
(5) objective is legitimate; and
(6) requirement is proportionate.

At paragraph 37 in *Bougnaoui* the Court emphasised that it is not the ground on which the difference of treatment is based but a *characteristic related to that ground* which must constitute a genuine and determining occupational requirement (see point (2)). In the context of manifestation cases, such as *Bougnaoui*, where dress code requirements are a characteristic related to the ground, criterion (2) does not pose a particular problem although the other five requirements may do. It works much less well for colour and sex (eg, black man to play Othello or woman to play Juliet). What is the characteristic related to the ground? Blackness or womaness/having breasts? This is almost offensive. The Court did not have to address this issue in *Bougnaoui* but its emphasis on characteristic related to that ground will generate problems in the future, especially in circumstances of a dementia patient, considered in section III.B above.

Returning to religion/belief, the Court did recognise that 'in accordance with recital 23 of Directive 2000/78, it is only in very limited circumstances that a characteristic related, in particular, to religion may constitute a genuine and determining occupational requirement'.[99] This means that such a characteristic may constitute such a requirement only 'by reason of the nature of the particular occupational activities concerned or of the context in which they are carried out'.[100] This must be 'objectively dictated by the nature of the occupational activities'.[101] So this might cover allowing a non-ethos based university or college to advertise for a Catholic priest or an Imam to serve the needs of Catholic/Muslim students. It cannot, however, cover 'subjective considerations, such as the willingness of the employer to take account of the particular wishes of the customer'.[102] This was discussed in section III.B above. However, it may

[99] Case C–188/15 *Bougnaoui* (n 6) para 38.
[100] ibid, para 39.
[101] ibid, para 40.
[102] ibid.

be difficult going forward to distinguish between legitimate objective considerations and illegitimate subjective considerations.

V. WHAT IS THE PURPOSE OF DISCRIMINATION LAW?

So, we have looked at the strengths and weakness of the judgments in *Achbita* and *Bougnaoui* and how the Court responded in *WABE*. These cases raise, at heart, the fundamental question of what is the purpose of EU discrimination law? There are three ways of looking at this. The first and narrower way is to see that prohibiting discrimination is an important vehicle for ensuring labour market access for all. Employment opens the door for income, security, identity/self-fulfilment and participation. The labour market perspective seems to be the principal objective underpinning the Directive. The ninth recital says: 'Employment and occupation are key elements in guaranteeing equal opportunities for all and contribute strongly to the full participation of citizens in economic, cultural and social life and to realising their potential.' As Vickers puts it, equality

> sees the harm in terms of economic disadvantage, rather than individual or collective dignitary harm. A correlation between religion and belief and economic disadvantage can be identified; economic activity varies according to religion, with the 2011 UK census showing that Muslims have the lowest rates of economic activity.[103]

This approach elides with a model of equality 'based on inclusion and participation in society. It suggests that lack of recognition and economic disadvantage can impede full participation in social life, and that equality law provides a method to promote greater participation in society as a way to achieve broader social justice'.[104] There is a nod to this position in *Firma Feryn* when the Court said:

> The objective of fostering conditions for a socially inclusive labour market would be hard to achieve if the scope of Directive 2000/43 were to be limited to only those cases in which an unsuccessful candidate for a post, considering himself to be the victim of direct discrimination, brought legal proceedings against the employer.[105]

Advocate General Sharpston, in her shadow opinion puts this more eloquently. She noted that '[a]ccess to jobs matters. So does protection from discrimination within employment. Work is of fundamental importance, both economically and psychologically, for us as individuals and for our society as a whole.'[106] She continued:

> Those who are excluded from the employment market or ejected from a job that they hold – particularly if that exclusion takes place for a reason that is central to their

[103] Vickers (n 59) 235.
[104] ibid 236.
[105] Case C–54/07 *Firma Feryn* (n 41) para 24.
[106] Sharpston (n 8) para 40.

> identity and that they cannot or should not be asked to surrender – easily become discouraged, alienated and embittered. Emotional damage risks being added to financial hardship and economic vulnerability.[107]

She concludes: 'To the altruistic reasons for combating discrimination can be added some hard-nosed practical considerations. Creating pockets of deprivation and delineating racial or cultural groups that can readily self-identify as victims easily sets the scene for social unrest and worse.'[108]

The labour market approach sits more comfortably with the Court's previous social policy case law.[109] But focus on the labour market creates considerable space for arguments such as those in *Achbita and Bougnaoui* that (un?)due account should be taken of the employer's position since employers provide the capital and thus the work on that labour market.

A second approach to equality focuses more on the dignity of the individual. This coincides with traditional human rights reading of equality law. As Vickers puts it,

> [o]ne theoretical approach to equality focuses on the infringement of individual dignity that can occur when unequal treatment is identified. This encompasses an aim of equality based on recognition of the uniqueness of individuals, and an acknowledgement that inequality can arise not just in socio-economic terms, but in cultural and symbolic terms, too, leading to stigma and lack of self-esteem.[110]

This reading of equality law starts with the assumption that the individual has the right not to be discriminated against and the employer must work hard to justify limiting this right. Elements of this approach can be seen in *WABE* where the Court set a very high bar for the employer to justify restricting the employee's rights.

A third approach sees equality law as a means to help build 'democratic and tolerant societies which allow the participation of all persons irrespective of racial or ethnic origin', as the Court put it in *CHEZ*,[111] or 'the pluralism indissociable from a democratic society, which has been dearly won over the centuries' as the Court said in *WABE*.[112] This democratic state-building approach, imbued with Article 2 TEU values can be seen in the rhetoric but is still far from being delivered in practice, even in *WABE*. To western liberal eyes, the result in *WABE* is still to uphold, at least in principle, the employer's right to have a neutrality policy, a neutrality policy which is far from neutral and serves to reject diversity and difference. Why do customers need to be protected by the neutrality policy and not other employees? As Jolly puts it: 'This is really quite an extraordinary assumption in a modern, diverse and plural society.'[113]

[107] ibid.
[108] ibid.
[109] C Barnard and S De Vries, 'The "Social Market Economy" in a (Heterogeneous) Social Europe: Does it Make a Difference? (2019) 15 *Utrecht Law Review* 47.
[110] Vickers (n 59) 235 (footnotes omitted).
[111] Case C–83/14 *CHEZ* (n 62) para 74.
[112] Joined Cases C–804/18 and C–341/19 *WABE* (n 7) para 48.
[113] Jolly (n 81).

VI. CONCLUSION

Achbita and *Bouganoui* provided the Court with its first opportunity to start thinking about sensitive, divisive, difficult issues. It is perhaps better to say the judgments are staging posts on a journey, a journey which is challenging. It defaulted to adopting the managerial prerogative approach because it was, at first sight easier. In *WABE* the Court found a more intellectually rigorous, progressive and thoughtful course, underpinned by a richer understanding of human rights, but one which still leaves room for development. And so far, the Court has been faced only with the less controversial issues of headscarves, not niqabs. Nor has it been faced with cases concerning those expressing religious-based, but potentially divisive, views at work (eg, gay marriage should not be allowed), nor those engaged with proselytising at work where issues of freedom of expression are also engaged.

However, this journey is one that the Court of Justice must undertake with national courts. It may face resistance. When *Achbita* returned to the Belgian court the court found no indirect discrimination. It also said that had there been indirect discrimination the neutrality policy would have been objectively justified. It was also resistant to any attempt to read in a duty of reasonable accommodation, and it took a light touch review to proportionality.[114] As we have learned elsewhere, when the proportionality analysis is left to the national courts, they often upheld the national rule or practice.[115] The resistance to the Court of Justice's approach may be stronger in other Member States.

Yet the high profile of the Court of Justice's judgments in the headscarves cases might push employers to act on their own. The very public airing of these issues has precipitated debate with employers. In Belgium some employers such as AXA, a private bank, reaffirmed their inclusive diversity policy, by clearly stating publicly that 'employers should be themselves at work. That is what brings up their best talents'.[116]

So, are *Achbita* and *Bougnaoui* and *WABE* landmark decisions? It is perhaps too soon to make this judgment. However, they come at a time when culture wars, islamophobia, even xenophobia are on the increase. Politicians struggle with navigating this complex terrain; some may also be responsible for fanning the flames of division. The courts are inevitably dragged into this highly contested territory. By instinct they tread cautiously, often feeling ill-equipped to

[114] For strong criticism, see G Busschaert, 'End of *Achbita* Saga in Belgium: National Judge Rejects Indirect Discrimination and Criticises Duty to Look for Alternative Position in Case of Refusal to Comply with Neutrality Policy' (2021) 13 *European Employment Law Cases* 2.

[115] C Barnard, 'The Worker Protection Justification: Lessons from Consumer Law' in P Koutrakos, NN Shuibhne and P Syrpis (eds), *Exceptions from EU Free Movement Law: Derogation, Justification and Proportionality* (Oxford, Hart Publishing, 2016).

[116] I El Morabet, 'Neutrality Policies in Commercial Companies' (*Law Society of Scotland*, 19 June 2017) www.lawscot.org.uk/members/journal/issues/vol-62-issue-06/neutrality-policies-in-commercial-companies/ (accessed 23 April 2022).

proceed further and faster. Yet, as we have seen in *Achbita* and *Bougnaoui*, this very caution is in itself a policy position – favouring managerial prerogative over the interests of the individual worker. In *WABE* the Court was more nuanced. It identified clearly the value of pluralism in a democratic society and started to work out what this value means in the concrete circumstances of the workplace.

Taken together, these three cases have started the process of shaping future thinking on EU discrimination law, and they have helped paved the way for legal and, ultimately, social change. As with *Defrenne*, the journey may be long, difficult and slow but these three cases provide a starting point and for this reason, this line of case law may come to be seen as landmark.

Index

www.ingramcontent.com/pod-product-compliance
Ingram Content Group UK Ltd.
Pitfield, Milton Keynes, MK11 3LW, UK
UKHW020234290926
15470UKWH00002B/531

9 781509 944262